2

ADVANCE PRAISE FOR

The History and Heritage of
African-American

D0887384

"Absolutely mesmerizing...conta............... .... well-documented information about the unmistakable role of the Black church in the lives of African Americans in this country. In addition to the thorough research that has gone into this work, Dr. Whelchel has been personally involved in such a great deal of the history of the Civil Rights Movement. This work should be required reading for every college student, not just for Black students, for the Whites need to know this as well. An excellent piece of research and writing."

—Earle D. Clowney, Ph.D. (ret.), Clark Atlanta University

"An important contribution to the study of black churches by a pastor and a teacher."

—James H. Cone, Charles Augustus Briggs Distinguished Professor of Systematic Theology, Union Theological Seminary

"The title understates the scope of this work.... While the development of Christianity among the African Americans whose forebears came to North America as slaves is a principal subject of the book, Whelchel considers that development within the broadest possible context."

—*Booklist*, the book review journal of the American Library Association

"...an absorbing and soaring examination of African-American Christianity. In a sweeping interrogation, Dr. Whelchel affirms the sacred legacy of the children of Africa in the United States from our African ancestral inheritance to the modern black-led struggle for freedom in this country."

—Alton B. Pollard III, Ph.D., Dean and Professor of Religion and Culture, Howard University School of Divinity

"...a valuable asset to students, clergy, and lay persons to gain a deeper understanding of the significance of African American churches in the history of our country. I highly commend this resource without qualification."
—William P. DeVeaux, Bishop, Sixth Episcopal District (Georgia), African Methodist Episcopal Church

"...an uncommon look at the Black church in America, as he extends it from the far reaches of the Motherland, Africa. A must read for those seeking to understand the focus, dimensions, and community of the Black church."
—Rev. Arthur Agnew, Bethesda Missionary Baptist Church, Minneapolis

"This newest addition to the expanding literature and deepening legacy of the black religious experience in America, is not only most welcome, but fills a void felt by those seeking more scholarly interpretations of that experience."
—Othal Hawthorne Lakey, Bishop Christian Methodist Episcopal Church; author, *The History of the CME Church*

"I highly recommend for your reading and study this incisive historical survey of the Black Church experience in America. This scholarly presentation is important for all clergy and lay persons who want to know the full story of the Black Church's contribution to the development of American society."
—Bishop Henry M. Williamson, Sr., Presiding Prelate, Ninth Episcopal District, Christian Methodist Episcopal Church

"A key feature of *The History and Heritage of African American Churches* is the way the historical unfolding of the African American Church is placed within the world historical context. The black church is viewed not only from ancient African history; it is also related to world church history from its inception."
—Edward P. Wimberly, Provost, Interdenominational Theological Center

ADVANCE PRAISE (continued)

"As Africa is now becoming the epicenter of Christianity worldwide, and as emerging post-colonial readings, ethnic studies and mission histories are focused on dynamic church movements in Africa, Asia and Latin America, professor L.H. Whelchel does a tremendous service to the academy by calling our attention to one of the most dynamic church movements in the North American context—that of the African American churches. With meticulous scholarship and the inclusion of neglected and ignored historical data, the author has produced an invaluable resource for those who seek to critically and thoughtfully engage church history and mission theology from the trajectory of an independent church movement among African Americans. You will be so challenged by the thought provoking narration of the origins and challenges of African American churches, and especially their intercourse with seminal events in the history of America that whether scholar, student or minister, you will never again be able to view church doctrine, mission history, and church transformation as you did prior to encountering this research. Whelchel has made a great contribution to the worldwide study of Christianity."

—Dr. Snulligan Haney, Professor of Missiology,
The Interdenominational Theological Center

"Dr. Whelchel's book on African-American churches is a major work of scholarship and a valuable piece of religious and cultural history. Full of solid research, penetrating analysis, and exciting narrative, this book will be well-received by students, scholars, and ministry leaders. I highly recommend this monumental work for anyone who appreciates the contribution of religion to the African-American experience."

—Bishop Charles E. Blake, Presiding Bishop, Church of God in Christ

"Whelchel's text is an accessible, well-researched volume that will educate a new generation of students, clergy, and the general public."

—Dr. Robert Franklin, President, Morehouse College

The History & Heritage of African-American Churches

The History & Heritage of African-American Churches

A WAY OUT OF NO WAY

L.H. Whelchel, Jr.

PARAGON HOUSE

First Edition 2011

Published in the United States by
Paragon House
1925 Oakcrest Avenue
St. Paul, MN 55113

Copyright © 2011 by L. H. Whelchel, Jr.

Photograph of Ring Shout on page 83 from *Slave Songs of the Georgia Sea Islands*. Used with permission of University of Georgia Press.

Photograph depicting Richard Allen is courtesy of St. George's Church, and the photograph of J. A. Delaine, Sr., is courtesy of J. A. Delaine, Jr. All other photographs courtesy of the Atlanta University Center Woodruff Library.

Library of Congress Cataloging-in-Publication Data

    Whelchel, L. H. (Love Henry)
    The history & heritage of African-American churches : a way out of no way
    / by L.H. Whelchel, Jr.
        p. cm.
    Includes bibliographical references.
        ISBN 978-1-55778-893-1 (pbk. : alk. paper)
    1. African American churches--History. 2. United States--Church history.
    I. Title. II. Title: History and heritage of African-American churches.
    BR563.N4.W486 2010
    277.30089'96073--dc22
                              2010033237

The paper used in this publication meets the minimum requirements of American National Standard for Information Sciences—Permanence of Paper for Printed Library Materials, ANSI Z39.48-1984.

Manufactured in the United States of America
10 9 8 7 6 5 4 3 2 1

For current information about all releases from Paragon House,
visit the website at http://www.ParagonHouse.com

Dedicated to my supportive family:
Larma
April
Kenyatta
Noel
Love III
Quanda
Love IV

Contents

Acknowledgments

To God be the glory for all the good He has done for us.

I am most grateful to my grandmother, Martha Leslie, who was my first grade teacher in a one room rural school; my grandfather, Arthur Leslie, who taught me in Sunday school; my father, Love Henry Whelchel, Sr., who provided for his family as an itinerant C.M.E. minister in rural middle Georgia, and my mother Lennie Catherine Whelchel, who was an elementary public school teacher. From them I received my core values which informed and inspired my ministry of service in the church, the academy and the greater community for more than fifty years.

I am profoundly grateful for my college and graduate school training, but I am even more thankful for my secondary education at the Holsey-Cobb Institute in Cordele, Georgia. In high school I met Mr. Hiawatha Just, the brilliant yet modest son of the great biologist Earnest Everett Just. He planted the seeds and nurtured my passion for African-American history. I also met Mrs. Mercedes Felton who enlightened and inspired me. I have been blessed throughout my academic career to be exposed to exemplary mentors and teachers, including Lucius Holsey Pitts, Maurice Cherry, George Tutt, Mildred Longmire, Gladys Cherry, James Brown, E. Clayton Calhoun, Cecilia Sheppard, C. Eric Lincoln, James S. Thomas, Grant S. Shockley, Stuart C. Henry, Ray Gavins, Moody Smith, Robert Durden, Allan Knight Chalmers, Edwin P. Booth, Harold DeWolf, Harold Beck, Walter G. Muelder, and Howard Thurman.

As fate would have it, I arrived in Birmingham at the height of the Civil Rights Movement. I was fortunate to walk right into the middle of history-making events. This was the most exciting period of my professional career. I also benefitted from being able to work side-by-side with civil rights luminaries such as Martin Luther King, Jr., Fred L. Shuttlesworth, Ralph David Abernathy, C.T. Vivian, Hosea Williams, Joseph E. Lowery, A.D. King, James E. Robinson, Andrew Young,

Nathaniel Linsey, E.P. Murchison, Calvin Woods, Abraham Woods, Ocie Thompson, F.N. Nixon, Frank Dukes and others.

After leaving Birmingham, I was assigned to the following pastorates: Russell Memorial C.M.E. Church in Durham, North Carolina, Philips Temple C.M.E. Church in Dayton, Ohio, and Philips Temple C.M.E. Church in Los Angeles, California. Later, I became the chair of the Department of Religion and Philosophy at Clark Atlanta University. I inherited a talented cadre of scholars and I still cherish the many enlightening discussions I shared with various colleagues at the university.

Also, I owe a debt of gratitude to the librarians and archivists at several repositories who assisted my research efforts. A special thanks to Brad Ost, the theological librarian for the Interdenominational Theological Center, Karen Jefferson, archivist in Special Collections, and Andrea R. Jackson, head of the Archives Research Center, both at the Atlanta University Center Robert E. Woodruff Library.

I must give acknowledgement to the community activists and church leaders who responded to a questionnaire I sent out concerning challenges facing the Black church in the twenty-first century. These respondents included: Bishop Marshall Gilmore, Bishop Ronald Cunningham, Bishop E. Lynn Brown, Dr. Jeremiah A. Wright, Dr. Edward Wimberly, Dr. Asa Hilliard, and Dr. Henry H. Mitchell.

The support of my family, friends and the I.T.C. community has been critical to the completion of this book. In particular, I appreciate the assistance of Dr. Earle Clowney, Retired Chair Emeritus of the Clark Atlanta University Department of Modern Languages, for his editorial support. I would be remiss not to express appreciation to Dr. Michael Battle, President of I.T.C., and Dr. Edward Wimberly, as well as my colleagues on the I.T.C. faculty for their support and encouragement.

The work on this book has been an arduous task, covering about three years since the project was first conceived. But it has also been one of my most enjoyable endeavors, because I was able to work with the assistance and support of my son, Noel.

Finally, I am grateful and deeply indebted to our African-American ancestors, those who endured and transcended the brutalities of the Middle Passage, the horrors of chattel enslavement, the cruelties of mob lynching, and the humiliations of segregation, and yet refused to abandon their faith in the goodness of God, and in the healing powers of our community, and in the ultimate triumph that belongs to those who persevere for righteousness' sake.

Be who you is, cause if you ain't who you is then you is who you ain't.

—Martha Leslie

Introduction

In this work we present the story of a tradition which represents the soul of a people. When we refer to the Black church or the African-American church, we refer to more than a particular ecclesiastical body, denomination or single organization. The Black church is an evolving, dynamic collective historical presence of a people and their patterns of expressing their beliefs and spirituality. The uniqueness of the Black church is found in the way enslaved Africans took the hybrid Christianity offered them by their oppressors and made it relevant and meaningful to their needs. Historically, the Black church started out as an "invisible institution" without walls, without written doctrines, without pompous and ostentatious displays and without sanction from White authorities. It was conceived and delivered in the hearts of a people who were struggling to come to terms with the most difficult of circumstances. The Black church was inclusive of the entire Black community, and nobody was outside of the care and concern of early congregants. The church became the face of the community, and its mission and purpose were not self-serving but served the needs of the people. This "extended community" concept of church lasted well into the twentieth century for many African Americans. As a former church pastor, I can recall that some of the largest funerals and most anticipated weddings were officiated for people who were not on the church membership rolls. Following the example of Jesus, the churches ministered to the needs of the people without respect to religious affiliation; Jesus, after all, was a servant of the people and not a particular organization. Historically, in times of greatest trouble, Black people have had nowhere else to turn but to their own families, communities, and their churches. The churches were not missing in action; they were places where the real action was going on.

The corpus of this work covers more than 30 years of teaching college and seminary students, lecturing, preaching, studying, and reflecting on the history of African Americans, their churches, and the story of Christianity in general. Rather than spending a great deal of time addressing the minutiae of denominational history, we have provided a chronological overview of Black church history as we attempted to present a narrative that links the history of the churches to the general flow of world history and the African-American experience.

Meaning and value are always contingent upon context. Thus, understanding the history and heritage of African-American churches requires an appreciation of the historical and cultural context out of which the churches developed. African Americans did not suddenly appear *ex nihilo* in the seventeenth century, and they did not emerge as mere spiritual and cultural destitutes. It was the early African settlers who laid the basic foundations for the prosperity that America enjoys today. Many of the Africans who were captured and brought involuntarily to America were skilled craftsmen, agriculturalists, griots, priests and priestesses, and some were members of royalty. In comparison with Europeans who were free and able to retain their religion, history, culture, beliefs, and family names, the Africans were systematically denied their freedom, family names, history, culture, religion, and in essence their humanity. Currently, so much public commentary about Africans and African Americans tends to completely ignore historical context; thus we found it necessary to give extensive analyses in some of the endnotes.

THE ROAD AHEAD

We cannot look forward intelligently or effectively plan for the future without a careful review of the past. All events arise from the confluence of some kind of antecedents; failure to appreciate the past eliminates the possibility of foresight. The "myth of the Negro" as described by the scholar Melville Herskovits will not be completely neutralized until the truth of the African is revealed. As the African-American experience is fundamentally shaped by a rich ancestral past as well as by responses to racist hostility, our study of African Americans must necessarily consider the history of Africa. And as suggested by the historian John Henrik Clarke, a historical review for any people of African descent or the African Diaspora, ought at some point, to consider their beginnings in Africa. To be human involves expression or representation of some kind of genetic, cultural, and historical experience, and for people of African descent that experience reaches back to the beginnings of civilization and even to the origin of humanity itself. Indeed it is questionable whether there can be any comprehensive knowledge or deep insight into the human condition absent an appreciation of African history and culture. Certainly, racist doctrines, attitudes, and structures cannot be adequately addressed until there is a full discussion of the African origins of humanity and human civilization. And contrary to the manipulative assertions of some and the naiveté of too many, race and ethnicity count; general phenotype or broadly similar physical appearances together with unifying cultural expressions are primary factors in the development of human societies. The history of the world is in part the story of how various ethnic, racial, and national groups have conceived of themselves and then made efforts to project their image onto human consciousness. One cannot meaningfully address human history without a comprehension of collective identity and the various racial and ethnic differences.

The designation of race and ethnicity, always fraught with some difficulty in modern times, has been a special concern for African Americans who have endured a practically continuous identity crisis. Among the professional classes and social status seekers, the propensity has been always to denigrate and repudiate those features marking them in contradistinction to the dominant social group, while qualities similar are accentuated and celebrated. With the collapse of European colonial empires in the aftermath of World War II, the centers of European and American power elites began to realize that their presumptions of racial superiority and White privilege could no longer withstand committed and persistent challenges from the world majority of people of color. Since the 1960s and the end of openly-declared White supremacy regimes, there has been an organized effort in public discussions to diminish and downplay racial identity for notions of individualism and to abandon discourse fostering racial and ethnic solidarity, removing these considerations as a basis for political action. Some have taken to neutering their racial heritage and proclaiming themselves just-happen-to-be-black folk, an accident of nature. But it may not be necessary to rush headlong from one extreme to another, from the strict hierarchical racial categories of the nineteenth century to the repression of any sense of collective identity and presence.

It should be understood that for better or worse, in the modern world all racial and ethnic classification schemes are informed by the last five centuries of European global conquest and colonialism. It may be true that race was never really a well-defined objective conceptualization. But race certainly has utility as a social construct, as an intuitive awareness of collective identity not altogether reducible to material factors, and as a dynamic upon which people may sometimes mobilize and organize. Otherwise, the last 500 years would be no more than a figment of our collective imagination. Can we seriously doubt that those vested interests now loudly proclaiming to support color-blindness and race neutrality would not turn on a dime and suddenly discover intriguing new rationales for pointing out racial distinctions if they believed that doing so was to their advantage? The very same group of people, anthropologists, philosophers, historians, and other social scientists ensconced in the dominant group's academic institutions, who defined and propagated concepts of race in order to rationalize the pursuit of slavery and imperialism, have now in their erudition deemed race to be a nonissue as they do their best to obscure racial designations.

What is the value of diversity if ancestral heritage has no value? In a modern globalized world, how might we determine whether the transcendence of superficial skin coloration has become a reality or whether instead such proclamations actually represent a triumph of superficiality? The study of human history may prove helpful. And we should be wary of those propositions promoting the postmodern deconstruction of any distinctive sense of community in the interest of a conjectured universality devoid of historical antecedents. Circumspection is called for since the failure to make critical discernments and appropriate distinctions is at least as dangerous as fixating on material particulars or differentiating by unwarranted presumptions. Universal comity and cooperation are noble pursuits, but such lofty goals are not likely to be obtained by leaping mindlessly from the sometimes precarious perch of ancestral perceptivity into an abyss of utter meaninglessness. What is certain is that the socioeconomic condition and life prospects for the masses of the people remain exactly the same in this new global-village, postmodern, postracial age as they were in the previous age of White supremacy.

In any case, clarity demands a consistent application of nomenclature for any historical presence or collective identity, although with the understanding that human beings individually or as groups may occasionally alter their cultural personas in order to suit the prevailing social customs of a given era. To detach human beings from their history and cultural heritage is to dehumanize those people; it is in effect to call them out of their name. And thus we refer to the "Blacks" as one of the several names for that historical group of people so identified, i.e., Africans, African Americans and other peoples of African descent.

The first chapter, "Our Mother," examines the African origins of humanity and human civilization. Instead of calling Africa the "Dark Continent," it would be more appropriate to call Africa the continent where the world first saw the light. The British philosopher John Stuart Mill recognized Africa as the earliest known seat of civilization and that the Greeks were indebted to this civilization for much of what they knew. Western scholars have often referred to traditional African religions and cultures as primitive, and though they may have meant it as a slight, their description may not be far off since the word primitive is derived from the Latin root *primus* which means primary or original.

Although substantiated by the most up-to-date scientific data, the African origin of humanity is not often discussed in classrooms by historians and scholars. Currently, there is no serious objection to an African origin of humanity in the scientific community. While there may one day be data indicating human origins aside from the African genesis, it is undoubtedly the case that Africans are the oldest representatives of humankind and they are most likely the progenitors of all of current humanity. The African origin of human civilization, seemingly a natural consequence of the African origin of humanity, is somewhat more controversial, but there is still a large and growing body of evidence supporting this view. We give a brief overview of the material demonstrating the African origins of civilization.

The second chapter, "Christianity in Transition," focuses on the shift in the locus of authority from the early church in North Africa to Europe and the emergence of Roman Imperial Christianity. Christianity may have benefitted from the association with the Romans in terms of growth and prestige, but much was lost as well in terms of the original mission and purpose. There was an immediate cessation of the persecution of the Christians after Constantine's conversion. The famous Roman roads were now opened to spread the gospel. The church's teachings and belief in an exclusive monotheism boded well for the hierarchical polity of the Roman authorities, and Constantine shrewdly used Christianity to enhance his control of the empire. This chapter covers how the church summoned its best minds to craft an official theology to support the marriage between the temporal and spiritual authorities. Eusebius even argued that Constantine had been chosen by God to bring peace and restoration to both the church and the empire. Constantine also had an impact on the church as worship became more formal and the pulpit took on the appearance and aura of a throne. Church worship began to mirror imperial forms of ceremony with the burning of incense, and officiating ministers adorning themselves with clerical garb as they opened worship services with grand processionals and closed them with equally grand recessionals. The more communitarian and egalitarian aspects of the early church began to fade away.

In this chapter we will also demonstrate how the secular authorities and materialistic prerogatives began to gain influence in Christianity at the expense of the more spiritual beliefs and practices of the early church. With the growing influence of secular authorities and materialism in the now Roman-dominated church, the African wing of the church eventually broke away from Western Christianity. The African leaders had been at the forefront in developing the basic doctrines of Christianity but their influence was now greatly diminished. In response to losing their influence, the African churches began to look to monks and monasteries for spiritual mentoring and inspiration.

In the third chapter, "The European Slave Trade," we examine the slave trade, which is linked to the discovery of America and the genesis of the modern global trading system. Columbus and his crew landed in Haiti in 1492. Three years later, Columbus was required to go back to Haiti in order to put down an uprising of the native people of that island who had declined to accept the European intrusion and hegemony imposed upon them. Columbus and his militia unmercifully massacred these people, whom they called Indians. A Roman Catholic missionary to the Indians, and later priest of the Dominican order, Bartolome de Las Casas, gave birth to the idea of enslaving Africans and bringing them to the Americas to serve as the work force in place of the rapidly diminishing population of Indians.

During the last decade of the fifteenth century, the Portuguese were exploring the coast of Guinea, and eventually reached the Cape of Good Hope, an accomplishment they somehow concluded gave them exclusive rights to the whole continent of Africa. In spite of reservations from King Ansah in Ghana, the Portuguese built the slave port Elmina, the first fort built on the Gold Coast of Africa. The Europeans exchanged guns, gun powder, whiskey, and other materials for human beings as they began their massive systematic enslavement of Africans and their international trade in black gold. The Europeans quickly learned to encourage the Africans to fight against one another, leading to their self-destruction and vulnerability to further exploitation. The strategy of corrupting the leaders while dividing to conquer continues to plague African people on the continent and throughout the Diaspora. This chapter also exposes the horrors of the Middle Passage. The mere survival of Africans with any sense of dignity at all after the deadly voyage across the Atlantic to the Americas is as much of a miracle as the crossing of the Red Sea by the Hebrews in Exodus. The perpetration of the European Slave Trade, including the Middle Passage, was one of the most inhuman acts ever committed. It has been estimated that up to one third of these Africans captured for enslavement are buried in watery graves beneath the Atlantic Ocean. The psychological trauma of being ruthlessly uprooted from their homelands and physically brutalized was so devastating that 145 years after Emancipation, African Americans are still struggling to deal with the aftermath.

In the fourth chapter we discuss the conversion experience of African Americans to the practice of American Christianity. Contrary to much academic and popular opinion, the adoption of Christianity was not simply a matter of the dominant Whites forcing some religion upon their hapless slaves. The program of Whites to Christianize the Blacks did not completely produce the desired results and expected outcomes. Africans did not accept Christianity in large numbers until the Great Awakening, and many of the early plantation slaveholders were reluctant to have their slaves converted as they were suspicious of religious teachings that might suggest the slaves were something other than chattel. In time, Africans began to perceive Christianity as a springboard to literacy, social advancement, and community development. And as we shall demonstrate at length, African Americans fought long and hard to establish their own churches.

The fifth chapter, "The Black Church and Black Reconstruction," introduces the Black church and those religious leaders who played a role in the emergence of independent Black churches and Reconstruction. The chapter opens with General William Tecumseh Sherman's march to Savannah and the liberation of Black churches, which took place along the way. Black churches then began to play a central role in the development of African-American communities, a role which continues to the present day.

In the sixth chapter, "The Struggle in the Wilderness," we describe and explain the emergence of color consciousness among African Americans, which can be related to classism and elitism as well. From the 1880s to 1950s, African Americans were no longer enslaved but they also were not fully recognized as citizens either. It was during this period that with numerous starts and turns there eventually emerged grassroots civil rights protests, which added to the long and storied tradition of Black preachers leading their people toward social justice and a higher sense of human worth. Elitism played a role in reducing the effectiveness of some churches and hampered the move to social justice. The struggle for justice would continue nevertheless, and many Black churches and ministers would play critical roles in the advance toward civil rights. This chapter shows how the elites, initially the mulatto elites, tried desperately to differentiate themselves from the Black masses, many aspiring to be completely assimilated into White society. They would be rebuffed, and a protracted grassroots protest movement would then emerge.

In the seventh chapter, titled "The Civil Rights Movement as an Outgrowth of the Black Church," and the final chapter, "Conclusions," we consider the seminal role of the Black church in the dramatic move toward social justice in America. Black churches provided much of the leadership, moral support, organizational structure, ground troops, public platform, and monetary resources for the civil rights struggle. Although overlooked or ignored by many scholars, African-American churches were central and not peripheral to the achievements of the civil rights era.

Over the years of my professional career I have embraced a holistic approach to the study and teaching of history. The holistic approach involves investigating interrelationships in comparison to expressions of an organic whole more so than looking for isolated phenomena subjected to external controls. The study of history should be more than just peering into the stagnant and stale past, and properly conceived, history is far more than the listing of events, dates, and iconic personalities. In this work we have attempted to tell the story of the African-American church in the context of unfolding social, political, economic, and cultural events by examining interrelationships of the African-American experience with aspects of American and world history.

Our African ancestors retained some collective memory of their African past and heritage, which ultimately extends back to the origin of humankind and civilization. One does a disservice to African Americans when one attempts to explain their experience without noting their retention and adaptation of African cultural forms, their capacity to survive, adjust and eventually rise out of chattel slavery, and their relationships to other peoples and events in American history. It is also true that Europeans have significantly influenced the social identity of African Americans and shaped the contours of the institutional life of Black churches. But influence is a two-way street; any effort to manipulate or control another requires the manipulator to observe and respond to the actions of the subject of manipulation. Black religious expressions and forms have evoked reactions from Whites, both negative and positive, and Blacks have had an impact on the way that Whites perceive of themselves in their religious practices and in their relationships with others.

CHAPTER 1

Our Mother

THE AFRICAN ORIGINS OF
HUMANITY AND CIVILIZATION

Mother is the best metaphor for describing Africa in relation to world history. When tracing our African roots, we arrive at this inescapable conclusion: Out of Africa came all entries into the world. She is the mother of all that from which or in which or on which continent the human race, human civilization, and the foundations of religion were conceived and delivered into the world. Mother Africa is the term used to describe Africa as the "matrix" or "womb" from which all else concerning humanity developed.

From time immemorial, Africa has been identified as the native soil of the original people. The term Africa itself is believed to have Roman origins. The Greeks have supplied us with the term Ethiopia which literally means "land of burnt-faced people," i.e., homeland of the Blacks. But, this term seems to have not only been applied to the people within continental Africa, but also to those Blacks or people of African descent who occupied much of Western Asia in ancient times. The ancient Greek writers Herodotus and Homer each identified the people of Egypt, Arabia, Palestine, and India as Ethiopians. The term Kush was used by the ancient Hebrews to indicate those people to the South of Egypt. The word Sudan, which refers to the "land of the Blacks" in Arabic, was once used to designate most of the regions throughout northern and western Africa. Black-a-moors was the name given by Europeans to those African and Arabic invaders who occupied the Iberian Peninsula. And the Portuguese later gave us the term Negro which also references this characteristic feature of people of African descent.[1]

1

In the beginning the whole earth was one super land mass centered on Africa. The continents as we now know them all broke off from the central African land mass millions of years ago. Geographically, about 175,000,000 years ago, we find Africa at the center of the original super-continent, a conglomerate land mass some geologists refer to as Pangaea, that places Africa in the center of the earth's four quadrants or in all four hemispheres. Subsequently, by way of the continental drift, the continents have evolved into their present formations, including Antarctica, Australia, North America, South America, Asia, and the peninsular formation of Asia currently known as Europe. Africa as the geographical center is a perspective that can be further understood when we consider two additional facts: (1) The center of movement of the earth's continental drift has been proposed to be in southern Africa, and (2) Africa lies across the equator, the centerline of the earth's spherical surface and the northernmost and southernmost extremes of Africa lie equidistant from the equator (37° north and 37° south respectively.)[2]

In agreement with the myths of the ancients, current scientific evidence points to Africa as the birthplace of humanity. Only on the continent of Africa have all of the earliest human prototypes been located by anthropologists. For more than three centuries, naturalists and anthropologists have drawn the conclusion that Africa is the birthplace of the human race. In 1924 Raymond Dart unearthed ape-like skulls with human-like features in South Africa.[3] He later also found evidence of man's early ancestors in northern Tanzania in eastern Africa, in the Great Rift Valley of Kenya, and in northern Ethiopia. The great Senegalese polymath, Cheikh Anta Diop, maintained that Africa was the singular birthplace of humankind. Diop advanced the following argument based on his study of the archeological evidence: (1) Of six basic prototypes of man—*Ramapithecus australopithecus, Australopithecus gracilis, Homo habilis, Homo erectus, Homo sapiens* and *Homo sapiens sapiens*—only the last two are found in the Americas, only the last three are found in Asia and Europe, but all six are to be found in Africa. (2) As a general evolutionary principle, "nature never strikes twice"; that is, a distinct type of being or creature emerges from only a single geographical region and in one and only one epoch of time.[4] A delineation of the development of humankind based on this model is illustrated in Table 1.

Table 1: Development of Humankind

Prototype	Ramapithecus australopithecus	Australopithecus gracilis	Homo habilis	Homo erectus	Homo sapiens	Homo sapiens sapiens
First Emergence	5–6 million years ago	3.2 million years ago	2.4–1 million years ago	2 million years ago	1.5 million–500,000 years ago	200,000–240,000 years ago
Eventual Outcome	*Prototypes of humankind found only in Africa that never left the continent before extinction*			*Left Africa 1.5 million years ago and eventually went extinct*	*Left Africa 100,000 years ago and eventually went extinct*	*Left Africa 30,000–40,000 years ago and populated the planet*

There have been several important developments since the time of Diop's writings, and various scholars offer differing views on the archeological record and the process of development for humankind. But, the theoretical account provided by Diop remains instructive; interpretation of some details may vary, but his model gives us the basic organizing principle for humankind's early development. The earliest prototypes of humankind are found in Africa; later representatives also arise in Africa and then migrate out to Europe and Asia; only the most recent representatives of humanity can be located in the Americas; and all may be traced back to an African origin.

Scholars continue to find archeological evidence to support the "Out of Africa" theory of human origination. Recently, geneticists have contributed to the body of evidence. They have collected samples of DNA from people all over the world, and after testing they have concluded that, based on genetic variation, African genes have been around longer than any other kind of human genes.[5] Some geneticists have even hypothesized that the human "Eve" was an African woman who lived around 230,000–240,000 years ago. DNA samples from people all over the world seem to be traceable to a single African ancestral source. They have proposed that it is quite possible that all humans alive today are the ultimate progeny of one Black woman.[6] The famed paleontologist Stephen J. Gould maintained

that all human beings are members of a single great family that originated in Africa. He traced the origin of Neanderthals in Europe and Java
Man along with Peking Man in Asia back to their African roots. Human
beings as we know them today, *Homo sapiens sapiens* have been around for
230,000–240,000 years, but of that time they have only lived outside of
Africa for a relatively brief period. Human beings first left the continent
30,000–40,000 years ago. It was only after the ice sheath receded from the
last glacial age that humans finally migrated into the other continents that
had broken off from Africa.[7]

As has often been stated, "Man is a tropical animal." The human race
was born in the warm tropical climates of Africa. It is in these moderate
climes that men and women have ready access to abundant supplies of
food, fresh water, and sufficient material to make clothing and tools needed
for survival. The almost continuous sunshine of the tropics then accounts
for skin which is abundant in melanin—the black skin of the Africans—
which is most advantageous for protection from the sun's ultraviolet rays
as well as for preserving the important B vitamin folate. Diop and other
African scholars have also speculated that the sunny African paradise also
afforded our early ancestors a sunny and hopeful attitude toward nature
and a vibrant communal spirituality, as they were so frequently showered
with nature's many blessings. Diop goes on to indicate that some of the
early people who left Africa and settled in Europe were trapped there after
the onset of the last ice age. These people lost the capacity to produce
melanin in sufficient quantities to maintain their skin pigmentation, and
perhaps they underwent psychological alterations as well. Diop contrasts
the hopeful outlook of the people in what he terms the southern cradle of
civilization, or Africa, with the much more aggressive disposition developed by Caucasians in the Eurasian or northern cradle of civilization. In
the North, people were much more prone to individualistic and violent
behavior patterns which were perhaps, due to their inhospitable climate.
With migrations from Africa to different climates around the globe,
human beings developed different physical features and cultural expressions; but nevertheless, all of them can trace their origins back to Africa.[8]

Perhaps owing to the harsh, cold climate of the North, civilization
came late to Caucasians, i.e., the offspring of those Africans who had

earlier migrated northward to Europe. The earliest stirrings of advanced social structures—evidence of the farming of plants and animals— that we might call civilization occurred in the Nile River Valley around 10,000–16,000 B.C.E. The nations of Kemet (Ancient Egypt), Nubia (in the region of present-day Sudan), and Punt (in the region of present-day Kenya) arose out of the Nile River Valley cultures. Dates for the rise of Dynastic Egypt range from 5,000 B.C.E. to 3,200 B.C.E. There is evidence of advanced civilization in Mesopotamia (the Fertile Crescent) about 3,000 B.C.E., the Indus Kush River Valley in India around 2,800 B.C.E., and the Yellow River Valley in China about 2,500 B.C.E. The Greeks began their cultural ascent around 750 B.C.E. followed by the Romans in 500 B.C.E.[9]

Prior to the emergence of these advanced cultures, we find in Africa abundant evidence of man's early development with numerous remains of tools and the early instruments that were used. Until recently it was held by many scientists that tool-making and major cultural skills first emerged in Europe about 40,000 years ago. But, Sally McBrearty, an anthropologist, made some startling discoveries while working in Lake Baringo in Kenya. She and her researchers discovered stone blades buried beneath volcanic ash, and these were hand-made tools showing signs of careful shaping which took considerable planning to produce, and they were dated at 240,000 years old. They also discovered other African archeological sites that yielded stone spear points and rhinestones that date to more than 130,000 years ago.[10] And this was long before the first documented cultural artifacts, or even the first human beings for that matter, were located in Europe. Prior to these recent findings there was a series of startling discoveries near the Olduvai Gorge in Tanzania by nineteenth- and twentieth-century anthropologists as they excavated evidence that shows that African people were the first to use fire. These seminal inventions originated in Africa and later spread to Asia and Europe. The first signs of cooperative hunting and seasonal campfires are found in Africa, along with the first shelters made of branches, grass, and stone. Over 10,000 years ago, Africans developed a high level of hunting and gathering food. Hunting was not only a source of food; the bones were used to make tools and ornaments, while animal skins could be used for garments. In some parts of Africa people found shelter in caves. Painting and engraving originated in Africa. There are numerous examples throughout the continent of pristine paintings from the Stone Age depicting humans and animals with religious themes concerning life, death, and the spirit world.[11]

Farming has an African origin; the domestication of plants and animals originated in Africa over 12,000 years ago. With the advent of agriculture, humanity was able to progress to more advanced forms of culture as (1) people were able to settle in one area with a steady food supply, which led to an increase in the population; (2) people developed more extensive families and support systems as they now lived in stable communities; (3) family structures provided the basis for more effective social organization which led to more labor to produce crops, and more effective means to care for and protect one another; and (4) the increasingly stable and secure environs allowed time and opportunity for more creative productions. In the Congo, archeologists have unearthed remains of the civilization of the Ishongo people, who lived there about 8,000 years ago and who used a type of abacus to perform mathematical operations, including multiplication. It is believed to be the oldest such calculator in the world. Africans were the first people to use iron, copper, and gold for forging weapons, creating jewelry, and building furniture and houses. The transition from food gathering to food producing empowered Africans to become the first people to build communities and establish the foundations of what we now recognize as governments, educational institutions, and religious systems.[12]

Finally, the world's first great centers of learning were in Africa. The first illustrious seat of learning on record was in the city that the Africans of that time called Nowe or Waset (referred to as Thebes by the Greeks and also called Luxor). Nowe was in southern Egypt on the banks of the Nile River. This center of learning flourished over 4,000 years ago.[13] Later, Alexandria would become a great center of learning in the northern part of Egypt. The great library of Alexandria was one of the wonders of the ancient world. Egypt as a center of learning is important to European history, because it is in Egypt that many of the Greek philosophers first got their training in higher education. Pythagoras studied in Egypt for 22 years before he returned to Greece to start his own school. Herodotus even gives an account of Pythagoras bestowing gifts upon his African teachers prior to his return to Greece. And of course Pythagoras did not "discover" the Pythagorean Theorem until after his education in Egypt. Plato, Solon, Democritus, and a host of other Greek philosophers also whetted their appetites for learning in Africa.[14]

In summary, we find that in practically every significant way, Africa is the progenitor of those activities that are found to be essential for modern societies, from the cultivation of crops to the formation of cities to creating institutions of higher learning. The great nineteenth century African-American leader Frederick Douglass expressed his pride when he addressed the debt that the world owes Mother Africa as he wrote:

> It is pleasant to know that in color, form and features we are related to the first successful tillers of the soil; to the people who taught the world agriculture; that the civilization which made Greece, Rome and Western Europe illustrious, and even made our land glorious, sprang forth from the bosom of Africa.[15]

In terms of theological and doctrinal antecedents, Africa is rightly considered the birthplace of the three Abrahamic religions—Judaism, Christianity, and Islam.[16] This can be seen in the myths and stories of traditional African cultures which existed in some cases thousands of years before the emergence of Judaism. The Dogon people of Mali are believed to have migrated out of the Nile Valley region as that center of early African civilizations was falling apart due to the repeated invasions from Asia and Europe. The Dogon creation myth is strikingly similar to the creation story in the Hebrew Bible. The character Nommo in Dogon cosmology is a prototypical Christ figure—a divinity who sacrifices his life in order to save the world.[17] From ancient Kemet we are provided with the story of a divine family which has remarkable parallels to the story of the Holy Family in the Bible. In the Kemetic story, the good king Ausar (called Osiris by the Greeks) is murdered by his evil brother Set who wishes to sit upon the throne. Ausar's wife Auset (called Isis by the Greeks) is overcome with grief. Upon finding her husband's remains she is moved to "immaculately" conceive his child, Heru (called Horus by the Greeks and from which the word hero is derived). Heru later challenges Set for control of the kingdom. Heru is eventually able to retake the throne once held by his deceased father, Ausar, who then sits in judgment of the dead in the netherworld. The Bible, the story of Ausar, and the Dogon mythology all focus on the great themes of creation, rebellion, and salvation or redemption.[18]

Africans are mentioned throughout the Bible. The Hebrew Bible alone cites Ethiopia over forty times and Egypt over one hundred times. In contrast, there is no mention of European countries in the Old Testament. Indeed the first Europeans of any international consequence, the Greeks, did not emerge into historical record until the time period covered by the Hebrew Bible was almost over. One will not find a single reference to England, Germany, or Spain in the Hebrew Bible.[19] It is only in the New Testament that Europeans begin to play a significant role in biblical events, but even then not one of the central characters is European. The fact of Africa's prominent role in the Bible would come into play later in the sixteenth century as Europeans initiated their massive enslavement of African people. They wished to rationalize their behavior, and it was the Portuguese, the first Europeans involved in the enslavement of Africans, who coined the term Negroes, or the Blacks.[20] Prior to this time, Europeans mostly referred to Africans as Moors or Ethiopians. The Moors were despised as they had just been overthrown after ruling over most of Hispania (the Iberian Peninsula) for the preceding seven hundred years. For the Portuguese, using the term Negro helped to obscure the fact that Africans, via the terms Ethiopia or Egypt, were repeatedly mentioned throughout the Bible. They did not want to reference the fact that they were in the process of enslaving the very people who were so often mentioned in their own holy book. To acknowledge that they were enslaving Ethiopians, people who are praised and honored in the Bible, would have been at the very least quite disconcerting.

The Biblical narrative found in Genesis 2:8–14 indicates that the first two rivers of Eden were in ancient Kush. Genesis 2:11–12 connects the Pishon River with Havilah, a direct descendant of Kush (Genesis 10:7). The Gihon River is cited in Genesis 2:13 as the second river in the Garden of Eden, and it is described as surrounding the whole land of Kush. The precise location of the biblical Eden has been a matter of some debate. However, as the above passages clearly indicate the location of Eden was at the very least quite close to Africa, if indeed it was not on African soil proper. It was certainly within the historical "Land of the Blacks," or Kush, which in deep antiquity included Western Asia.[21]

In the Christian Bible, according to the historical account of the Book of Acts, second chapter, Africans were charter members of the original church. These are they who were present on the Day of Pentecost, the beginning of the early Christian church:

- Parthians and Medes and Elamites and dwellers in Mesopotamia and in Judaea, and Cappadocia in Pontus and Asia (v.9)

- Phyrgians and Pamphylians in Egypt, and in the parts of Libya about Cyrene, and strangers of Rome, Jews, and proselytes (v.10)

- Cretes and Arabians, we hear them speak in our tongues the wonderful works of God. (v.11)

Kemetic texts from 1,300 B.C.E. have been discovered that refer to one of their provinces called Canaan, which was located in the land that we now refer to as Israel or Palestine. In the Bible, the character Canaan was the son of Ham, the mythological progenitor of the Blacks—the word "ham" meaning hot or heat and by inference referring to the color black, and the other biblical sons of Ham being Egypt (Kemet), Libya, and Ethiopia. (See Genesis 9:18–29) In prehistoric times African people migrated out of Africa and into Western Asia, the region of present-day Palestine, the Arabian Peninsula, and the Fertile Crescent of Mesopotamia. They later moved on into the Indus Kush Valley in India and further into Asia. Later in history, about 500 B.C.E., Diop indicates that Egyptian priests, having been chased out of their own country by the persecutions of Cambyses, may have then spread their teachings throughout much of Asia giving rise to Buddhist, Confucian, and Zoroastrian traditions.[22] Thus, it is not surprising when we find similar myths and stories by the people in these different regions as they may well have all had an origin in Africa.

The act of someone being "called out of Egypt" is a repeated reference in the Bible, and it may be a conceptualization of Africa as the archetypal mother, the primordial source of spirit and substance. During the Patriarchal Period, Jacob and his family go into Egypt.

And God spake unto Israel in the visions of the night, and said, "Jacob, Jacob." And he said, "Here am I." And He said, "I am God, the God of thy Father, fear not to go down into Egypt, for I will make thee a great nation." (Genesis 46:1–2)

Later the prophet Hosea reports, "When Israel was a child, then I loved him and called my son out of Egypt." (Hosea 11:1) After Jesus was born in Bethlehem, his parents believed that their child's life was threatened, so they traveled into Egypt for safe haven. Thus it is written, "I shall call my son out of Egypt." (Mathew 2:15) It should also be noted that the scripture, "Princes shall come out of Egypt, and Ethiopia shall stretch forth her hands unto God" (Psalm 68:31), was frequently quoted by Black preachers and community leaders to encourage the people during the darkest days of slavery and segregation.

Further evidence of a strong African influence on early Judaism can be found in the stories of Moses and the Queen of Sheba. Moses was of course born in Egypt. He even became a part of the Pharaoh's royal court. After Moses was forced to flee Egypt, he went into the land of Elam, which is south of Egypt in the region of present-day Ethiopia. In Elam, he meets Zipporah, an African woman and he marries her. Scholars have also pointed out that (1) as Moses grew up as a member of the royal family of Egypt, he would have been trained in the religious system of the Egyptians, which surely influenced his own later religious teachings; and (2) the Jews resided in Egypt for 400 years, and as they were small in number upon arriving but great in number when they left, they were likely influenced by the Egyptians both culturally and genetically.[23]

Makeda, the Queen of Sheba, ruled over much of modern-day Ethiopia and perhaps parts of the Arabian Peninsula and southern Egypt as well around 1,000 B.C.E. She visited King Solomon of Israel. (I Kings 10: 1–13) According to longstanding Ethiopian tradition, the queen bore a son after her visit, the seed of Solomon, whose name was Menelik. Menelik became the first Emperor of Ethiopia, bearing the royal title, "Conquering Lion of the Tribe of Judah." The descendants of Menelik ruled in an unbroken line of succession until the fall of Haile Selassie in 1974.[24]

In the traditional lore of Ethiopia, Solomon failed to pay the proper homage to the sacredness of the Ark of the Covenant which was housed in the Holy Temple of Jerusalem. In response to his father's carelessness, Menelik brought the Ark of the Covenant to Ethiopia for safe-keeping. To the present day the officials of the Ethiopian Tewahedo Orthodox Church claim to have in their possession the original Ark of the Covenant and they profess to be its guardians.[25] We also find that the Ethiopian eunuch, Finance Minster of Queen Candace, who met the evangelist Philip as told in the Bible, was an African Jew. The document he was reading from when he came upon Philip contained the teachings of the prophet Isaiah. And this indicates that the Ethiopians of that time were familiar with Jewish literature.

African Jews have a long history of residing in Ethiopia. These people are sometimes called Falashas by other Ethiopians which means "foreigner." But the name Falasha is considered by them to be derogatory. The Ethiopian Jews refer to themselves as Beta Isra'el or "The House of Israel." They are phenotypically African (i.e., appearances tending toward black skin, curly hair, and full lips and noses), and it is possible that they are the remnants of the original Jews from the time of Moses. The Beta Isra'el may be traced by historical documentation back to at least 586 B.C.E. and the destruction of the first Holy Temple in Jerusalem, which they commemorate annually with a feast.[26] The Black Jews possess an ancient spiritual literature and a sacred language which is called Ge'ez. Ge'ez is more ancient than Hebrew and it may well be a precursor for both the Hebrew and Arabic languages. Ge'ez is also used as the liturgical language of the Ethiopian Orthodox Tewahedo Church. It plays a role similar to the Latin language in the Roman Catholic Church. European Jews or Ashkenazim now dominate Judaism and they were reluctant for many years to recognize the Ethiopian Jews. But, they have since relented, and currently the Black Jews are recognized as a part of worldwide Jewry. Many Ethiopian Jews have resettled in present-day Israel.

Finally, we note that many of the teachings and symbolisms of Christianity have analogous conceptualizations within traditional African spiritual systems. Some African Americans who have adopted Islam or returned to traditional African religions have supposed that Christianity is incompatible with the traditions of Africa. And many Christians, prompted by Eurocentric propaganda, have presumed their religion to be superior to the beliefs and practices of traditional Africa. Ignorance mixed with arrogance can leave one dangerously susceptible to foolish assertions. Those mature in their faith are prepared to dispel misconceptions and remedy misdeeds as they calmly reclaim the sacredness of their traditions from those who would exploit religious facilities to further irreligious activities. There are many important differences between the modern practice of Christianity and the various evolving, living spiritual traditions of Africa; each has developed over the centuries according to the needs and prerogatives of their respective practitioners. But, there are also similarities of underlying basic concepts and more than a few striking parallels in symbolism. Among the Yoruba, the divine attributes of Ifa, which represent the central tenets of that tradition, have some of the very same attributes of God as found in the Bible. For example, there is Obatala, deity of the Yoruba Orisha pantheon, who was permitted by Oludumare, the Supreme God, to provide solid dry ground and a living space for the beings of the earth, after which he fashioned humankind out of clay. One story about Obatala is summarized as follows:

> One day Obatala determined to travel on a journey to visit his friend Shango. Obatala who was well known for his beautiful, radiant flowing white robes, was greeted along the way by Eshu, an often mischievous deity, who tricked Obatala into soiling his robe. Undaunted the King in White Robes continued on his journey to meet his friend. However, with the now dirty garments he was mistaken for a thief, and so he was beaten and then taken into captivity. Obatala is unjustly forced to endure imprisonment. Finally, after these ordeals Obatala is released, but despite his suffering and abandonment he nevertheless demonstrates great compassion and bestows his blessings upon the land and heals the people. [27]

In Isaiah 53:2–5, the passage of the suffering servant provides a description of the Savior as follows:

> For He shall grow up before Him as a tender plant, and as a root out of dry ground ... and when we see Him, there is no beauty that we should

desire Him. He is despised and rejected by men, a Man of sorrows and acquainted with grief.... Surely He has borne our griefs and carried our sorrows; yet we esteemed Him stricken, smitten by God, and afflicted... He was wounded for our transgressions. He was bruised for our iniquities, the chastisement for our peace ... and by His stripes we are healed.[28]

Teachings that conceptualize a benevolent Supreme Being, the dead coming back to life, justice for wrongdoers and vindication for those who persevere in righteousness are central to both African traditions and Christianity.

THE AFRICAN DEFENDERS OF THE FAITH

In discourses on scripture, too often Bible teachers, ministers, and even seminary professors quote scripture and then immediately jump to analogous circumstances in the present day without ever giving due consideration to the intervening period and especially the development of the early Church and how those developments continue to inform our Christian beliefs. When this occurs, not only is proper historical context lost but the following two key developments are omitted: (1) the African contributions to shaping the basic doctrine and theology of the faith, contributions which still deeply influence the contemporary church, and (2) the struggles, sacrifices, and martyrdom of many African Christians in the early church—those who sealed their witness with blood and by their witness they helped to spread the faith.[29]

The singular mission of the early church was to witness the power of the Holy Spirit to the uttermost parts of the earth:

> But, ye shall receive power when the Holy Spirit has come upon you; and ye shall be witness unto me both in Jerusalem and in all Judaea, and Samaria and unto the uttermost parts of the earth. (Acts 1:8)

African thinkers and theologians became the primary contributors to shaping the foundational doctrine, practices, and rituals of the Church. Tertullian of Carthage (160–220 c.e.) was one of the most able theologians of the early church. He strongly opposed the confluence of Christianity with Greek philosophy. Like Paul before him and Martin Luther many centuries later, he believed that the struggle against sin was the central focus of the church and that this focus must not be diverted by engaging in fanciful speculations or materialistic pursuits. He felt that there should be a holiness and purity about Christianity that set it apart from secular philosophy and thought. The father of Western theology who helped to fashion the sacred Latin script of Roman Catholicism was not from Rome or Greece but was a native son of Africa. The most basic theological concepts and vocabulary of the church were formed in the minds of Africans like Tertullian, Augustine, and Cyprian, among others.[30] Tertullian was a most insightful theologian. He foresaw the inherent conflict in the "love thy neighbor as thyself" teachings of Christianity which might lead the church to trying to become everything to everybody; loving thy neighbor must not mean the loss of thyself. He argued that Christianity did not need philosophy to augment its mission and teachings. Tertullian concluded that "the soul is by nature Christian. Christians are no longer seeking the truth; you do not need to seek what you already have." A century prior to the heresy of Arianism, Tertullian envisioned such a heresy creeping into the church. Tertullian was a traditionalist; he opposed relaxing the basic teachings of Christianity to accommodate the profundities of Greek philosophy, which were held in such high esteem by the learned of that day.[31]

Justin (100–165 c.e.), whose martyrdom sealed his witness with blood, embraced the idea of connecting classical Greek philosophy with Christianity. In an attempt to find a common ground with Greek philosophy he made an effort to connect the concept of Logos (universal reason) which was first espoused by the Greek philosopher Heraclitus in the sixth century b.c.e., to the doctrine of the faith. Justin attempted to build a bridge between reason and faith. There was lively debate between those Christians who took the view of Tertullian and those who agreed with the efforts of Justin. Despite the controversy, by applying Logos to the Gospel, Justin did pave the way for those who were influenced by Greek philosophy to become Christians.[32] Tertullian and other African thinkers such as Tatian (110–172 c.e.), responded negatively to any attempts to associate Christianity with Greek philosophy. Tatian rose to strongly oppose the views of his renowned teacher, Justin. In the midst of the controversy, Tatian delivered a blistering critique of Greek arrogance and culture in his famous Address to the Greeks which he delivered in the last decade of his life:

> Be not, O Greeks, so very hostilely disposed toward the Barbarians, nor look with ill will on their opinions. For which of your institutions has not been derived from the Barbarians? The most eminent of the Telmessians invented the art of divining by dreams; the Carians, that of prognosticating by the stars, the Phyrgians and the most ancient Isaurians, augury by the flight of birds; the Cyprians, the art of inspecting victims. To the Babylonians you owe astronomy; to the Persians magic; to the Egyptians geometry; to the Phoenicians, instruction by alphabetic writing. Cease, then, to miscall these imitations inventions of your own. Orpheus, again, taught you poetry and song; from him, too, you learned the mysteries. The Tuscans taught you the plastic art; from the annals of the Egyptians you learned to write history…. Wherefore lay aside this conceit, and be not ever boasting of your elegance of diction; for, while you applaud yourselves, your own people will of course side with you. But, it becomes a man of sense to wait for the testimony of others, and it becomes men to be of one accord also in the pronunciation of their language…. On this account we have renounced your wisdom, though I was once a great proficient in it; for, as the comic poet says—These are gleaners' grapes and small talk, Twittering places of swallows, corrupters of art.[33]

The supremacy of the Hellenistic culture and language was a notion promoted by the Roman emperors who used the erudition of their Greek learning to intimidate and promote their dominance over their subjects; those who did not speak the Greek language were called barbarians. Tatian ridiculed the presumed cultural superiority of the Greeks and exposed their boasted achievements to in fact be a long list of borrowed or stolen inventions. Furthermore, he found that the Greeks were inclined to use their great learning for deceptive and ignoble purposes.

Persecution and martyrdom did not suppress the spirit of the early church. To the contrary, the witness of the martyrs somehow always seemed to inspire ever greater evangelism. It was the persecution of the gathered church that scattered the witness of Christianity to Judaea and Samaria and the uttermost parts of the earth. It was from Africa that the theologian Tertullian spoke for the church as martyrs were being ripped apart and thrown to the lions:

> We grow up in great numbers, as often as we are cut down by you. The blood of the martyrs is the seed of the church. We are of yesterday, and yet we have filled every place belonging to you—cities, islands, castles, towns, assemblies, your very camps and companies, palaces, senate, forum; we leave your temple only. [34]

Saint Augustine, the African who was of great influence in shaping the doctrinal character of the Roman Catholic Church, once wrote that the church owes Paul to the prayers of Stephen, who while he was being stoned to death, prayed for the forgiveness of his executioners. Prior to Paul's conversion, he terrorized early Christians, but he could never forget the way Stephen died. It was Paul's conversion that led him to write half of the books of the New Testament. He is frequently called the greatest missionary of the church. The Pauline letters and the didactic teachings of the Twelve Apostles provide a guideline for worship and practical Christian living.[35] In the early stages of Christianity, the teachers and group leaders were focused on addressing the practical issues of survival confronting the church. The more challenging theological controversies did not arise until the third and fourth centuries after the death of Christ as heretical doctrines and beliefs began to proliferate throughout the church. It should be noted that the New Testament was not established as the official doctrine or canon of the church until 397 C.E. in Africa, at the Synod of Carthage. Until that time the various communities of the early church used different Gospels, various letters from the apostles and an assortment of other texts instead of a fixed body of sacred literature. The use of different texts by different churches was obviously going to be problematic over time as the religion spread to new regions and various interpretations of scripture proliferated.[36]

The earliest Christians did not believe that they were a part of some new religion. They were mostly Jews who were convinced that they were followers of the long-awaited Jewish messiah. The believers saw their movement as the fulfillment of the promise God had made to Abraham. For the early Christians, the Old Testament was the New Testament concealed, and the New Testament was the Old Testament revealed. Paul became the apostle to the Gentiles (non-Jews) and invited them to become children of Abraham by faith, as it was not possible by flesh. It was then the mission and vision of the early church that, through the coming of Jesus Christ, all nations would be brought unto Zion. Christianity was conceived not to be a rival to Judaism, but the fulfillment thereof. Even those Jews who rejected Christianity did not see this new faith as a new religion at first but instead thought it just a heretical sect of Judaism.[37]

At the dawn of the Christian era, the Romans stayed out of the feud between the Jews and the Christians. However, Christianity as an actively proselytizing faith grew quickly and soon the Gentiles outnumbered the Jewish Christians. Before long, the Romans began to recognize a clear distinction between Christianity and Judaism.

The phenomenal growth of Christianity in the Roman provinces was alarming.[38] The early Christians embraced a peculiar, disciplined lifestyle, and they rejected tribute to the corrupt authorities of the then prevailing religions. Their emphasis on modesty and egalitarian communal living was both unusual and appealing to the masses of oppressed humanity. They invited all, both the slave and the Roman citizen, to enjoin their party and they held the strange notion that a person was created as a new creature upon a conversion experience. Christians were unusual because they gathered before dawn to sing and pray to Christ and they declined to engage in the gluttony and sexual promiscuousness that was common throughout the Roman Empire at that time. What's more, the early Christians shared their property and regularly shared in a communal meal. All of this stood in sharp contrast to the materialism and dominant lifestyles of that day, which emphasized sensual gratifications of all kinds.[39] This behavior of the Christians was soon recognized as a threat to the established social order and so the persecutions of the early church began. The persecutions of the Christians extended from the reign of Emperor Nero, who blamed them for the mysterious burning of Rome in 64 c.e., to the conversion of Constantine which occurred in 313 c.e.[40]

The persecutions under Rome evolved through several stages. Initially, there was no formal and systematic persecution of Christians. Harassment and mistreatment of Christians was carried out randomly and arbitrarily as local officials became annoyed with their peculiar ways. There were no specific rules or laws enacted for arresting Christians; their behavior was a nuisance but not yet criminalized. But, this left Christians vulnerable. If someone wanted to bring harm to another person, they needed only to go to the authorities and accuse the other person of belonging to the Christian sect. Prejudice and disdain for Christians was based upon rumors that the Christians were ignorant, cannibalistic, and barbaric. These charges were generally not easy to refute as the accused were primarily from the lower echelons of society. In many cases when charges were made against Christians, the Roman authorities were left in a quandary as to how to handle the situation. Even though the accused Christians had committed no criminal act, they might still be considered a menace to Rome.[41]

In the second century during the reign of the Roman Emperor Septimus Severus, an African and native son of Carthage, the persecutions of the Christians began in earnest. The emperor issued an edict that required all Roman subjects to worship Sol Invictus (the Roman sun god and patron of the city of Rome). Severus was the first emperor to make a concerted effort to impede the spread of Christianity.[42] The official persecution of the Christians came at a time when Rome was losing much of its grandeur, as the empire was being threatened by marauding tribes from central Europe.

The Roman Emperor Decius, who reigned about 40 years after Severus, believed that the problems besetting Rome were the result of the empire abandoning the ancient gods. The emperor required all subjects, including Christians and Jews, to worship the gods of the Roman pantheon. The emperor took this measure in response to the now obvious decline of the Roman Empire. Decius believed that returning to the worship of the gods by his subjects was necessary for the empire to be blessed. Consequently, the emperor made it mandatory for Christians and Jews to sacrifice and burn incense before him. Those subjects who obeyed were awarded certificates and those who refused became outlaws, many of whom were imprisoned or martyred. The act of worshipping the Roman sun god would be a clear violation of the Christian faith and there were many who openly defied this decree, but there were many others who were not so firm in their faith. Those Christians who refused to obey the emperor's edict were called the *confessors;* those who complied and worshipped Sol Invictus were called the *lapsed.*[43]

In the aftermath of this program of persecution, the church was faced with the problem of restoring those who wavered and gave in to the decree of the Roman emperors. The confessors felt that they were in position to decide the status of the lapsed and whether or not they could be restored to the church body. Particularly in Africa, the confessors mostly wanted to return the lapsed to the fold, but there was opposition among some of the bishops and clergy, as they had also been forced to flee the Roman persecutions.[44]

The African wing of the church was most prominent in pushing for the readmission of those Christians who wavered under Roman persecution. Cyprian, the bishop of Carthage, was a protégé of Tertullian and trained in the art of rhetoric. He had been forced to flee and find a secure location during the persecutions, though he maintained counsel with his congregations through letters. Some of the confessors questioned Bishop Cyprian's authority to restore those who had lapsed, claiming that he too had wavered in his faith by fleeing rather than staying to face the wrath of the persecutors. Cyprian proclaimed that he was not a coward and that he had fled for the good of the faithful. Cyprian crafted a theological defense for his position. He argued that the church was necessary for salvation and the unity of the church must be maintained. He defended his belief that, "There is no salvation outside of the church." And since there could be no salvation outside of the church, the lapsed must be allowed to return. Cyprian is also credited with saying, "No one can have God as Father who does not have the church as mother." He used his scholarly acumen to craft a uniform policy of restoration in order to preserve the unity of the church.[45]

Novatian strongly opposed Cyprian. He believed that for the apostates, those who yielded and bowed before the sun god, there could be no restoration in this life. The rigid view advanced by Novatian and others was a minority view. However, the issue divided the church for centuries and it was not settled until the seventh century. The problem of backsliding and falling from grace, always an issue as Christians like any other human beings were imperfect, eventually led to the penitential system in the Roman Catholic Church and the seven sacraments. (Incidentally, the penitentiary or prison is a derivative of the penitential system devised by the church.)[46]

The bishops who handed over the scripture to the emperor and compromised their faith were called the "traditores." Danatus of Casae, Nigrae (? – 355?), also known as Donatus Magnus, presided as the bishop of Carthage for nearly fifty years, at least in the eyes of the Africans. His refusal to abandon church tradition prompted authorities in Rome to declare that Caecilian, not Danatus, was the true bishop of Carthage and that Danatus was a usurper.

Danatus and his supporters contested the appointment of Caecilian. Danatus contended that one of the three bishops who consecrated Caecilian was a traditore, which rendered his consecration invalid. The Caecilian backers argued that Bishop Caecilian was not himself a deserter of the faith, and that the validity of his consecration did not depend on the worthiness of those who performed the consecrating act. Caecilian's supporters maintained that it is impossible to know the true character and worthiness of the person who administers sacraments.[47]

It is axiomatic of the traditional African view that, "In the beginning there is Spirit," which means that spiritual reality always encompasses and transcends whatever is material in nature, while the divine always takes precedence over whatever is human; it is the presence of the Spirit which gives meaning, authenticity, and life to material reality.[48] This view influenced the supporters of Danatus as they held that any rituals carried out by a corrupt priest are invalid, as the spirit of the divine cannot work through the agency of corruption. However, the more materialistically inclined European mind was willing to allow that as long as the proper ritual rules and procedures were followed, there had been an appropriate laying on of hands, and the correct words were spoken, then the blessings of an ordained priest were assured no matter how immoral and ungodly his behavior might otherwise be. The materialistic approach or outlook may be encapsulated with the statement, "Whatever it is, it's either exploitable (usable for some kind of stimulation or sensual gratification), it's worthless (not usable for such aims) or it's dangerous (it might curtail or prevent further exploits)." Western materialism confines reality to material things and attempts to suppress spirituality, which it is unable to grasp and control.

Material reality becomes the sum total of reality rather than an expression of something far greater. The materialistic view, which is antithetical to the traditional African perspective, was more attractive to the European way of thinking. This view pervades much of modern scholarship and heavily influences the thinking of most Westerners and those who have adopted the ways of the West.[49] The Emperor Constantine (272 – 337 C.E.) eventually intervened to settle the controversy in 311 C.E. He declared Caecilian to be the legitimate bishop of Carthage and he gave tax exemptions to those clergy who supported Caecilian.[50]

The unprecedented intervention of Constantine into the affairs of the Church inflamed the class and geographical divisions of Christianity. By this time the Roman Empire had begun to split between the eastern and western empires. Widespread corruption, disputes over who should be emperor and unchecked greed inevitably led to war. Constantine needed to consolidate his authority after defeating his rivals for power in 312 C.E. He made a political calculation that by intervening in the church dispute, he could maintain some semblance of stability and strengthen his empire. But, while this act may have been good for the empire it was destabilizing for the Church. Constantine's intervention served to deepen the regional, ethnic and doctrinal divides already present within Christianity. Those Christians in the far west, the African Christians, and those less affluent generally supported Danatus, but the well-off and well-connected mostly favored Caecilian and the Roman establishment. Those left out of the imperial circle of power and those on the margins of society perceived that they were being shut out and some decided to take matters into their own hands. A militant group of Danatus's disciples emerged. They were mostly peasants who believed that martyrdom ensured salvation. These radical followers of Danatus were called the "Circumcellions," and also referred to as Donatists, while those who opposed them were called anti-Donatists.[51] The Donatian controversy divided the church along racial or ethnic lines as well as by socioeconomic class. European Christians and the more affluent and well-connected sided with the anti-Donatists, while the Africans and the lower classes mostly embraced the Donatist position. The controversy exacerbated the tensions that already existed within the church over the role of material wealth in the life of the church. Since the time of the apostles, many Christians believed that it was not truly possible to be both a Christian and rich in worldly goods simultaneously. The Romans ruled the ancient Mediterranean world with a heavy hand and Christians had suffered greatly under their rule. To become wealthy or successful in worldly affairs meant to be in good standing with the Romans, but it was the Romans who had executed Christ. The situation was only intensified by the intervention of Constantine. Prior to Constantine, controversies within the church were left to the faith community to resolve and although they regarded the Christians with general contempt, the civil authorities paid little attention to the specific beliefs and practices of the early Christians.

Constantine's conversion to Christianity just prior to his battle against Maxentius is controversial. Invoking the deity to act on one's behalf before going to war was the act of a pagan, not of a Christian. Yet Constantine declared that his military victory had been ensured by the same Christ who had implored His followers to love their enemies. As the first civil authority to become deeply involved in the affairs of the church, Constantine continues to be a topic of endless discussion and speculation. The debate revolves around whether his "battlefield conversion" was authentic or an act of political expediency designed to solidify his control over the Roman Empire. His conversion raises suspicion because he was never under the tutelage of one of the early bishops. Indeed, despite no religious training and only a cursory understanding of the faith, he reserved the right to determine religious practices for Christians and to set policy for the church. He retained the title *pontifex maximus*, chief priest of the pagan cult of Rome and he declined baptism until he was on his deathbed. Yet, he had no inhibition in considering himself to be the "Bishop of Bishops."[52]

Constantine envisioned a united empire with himself as the head of both church and state. He also attempted to end the social division between those considered Greek and those considered barbarian. In his view, everyone in the empire should be of equal status—all equally beneath his authority. The invitation to assimilation as a citizen of the empire was quite appealing to many people of that day. The Romans controlled the Mediterranean world and acceptance by the empire was the surest route to material wealth and security.[53]

When heresies surfaced, African theologians and church leaders were major proponents on both sides, they were in the forefront of shaping the meaning of the faith. When Constantine came to the throne, the Arian controversy was at its apogee. The first major heresy, Arianism, erupted in Alexandria, Egypt, and caused a conflict between the Bishop of Alexandria and a local pastor. The main focus of the controversy was the nature of the divinity of Christ. Was the divinity of Christ equal to that of God the Father or was He in some way subordinate? The local pastor took the position that no creature or entity could be equal to God the Father; none could possibly rival the magnificence of the Creator, not even Christ. Arius took the position that, "there was when He (Christ) was not."[54] The Bishop held the traditional view that God the Father and God the Son were of the same substance. The controversy permeated the church and threatened the stability of both civil and religious institutions.

To address the Arian controversy among other issues, Constantine convened the first great ecumenical council, the Council of Nicea. In 325 C.E. he summoned all 1,800 bishops to Nicea in northern Turkey, although only about 300 were able to attend.[55] The Arian heresy challenged the unity of the church as Arianism was seen to question the absolute divinity of Christ. The Arians maintained that Jesus, the Son, was less than God the Father, which was contradictory to the traditional teachings of the church. The traditional teaching was ably defended and best articulated by the African Athanasius. Athanasius was the secretary to Alexander, Bishop of Alexandria. Although a man of small physical stature who was even called the "black dwarf," Athanasius was a towering figure at the Council of Nicea. Arius was not a bishop so he was represented at the council by Bishop Eusebius of Nicomedia. Alexander, the leader of the group against Arius, was able to speak for himself at the council. For the most part, the bishops of the Western Church and Africa were supporters of the traditional view, while some bishops of the Eastern Church embraced the teachings of Arius. Constantine came down in support of the traditionalists and he paid the expenses for some of the supporters of Athanasius to travel to the council. For the most part the bishops of the Western Church had little interest in a theological debate since in their minds the divinity of Christ was a settled matter. Tertullian a century earlier had already expounded on the doctrine of the Trinity which held that the godhead was composed of "three persons in one substance." After the debate, most of the bishops at the Nicean Council came away in support of the position held by Athanasius; only two voted with Arius.[56]

Athanasius was groomed by Bishop Alexander to become his successor. Athanasius spoke the Coptic language that was native to Egypt and the common language of the Egyptian people at that time. Athanasius was an unpretentious man, and upon the death of Alexander, he fled into the desert in order to escape selection to the office of the episcopacy. But by the popular demand of the people, he was brought back and named bishop of Alexandria in 328 c.e. Bishop Athanasius' unshakable conviction helped to preserve the teaching of the Trinity in the Apostle's Creed and inspired the Nicean Creed. Athanasius articulated the central theme of Christianity as the incarnation and presence of God in history through the person of Jesus Christ. He was Arianism's most formidable adversary and he was the decisive voice in the first and most important Christological debate.

Athanasius' unyielding stand against Arianism inspired animosity against him by those who supported the heresy. Arianists circulated rumors that he was a magician who killed Bishop Arsenius and cut off the prelate's hand in order to use it in one of his nefarious rituals. For this charge Athanasius was summoned to court. He soon discovered that his enemies had conspired against him and would not give him a fair hearing. He decided to appeal to the emperor in an unconventional manner. He jumped in front of the emperor's horse and demanded an audience. Eusebius of Nicomedia, a supporter of Arianism, used this incident to argue to the emperor that Athanasius was fanatical and dangerous. Constantine therefore sent Athanasius into exile in Trier. Shortly after sentencing Athanasius, Constantine died. He was succeeded by his three sons, Constantine II, Constans and Constantius. The three new co-emperors had been raised as Christians, and they issued a decree freeing all bishops from exile.[57]

During the exile of Athanasius, Alexandria was presided over by Bishop Gregory, an Arian. Upon his return however, Athanasius was greeted by the people as a returning hero, and Gregory was removed from office. As long as Constans lived, he supported Bishop Athanasius, but upon his death his brother Constantius became sole ruler and he unleashed a pro-Arian campaign. The emperor was jealous of Athanasius due to his great popularity. Constantius ordered a synod to condemn Athanasius. The bishop responded that it was not possible to condemn someone without a hearing as was stated in canon law. Emperor Constantius's infamous reply was: "My will is canon of the church." The Arians threatened many bishops forcing them into resigning, while those who refused were banished. The struggle against Arianism continued for many years and there was found to be need for another ecumenical council, the Council of Constantinople called in 381 c.e.[58]

As the situation developed there were basically two schools of thought. First, the Antioch Christians believed that Jesus' divinity was bonded to human form with a mind, soul, and body in a manner in which each nature retained its integrity. Those who held this view in effect made the humanity of Jesus subordinate to the divinity of God. The opposing view held by the Alexandrians found that the divinity and humanity in Christ were integrated into a "hypostatic union."[59] The body of Christ served as a facilitator for the expression of divinity, but there was only one essential nature shared by the two. There was no division between divinity and humanity in Christ as they were deemed to be indivisible.

To address the continuing controversy between the two camps, the third ecumenical council was called in 431 c.e. St. Cyril represented the position of the Alexandrians by affirming that the Virgin Mary was *theotokos*, meaning "God bearer" or the "Mother of God." In other words, Mary gave birth not merely to a human being closely related to God, but to a single undivided entity of one divine substance; Mary gave birth to God Himself. Nestorius, the bishop of Constantinople favored Antiochean Christology. Nestorius argued that Mary was *Christokos*, which means that she was the "Mother of Christ" but not the "Mother of God." Nestorius also drew a sharp contrast between the divinity of Christ and the humanity of Jesus. Nestorius was condemned as a heretic by the Council of Ephesus. But, still the official outcome of the council did not end the controversy and debate which prompted a fourth ecumenical council known as the Council of Chalcedon in 451 c.e. By this time, the Alexandrians were willing to argue with the Antiochenes that Christ is "from" two natures but not "in" two natures. This council reaffirmed that Christ is "perfect in Godhead and perfect in humanity," and He is made known to us through each of His two natures. After the Council of Chalcedon, those who still embraced a clear distinction between the divine and human nature of Christ were called Nestorians.[60]

The doctrine of the Trinity is the central theological position of the Christian Church. This doctrine establishes the unity of the Godhead with Father, Son, and Holy Spirit. The development and defense of this concept of orthodox Christianity was primarily carried out by African bishops and theologians, not least of all Tertullian, who coined the term Trinity.[61]

The outcomes of the various councils did not end the controversies mostly because these disputes were not simply about semantics or an interpretation of scripture, but they reflected a struggle for political control of the church. Since the beginning of Christianity there had been a strong African presence and influence in the church. In addition, church affairs were administered by church officials, and the civil authorities generally did not meddle in the church. But, Constantine's actions began to change these circumstances dramatically. Even though he ostensibly sided with the African bishops at the Council of Nicea, by the very act of calling a church council, Constantine, a Roman Emperor who was not a church official, set the precedent of civil authority taking the initiative to create church policy. Also, many eastern bishops saw the Arian heresy as a way to wrest control of the church doctrine and church leadership away from the Africans. By this time, African political power was in steep decline in the Mediterranean World. Ancient Egypt, or Kemet, had lost its political power and had been declared a province of Rome in 30 C.E., once mighty Carthage had also been reduced to a vassal state of the Roman Empire, and the Phoenicians were by this time a distant memory. Nevertheless, the historical and cultural heritage of Africa was still held in high regard. Ancient Africa was viewed as a land of learning, wisdom, and ingenuity, and the African church officials were regarded with great esteem. Of course Africans were major figures on both sides of the various debates, which demonstrated their strong presence in the early church. For the first three hundred years after the death of Christ, African bishops, theologians, and church leaders had been the primary architects who shaped the character and direction of Christianity. The Arian controversy was divisive and it opened the door for Europeans to play a more assertive role in the new religion, and so the controversy continued long after Constantine's death.[62]

In this chapter we have outlined what may be called the African roots of Christianity by establishing that (1) the early seminal developments of Christianity took place primarily in Africa among African Christians and (2) there are many parallels in allegorical teachings and symbolic representations between biblical stories and the various African traditions, some of which are much older than Christianity. The symbolism and basic concepts of the Holy Family, the Holy Trinity, the Virgin Birth, the suffering Savior and the redemption of the lost were first formulated by Africans, incorporated into Christianity, later adapted by Europeans, and reconfigured by them to lend support to their assertions of political and cultural dominance. In modern times, the main thrust for the propagation of Christianity has come from Europe, not Africa, and the world's Christians look primarily to predominantly European denominations for institutional models, resources, and church leadership. Still, the historical role of the early African Christians is indispensible to the development of Christianity. The African roots of Christianity help to give us some understanding of how it was possible for the historians George Washington Williams and Bishop William Jacob Walls to maintain that Africa was the real birthplace of Christianity. We may now see why the Kenyan theologian John S. Mbiti could remark that, "both Christianity and Islam are 'traditional' and 'African' in a historical sense, and it is a pity that they tend to be regarded as 'foreign' or 'European' and 'Arab.'" Mbiti maintained that Christianity and Islam are just as much indigenous to Africa as anywhere else.[63] And there should now be some appreciation of Professor John Henrik Clarke's contention that both Judaism and Christianity were basically founded upon African folklore.

Chapter 1 – Our Mother

DISCUSSION & REVIEW QUESTIONS

1. Genetic studies indicate that the African people are the oldest people on the planet, i.e., Black humanity is the original humanity. Also, the domestication of plants and animals first began in Africa. Give an argument for how human beings and human civilization might nevertheless have originated somewhere outside of Africa.

2. Describe and explain five of Africa's major contributions to the progress of human civilization.

3. Who are the Beta Isra'el people? How is it that they came to settle in Ethiopia?

4. What was the argument that Athanasius gave to refute the Arianists? What impact does Athanasius's argument still have on Christian theology?

CHAPTER 2

Christianity in Transition

ROMAN IMPERIAL CHRISTIANITY

Constantine sought religious unity as a means to strengthen his empire. The Christianity of that day, with its enthusiastic proselytizing, a reputation for fiercely resisting corruption and a unified monotheistic outlook, seemed well suited for his political aims. The empire was rife with corruption, and the people had lost confidence in the civil authority's capacity to maintain the peace. Imperial Rome was losing its luster and vitality. The relatively new upstart religion of Christianity was able to inspire hope and confidence in people in a way in which the empire no longer could. Christianity would serve as a means to breathe new life into the empire. Also, the monotheism of Christianity offered the additional benefit of being easily adaptable to the patriarchal inclinations of the Roman authorities. Constantine would use Christianity to reinforce the control he had obtained by brute force. Imperial Rome now had an imperial religion. The heretics, including the Arians and Nestorians, now represented a threat not only to the unity of the church but also to the empire, and they were persecuted. To avoid persecution, the Nestorians went into exile outside the boundaries of the empire and they found refuge among the Persians.[1]

In response to the imperialism, materialism and militarism taking hold in the now Roman-dominated church, the Syrian church, which was composed mostly of Nestorians, became the first church to break away from what had been a unified or catholic (universal) church. This fifth-century schism was a significant and crucial event in the history of Christendom. With this defection and separation, communication between Christians in North Africa and the Near East with those in Europe began to decrease. With the rise of Islam two centuries later, communication would be completely cut off for almost one thousand years. The Nestorians were a dissident sect that was excommunicated by the Roman Catholic Church. But they found acceptance and prosperity in the east under the Persians. Later in the 13th century the nestorians would flourish. The Syrian Church experienced rapid growth under the leadership of the Patriarch Rabban bar Sauma. He presided over 25 metropolitan cities and supervised two hundred bishops from Persia, Mesopotamia, Khorasan, Turkistan, India and China. The Nestorian wing of Christianity boasted the largest missionary expansion of the Church prior to the nineteenth century.[2]

Christianity had taken firm root in North Africa and, besides Alexandria and Carthage, early Christianity also flourished in the areas now called Tripoli, Tunisia, Morocco and Libya. By the third century, the African Christians had more than 500 bishops extending across North Africa. But, with the advent of Constantine's imperial church many Christians felt that the church was drifting away from its original mission and purpose. A split soon developed among those Christians who believed that materialism and secular authority were stripping the faith of its authenticity and those who more readily embraced the protection and approval of the Roman authorities. Many church leaders soon began openly competing for ecclesiastical positions, and they joined the Roman emperors in the ostentatious display of wealth and power. The more spiritually inclined Christians were unhappy with the growing role of politics in the church. African leaders were at the forefront in raising the question: How can the Lord's church have leaders who live in a sea of plenty while the people they serve live in a desert of poverty?[3]

Some Africans responded to the opulent lifestyles, materialism and increasing corruption within the church by establishing monasticism. The monastic lifestyle became a refuge from the growing excesses of materialism and worldliness of the imperial church. It was a call to humility and self-denial in a time of excess and corruption. According to tradition, it is said that Paul and Anthony founded the first monastery in the Egyptian desert around 250 C.E. and they were the first monks. At the beginning of the fourth century there was a growing clamor for a deeper spiritual encounter, and thousands withdrew to the monastic shelters in the desert. Many bishops lived in great luxury with large residences and vast wealth. Some were not above bribes and licentious behavior. Consequently, the church lost much of its moral authority, and the people began to look to the monks for spiritual leadership and inspiration. One of Athanasius' most notable contributions was to bring the solitary monks and female ascetics under the authority of the church. By empowering monasteries with parishes, Athanasius integrated them into the church, and in turn the church benefited from the monks' spiritual discipline, cultivation of learning, and administrative skills. The ideals and virtues of the monks and ascetics inspired Bishop Athanasius to chronicle the life and ministry of the first monk, St. Anthony.[4] These African leaders in effect challenged the greed and corruption that had quickly become rampant in the church hierarchy.

Monasticism, which has its roots in the African church, made an enormous contribution to church and society. Monasticism eventually reached Europe, and the monks helped to preserve learning and cultural heritage in Europe during the Dark Ages. The monks taught European farmers how to reclaim wasteland and improve farming techniques. During the long period when Europe was mostly cut off from the rest of the world, residing in isolation and stagnation, it was the monks who wrote books, copied ancient manuscripts, maintained schools and libraries, and founded hospitals.[5]

By the fifth century, the Roman Empire was facing increasing pressures both from without and within. Besides the rampant corruption and constant political intrigues and coup attempts, marauding Germanic and Eastern European tribesmen began to threaten from the North, and soon Islam began expanding in the south. The power of the Roman emperors finally collapsed in the fifth century but the relief this provided for the North Africans would be short lived. The Arab invasions of North Africa were launched shortly after the death of the prophet Muhammad in 632 c.e. Under the banner of Islamic jihad, or holy war, Arab tribesmen quickly spread across northern Africa to the west and also to Central Asia and India in the east. The Arab Muslims gave no quarter to the Africans, demanding that they convert to Islam, be reduced to slavery, or be slaughtered. The Jihadists enslaved or murdered countless numbers in their brutal assault. Many Africans were converted at the point of a sword; many others died in the aftermath of the invasions and the social upheaval. Slavery was tolerated if not promoted by Islam from its very beginning.[6] And it should be noted that the first massive enslavement of Africans was initiated by Arab Muslims, to be followed 800 years later by European Christians. Both took the lives of millions of African people and both wreaked untold destruction on African societies. The Arab-led enslavement and racial subjugation of Blacks among other things set an unfortunate example that Europeans would later eagerly follow.[7] Africa and Africans were increasingly viewed as fair game for those who engaged in predatory endeavors of human exploitation. Also, the removal of millions of Africans from North Africa disrupted long-established societies and cut off trading routes, which helped to isolate and weaken societies in West Africa.

Prior to the emergence of Islam and the Arab invasions of North Africa, the Arab tribesmen were largely nomadic and removed from the opulence and culture of the great cities of the world. They now eagerly grasped this new opportunity to achieve wealth and status. The Eastern Roman Empire based in Constantinople was crumbling, and the emperors could no longer field sufficient legions to protect the borders of the empire. The Western Empire had already fallen, and Rome had been sacked first by the Visigoths in 410 c.e. and again by the Vandals in 455 c.e. The once influential African churches were completely engulfed by the Islamic onslaught. Only a remnant of Coptic Christians in Egypt, Sudan, and Ethiopia remained. This also marked the beginning of the change in ethnic and cultural composition in much of North Africa from mostly Black or African to predominantly Arab. And with the Arab invasions effectively severing Christianity from its African roots, the religion would now begin to take on a decidedly more Eurocentric character.[8]

For many African Christians it was not difficult to convert to Islam. Christianity and Islam both have their origins in the same region of the world and share monotheistic doctrines, both emphasize piety and faith in religious expression, and both trace their heritage back to Abraham. Common ground can be found in theology and scripture as there are similar stories and parallels in the Hebrew Bible, the Christian Bible, and the Muslim Koran. The African influence is readily seen in both from the commandments of Moses, which are paralleled in Ancient Egyptian sacred texts, to the doctrine of the trinity to the example of Bilal Ibn Ribah, or "Bilal the Ethiopian," the African who was the first to call the faithful to prayer and who was called by the prophet "one third of the faith." There are deep African roots for each of these religions, and Africans played pivotal roles in the development of each. Some African Christians willingly converted to Islam, which they viewed as a version of Christianity. Another appeal of converting to the new religion was that those who converted could avoid slavery and death. There were and there remain anti-Black sentiments and racism in Arab-centric Islam, although historically such sentiments have not been nearly as rigid or as polarizing as the racism European Christians would later apply in the aftermath of the European Slave Trade.[9]

To understand the appeal of Islam to many Africans we should consider the following: (1) the Islamic confraternity proved to be able to provide some political and economic stability along with physical security for people of diverse backgrounds; (2) the people of the Islamic faith did not always live up to their ideals any more than did Christians, but they were more consistent than Christians in providing equality within their community of faith; (3) adopting Islam allowed African leaders access to the valuable trading routes with the East which were now controlled by Muslims; (4) Muslims embraced plural marriages and extended families, which were already part of traditional African cultural systems; (5) in many cases Africans were able to modify and adapt Islamic beliefs to fit into their own spiritual traditions. African Muslims especially in West Africa could still adhere to beliefs in ancestor veneration and divination without great difficulty; (6) the names and attributes of God in some African traditions were similar to the names and attributes of Allah in Islam. Captured and enslaved Africans who practiced Islam in Africa were brought to America and introduced to Christianity. Some of them attempted to synthesize Islamic and Christian practices. "'God', say they, 'is Allah and Jesus Christ is Muhammad—the religion is the same, but different countries have different names.'"[10]

The sixth century was dominated by an atmosphere of upheaval and turmoil everywhere in the Mediterranean World. There were growing theological controversies between Christianity in the East and in the West. The rise of the Monophysitism in Egypt and the continuing controversy over Donatism in Africa exacerbated a climate ripe for defection and division. These theological differences were accentuated by underlying tensions caused by imperialism, materialism and ethnic conflicts. In Egypt, once the seat of the African wing of the church, the radical Christians were called Monophysites, and those who wanted to return to the roots of the faith were called the Donatists. Those who aligned themselves with the imperial church were known as the "Melkites" or "King's Men." The Melkites took pride in speaking the Greek language and eschewed the Coptic language, which was native to Egypt, in liturgy and preaching.[11]

With the completion of the Arab conquest of Egypt in the seventh century, the Coptic Church sought to make peace with their new rulers. The Coptic Church chose to side with the Muslims rather than the Roman Catholic Church as a political expediency and survival necessity, as the church in Rome by this time had too many problems of its own and could not assist them. But, there was also the fact that the European-dominated church was increasingly becoming arrogant and paternalistic. The ideology and systematic practice of White supremacy was not formally established until the Age of European Imperialism and Colonialism in the eighteenth century, as scholars Carl Linnaeus, Johan Friedrich Blumenbach, Georg Wilhelm Friedrich Hegel and others developed the contours of the racial classification scheme that still largely holds sway today. Yet, as demonstrated in Tatian's "Address to the Greeks," the European cultural personality already exhibited an intense egotistical outlook along with a troubling tendency to disrespect and disregard the natural rights and prerogatives of other people. The Roman Catholic Church closely identified with the Empire and thus they lost the allegiance of most African and Western Asian Christians. After the ascension of the Arabs, many African Christians became Muslims, and many churches were converted to mosques or fell into disuse and ruin. From the inception of the Christian church, African scholars and theologians had played a strong and productive role in the leadership of the church and the various ecumenical councils, but this role was now coming to an end. As a result of separation, desolation, and isolation, the African influence on shaping the doctrines and character of the Christianity, which had been waning since the fifth century, came to a close in the seventh century.[12]

By the end of the fourth century the African bishops and church leaders had helped to make Christianity a vibrant presence throughout the

Mediterranean World. They had made Christianity into a prize coveted by Constantine and the other Roman emperors. Yet, culturally and politically, Africa was never given any more consideration than colonial status. In spite of the contributions of African thinkers, it was Latin that became the official language of the church, not Ge'ez, Coptic, or some other African language. Increasingly, Africans were only accepted in the church as followers and subjects and not leaders or equals. But severing the church from its African roots would also have the consequence of separating it from its original mission and purpose.

AFRICAN DEVELOPMENTS APART FROM FOREIGN INVASIONS AND COLONIZATION FROM 300 TO 1450 c.e.

Ancient Nile Valley Civilizations, and in particular Ancient Egypt or Kemet, emerged as outgrowths of traditional Africa. The civilizations of the ancient Nile valley sprang from cultures in the interior of Africa that were exceedingly ancient, stretching back to prehistoric times. The inhabitants of Kemet benefited from the copious overflows of the Nile River which fertilized their land. They built a civilization and excelled in creative arts, craftsmanship, engineering, and architecture as exhibited in the building of pyramids, temples, and tombs. Their reverence for nature inspired them to deeply probe for answers concerning the character of humankind and the nature God. They eventually extended their influence over wide areas, influencing the inhabitants of many lands.[13]

Egypt's fertile black soil is the recipient of a natural irrigation system from the annual floodwaters of the Nile. Its strategic location prompted the ancient Greeks to call Egypt the "Gift of the Nile." The Ancient Egyptians themselves used many names for their country, one of the most common being Kemet, or the "Black Land." Some scholars have suggested that this reference was meant to indicate the blackness of the soil as opposed to the ancestral heritage of the people. But, we note that the hieroglyphic symbol for Kemet, the Black Land, was made using a burnt or charred piece of wood followed by the image of a man and a woman, a symbolic reference. Futhermore, the Ancient Egyptians consistently applied the hieroglyphic symbol for blackness (kmt), which they used to identify themselves, to also reference the divinities of their religious system. Thus, the people of the Black Land venerated and worshiped the Black gods.[14]

The origin of many of our contemporary beliefs and customs can be traced back to Ancient Egypt. The Egyptians have been credited with creating one of the first religious systems to embrace life after death. In addition to introducing refined stone architecture, they produced writing materials made out of papyrus. We are indebted to the Egyptians for the 365-day solar calendar. They also gave the world the fundamental principles of geometry, a philosophical theory of being, and the practice of medical diagnosis according to physical examination, along with a variety of surgical techniques.[15]

The Nubians were Egypt's neighbors to the south, located mostly in current-day Sudan. The Nubians had an abundance of wealth in gold and cattle. There is also evidence that the Nubians initiated the pharaonic system of governance centuries prior to the Ancient Egyptians. In 750 B.C.E. kings from the region of Nubia or Kush conquered Egypt and expelled foreigners who had overrun that land. They ruled until 670 B.C.E. The pharaoh Tirhakah, who was one of the Nubian rulers during that time is mentioned in the Bible in Isaiah 37:9.[16] Christianity was planted in Nubia as early as the sixth century and a strong Christian presence remained in that region until the sixteenth century when it was conquered by Arab invaders.[17]

With the gradual decline of the African kingdoms to the north and the migration of Blacks out of Egypt, there arose new kingdoms to the south of Egypt in the regions of Sudan and Ethiopia beginning around 800 B.C.E. with Axum, followed later by the Three Christian Kingdoms of Nubia—Makuria, Nobadia, and Alwa. Nobadae eventually became a part of Makuria. Axum was a major distribution center with Africans from the interior of the continent bringing in iron, tortoise shells, lions, elephant hides, rhinoceros horns, gold, and slaves to be exchanged for iron tools, weapons, copper implements, cloth, and wine. Axum was a cosmopolitan city of that era with people from Egypt, the Eastern Roman Empire, Persia, and India within its borders. They engaged in a robust trade from the Mediterranean to the Indian Ocean. The kingdom reached its apogee during the fourth century when King Ezana unified Axum, brought Iflemen into the kingdom, and conquered the rival Kushites. As Axum grew in international stature and trade, the kingdom began to develop a vibrant society, with Christianity being a centerpiece of its culture. There was a close connection between the Coptic Church of Egypt and the various churches of Sudan and Ethiopia, which continued even after the Arab Muslim ascendance in Egypt. The scholar Chancellor Williams gives an account of how the Patriarch of the Coptic Church was once rescued by the Blacks from Sudan. In 745 c.e. the Arab governor of Egypt began to pursue a persecution of the Christians, and he arrested and detained the Patriarch of the Egyptian Coptic Church. After their calls for diplomacy were dismissed, the Africans of Makuria marched 100,000 troops into Egypt. Omar, the Arab governor, quickly released the Patriarch. Cyriacus, the Black "king of kings" who ruled over Makuria, then extracted a promise from the governor that Christians in Egypt would be better treated. Alwa would the last of the ancient Black kingdoms to hold out against the tide of invasions and enslavements. That kingdom finally yielded to foreign encroachments and invasions in 1504 c.e.[18]

The seeds of Christianity were planted in Ethiopia before it was recognized as the official religion of that country. According to tradition, the Ethiopian conversions began when the gospel writer Saint Matthew preached in that country. There is also the Bible story of the Apostle Phillip's contact with the Ethiopian eunuch and treasurer to Queen Candace (Acts 8:26-40).

The preaching of Saint Matthew and the conversion of the Queen's Treasurer helped to open windows of opportunity for Christian traders to the ports of this region. In the fourth century, a Christian trader named Fromentius came to the capital of Ethiopia to engage in commercial trade. While in the city he was involved in an accident, which delayed his departure. During this time, the king of Ethiopia died and the Queen inherited the throne. She summoned Fromentius to assist her new administration. He used his cabinet position to promote Christian education of the princes and implemented the building of prayer houses. Fromentius was later appointed Bishop of Ethiopia by Athanasius. Fromentius is credited with converting King Ezana who reigned over Ethiopia in the fourth century.[19]

The fourth century was the period during which the great Christological debates in Christianity came to the forefront. These debates revolved around the nature of Christ and his relationship to God the Father. The Ethiopian Christians supported the official ruling of the Council of Nicea (325 c.e.), in which it was held that Christ is fully God and fully human, and never did there exist a time in which He did not exist. Later, the Ethiopian Church opposed the Council of Chalcedon (451 c.e.) which embraced the view that Christ was of two natures, one divine and one human. The theological disagreement between the Roman Catholic Church and the Christians of Egypt and Ethiopia presaged the eventual split between the Church in Rome and the African wing of Christendom. Many of the African Christians continued to insist on the one divine nature for Christ and they became known as Monophysites. In the aftermath of these debates and the eventual schism of the Church, the Egyptian Christians established the Coptic Church while the Ethiopians established the Ethiopian Orthodox Church, which was nominally under the Coptic Church.[20]

The Council of Chalcedon condemned the Monophysites as heretics, and they became persecuted. Many traveled across the African continent to find refuge in Ethiopia. This led to a cultural renaissance in the Ethiopian Church during the fourth century. Christianity flourished in Ethiopia as an influx of talented Christians moved into that country seeking safe haven. Some pre-Christian temples were converted into churches, and many new churches were built during this time. These activities also attracted more and more local people to the faith.[21]

The civil authorities in Ethiopia began to actively support Christianity. In the sixth century, King Gabre Maskal presented land to monasteries so that they could expand. With the support and generosity of the monarch, monasteries proliferated and became leading depositories of learning and scholarship. The Ethiopian kingdom of Axum was a safe haven for the Nine Saints including Za-Mikael, Aregawi, Pantalewon, Afse, Garima, and Libanos, who were fleeing persecution in the Eastern Roman Empire in the aftermath of the Council of Chalcedon. They translated the New Testament and other religious literature into the native language, Ge'ez, giving the Ethiopian Church one of the earliest versions of the Holy Bible. The spiritual discipline and solitude of the monastic life produced the Ethiopian scholar Yared, who compiled a hymn book designed for use with the sistrum and the drums to accompany singing.[22]

One of Ethiopia's most impressive cultural achievements occurred in the thirteenth century, when the famous rock-hewn monolithic churches were constructed in the reign of King Lalibela. These churches were carved out of solid rock mountains starting at the top and chiseling down to depths of 40 feet. The interiors of the churches were decorated with colorful religious figures. These churches were so remarkable that they have been called one of the wonders of the world. The British scholar Ivy Pearce called these stone churches "the greatest historical cultural heritage of the Ethiopian people."[23] The Ethiopian Christians and the Coptic Church in Egypt have been able to maintain a continuous heritage of Christianity going back to the time of the Apostles.

As the Islamic conquerors swept across North Africa in the seventh century, the Axumite Empire became isolated from other bodies of Christendom. Ethiopia ceased to engage in the robust commercial trade that was taking place along the Red Sea and Indian Ocean, as now these routes were dominated by Muslims. Centuries of isolation and religious inversion were observed by the historian Gibbon as he wrote: "The Ethiopians slept for close to a thousand years, forgotten."[24]

The churches of Tigray, Ethiopia, are depositories of rare manuscripts dating back to medieval times. Stowed in these ancient churches were the rudiments of the beliefs and practices of the early Christians. The robes, chants, singing, preaching, pomp, and ceremony practiced in these churches were originated, observed, practiced, and refined in Africa long before the establishment of the Vatican or Westminster Abbey, before Martin Luther, John Calvin, King James I, or any of the other European fathers of the faith. Christianity is rooted in African soil and particularly in Egyptian and Ethiopian soil, and this establishment predates the establishment of the European church.[25]

Northeastern Africa has a history shaped by the geographical impact of proximity to Asia and Europe, along with the Nile River, which served as a cultural highway bringing contacts and influences from the interior of the continent. Western Africa on the other hand was largely insulated from foreign incursions prior to the fifteenth century due to the rugged terrain of the Sahara Desert and the immensity of the Atlantic Ocean. However, there were many cross-cultural and commercial contacts between

West Africa and the rest of the continent. Over time the people of West Africa developed many large, relatively stable and peaceful societies of their own. As foreigners, people from outside of Africa, began to overrun North Africa, Africans were pushed southward, and various groups like the Dogon of Mali migrated westward. Thus, many West African cultures trace ancestral connections to North African and the Nile River Valley cultures.[26]

Carthage, which was called Khart Haddas by the people who founded that great port city, had cultural and commercial ties to West Africa. Like Egypt, Carthage benefited from its location along the Mediterranean Sea to become a major distribution center for commodities. For centuries, Carthage dominated most of the western Saharan trade. In the sixth or fifth century B.C.E., under the command of Hanno, the Carthaginians engaged in an ambitious expedition to explore the west coast of Africa, and they set up trading posts along the way.[27] The Carthaginians, like their progenitors the Phoenicians, excelled at ship building, sailing and navigation.

The prosperity and influence of Carthage was brought to an end by the Roman conquest of 146 B.C.E. The Carthaginians at one point challenged Rome for the supremacy of the Mediterranean World. As the Romans expanded their power and territory, they could tolerate no rival. This is the time period during which the intrepid general Hannibal Barca made world history. In an ingenious and daring military campaign, Hannibal struck at the seat of the Roman Empire as he led his African army across Spain, southern Gaul and over the Alps to the very gates of Rome. Using war elephants obtained from the interior of the continent, he dealt one crushing blow after another to the retreating Romans. He was only defeated as his forces were finally exhausted after their long march. The Romans and the Carthaginians fought three wars, called the Punic Wars, which ended in the final defeat of Carthage. Under Roman rule, Carthage continued to attract merchants from the Sudan and other regions of the Sahara. However, Carthage was no longer an independent state but was a dependent vassal state of Rome.[28] The indomitable spirit of the indigenous Africans of that region, along with the Berbers who are of African and Asiatic background, enabled them to retain much of their ethnic identity, language, and culture after assimilating Islam. The Berbers would eventually become the core group within the Moors who would later rise to conquer the Iberian Peninsula.[29]

To the south of Carthage in the Western Sudan, the region from Lake Chad to the Nigerian Delta, the people engaged in the development of agriculture and the domestication of various plants and animals. There are indications that cities in West Africa were prosperous and vigorous going back as far as the period of Dynastic Egypt. Three towering kingdoms arose in West Africa during this time, Ghana, Mali, and Songhai. The history of Ghana extends back at least to the fifth century c.e. The proper name of this ancient kingdom is Wagadugu. The kings of Wagadugu were addressed by the title Ghana, or "warrior king," and also by the title Kaya Magha, or "king of gold," among other titles. Ghana peaked during the eleventh century before finally collapsing around 1240. Mali arose and took up where Ghana left off. Mali was founded between 1230 and 1235 and reached its peak in the fourteenth century. Songhai next emerged to become the largest and most powerful of the three kingdoms. It came into fruition in the mid 1400s and reached its apogee during the latter part of the sixteenth century. These three kingdoms had many similarities in governance structure, which included hierarchical bureaucracies headed by royalty, regional districts, and villages with local leadership.[30] A temporal leader invested with spiritual authority was the rule rather than an anomaly for Africans. Africans have traditionally recognized an interaction between spiritual and temporal matters, and there could be no rigid separation between the sacred and the profane. This cultural sensitivity or world view continues to be widely reflected in the social organization and spiritual practices of Africans, both on the continent and throughout the Diaspora.

During the early period of Ghana, Berbers from the north ruled the native people of Soninke. Ghana's most illustrious history began when the Soninke took control of their own country and established a government that lasted for about 500 years. The kings of Ghana amassed wealth by assessing import and export duties which were to be paid in gold. The kings also laid claim to any gold that was found in the kingdom. With this wealth they were able to maintain a strong army which kept trading routes open, and iron was made available to them in order to fashion weapons for their army. In 1065, King Tenkaminen of Ghana had an elaborate court and boasted an army of 200,000 soldiers. With a military apparatus of this magnitude, Ghana extended its influence over a large region of West Africa.[31]

Mali emerged in this same region just as Ghana was falling apart. At its zenith the Empire of Mali controlled most of present day Gambia, Guinea, Senegal, and parts of Mauritania, Niger, and the Upper Volta region. Mali had trading routes that stretched from Gao in the eastern buckle of the Niger River and across the Sahara to Tunis. A variety of commodities were transported on these routes, including gold, salt, shells, animal skins, ivory, cloth, and nuts. Mali continues to produce some of the world's best quality cotton.[32]

In the thirteenth century, Sundiata, the King of Kangaba, conquered the land of Sasso and built the city of Mali, which became the new capital. Mansa Musa ascended to the throne in the fourteenth century. He became the most influential and most well known sovereign of Mali. Mansa Musa converted to Islam, and he distinguished himself by leading an ostentatious pilgrimage from western Africa through Egypt to Mecca. The king took along with him an impressive entourage of 80,000 people carrying gold bars and sacks of gold dust. While on the pilgrimage the king persuaded Muslim scholars, jurists, architects, and other artisans to return with him to Mali. The great university of Sankore in Timbuktu was established, and students and teachers were attracted from across North Africa and Western Asia to attend. After Mansa Musa the kingdom of Mali began to decline. Around 1400, Songhai and other states overran Mali's territory and trading routes. Tuareg raiders captured southern Saharan market towns. In 1494, Portugal penetrated the continent and established diplomatic contacts with Mali, but by 1520 Songhai controlled most of the territory once governed by Mali.[33]

Upon the decline of Mali, Songhai ascended to become the next great West African kingdom of this period. In 1468, under the reign of Sonni Ali, Songhai became the greatest of the Sudanic kingdoms. The strategic trading routes included the fertile regions of the Niger River. During the reign of King Askia Muhammad the empire extended from the Atlantic coast to well into present-day Mali. Askia Muhammad's fame would rival that of Mansa Musa. He too made a pilgrimage to Mecca carrying gold, which he distributed along the way. He also returned from Mecca with a cadre of talented people who made an impact on his country. It was also during this time that the great African scholar Ahmed Baba composed many books on various subjects, including one on Islamic law and a dictionary.[34]

Songhai was to be the last of the great West African kingdoms. El Mansur of Morocco precipitated the decline of Songhai in 1591 when he dispatched a large army to attack that kingdom and seize control of its rich gold mines. However, after defeating the armies of Songhai at the Battle of Tondibi, Morocco discovered that they still did not control the rich gold mines of the forest regions. The Africans launched a type of guerilla warfare against these invaders, and it prevented the Moroccans from fully subduing the region.[35]

Large regions of the Western Sudan escaped Arab domination and influence during this period and many societies were never incorporated into one of the larger African kingdoms. Various groups of people came together to form cultural confederations for their mutual support and protection, and there was a confluence of different spiritual traditions. Indeed such circumstances were not uncommon throughout the continent starting in ancient times, as large regions often lacked a centralized governing authority, but there were nevertheless well-organized social structures present. It is usually supposed that those societies that existed without strong central governments were somehow less developed. But the capacity to effectively organize large groups of people based upon shared cultural values as opposed to systems of military domination and enforcement may actually indicate a culturally and morally more advanced state of civil society, although the development of military skill and prowess in such societies is likely to be retarded. Africans developed mostly cooperative communities with a strong sense of spirituality, including various councils of elders and respected wise men and women to settle disputes and keep the peace.[36] General concordance and peacefulness flowed naturally and without much need for coercion from circumstances in which people were able to expect just dispensation for any wrongdoing and where there was widespread observance of basic moral values.

These cultures contributed to vibrant spiritual and oral teaching traditions in Africa. One of the largest and most influential such of traditions belongs to the Yoruba people. The heart of Yoruba life is the spiritual teachings of Ifa, which come from Ile-Ife, a city they consider to be the cradle of human existence. The Yoruba fashioned a complex metaphysical system which explores the relationship between humanity and the universe. This metaphysical system was accompanied by a ritual system and the two served as means of sanctioning the right of rulers and supporting a rich religious life for the people. Yoruba culture is also known for its bronze and terra cotta sculpture. The features are naturalistic and many are life-sized. Art work in Yoruba tradition was held in high regard, and being an artist was considered a spiritual calling as many of the art works were completed incognito. The people of Benin, also on the west coast of Africa, were known for their artwork and craftsmanship.[37]

The traditional priest or ritual leader was a major figure in West African cultures. The diviner was the mediator between the people and the ancestors or the gods. In West Africa the spiritual leaders were skilled in predicting the fate of individuals and interpreting the will of the ancestors. They performed these rituals by interpreting omens or dreams, reading the entrails of a fowl, or gazing into waters. In the Yoruba Ifa system, a Babalawo, or "Father of Secrets," casts a chain of eight halves of palm nuts or sixteen separate nuts; then the priest would read the pattern of the casts and would mark the changes. These priests had to memorize 256 different readings or sayings called odu, which consisted of verses or a story that gave some insight into the matter at hand, each odu corresponding to a different pattern of the cast nuts. Such practices indicate that Africans generally did not separate themselves from the wisdom and intelligence that maintains the universe, and they appealed to this intelligence to assist them in various affairs.[38]

Since ancient times, the history of African people has often been a story of people struggling to contend with one foreign invasion or imposition after another. This can be observed by considering the history of the Carthaginians. The Canaanites were apparently a colony of Ancient Kemet. Upon the destruction of Canaan by foreign invasions, the remnants of the Canaanites reconstituted themselves into various city-states, and they were then called the Phoenicians. The Carthaginians then arose from the leading remnant of Phoenicia around the time that the Phoenicians lost their homeland.

The spread of Phoenician influence started when the Phoenicians migrated from the region around present-day Syria and Lebanon. Phoenicia is the name given to these people by the Greeks. The origin of the name Phoenicia is apparently derived from the root of the word Canaan, and it means the "land of purple." This is apparently the source from which the Romans and later the Christians got the notion that the color purple should be associated with royalty or elevated ecclesiastical office. In the ancient world, the Phoenicians distinguished themselves as great sailors, navigators, and traders. Western Europe is indebted to the Phoenicians for the alphabet, among other things.[39]

Conceptually, if not physically, Africa is the birthplace of the world's three great monotheistic religions—Judaism, Christianity, and Islam. Understanding the history of North Africa and its relationship to the rest of Africa is crucial when examining the origin and development of Christianity. Blacks are native to North Africa just as they are to the rest of the continent, although presently they are politically and culturally subordinated in their homeland. Africans of Egypt and Carthage were primarily responsible for the birth and early nurturing of Christianity. Even though Christians make their pilgrimages to Israel and not to Egypt or Ethiopia, it would not be too much to say that Christianity would not exist without the ancient churches of North Africa. By 451 C.E., the rift between the African wing of the church and the Roman-dominated church became too great to maintain any semblance of unity. The African wing disagreed with the outcome of the Council of Chalcedon; thus the Coptic Church of Egypt (the Orthodox Church of Ethiopia was nominally under the patriarchate of the Egyptian church at that time) set for itself an independent course of development.[40]

This chapter demonstrates the vitality and continuity of various African societies as they struggled with the loss of influence in the Mediterranean World and against foreign impositions to nevertheless survive, develop, and prosper. The history and heritage of Africa has been distorted, obscured, and falsified by modern Western scholarship—which is still seriously infected with notions of White supremacy. But, the rich historical heritage and legacy of Africa ought not be treated as a forbidden fruit. Africans, apart from foreign incursions, developed their own languages and educational systems, produced great works of art, and fostered rich spiritual systems, they fashioned various governmental bodies and social structures in order to resolve their differences, and they were able to organize millions of people into mostly peaceful societies, some of which lasted for centuries.

Figure 1: Timeline 146 B.C.E –1500 C.E.

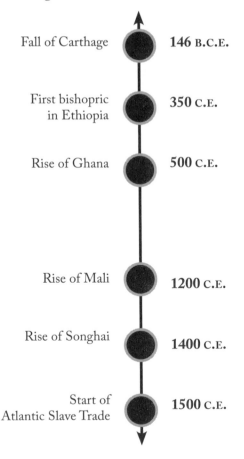

Fall of Carthage	146 B.C.E.
First bishopric in Ethiopia	350 C.E.
Rise of Ghana	500 C.E.
Rise of Mali	1200 C.E.
Rise of Songhai	1400 C.E.
Start of Atlantic Slave Trade	1500 C.E.

Chapter 2 – Christianity in Transition

DISCUSSION & REVIEW QUESTIONS

1. What major factors contributed to the development of Christianity in Ethiopia?

2. Compare and contrast the Arab-led enslavement of Africans with the European-led enslavement. What were the factors that facilitated the conversion to Islam by North Africans?

3. Describe and explain how the North African Church became separated from the Church of Rome.

4. Describe governments, commercial activities, and significant historical events of the kingdoms and cultures of West Africa prior to the slave trade. Why was the charge made that these people were savage and uncivilized?

CHAPTER 3

The European Slave Trade

PRELUDE TO THE GREAT CALAMITY

What's in a name? A name may either conceal or reveal meaning depending upon its usage. Words in general—and names in particular—can be used to enlighten, deceive, or manipulate. And manipulative names are sometimes used to remarkable effect against those who are unaware of the power of name-calling. The calling of the name of a person or thing, evokes that entity, at least in the subjective sense, or a mental image. Demeaning words can hurt, soothing words can placate, and the use of names or titles can sometimes dramatically transform perceptions of status and identity. Thus, the power to name is at least to some degree, the power to create, and implicitly it is also the power to destroy. And so in naming realities, the discerning will do so with particular care, as they realize that the capacity to successfully navigate reality and establish meaningful relationships grows out of an ability to clearly distinguish that which illuminates greater self-awareness from that which distorts, obscures, or obliterates the same. Surely this is one reason why oppressors have always insisted on imposing their language systems upon the oppressed. If we are deeply troubled, perplexed, overwhelmed, or frustrated by some matter this may ostensibly be due to many different reasons, but inherently such agitation indicates that we have yet to perceive the agitating phenomenon as reflective of the comportment, constancy, and capacities of our own being; we have yet to identify and name the phenomenon meaningfully in relation to ourselves.

We refer to the European Slave Trade to describe the events that are currently most often referred to as the Transatlantic Slave Trade or the Triangular Atlantic Slave Trade. But the holocaust committed against African people during the period from the middle of the fifteenth century to the nineteenth century, did not occur simply because of an accident of geographical location, nor is the particular geometrical shape of the shipping routes of any essential importance. Both terms tend to obscure the historical reality of a consciously-planned enterprise ruthlessly carried out at the expense of a specific group of human beings, and which was perpetrated primarily for the benefit of another specific group. There are attempts at diversion with comments like, "Everybody practiced slavery," or "Africans sold slaves too." Some people may find it uncomfortable or disturbing to identify by name or by denominational, national, ethnic, and racial origins those who planned, initiated, and systematically carried out the project of chattel enslavement imposed upon tens of millions of Africans over a period of four centuries. The scale and scope of these horrific events is indeed astounding. Nevertheless, their feelings of embarrassment or discomfort pale in comparison to what was felt by those Africans who were so abused. In consideration of the continuing disastrous consequences of the European Slave Trade still experienced by the progeny of those who were enslaved, we may dismiss such concerns. Far beyond merely assigning blame, we must thoroughly understand the factors that facilitated such a monstrous deed should we ever hope to fully neutralize and transcend the negative behaviors engendered during the slave trade. We are most unlikely to resolve problematic conditions if we are unable to substantively describe them, accurately identify contributing factors, or to even acknowledge that the conditions exist. Indeed, it appears that many of the misconceptions and erroneous behaviors initiated during the slave trade might well be reduplicated in perpetuity unless properly delimited.

With the loss of the Copts in the seventh century, the main body of Christianity for the first time became predominantly European and White. For the next 1,000 years Christianity flourished almost exclusively on the European continent. This has led to the misconception that has persisted even up to the present day that Christianity is basically a "white man's religion."[1] People began to identify Christianity with Europe, not Africa and this perception was purposely propagated by many European scholars after the 1500s as they sought to rationalize Europe's manifest destiny to dominate the rest of the world. Thus, Africans, the historical parents of Christianity, now became the children. Western Christianity (now referencing only Western Europe) had gained the world but in many ways lost its soul. The African roots were forgotten or purposely erased along with the memory of a once much more inclusive church. Without the African presence, Western Christianity adopted a decidedly more materialistic gospel, the church became more intertwined in European politics, and things would not change much for the better until the Protestant Reformation. In the 1500s, for the first time, Europeans began to depict Christ in their own physical image as the Black Madonna, still venerated even today throughout Europe, miraculously gave birth to a blond-haired, blue-eyed Jesus.[2]

At the dawn of the European Slave Trade, European Christianity had lost contact with African Christians for a millennium. When European Christians reestablished contact with Africans it would not be for the purpose of renewing Christian fellowship. In the first half of the fifteenth century, Portugal led the way in the exploration of Africa. This should be no surprise since the Iberian Peninsula, which includes Portugal and Spain, had been occupied for over 700 years by the Moors, including Africans who had converted to Islam. These black-a-moors maintained the light of civilization in Europe during the Dark Ages by promoting learning and grand architecture throughout Spain and Portugal. Prince Henry the Navigator was no doubt intrigued by the source of the wealth, knowledge, and power of these Moors or Berbers who came from present-day Morocco, Algeria, Niger, and Mali. He initiated a number of unsuccessful attempts to round the coast of Africa in order to find a trade route to the Far East. The Portuguese were determined to establish a foothold in Africa. It took 80 years, but they were eventually able to erect the Elmina castle which gave Portugal a head start in the slave trade.[3]

There were several motivations for the explorations of Prince Henry and the other Europeans. One was the hope of reaching the Orient, crossing the African continent and thereby bypassing the Arab Muslims who controlled the direct land routes to the Far East. Also, after centuries of isolation, poverty, hunger, and disease during the Dark Ages, Europeans were eager to move out of their homelands, find new resources to exploit, make new trading partners and explore the world. There were rumors about an ancient Christian kingdom in Ethiopia. The European courts were hoping to find that kingdom and establish an alliance to launch a crusade against Muslims. The Europeans quickly discovered that they had a decisive military advantage over Africans. During the 1300s Europeans had learned the use of gunpowder in warfare. They had also developed the technology to build large seaworthy ships. They expressed an insatiable desire to obtain material wealth and social status, an animus which had led to a state of practically continuous internecine warfare on the European continent and would now be turned outward onto the rest of the world. With the "discovery" of the Americas by Columbus in 1492, and indigenous peoples who, like Africans, had only a limited capacity to resist these aggressions, Europeans understood that they had a golden opportunity to acquire enormous material wealth and power. And thus began the colonization of the Americas and the forced importation of African labor to build and maintain the colonial infrastructure.

It is deeply ironic that the rationale of converting Africans to Christianity was used by Europeans to defend the European Slave Trade. All of the major European powers from the sixteenth through the eighteenth centuries were involved in the slave trade which they defended on the grounds that Africans must be converted from paganism and barbarism in order to become European-style Christians and "enlightened" by European civilization. If the African churches had not been separated from Western Christianity, the Atlantic Slave Trade may still have occurred, but the rationale used to support it would have surely been different. Nevertheless, Eurocentric or Western Christianity stands indicted for its three-century complicity, defense, and support of the slave trade.[4]

The European Slave Trade brought millions of Africans to the Americas, and left millions more dead due to starvation, disease, and war.[5] Africans who were brought to the Americas were mostly kidnapped from the coast of West Africa, but there were also some taken from the regions of northern, central, and eastern Africa. The captured Blacks were forced to undergo a horrific voyage across the Atlantic Ocean in chains. They were subjected to beatings, rapes, and wanton murder during this Middle Passage from Africa to the Americas. It is estimated that more than one third of those Africans captured died on the continent or during the 6–10 week voyage across the Atlantic. The worst trauma came from being uprooted from their homelands. Stories abound of how captured Africans would grab handfuls of dirt to swallow prior to being forced onto slave ships. The movement of Africans to the Americas during the European Slave Trade was the most massive movement of human beings from one continent to another in human history.

Typically the voyage of slave ships would originate at some European slave port such as Liverpool, Lisbon, Marseille, or Barcelona. The ship would then travel to the coast of West Africa to pick up the black gold to be transported to its next destination in the Americas before returning to Europe with a cargo of raw materials.[6] Later, during the seventeenth century, there were direct routes from the North American colonies to slave ports in Africa. The slave market in Rhode Island took in slaves directly from Africa via ships that were based at the port of Newport. The shipbuilding industry and rum distillers in Rhode Island found the profits associated with slave trading to be irresistible. Ships exported liquor to Africa in exchange for people who were captured and brought to America. Slave trading was good business for the colonists and it was supported by the leading citizens of colonial society. Presidents Washington and Jefferson were slaveholders. John Adams, the second President of the United States, proclaimed his personal opposition to slavery even as he signed off on the political compromises that allowed slavery to flourish. The noted philanthropist John Brown, one of the founders of Brown University, amassed much of the wealth he would later philanthropically disburse through the buying and selling of slaves. In 1773, Moses Brown, the brother of John Brown, resigned from the family business of trading in human beings as he had become an abolitionist. He freed his own slaves and he admonished his brother to also give up the cruel enterprise of slave trading.[7]

Greed was the psychological motive behind European slavery, and once the economic and political forces needed to sustain the endeavor were unleashed, they would prove to be difficult to subdue. Religious rationalizations were also concocted in order to legitimize slavery. Conquest, conversion, and slavery were inseparable factors of European colonial expansion from the early 1500s, as Portugal and other European powers came together in pursuit of a policy designed to break the Muslim monopoly of trading routes through the Red Sea and across the Indian Ocean. The Europeans were highly motivated and determined to penetrate

Africa as a way of bypassing Muslim influence. Prince Henry the Navigator of Portugal began to formulate a plan to outflank the Muslims by circumnavigating Africa. His plan was to buy into the African trading routes and thereby avoid the high prices demanded by the Venetians who at that time dominated European trade in the Mediterranean. He also hoped to establish political and economic links with African Christians, who by this time Europeans knew only through myths and incomplete historical records.[8] Europe was just emerging from the Dark Ages, and those who went to Africa in the fifteenth century were unaware of the origin of Christianity in Africa. They were largely ignorant of the fact that centuries before the rise of Islam, Christianity was well established in North Africa and flourished in Egypt, Ethiopia, and parts of the Sudan. The religion that Europeans thought made them superior to Africans was in fact the product of African theologians such as Tertullian of Carthage, Origen, Clement of Alexandria, Augustine of Hippo, and others.[9]

During the final decades of the fifteenth century the Portuguese began to explore the coast of Guinea and they would eventually reach the Cape of Good Hope in southern Africa. After they reached the Cape Verde Islands, they continued their explorations into the mouth of the Senegal River, and by the late 1400s they had discovered a rich gold trade. This is how part of the West Coast of Africa became known as the Gold Coast. The Portuguese discovered a great abundance of natural resources, and their materialistic and acquisitive mindset led them to claim rights to the entire continent. These explorations initiated the sharp contrast in technological development we now see between European and African nations. Many of the African nations and societies of the 1400s were just as civilized, advanced, well-organized, and prosperous as the concurrent nations of Western Europe. These African societies had long traditions of governance by ritual and consensus building, they developed natural resources, they had magnificent oral traditions of education, they traded with foreigners in Arabia and India, and, save for skill in warfare, they were generally just as far along as their European counterparts. But Europeans would relentlessly exploit the people and resources of Africa as they pushed to build worldwide colonial empires propelling them into the Industrial Age. People and natural materials were removed from Africa in massive numbers and amounts for the benefit of Europeans, a process that was much to the detriment of the long-term development of African nations.[10]

The Portuguese eventually built Fort Elmina, "The Mines," which was the first slave hold depot on the Gold Coast. The African King Kwame Assa welcomed trade with foreigners in his country, but he did not intend for the Whites to have a permanent presence. He attempted to discourage the building of a fortified trading post in his country. The Portuguese, however, pushed to obtain the trading post as they were determined to establish a foothold in Africa. After the king reluctantly consented, the Portuguese broke ground for an elaborate fortress. Many of the local people were alarmed by the presence of the Portuguese and resisted the efforts of these belligerent foreigners. It took 80 years, but the Portuguese were finally able to build and equip Elmina with towers, cannons, and a dungeon for slaves. The king of Portugal, Juan II, was elated with this accomplishment and he called the castle, "Lord of Guinea." Portugal's achievement became the model for European conquests and colonization during the Age of European Imperialism. First, explore the land to locate any natural resources and find a suitable area for building a fort. Next, curry favor with the local chiefs or leaders and inspire intrigues among them. Finally, once a foothold is established, begin a systematic process of exploiting everyone and everything that is usable.[11]

Building slave ports on the west coast of Africa enabled European nations to establish a colonial presence and allowed them to more efficiently engage in slave trading. The ports provided Europeans with large, partly self-sufficient communities that could orchestrate and manage the enterprise of capturing and selling human beings. The fort at Elmina was well-staffed with secretaries, merchants, craftsmen, physicians and soldiers. Elmina functioned both as a military base and an embassy. The fort was also staffed with a chaplain. Some of the Portuguese men began to have children with the local women. The chaplain would bring some of these children into the castle to be trained in the ways of Europe. Thus, the Portuguese initiated a key strategy of the European project of conquest and domination—that of introducing confusion and discord among indigenous populations through the manipulation of the offspring of "mixed" unions. The divide-and-conquer approach that had earlier been employed against Africans in the north by the Arabs, was made possible because Africans, with their traditional matrilineal customs and xenophilic tendencies, wanted to accept all of the children as welcome members of the tribe, while the Europeans viewed them as objects to be exploited. Unfortunately, over the centuries this stratagem has met with significant success as many have preferred the material benefits of accepting a subhuman status as "mixed" or as a "lesser white" rather than embracing their indigenous heritage and the protracted struggle against injustice and oppression that embrace would necessarily include.[12]

The European expansion and intrusion into Africa had the blessing and support of the church and the royal governments. The missionaries and military commanders coordinated their activities in order to more effectively penetrate Africa both physically and culturally. Conversion and conquest went hand in hand. An early Portuguese slaver summed up the effort by relaying that their mission was "to serve God and His Majesty, to give light to those in darkness, and to grow rich as all men desire to do."[13]

THE MIDDLE PASSAGE FROM FREEDOM TO SLAVERY

In order to maximize profits, crowding slave ships to the absolute limit of the available space capacity was the norm. The Roman Catholic priest, Dionigi Carli de Piacenza described the human cargo on a Portuguese ship in the late seventeenth century as "herring in a barrel" and said "if anyone wanted to sleep, they lay on top of each other." The enslaved males were paired in chains, the right ankle of one being connected to the left ankle of the other, and when it came time to relieve themselves they were forced to defecate and urinate upon one another. Many of the enslaved experienced difficulty breathing in the overcrowded conditions. On some ships, those who got seasick were forced to hold rice in their mouths to the point of strangulation. Olaudah Equiano was an enslaved African prince who later wrote of his experiences. He described the journey across the Atlantic on overcrowded ships as all but unbearable. He reports that "the ships were so crowded that the people suffocated and died." The over packed death ships diminished the space available for food and many of the enslaved suffered from malnutrition and starvation during the 6–10 week journey to the Americas.[14]

A special section of the back cabin of the ship was designated for pregnant women and children. Children and young people were cherished commodities, and they would demand a high yield on the slave market. Some females were pregnant before they were captured and gave birth aboard the slave ships. The case of an African woman aboard the vessel *Bristol,* captained by William Lugen, was typical. The infant she gave birth to aboard the slave ship died and the captain ordered the body thrown overboard.

So as not to undercut the propaganda and political power of the slave-holders, the magnitude of the deaths associated with slave trading and the frequency of slave revolts were purposefully underreported. According to one English surgeon in 1790, two-thirds of the deaths of slaves were complicated by a condition he called "bango," or a mortal melancholy and involuntary suicide. Other diseases which took their toll on the enslaved Africans included dysentery, dehydration, smallpox, scurvy, and syphilis. Countless deaths occurred in violent brawls and rebellions. The slave ship captains and crew knew that they were under constant threat from their captives. Thomas Phillips of the *Hannibal* wrote in 1674 that some of the commanders would cut off the legs or arms of rebellious slaves in order to terrify the others. Rule by terror was necessary, as slave trading required small numbers of Whites to work in proximity to large numbers of Blacks.[15] From the beginning of the European Slave Trade, Africans rebelled frequently and repeatedly, and many clung tenaciously to the belief that they would be returned to their homeland. Resistance to enslavement was continuous, and almost no year went by during the period of the European Slave Trade in which there was not a major uprising or some ongoing resistance being carried out by the Africans.

The slave ship captains were charged with keeping accurate records of their human cargo. The ship records included a "death book" to document the loss of any property. It is from a review of these records that some researchers have concluded that there was a slave insurrection every eight to ten voyages.[16] A slave rebellion was documented on the *Marlborough* in 1725. There were about 400 slaves aboard the ship at the time of the uprising, some coming from Bonny and some coming from the Gold Coast. About 30 of the slaves from the Gold Coast were moved on deck while the sailors went below to wash out the filth that had accumulated. The Africans took the opportunity to free themselves as they seized some of the arms and they then proceeded to shoot most of the crew of thirty-five. The seven unharmed crew members were ordered to sail back to Bonny and they complied. Upon hearing news of this successful slave revolt and repatriation, the captain of the slave ship the *Hawk* set out to attempt a recapture of the Africans. The Africans again had to fight for their freedom and they were able to overcome the crew of the *Hawk*. The men from the Gold Coast then ordered the White sailors to take them back to their homeland, and after disembarking there they dispersed, not to be seen again.[17]

Those Africans who rebelled could expect only torture and death if they were unsuccessful. On one occasion, three insurrectionists were captured. The ring leader was forced to eat the hearts and livers of his compatriots before he was killed. To terrorize the Blacks, the hands and feet of rebels would often be cut off and displayed before them. When Blacks rebelled by refusing to eat, slave ship captains would sometimes apply a red hot iron to their lips forcing them to open their mouths. In the slave markets of New York, Boston, and Charleston the "vile smell of vomit, sweat, stale urine, and feces wafting over the port" would signal the arrival of a new cargo of African humanity.[18]

The brutality and hardship of the Middle Passage violently displaced the African cultural identity and helped to initiate conditioning for a life of servitude. The sheer terror of the Middle Passage is almost incomprehensible. Africans were placed aboard a ship with little or no clothing, without a clue as to the reason for their captivity, and no knowledge of their ultimate destination. Scenes of inhumanity, including rapes and vicious beatings, could be witnessed all around. The Middle Passage left an indelible mark on the psyche of all who experienced it. The journey aboard the overcrowded death ships could last over two months, depending on the weather and the seafaring skills of the captain and crew. Thus were the mothers and fathers of humanity packed like books on a shelf, each with a space about the size of a casket. Typically, slave ships had two decks, and the hole was reserved for slaves and other commodities, such as barrels of food and whiskey. These ships meandering across the Atlantic Ocean were appropriately termed death ships. Blacks were chained together and they often had to witness the death of another captive, and it would sometimes be days before the corpse was removed and tossed overboard. In one incident it was reported that a young infant was unable to consume the boiled rice given to the slaves as food. The slave ship captain accused the infant of being stubborn and willful. As punishment for this act of "willfulness," the captain tied a 12-pound stick of wood around the infant's neck. A few days later the captain whipped the child to death and forced the mother to toss the body overboard.[19]

The crew members on a slave ship ranged in number from 20 to 60 men, depending on the size of the ship. The crew members were disciplined in a way that was similar to naval sailors, and they were under the command of the ship's captain. Job functions of the crew included a notary to record the trading of slaves, a cleaning crew, carpenters to effect needed repairs, cooks to prepare the food, and a surgeon. It was not out of the ordinary also to have a ship's chaplain. Most of the crew would be young men in their twenties, while the captains could be anywhere from 30–60 years in age. The young men who worked on the crew were most often from the lower echelons of European societies—and they were frequently hard pressed to find employment elsewhere outside of the slave trade. Being a sailor aboard a slave ship was a low-end job for lower-class Europeans. However, by the early sixteenth century there would also be a few free Blacks and some enslaved Blacks who would serve as crew members on slave ships. In 1505, half of the fourteen crew members on the slave ship *Caravel Santa Maria Las Neives* were Black. Black crew members were more likely to be found traveling on ships from Africa to Europe than from Africa to the Americas.[20]

There were even a few rare voyages of slave ships in which the crew was all Black. On such occasions the White ship's captains would be more judicious in their treatment of the captives. It is reported that about half of the 350 slave ships from Brazil included enslaved Blacks among their crew. Many of the Blacks acquired skills and knowledge of sailing that surpassed that of their White counterparts. But, regardless of ability, the Black crew members were always barred from becoming officers or captains aboard slave ships. One of the amenities of holding the office of captain on a slave ship was to be awarded two or three "privilege slaves."[21]

The determination and skill of the captain was key to the success of any slave ship voyage. On the business side, it was the captain's responsibility to negotiate the prices of slaves with the African merchants or local chiefs. The captains needed both political skill and physical stamina in order to survive arduous sea journeys, disgruntled crew members, and frequent slave rebellions. The careers of most slave ship captains were short-lived. Few captains made more than three voyages across the Atlantic before they retired. But the slave trade was very profitable, and a captain could make enough money to invest and become a ship's owner after just a few voyages. Also, captains had the option of selling their privilege slaves to make additional income. Many captains attempted to rationalize their involvement in the trading of human flesh. Hugh Crow was the captain of a slave ship owned by the Assinalls of Liverpool, England, and he justified his behavior by saying that African slaves in the West Indies are happier than when they lived in their own country, "subject to the caprices of their native prince."[22] Captain Joseph Hawkins was based in Charleston, South Carolina. In 1793 he traveled to the west coast of Africa and saw the barracoon where the Blacks were held while waiting to be sold and shipped out. After witnessing the deplorable conditions, he claimed that removing the people he had purchased was better than leaving them in such a wretched circumstance; he convinced himself that he was doing the poor Africans a favor. He did admit, however, that "the majority were afflicted with grief at their approaching departure." Some captains felt a twinge of guilt and they questioned the proclaimed virtues of the slave trade, although the momentary outburst of conscience did not stop them from continuing to profit from slave trading. Captain Thomas Phillips of London expressed some misgivings when he observed, "Nor can I imagine why they should be despised for their colour, being what they can not help.... I can not think there is any intrinsic value in one colour more than another, that white is better than black, only we think it so, because we are prone to judge favorable in our own cause."[23]

The practice of slavery in America has a European origin. The ancient and ubiquitous practice of slavery would find its most extreme and intense expressions in the "New World." Before the arrival of Europeans, slavery had been practiced in Africa for centuries, but it was qualitatively different from the much more brutal forms of slavery that would be imposed by Arabs and, later, Europeans. The Arab invaders were interested primarily in cultural and political domination in Africa. Those Africans who refused to submit to Arabic culture were persecuted and many were enslaved. Europeans were interested in the exploitation of Africa for slave labor. Africans could adopt European cultural values if they wished; they would nonetheless be enslaved.

Early on in the European Slave Trade there were slaves of other racial backgrounds besides Blacks, including Native Americans and Whites. But, there would soon be a premium placed on the Blacks and they became the slaves of choice. The demand for Black slaves was clearly articulated by the procurator-general of Lima, when he wrote in 1646: "The shortage of blacks threatens the total ruin of the entire kingdom, [for] the black slaves are the source of wealth which the realm produces." There was even recognition that the hearty Africans, already accustomed to arduous agricultural labors, were superior workers in many ways. Avear Monrique de Zirnigo, a Mexican laborer, told of working on a sugar plantation and relayed that "difficult and arduous work" was only for Blacks and not for them [mestizos or persons of mixed race] or "weak Indians."[24]

Slavery was practiced in West Africa prior to the arrival of Europeans. Africans enslaved by other Africans generally had the status of persons that Europeans would call indentured servants. Africans did not view slaves as commercial property until after the arrival of Arabs and Europeans. Those who were enslaved in Africa prior to foreign intrusions were usually not perpetually enslaved and their offspring were not condemned to a life of slavery. And of course they were not subject to color prejudice, which would later be the case with Arabs and even more so with Europeans. Africans enslaved other Africans for the following reasons: (1) Being a prisoner of war. Europeans would later instigate and incite warfare among the Africans in order to generate more captives for slavery. (2) Being a criminal. Africans did not have prison systems, and the imposition of slavery was a way of meting out justice for a criminal act. Criminal acts in fifteenth-century Africa included theft, adultery, and showing disregard for a sacred taboo. Only a few criminals were ever sold to Europeans, and the adjudication of criminal acts became irrelevant in the midst of the upheaval of African societies that ensued once the European Slave Trade was in full swing. (3) Being unable to pay off a debt. Slaves in pre-colonial Africa lived and worked with the family to which they were attached. There were well-established rules against abusing slaves, and slaves would frequently marry into the slaveholding family, thereby becoming fully accepted as family members.[25]

There were many African chiefs who engaged in slave trading with Europeans. They viewed slavery as an opportunity to increase their wealth and status. The chiefs of Africa were not infrequently corrupted by alcohol, guns, and lust for various material comforts. Their shortsightedness and greed paved the way for European slave trading in Africa, for the destructive, fratricidal wars to produce more slaves, and for the resultant weak political and economic disposition of African nations that persists to the present day. Many members of the African ruling classes were implicated in international slave trading. A few African leaders resisted the temptation, but others sold their neighbors in exchange for guns, textiles, liquor, and other products.

Several of the larger and better-organized African societies, particularly among the Yoruba, the Dahomey, and the Ashanti, actively engaged in slave trading at the expense of their neighbors. Many of the African leaders were well aware of the great harm that slavery was causing their societies but they seemed unable to mount a unified effort against the European aggressors. And once the slave trade began in earnest by the end of the sixteenth century, it was too late. The coast of West Africa became a kind of no-man's land where the local people were forced to kill and capture or be killed and captured in order to supply the voracious appetite of the slave traders.

Pre-colonial Africa was no utopia; slavery was practiced and there were occasional conflicts including wars among the various indigenous culture groups. But slavery was never a predominant means of supporting economic activity among African people. They managed without the wholesale reduction of large portions of the populace into perpetual servitude, chattel or otherwise. Also, they frequently worked out means to settle their disputes peacefully through various ritual systems, councils of elders and the consultation of chiefs. When warfare did break out, there was relatively little bloodshed compared to the more intense and unrelenting mode of warfare practiced in Europe.

It is appropriate to point out the weaknesses and failings of the Africans in regard to slave trading, but we must be mindful of and not duped into placing the primary culpability for this assault on the people who were assaulted. It was not Africans who planned and initiated the European Slave Trade. There were many factors contributing to the perpetration of the slave trade, including the fallibility of the Africans, but absent the felonious mindset and covetous motivations of the Europeans, none of the other factors matter. It was the avarice and inhumanity of European slave traders that drove the slave trading. And for Europeans, becoming wealthy by enslaving Africans became a continent-wide project. Slavery was supported by governments, corporations, and churches in Europe. There was a general consensus that the exploitation of Africa was an economic and political imperative.

The Renaissance in Europe focused on the rebirth of the European spirit of material acquisition and cultural refinement, but as the scholar Hugh Thomas notes, there were no "humanitarian pretensions" about altering or changing the practice of slavery.[26] The Renaissance ushered in the rebirth of slavery because free labor was seen as the way to fuel the prosperity of Europe. This sentiment was echoed by the Flemish diplomat, Ogier-Ghislaine ele Busberg, who lamented in the sixteen century that there was a shortage of slaves: "We can never achieve the magnificence of the works of antiquity and the reason is that we lack the necessary hands, that is, slaves."[27] Even the revered father of the Reformation, Martin Luther, believed that the earthly kingdom could not survive unless some men were free and others were assigned to slavery.

There were also a number of African leaders who fiercely resisted slavery. King Ansah of Ghana (1470–1486) had his people watch out for European ships approaching the shore, and they tried to prevent them from landing and entering Africa. King Agadja of Dahomey warned the English in 1777 that if they entered his kingdom looking for slaves they would be killed. King Almammy of Senegal in 1786 issued a decree declaring it to be illegal to transport slaves through his kingdom and he returned presents that French slave traders had sent him as bribes. One of the most determined resistances to the European Slave Trade was engaged by the African monarch Queen Nzinga of Angola. She declared her kingdom to be free of slavery and a safe haven for all who would be enslaved. She became renowned for a tenacious guerilla war which she fought against the Portuguese and which lasted for 30 years until a treaty was negotiated in 1656.[28] Then there is the case of King Jaja of Opobo in present-day Nigeria. As a boy Jaja was sold into slavery by a Bonny trader and he was given the name Jubo Jubogha (the British later referred to him as Jaja). The boy Jaja was sold to the chief of the Opobo people as a slave. His natural talent for business allowed Jaja to rise to a position of leadership among the Opobo. He eventually became the king of the Opobo and he fiercely defended the independence of his people against encroachments by the British.[29] Nowhere in the history of Europe or America do we find a former slave rising to become the head of state over the very nation of the people who had enslaved him.

THE AMERICAN PRACTICE OF SLAVERY

Contrary to the free market propaganda currently proclaimed by Western governments to the developing nations of the Third World, European and American economic strength was built through conquest, colonization, enslavement, and strict control of the markets. British plantation owners got legislation passed in parliament to give them a monopoly over the exportation of sugar from the Caribbean. In fact, they passed laws to monopolize the trading of tea and coffee as well. The residuals from these monopolies helped to finance the first coffee house in London in 1652 and the first teahouse in 1658.

The behavior of the American colonists with regard to slavery differed from their European counterparts only in that they were even more inclined toward brutality. The Europeans who settled in the Americas were motivated by many factors, including the desire for religious and political freedom and to escape from the oppressive regimes of Europe. Many Europeans were forced to come to early colonial America as punishment for crimes. But first and foremost, the European settlers were driven by an all-consuming desire for material wealth and social advancement. Slavery as practiced in the region that became the United States would become the most inhuman form of human bondage.[30]

Most slaves captured by the British were forced to undergo a "seasoning process" in the Caribbean that acculturated them to a life of servitude. The seasoning process sometimes lasted for 2–3 years and included separation from their countrymen, being inspected and sold, frequent beatings, and field work. Later they would be shipped off to various ports in North and South America to serve as field laborers, builders, craftsmen, and home servants.

The presence of large populations of Native Americans and Africans often outnumbering Whites in Latin America led to the development of a racial classification regime that tends to marginalize indigenous ancestry. Children with European parents were actively encouraged to abandon the cultures of their African or Native American parents. They were taught to prefer the social and religious values of Europe, usually Spanish or Portuguese, as a way of advancing in the colonial order. The Spanish and Portuguese promoted the creation of a mulatto "buffer" class between themselves and the indigenous masses. Native Americans were degraded as savage "indios" and along with Negroes were looked upon as something less than human. Today there are many millions of people in Latin America who are of African descent, but only a fraction of them acknowledge or claim an African heritage. Most people of African descent in Latin America, even some who have obvious African ancestry, prefer to follow the prevailing social custom that tends to maintain a small class of White elites in power while granting a few social privileges to those who accept a mestizo status, thus leaving the masses of indigenous people and Blacks at the bottom of the racial hierarchy.[31]

A different strategy of White supremacy and racial domination was applied in the United States, as the number of Blacks was only a fraction of the number of Whites and there was not much need for a racial "buffer." The rape and abuse of African women was common, and there were soon large numbers of "mixed-race" children present on slave plantations. To address this circumstance, slaveholders in the United States adopted the "one-drop rule" to apply to the offspring of Whites and enslaved Blacks. One drop of African blood was deemed powerful enough to make one Black. The one-drop rule effectively turned the wombs of African women into slave breeding machines, and it was not uncommon to witness the children of a slaveholder working in his fields as his own slaves. Even those who had predominantly European physical features, light skin, straight hair, and aquiline noses were nevertheless considered to be Black if they had even one provable African ancestor. Thus, African Americans tended to evolve a consciousness that readily accepted people of any skin color into their communities, many of whom would be classified as something other than Black in Latin American countries.

Slavery is inhuman wherever and whenever it is practiced, but the chattel slavery developed by the North American colonists was unrivaled in the utter intensity of its brutality. Slaves in North America were property, period. They had no recognized rights as human beings, and consideration was given only to what they could produce economically. This form of slavery was extreme when compared to slavery practiced in other countries, such as South America. Enslaved Africans in North American could be raped, beaten, maimed, or murdered without even the pretense of legal consequence for the Whites who perpetrated such acts. The British and their colonial descendants in America perfected the practice of turning human beings into commodities. In Latin America it was generally the practice that enslaved families could remain intact, allowing them to at least care for one another. However the British and Americans thought nothing of selling off family members, separating fathers and mothers and children at random. A family could be broken up and sold off on the whim of the owner.[32]

The Old World, or Europe, was the largest importer of African slaves until about 1550. The Portuguese distribution centers for enslaved Africans were Sao Tome, Santiago and the other Cape Verde Islands. Because of Africa's role in supplying the labor for the difficult physical tasks of building the colonies in America, a British scholar would argue that "America was saved by Africa." And the scholar would not have been wrong if he added Western Europe to the list of those "saved" by African labor.[33] As more and more slaves were imported to the Americas, the colonists found themselves facing the prospects of large populations of Blacks, both slave and free, living in their midst. "The problem faced by White Carolinians during the first and second generations of settlement was less one of imparting knowledge to unskilled workers [slaves] than of controlling for their own ends black expertise."[34] The Whites began importing so many slaves that they soon found themselves with a large and unwanted population of people. The greed of the slaveholders created circumstances in some areas in which Whites sometimes found themselves outnumbered by Blacks and in which poor Whites had to compete with Black slave labor for jobs. This eventually led some Whites to support repatriation of Blacks to Africa in the guise of various colonization schemes fostered by the American Colonization Society. Of course, most free Blacks were reluctant to abandon their new homes and their enslaved countrymen for uncertain prospects in Africa, so the American Colonization Society met only with limited success. However, the African nations of Sierra Leone and Liberia were outcomes of the schemes to remove Blacks from America. Sadly, many of those Africans who did return to the continent adopted the same attitudes and practices of Europeans toward their African brethren, and they horribly abused, mistreated, and enslaved native Africans in those areas in which they settled.

Africans not only provided the brawn but they also brought the brains needed to develop agriculture in the Americas. "Prior to the Atlantic Slave trade, rice, indigo, and cotton were widely planted in Africa."[35] Some of the enslaved Africans were from societies that had developed technologically advanced agricultural techniques that were superior to those then employed by European farmers. Beginning in the eighteenth century, the British colonists of the Carolinas learned of an agricultural process on the island of Barbados that was considerably more profitable than the processes they were using to produce rice, indigo, and tobacco. This discovery fueled the demand for slaves in South Carolina. The rapid increase in African slaves eventually led to a Black majority in that colony. Enslaved Africans brought with them across the Middle Passage knowledge of planting and processing crops from Africa, along with the skill to herd cattle in open ranges, and expertise in weaving and dying cloth.[36] Virginian slave holders made a similar discovery with tobacco, which fueled a new influx of slave labor. Whites and Native Americans tended not to work as well as the Africans in the tobacco and rice fields, since the Africans already brought with them much of the skills and knowledge needed for such tasks.[37] The large damp coastal low country of the Carolinas was perfect terrain for the lucrative rice plantations which demanded a vast population of Black laborers. Between 1721 and 1726 three and a half thousand slaves were brought into South Carolina. The numbers of Blacks increased dramatically so that by 1732 there were 14,000 Whites in the colony together with 32,000 Blacks. This large Black majority did not allow for strict control of their most intimate affairs as was mostly the case in the other American colonies.[38] Africans in South Carolina were thus able to preserve and maintain many traditional African beliefs and customs to a greater degree than elsewhere in the United States. They developed the Gullah culture which still has some influence in parts of South Carolina.

At the dawn of the eighteenth century, colonial South Carolina had discovered that the soil on the coastland was ideally suited for the production of rice on a large scale. They needed a large labor force to work the land, which eventually led to increasing numbers of Blacks. Some colonists began to question the heavy reliance on slave labor and there were fears of slave rebellions, which were frequent occurrences. The South Carolina Assembly passed a tax on each slave brought into the colony. But there were also many colonists who maintained that the colony could not manage without the labor of the Blacks.[39]

Christian nations, both Catholic and Protestant, were deeply involved in the slave trade. In the British Commonwealth, the major slave ports were Liverpool, London, and Bristol, and most of the slave merchants were Anglicans. Other major ports were Nantes, Bordeaux, Lisbon, Seville, Bahia, and Luanda, and most of the slave traders were Catholics. In La Rochelle, France, most of the slave merchants were Calvinist Huguenots. Even the pacifist Quakers were not entirely unsoiled by the trafficking of Black slaves. Quakers in Newport, Rhode Island, dealt in human flesh. The Wanton Family had a robust slave-trading enterprise in the 1760s. William Penn's Holy Experiment in Pennsylvania encountered a few Friends who were prominent slave traders, transporting slaves from the West Indies to the City of Brotherly Love. Some Quakers were quite active in the enterprise of human bondage. The Quaker entrepreneurs Farmer and Galton of Birmingham, England, sent a slave ship carrying 527 enslaved Africans to the West Indies in 1703.[40]

European Jews were also attracted to the profits of slave trading. Jews were invested in slave trading from its very beginnings in Portugal and Spain, and they played an important role in the slave trading that was conducted. In these two countries, Jews dominated the market for human slaves. There were Jews who were active among the Danish in the mid-1700s and there was at least one Jewish trader in South Carolina, which was the largest slave market in North America at that time.[41]

Slave trading was deeply entrenched in the social fabric of American colonies. Many of the leading citizens of colonial America and England were human flesh traders. They were members of Parliament in England and members of the Continental Congress in America. Philip Livingston of New York founded and endowed a professorship of divinity at his alma mater, Yale University, and he joined Barbara Heck in establishing the first Methodist society in America. These social luminaries of early America defended the practice of reducing human beings to animals as a benevolent practice for people who were unable to help themselves. In 1680, Jean Barbot, a Huguenot, stated the widely held rationale that it was better to be a slave in the Americas than to be free in Africa.[42] Another apologist for the European slave trade wrote: "At bottom the blacks are naturally inclined to theft, robbery, idleness and treason." William Chancellor of New York defended slavery in 1750 on the grounds that the slave trade was "redeeming an unhappy people from inconceivable misery."[43]

Africans were unequivocally and universally opposed to being subjugated under the capricious cruelty of European slavery in the Americas. There was nothing attractive about being violently uprooted from one's homeland and forced to work in the American wilderness to provide profits and comforts for belligerent foreigners. It was clear to the Africans before they left their homeland that they were in for unimaginable horror. At the various slave ports along the coast, African women and children were separated from the men so that they could be raped repeatedly. The flesh of Africans was burned and they were branded as property. They were held in unsanitary and overcrowded dungeons as the European slave ships waited at port to gather enough slaves to fill the ships before making a voyage to the Americas. A French businessman wrote near the end of the seventeenth century: "From the moment that the slaves are embarked, one must put the sails up." The reason for raising the sails was to serve as blinders so that the captured Africans would not look back upon their lost homeland in utter despair. Some slave merchants even observed that the slaves would die of grief and sadness during the journey to America. Many Africans at the beginning of the journey violently resisted. Some would hold their breaths until they passed out in an attempt to end their lives, others banged their heads repeated against the ship walls, some engaged in hunger strikes refusing all food in hope of dying of hunger, and others simply jumped overboard to drown. Occasionally, a ship's captain would try to console the captive Africans by standing before them to read scripture aloud.[44]

Before the cargo of the Blacks arrived at the slave market to be auctioned off, they would be cleaned, shaved, and covered with palm oil. Like cattle, they would be herded into a slave pen. The treasurer of the port, a magistrate, a tax collector, clerks, and guards would first inspect the cargo in order to determine its value. Once assembled, the naked and traumatized Africans would be counted and examined. The buyers would then make their inspections of the Africans along with a surgeon. Similar to the trading that takes place today in stock or commodities markets, most sales of enslaved Africans were made through brokers who typically would take a 2 percent payment while the buyer would be responsible for paying the property taxes. The Blacks were treated no differently than the other goods brought aboard the ship, and they were stored in warehouses near the ports along with other merchandise. *Manual do Fazendeiro*, a guidebook for plantation owners, was published in the 1800s and it informed buyers of what to look for when examining the Blacks. The manual insisted that it was important to inspect the teeth, tongue, and arms of slave merchandise before purchase. Readers of the manual were advised to pay close attention to the male's penis and to avoid those who had underdeveloped or misshapen genitals. Sick or maimed Blacks were sometimes unable to attract a buyer and they were left to die unattended at the ports of entry. James Morley, a White sailor in the 1760s, recalled seeing some of these kidnapped, maimed, and then rejected human beings "lying about the beach of St. Kitts market place and in different parts of town in a very bad condition and apparently nobody to take care of them."[45] The European Slave trade was in no way about charity for Africans or giving them the "benefits" of European civilization; it was a demonic enterprise in every respect and from start to finish.

The European Slave Trade was initiated by the Portuguese, intensified by the Spanish and French, and refined to commercial perfection by the Dutch, the British, and the Americans. The slave trade was an intercontinental business and some slave merchants and traders maintained a multinational presence. Slavery was protected and encouraged by legislation and it was supported by religious institutions. The slaveholders were well organized and politically well-connected, and the trade in human flesh was highly profitable for many traders. The European Slave Trade ended in the mid 1800s, but not before the nations of Europe and America had developed a system of international commerce that became the basis for the modern system of global trade.

John Newton once described the slave trade as a lottery in which every slave trader was trying to win the jackpot. Newton, the slave ship captain who later became a preacher and hymn writer confessed that there is "no method of getting money not even robbing for it upon the highway, which has so direct a tendency to efforce the moral sense...." However, it was not Newton's moral sense that forced him from the slave trading business but his poor health. Newton was a professing Christian while he was a practicing slave ship captain. He later became an Anglican minister. On one voyage taking slaves from Africa to the West Indies, Newton wrote to his wife about the danger and unpredictability of the conditions aboard the ship. He reported that the "innumerable dangers and difficulties which without a superior practitioner, no man could escape or surmount are by the goodness of God, happily over."[46] His jubilation at arriving safely to port was of short duration since two days after writing this letter he had to put down a slave rebellion. He stated that he was only able to overcome the rebellious slaves with "divine assistance." Newton was one of the slave ship captains who would read aloud prayers to the crew and captives. As a slave ship captain Newton employed use of the "thumb screw" in order to obtain confessions. John Newton was still a slave ship captain when he penned the popular hymn "How Sweet the Name of Jesus Sounds."[47]

With an intimate knowledge of European slave trading, Newton expressed profound insight about the demoralizing and corrupting impact that the enterprise was having on Whites. The slave trade desensitized the Europeans and White colonists to the plight of other human beings, who were mostly Blacks but also including Native Americans. Enslaving Africans appealed to the leaders of major institutions in European society because it was a lucrative enterprise that provided wealth to the elites, social mobility for professionals, and employment opportunities for the White masses. The "dirty work" of actually capturing and handling slaves was done by relatively few people in places relatively far away from the centers of refined European culture. This comfortable distance allowed for the illusion of being uninvolved in the evils of the slave trade.

By building colonies in the Americas, Europeans were able to dump criminals and malcontents into faraway lands. Often the young men who served as crew aboard slave ships would be recruited by "crimping." They would be enticed with alcoholic beverages at pubs or inns and while still in a drunken stupor they would be carried off to the slave ship, and the innkeeper who served the drinks would be paid off. Newton realized that the ill-treatment of Negroes numbed the hearts of those who engaged in it and rendered them unable to empathize with human suffering, even that of their fellow Whites.[48] Thus, the cruelty that started with the victimization of Africans was soon extended by the slave traders to their own countrymen.

The naming of the slave ships speaks volumes about the magnitude of the support that European Slave Trade had from religious institutions. All major institutions—governments, churches, universities and businesses—engaged in or benefited either directly or indirectly from the slave trade. First and foremost, slavery had the blessing of the churches. The conversion rationale was formulated to make a theological apology for slavery. Those countries primarily involved in the slave trade, Portugal, Spain, the Netherlands, France, and England, could declare that by converting Africans from paganism and barbarism to Christianity, they were engaged in a noble cause. The slave traders were free to invoke God's blessing upon their death ships, and they christened them with holy names like *Brotherhood, Charity, Gift of God, Morning Star,* and the principal ship *Jesus.*[49] Among the Portuguese, slave ships were frequently given the names of saints or incarnations of the Virgin, representing the blessing of the Roman Catholic Church. Portuguese ships had names including *Our Lady of Misericordia, Our Lady of Conceidas, Our Lady of Sao Tiago,* and *Our Lady of Sao Miguel.* Protestant Christianity was not to be left out of this hypocrisy as the slave ship *Reformation* attests. The *Perseverance* was the name preferred by Quaker slave traders for their ship.[50]

Insurance companies and banks financed slave trading activities, and they benefited from the interest earned on their investments. Some of these insurers and banks became international concerns, with offices in Antwerp, London, Paris, and New York. The immense profits of the slave trade helped to nurture the growth of European financial and industrial establishments for centuries. Financial institutions played a key role in facilitating the activities of the European Slave Trade.[51]

In 1781 a slave ship en route from Africa to Jamaica with 440 slaves aboard discovered midway across the Atlantic that there was a serious water shortage. The captain had a dilemma on his hands because they might all perish, both crew and captives, from dehydration if the water completely ran out. But, he did have an insurance agreement that stipulated that he would be paid for all cargo jettisoned overboard in an emergency. So the captain ordered 32 of the weakest African captives to be ushered to the deck of the ship and they were thrown to the sharks below swarming around the ship. The insurance company upon hearing of the circumstances in which this cargo was lost refused payment for the 32 captives and the case was taken to court. The court judge ruled in favor of the ship company and the captain on the grounds that the Blacks were in essence property and that the purpose of insurance was to protect the property value and pay for that which was lost.[52]

Figure 2: Timeline 1450–1791

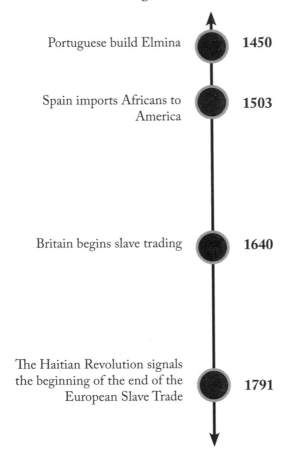

Portuguese build Elmina — 1450

Spain imports Africans to America — 1503

Britain begins slave trading — 1640

The Haitian Revolution signals the beginning of the end of the European Slave Trade — 1791

Chapter 3 – The European Slave Trade

DISCUSSION & REVIEW QUESTIONS

1. How did Europeans initiate and carry out the enslavement of Africans? What did they hope to gain?

2. Why did European Americans systematically suppress the language, religion, and names of those Africans who were enslaved?

3. What skills did enslaved Africans bring with them to America?

4. How did Africans resist the European enslavement? Why were slave rebellions relatively frequent?

CHAPTER 4

The Conversion of Enslaved Africans to the Practice of American Christianity

AFRICA'S FIRST ENCOUNTER WITH CHRISTIAN AMERICA

America is often called a nation of immigrants. The term immigrant implies the voluntary movement from one geographical region to another. And for Europeans, at least, this term is appropriately applied. Europeans were attracted to the Americas as they were looking for new beginnings, new opportunities for wealth and prosperity, and new freedoms from tyrannical regimes in Europe. The Africans who arrived in early America on the other hand had been ruthlessly uprooted and involuntarily forced to come in chains as the free labor source for the European colonists.[1] The European slavers crisscrossed the Atlantic Ocean to fuel the economies of Europe with free labor used to cut down the trees, clear the land, build the infrastructure, and plant and harvest the crops. In fact it has been documented that there were more Africans brought across the Atlantic by the British in the seventeenth and eighteenth centuries than there were Europeans who came as colonists.[2] The European Slave Trade gave birth to the modern global marketplace as rum and guns were transported to Africa, slave laborers were shipped to the Americas, and Europe was enriched with the raw materials transported from the colonies. Indeed this pattern of extracting wealth and resources, both human and material, from the so-called "Third World" to enrich the corporate and national interests of Europe and America continues right up to the present day.[3]

The contrast between the conditions and social prospects of the arriving European immigrants and that of the enslaved Africans was striking:

> Whatever the difficulties and anomalies of colonization, a broad range of religiously inclined Europeans—Puritans, Scottish Presbyterians, German Lutherans, Dutch Reformed Quakers and Jews—not only survived in America but often eventually prospered both individually and spiritually. But the rich religious systems of the Akan, Ashanti, Dahomey, Ibo and Yoruba societies—to name only some of the major sources of African religion in American—collapsed in the shattering cultural destructiveness of British slaveholding.[4]

In fact, the mainline White denominations offered Africans a degrading brand of Christianity, contributing to the process of eradicating African culture and religion. The religion that the colonial Christians offered the Africans did not allow them to openly integrate the memory of their ancestors and native religions into their lives. After being stripped of their heritage, they were denied their humanity as they were brutally forced into an animal-like existence devoid of the respect for their ancestry or cultural heritage. Although they had come from many different culture groups from across the African continent with distinct and complex social hierarchies and elaborate ritual systems, they were now thrown together into the same wretched condition without any respect for their previous social identities. There was an attempt made to obliterate the African cultural identity and completely dissolve the sense of community that the Africans brought with them from their homeland. They were forbidden to speak their native languages, use their African names, practice their customs, initiate their children into their ritual systems, or preserve their native beliefs and values.[5] The impact of this historically unparalleled cultural and spiritual holocaust on African people, which lasted for the better part of four centuries, is all but unfathomable. This is so because for African people, perhaps more so than for any other people, collective memory, social heritage, cultural tradition, and personal identity are inextricably intertwined. For Africans, history and culture runs in the blood. It is a basic precept of traditional African cultures that a people who do not express love and appreciation for their ancestors will surely die. But, how can the ancestors be honored if the people are not allowed to learn who they were? Expressing faith and love for someone else's cultural heritage while rejecting one's own is effectively an act of cultural and spiritual suicide. Yet, the Christianity offered to the Africans was intentionally designed to make them reject and forget the memory of their African ancestors and to accept the gods of those who had enslaved and colonized them. Converting Africans to the practice of American Christianity was an effort to coerce and co-opt them into embracing the gods and religion of their enemies, and in effect, to worship their enemies.[6]

Europeans began the process of enslaving Africans prior to their colonization of continental America. Thus, in early colonial America the enslavement of Africans met with only slight opposition. Even the minimal opposition offered was mostly silenced as the slaveholders and their supporters developed the rationale that the slave trade was a means of civilizing and Christianizing the heathens of the Dark Continent. The conversion motif crafted by the religious authorities "sanitized" the activities of the slaveholders and provided a moral basis for the slave trade. However, the excuse of enslaving Africans for religious reasons created unforeseen problems. The conversions and baptisms of Africans compelled colonial Christian America to face the question of the humanity of their Black slaves. If the Blacks could be baptized and converted, were they not then also created in the image of God? (imago Dei) It was a widespread English belief that there was a common need for conversion expressed in the saying "all men before God as sinners in need of salvation."[7] And this was applied to the Blacks as well. But acceptance of this concept forced a confrontation with the long-established English custom in both civil and church canon that held that no baptized person could be held in slavery.

The old English custom that prohibited one Christian from holding another in bondage had devastating economic implications for the slaveholders. The colonial governments were faced with contradictory theological and economical imperatives. To deny the conversion and baptism of the slaves would be to undermine the rationale for the slave trade. Yet, to embrace the manumission of slaves after conversion and baptism would destroy the slaveholders and wreak financial havoc on the ruling classes of the colonies. Consequently, the colonial authorities began to develop a conversion motif that would accommodate the interests of both the church and the slaveholding establishment.

Initially, conversion justified religious involvement in slavery on the grounds that Africans needed to be converted and civilized. Once enslaved Africans became Christians, a further rationale was required to justify their continued bondage. This new rationale was supplied by the religious authorities and scholars of the church, who claimed that Africans, already barbaric and heathen, had souls doomed to eternal perdition and destruction. Black skin color thus became a stigma, an inherent mark of slavery, inferiority, and godlessness. And baptism did not change the inferior status of the Africans as it was deemed an insufficient reason for emancipation. The slave status would remain with the Blacks despite their conversion status.[8]

The civil and church authorities worked together to enact a special legislation that would resolve the theological and economic dilemma of slave conversions. In 1664, Maryland became the first colony to enact laws explicitly denying slaves freedom based on their conversion to Christianity. Three years later, Virginia enacted a similar measure, which held that the freedom of the slave's soul after conversion did not also apply to his body. At first, the Virginia Assembly had protected Africans who were Christians prior to arriving in America as it also protected Whites who were indentured servants. However, that legislation was repealed in 1682 and replaced with a measure that declared that conversion before or after importation would not alter the status of slavery. During the colonial period, Maryland, Virginia, the Carolinas, New York, and New Jersey all agreed that the saving of an African soul did not merit release of the African body from bondage.[9]

The colonial establishment devised a particular language for slave conversion—differentiating the salvation of the soul from the freedom of the body—to give the institution of slavery the veneer of civility and legality. Attempting to justify the evil of slavery, the colonialists rhetorically separated the slave's soul from his body. The justification for the continued enslavement of the African's body was accomplished by the invention of the idea of the racial inferiority for the African. This doctrine posited that the biological, social, cultural and linguistic differences made it impossible for an African to ever be the equal of European Americans. This new language of conversion was custom-made for the peculiar nature of American slavery. It met both the economic and political needs of Colonial America and was supported by civil and religious authorities. To their satisfaction the American colonialists had answered the question: How can a Christian nation condone and conduct the institution of human slavery?[10]

Despite their attempt to legitimize and sanitize the slave trade, slaveholders were primarily interested in the use of free African labor to cultivate the vast natural resources that they had found in the Americas. Searching for a cheap or free labor force was the priority of Spain and England in the sixteenth century when they began trading goods for slaves in Africa. Africans emerged as a far superior source of free labor compared to Native Americans or European indentured servants. The Native Americans were familiar with the American terrain, which was after all their homeland, and they could more easily escape from servitude than the hapless Africans who found themselves lost on a new continent. Also, the colonists bitterly complained about the poor stamina of the Native Americans and their apparently diminished capacity to withstand the rigors of human bondage as compared to the Africans. The indentured Whites on the other hand could readily escape and easily blend in with White colonial population in ways in which the Blacks obviously could not. In addition, it was psychologically easier for Europeans to mistreat and brutalize people who were culturally and phenotypically so different from themselves. By the eighteenth century, Black skin color had become not only the evidence of slavery but also a badge of degradation and prejudice against the Blacks, which was engraved into American custom and law. Africans were considered an anomaly in the human race. Europeans would use the excuse of black skin to justify enslavement. They based their horrific treatment of the Africans on their skin color, and the stigma and legacy of color consciousness and bias became imbedded in the fabric of European-American society.[11]

There is evidence that Africans had arrived in the Americas long before the first Europeans, and people of African descent were included in the first groups of Europeans to arrive in the Americas.[12] However, the freedom and new opportunities enjoyed by the European immigrants would not be extended to the Africans. The historian Richard Hofstader gives a striking description of the implementation of the slave trade:

To Africans stunned by the long ordeal of the Middle Passage the auctions could only have marked a decrescendo in fright and depression....As one tries to imagine the mental state of the newly arrived Africans, one must think of people still sick, depleted and depressed by the ordeal of the voyage, the terror of the unknown, the sight of deaths and suicides, and the experience of total helplessness in the hands of others. What they had been and known receded rapidly, and the course of their experience to the withered husks of dead memories.[13]

It is seldom recognized or acknowledged that the religious instruction by the Colonial Christians given to the African Americans contributed to the suppression of their indigenous spirituality and piety as expressed in traditional African religion and culture. European Americans regarded African beliefs and practices, such as ancestor veneration, holy dancing and shouting, deity possessions, and drumming as expressions of paganism and barbarity. The slaveholders claimed that such behavior was offensive to their more refined and civilized sensibilities. Of course they also realized that such practices were vestiges of the African identity that must be destroyed if they were to exercise complete control over their slaves. Nevertheless, African Americans clung tenaciously to many of their native beliefs and practices, often expressing them in secret as they adapted and integrated these customs into the version of Christianity now being imposed upon them. During the early colonial period, few Africans were attracted to American Christianity. The first generation of Africans did not embrace American Christianity. However, later generations, particularly those Africans born in America, began to accept Christianity as they saw some educational, social, and economic benefits in converting. Also they soon learned how to alter the version of Christianity they were given to make it more spiritually compatible with their reality. In time, the vitality, imagination and creativity that the Africans brought to the practice of Christianity produced a unique religiosity that helped to shape American Christianity.[14] The American south was "harvested by God" as the African Americans brought forth a new and deeper spirituality and insight that began to have pervasive, though at first subtle influence on the course of American Christianity.

It was not until the Great Awakening (1730–1780) that a significant number of African Americans accepted Protestant Christianity. It is perhaps ironic that the African-inspired pietism and holiness that the European Americans had suppressed and attempted to destroy for more than a century sparked a transcontinental spiritual revival in both Europe and America. Prior to the Great Awakening, African Americans practiced a clandestine holiness while at the same time worshipping publicly in White churches under the supervision of the slaveholders. The religious services and teachings were conducted by White preachers who emphasized a heavenly reward for good slaves who were obedient to their masters. More important to the Blacks, however, was the "Invisible Institution," in which practices of holy dancing, shouting, spirit possessions, spirited testimonies, and exhortations were practiced in secret bush harbors away from the prying eyes of the overseers. Despite threats and punishments, African Americans persisted in holding secret praise services, usually at

The African-American Ring Shout was a counterclockwise circular movement of the shouters, who were slightly bent in posture and gracefully dancing to the rhythmic hand clapping of those standing outside the circle.

night in the midst of thickets and bushes or down by the riverside, "where you couldn't hear nobody pray."[15]

African Americans became excited about American Christianity in large numbers during the Great Awakening, a period that the eminent historian Carter G. Woodson labeled the "Dawn of a New Day."[16] A new form of personal, heart-warming, and experiential Evangelical Protestantism emerged during the Great Awakening and proved to be far more suited for the spiritual needs of Black people than Colonial Puritanism or Anglicanism had ever been. Prior to the spiritual fervor of the Great Awakening, African Americans characterized American Christianity as dull, spiritless, hypocritical and generally unappealing.

The spiritual fervor that accompanied the Great Awakening had visible elements that resonated with African religious expression—elements that appeared less frequently in more formal catechetical styles of religious transformation. The spirited shouting and singing, dancing, and Holy Ghost possessions that were present in many camp meetings during the Great Awakening were outgrowths of African-American spirituality that now began to be openly embraced by many Whites. There was a focus on a religion of the heart, including energetic expressions of music, dance, call and response, singing and preaching, hand clapping, and so forth, and that focus has continued to the present in many southern Baptist and Methodist churches. These African-American spiritual expressions served to provide a basis for commonality in the religious experiences of Whites and Blacks:

> The styles of Baptists and Methodists were less formalized and stereotyped than the Presbyterian or Episcopalian churches and the evangelical mode of preaching seemed to have a spontaneous appeal to Negroes; perhaps, they were disposed toward emotional-toned group meetings by their African background. They seemed to have a marked selectivity for the intensity and emotionalism of the Baptist and Methodist preaching.[17]

Whether slave or free, Black or White, there was a shared understanding that "all are sinners saved by grace." The spiritual fervor was precipitated by a shared need for change. As Robin Horton's article on African conversion points out, "spiritual hunger" was a driving force for conversion, and it ushered in a wind of change. Blacks and Whites who were converted were hungry for spiritual and physical renewal and transformation. Blacks were at the bottom of the social and economic structure of America, but it was poor Whites who were displaced by slave labor, and they were also generally excluded from opportunities for social advancement by the White social elites. The Anglican Church in particular catered to the social elites and failed to welcome poor Whites. And it goes without saying that Blacks were also generally excluded from the accordance of any status of respect within the church.[18]

Many of the scholars who have taken an interest in the conversion experience of African Americans have focused solely on their desire for deliverance from bondage, which was indeed a factor, but to reduce African-American conversions to their desire to address material needs would be an oversimplification. Blacks, like their poor White counterparts, wanted desperately to be relieved of harsh living conditions and liberation from their sins. The Reverend Samuel Davies, in 1757, expressed the ambiguity that was apparent during many African-American conversion experiences: "Many of them seem only to desire to be they know not what. They feel themselves uneasy in their present condition and therefore desire a change."[19] In keeping with their deeply rooted African spiritual heritage, African Americans required a holistic change, which included both physical release and spiritual rebirth. More than Native Americans, who at least still had some semblance of their traditions and culture, or poor Whites, who at least had the "right" color if not much else, African Americans needed a deeper and more radical spirituality that would allow them to both morally transcend and physically withstand the conditions to which they were subjected. To be "born again" was the conversion language best suited to the African-American religious experience. The new birth meant even more than liberation from slavery and physical bondage, as important as that was. Reverend Davies estimated that over seven thousand African Americans attended his ministry at different Virginia churches because they were eager for spiritual and physical freedom. He quoted the words of the psalmist to describe his impressions of Black spirituality: "Ethiopia has stretched forth her hands unto God."

Conversion to Christianity did not mean the same thing to all African Americans. Likewise, the terms used for conversion varied according to differing perspectives. For some, conversion meant recriminations and a coming to terms with their degradation. For others, it was a way to express defiance toward the slave masters and the institution of slavery. Still others may have believed some of the words of the fire-and-brimstone preaching of White evangelists and sought forgiveness of their personal sins. And for many there was a combination of factors causing them to seek the conversion experience.

The institution of slavery forced African Americans to reconcile two levels of religion. As more Africans learned English and became more acculturated to American customs, each successive generation became further estranged from traditional African cultural forms and practices. Enslaved Africans were put into situations where they had to struggle to retain even the smallest amount of dignity and self-esteem as they adopted the culture and beliefs of their tormentors. Consequently, Blacks were put into the position of having to develop contradictory patterns of conduct and values. On the one hand, they were expected to conduct themselves obsequiously and submit to subhuman treatment. However, the nature of conversion and the "new birth" implied a cosmologically enhanced status and a relationship with God. Such a relationship and status many African Americans already felt anyway as evidenced by their conversion testimonies. Europeans attempted to limit the conversion experience to one of acceptance of docile, childlike obedience during slavery. Africans had the arduous task of grappling with these conflicting messages and values.[20] This conflict was partially resolved by feigning acceptance of obsequious behaviors toward Whites as a survival tactic while strongly identifying with the unassailable and ultimate liberating powers of an omnipotent Savior. Great faith in the liberating and sustaining powers of the Holy Ghost among African Americans can be understood as far more than a compensatory device when we consider the strong emphasis on spiritual capacities found throughout traditional African societies.

For the enslaved and the slaveholders, different experiences shaped patterns, norms, and forms of individual expression of spiritual conversion. Consequently, the conversion of African Americans differed from that of the of slave masters, even when converted during the same worship service. The conversion experience was much more radical for the Blacks than for the slaveholders. For most Whites, conversion meant fellowship with Christ and forgiveness of personal sins such as drinking and smoking, but their conversion did not alter their hearts or minds to the degree that they would free their slaves or attempt to address social ills. In fact nothing was fundamentally at stake for the slaveholder in the conversion process. The White converts wanted a better relationship with Christ, but not necessarily with their neighbors, especially if those neighbors were Black. On the other hand, the slaves were looking for a more holistic conversion experience that would liberate them spiritually if not also physically. Being "born again" best describes what conversion meant to the enslaved. Spiritual birth, like physical birth, was a crucial and decisive event not to be taken lightly. It was like waking up after a long deep sleep. Failure to awaken was ruinous, as all the plans for living would then no longer matter. Like the day of physical birth, the time and place of spiritual birth was thought of as an event to be remembered and celebrated. Just as a mother experiences labor pains in childbirth, the enslaved encountered a psychological turmoil full of pains and sorrow over sinful acts, trepidation and fear of being in the presence of the Holy Ghost, and the anticipation of coming forth as a new being. The conversion experience for Blacks was in this way not unlike the initiation rituals of traditional Africa. It was a struggle and a trial, but it was a struggle that led to deliverance, and this experience was inscribed upon the memory forever. They never forgot the day nor the hour when they "came through." And this tradition of ecstatic and dramatic conversion experiences continued among Blacks, especially in the American South, through the middle of the twentieth century. Many southern Blacks could recount the moment of their conversion, and there were popular revival songs commemorating the day and the hour when they encountered their conversion experience. One of the enslaved recalled the vision she received during her conversion experience:

> As I prayed an angel came and touched me, and I looked at my hands and they came new. I looked and saw my body suspended over a burning pit by a small spider web. I again prayed and there came a soft voice saying, "My little one, I have loved you with everlasting love. You are this day made alive and freed from hell." [21]

Africans who survived the horror of the Middle Passage became the primary victims of the institution of American slavery. American slavery is in many respects unique in the long and sordid history of human slavery. The harshness of American slavery was unknown to any previous English law, Spanish tradition, or African custom. The American version of slavery stood out in its brutality, its inhumanity, its intensity and its duration. Because many of the American slaveholders professed Christianity, the need to justify slavery as a benevolent institution became as important to the slave masters as it had been to the slave traders. The Africans' need for conversion and civilization continued to captivate the minds of the slaveholders as the most humane rationale and defense of slavery. The conversion motif inspired the religious and civil authorities to provide religious training for slaves, which gave slaves not only the possibility to become Christians but also the opportunity to become literate.[22]

To support these justifications, White Christians encouraged evangelical activities among the slaves. The evangelical appeal focused on exposing Blacks to the Christian symbols, customs, and practices and was at least nominally supported by many slaveholders who wanted a Christian "blessing" for their activities. Many religious leaders and colonial officials endorsed religious training for the slaves, which meant teaching slaves to read and write—also called "religion with letters." In the early eighteenth century many opponents and proponents of slavery had a mutual interest in the religious training of slaves. An early printed protest against the brutalities of slavery by the New Englander Cotton Mather admonished slaveholders not only to set the captives free but also to "teach [Blacks] to read and give them Christian Education." Carter G. Woodson, the initiator of Black History Month, said, "The first real educators [to enlighten] American Negroes were clergymen interested in the propagation of the gospel among the heathen of the New World."[23]

For the enslaved, the hunger for getting an education was as great as the hunger for salvation. Indeed, the two were interrelated and they complemented each other. There is the story of the Black family and mourners who were gathered around a grave site in Port Royal, South Carolina. While there, the children had school books in their hands and they sang their ABC's over and over again. These children considered their school

One of the early structures used by the Silver Bluff Church Congregation

studies to be work a kind of religious exercise.[24] The first schools for Blacks were in fact in churches. Historically, Black educational institutions are the offspring of Black churches, and there has been an enduring and inseparable bond between them.

The early education of the slaves in Colonial America was under the auspices of the Society for the Propagation of the Gospel (S.P.G.). The society was organized in 1701 as the missionary arm of the Anglican Church, and it provided religious training for Blacks and Native Americans. Also with the teachers, the society provided Bibles, the Book of Common Prayer, and religious literature, and they provided Blacks with their first textbooks. The strong desire to know the Word of God inspired and motivated many African Americans to learn how to read. The original intent of the S.P.G. was to evangelize and thereby culturally subdue Native Americans. At this time, native people were in the process of being removed from the east coast of America, isolated on reservations, or simply exterminated. Despite opposition from some of the plantation owners, the first school for Native Americans was established in the colony of Virginia, in Accomack County. After the general demise of Native Americans in the early colonies, the

S.P.G. turned its benevolent attentions toward Africans.[25] The Church of England devised a system for the plantations which combined Anglican Christian order and paternalism with the oppressive brutality of slavery. Despite support from colonial legislatures and the favor of the colonial elites, Anglican Christianity was unable to stamp its liturgy, doctrine, or ministry upon what became the American South. As the enslaved Africans had brought the original Holy Ghost with them from the Motherland, they found it difficult to internalize the sterile and hypocritical teachings of the colonial Christians. The orthodox Calvinists and Anglicans had begun to exile and ridicule the "new birth" Baptists and the "heartwarming" Methodists who verbalized and dramatized the new birth. But, because of the emphasis on a personal encounter with the Savior, the Methodists and Baptists had a more compelling presentation as they met in camp meetings, love feasts, and other protracted gatherings.[26]

In slavery, Blacks all but worshipped the Bible itself. The Bible stories and characters were centerpieces of sermons by slave preachers. These biblical stories, characters, and images from the Bible saturated the preaching, praying, and singing of the slaves. Eventually the slaveholders realized that teaching slaves to read and write did nothing for the capacity to control their captives, and there were bans on literature for the slaves. The Blacks resisted and continued to pursue literacy. William McWhorter recalled the following: "Dey jus' beat 'em up bad when dey catched 'em studyin', readin' and writin'...Folks did tell 'bout some of de owners dat cut off one finger erry tim dey cotch a slave tryin' to get larnin'. How-some-ever, dere was some Niggers dat wanted larnin' so bad dey would slip out at night and meet in a deep gully whar dey would study by de light of lightwood torchers; but one thing sho, dey better not let no white folks find out 'bout it and if dey was lucky, nough 'til dey larned to read de Bible, dey kept it a close secret."[27] Many enslaved Blacks had an insatiable hunger for literacy, and some of them would put their life on the line to learn to read. One slave who was a nurse for her slaveholder family had been taught by one of the children to spell the name Jesus and to recognize it in text. At every opportunity the woman would spend time, "taking the Bible and searching for the name." She travelled with her finger along line after line and page after page until she found "Jesus."[28]

The Bible was the key to early acquisition of literacy among African Americans. Frederick Douglass wrote in his autobiography:

> The frequent hearing of my mistress reading the Bible aloud … awakened my curiosity in respect to the mystery of reading, and roused in me the desire to learn. Up to the time I had known nothing whatever of the wonderful art, and my ignorance and inexperience of what it could do for me, as well as my confidence in my mistress emboldened me to ask her to teach me to read…. In an incredible short time, by her assistance, I had mastered the alphabets and could spell words of three or four letters…. [My master] forbade her to give me any further instruction … [but] the determination which he expressed to keep me in ignorance only rendered me the more resolute to seek intelligence. In learning to read, therefore I am not sure that I do not owe quite so much to the opposition of my master as to the kindly assistance of my amiable mistress. [29]

CONVERSION AND THE INSPIRATION TO LITERACY

Early on in America, the enslaved began to associate literacy with liberation and self-esteem. Education and literacy have been a consistent value among African Americans as a sure ticket for survival and progress in a hostile environment. Education was seen by those enslaved as freedom from ignorance and freedom from a menial existence. Literacy reinforced self-worth. Lucius Holsey, a towering figure in the Christian Methodist Episcopal Church (C.M.E.), took pride in learning to read and exhorted his people to strive for excellence, saying that "books were the path to improving any man."[30]

The inextinguishable desire of the Blacks to learn to read revealed their tenacity in attempting to maintain a sense of self-worth and self-determination under chattel slavery. Seeking literacy was a personal, communal, and political demonstration of resistance to degradation and bondage. To read the Bible opened the slave to a new world of ideas and possibilities, which inspired their curiosity to learn even more by reading newspapers and pamphlets. This eventually caused some to aspire to become preachers, abolitionist leaders, and race leaders. Reading the Bible helped the slaves to gain a sense of freedom long before most of them would actually be free of physical chains.

Learning to read was not only a path to God but was a means to witness and save others. Jupiter Hammon was seventy years old but he was literate and he felt a duty to admonish other enslaved to learn to read. "Get those who can read to learn you but that if there was no Bible it would be no matter whether you could read or not. The Bible is the 'Word of God' and tells you what you must do to please God, it tells you how you may escape misery, and be happy forever."[31]

Blacks recognized the Bible as much more than a book, they viewed it as a library in itself, an opening to a new reality. Alexander Garden, a committed proponent of training slaves, noted the eagerness of the Blacks to attend "the school, but probably for opportunity at literacy rather than religious instruction."[32] In spite of the impediments and reluctance of slaveholders to consent to their learning to read, growing numbers of Blacks became literate throughout the seventeenth and eighteen centuries. The Great Awakening sparked the growth of independent Black churches, the emergence of the Black preacher as a community leader, and even more avenues for Blacks to become literate and socially aware.

The education and socialization of Native Americans and Africans became the focus of the S.P.G. The Anglican sponsors of missionary work among the slaves believed that literacy was a necessary prerequisite for baptism and church membership as well as a way to acculturate the heathen to their new lot in life as the wards of a superior civilization. The Anglican Church sent the Reverend Samuel Thomas from England to the colonies to evangelize and provide training to the Blacks and Native Americans. The evangelistic efforts of Thomas did not go unnoticed. Captain Nairne and Reverend Robert Stevens of Goose Creek reported that "Mr. Thomas is instructing the Negroes … and they have books."[33] Stevens also reported that the slaves belonging to Governor Moore were provided with Bibles and the Book of Common Prayer by the Governor. Thus, the Bible and religious literature served as the first reading material for enslaved Africans in the Americas. Ironically, though the colonial leaders had intended to use American Christianity as a tool to perpetuate their dominance over Africans, it became a means by which the Africans would begin to form an independent new identity for themselves.[34]

Reverend Thomas had only five students at first, but the number quickly increased to 32. Soon, Thomas succeeded in teaching twenty of them to read. This notable beginning permanently settled the question in the minds of many in the S.P.G. of whether the slaves were capable of learning how to read. It also helped unsettle the notion that Blacks were innately inferior to Europeans. When Thomas unexpectedly died in 1706, the S.P.G. appointed Dr. Francis LeJeau as his successor to address the educational needs of the slaves. LeJeau appealed to the slaveholders' self-interest, promising that religious training would make better, more loyal, and more controllable slaves. He also presented slaveholders with a formal written statement reassuring them that conversion would not change the status of their slaves as property.[35]

Anglican Commissary Alexander Garden was another strong advocate for training Blacks to become literate. To diminish the fear slaveholders had for educating their slaves, Garden came up with the idea of training the male youth slaves between the ages of 12 and 16 and having them in turn train the other Blacks under his supervision. He erected the first school for Blacks in Charleston, South Carolina, in 1744, with Harry and Andrew serving as the first teachers. The school opened with sixty young students who were enthusiastic and possessed an insatiable craving for knowledge. The program was a success. It graduated more than thirty pupils who were well instructed in religion. They were capable of reading the Bible, and they would carry that knowledge home to diffuse to teach other Blacks.[36]

The efforts to train and prepare the enslaved to read and write were not without challenges and obstacles. The Stono Rebellion erupted on September 9, 1739. The Africans rose up to kill twenty-five Whites before the insurrection was suppressed. This rebellion stirred up deep-seated fears and anxieties among the Whites, and as a result of this violent uprising, the Southern establishment passed laws against teaching Blacks to read or write. Also, churches that seemed sympathetic to the plight of the Blacks were ordered to be closed. William Heard of Elberton, Georgia, was an enslaved Black man who later became a bishop in the A.M.E. Church. Heard attended a White-controlled Sunday school which refused instruction for Blacks on how to read or write. He reported, "Any slave caught writing suffered the penalty of having his forefinger cut from his right hand."[37]

After the Stono Rebellion, new laws were enacted and the social environment became hostile toward educating slaves. But the laws did not eclipse the efforts of the Anglican missionaries to try to meet some of the needs of some of the slaves. Nor did colonial legislation impede the motivation and determination of many of the enslaved to achieve literacy; there was no turning back the tide of history and the advance of Blacks in learning to become socially competent in American society. An outstanding example of the desire of enslaved Blacks to become literate despite obstacles was L.H. Holsey. L.H. Holsey was a house slave in Georgia, most likely the offspring of his slave master, and he would later go on to become the third elected bishop of the C. M. E. church. He made literacy a priority in his early life despite his bondage. In his spare time he collected and sold rags and soon had enough money to buy five books—two Webster's blue book spellers, a school dictionary, Milton's *Paradise Lost* and the Bible. Holsey relied on some White children and elderly Black women who taught him how to read and write:

Bishop Lucius H. Holsey (1842–1920)

Day by day, I took a leaf from one of the spelling books, and so folded it that one or two of the lessons were on the outside as if printed on a card. This I put in the pocket of my vest or coat, and when I was sitting in the carriage, walking the streets, or working in the yard or using the hoe or spade, or in the dining room I would take out my spelling leaf which was finished by this process. I would refold it ... with a new lesson on the outside.... Besides, I could catch words from the white people and retain them in my memory until I could get my dictionary. Then I would spell and define the words, until they became perfectly impressed upon my memory.[38]

The Blacks conceived of creative ways to become literate, which many considered a divine imperative. There was nothing more exhilarating than for an enslaved person then achieving a firm command of the English language. At the age of 90, a woman recalled how she learned to read while caring for her slave master's baby who was playing with alphabet books. Her efforts to learn to read did not sit well with her slave master. One day he came home from working in the field wearing muddy boots and he caught her attempting to read. He responded by viciously kicking her with the muddy boots. Despite the punishments and threats, the woman was undaunted as she clandestinely practiced her writing skills whenever she could. She never forgot the day when she found a hymn book and was able to spell out and read. She could not retain her jubilation. "I was happy when I saw that I could read, then I ran around telling the other slaves that I could read."[39] Learning to read became a status symbol for enslaved Blacks and a ticket to recognition and leadership in the Black community. Consequently, many had an insatiable craving for knowledge and learning. They were known to carry books around, especially the Bible even before they had learned how to read. The Bible and the church became the central symbols of self-worth and positive identity for their lives and their community.

Most Blacks at this time never did learn to read, but the lack of literacy did not stop them from preaching and teaching Bible stories. As they learned Bible stories read and taught by White preachers and teachers, these stories became a part of their oral tradition. White teachers were often amazed at the astonishing memorization capacity exhibited by many of their Black students, for the students listened attentively to every detail and would repeat Biblical stories with great clarity and conviction. As one missionary reported, "To those who are ignorant of letters their memory is their book.... In a recent examination of one of the schools, I was forcibly struck with their remembrance of passages of scripture. Those questions which turned up and called for passages of scripture the scholar answered more readily than any other." William H. Heard recalled, "In ... Sunday School, we were taught the Bible and catechism and committed much to memory by having the same repeated to us in Sunday School, and then the white family continued to teach the lesson during the week, so that there were those of us who could repeat whole Psalms and chapter after chapter in the shorter catechism."[40] The Reverend S.G. Whiton reported that Uncle Peter had a remarkable memory, "he can repeat a great many chapters entire. This morning among others he repeated the first chapter of Matthew, hardly making a single mistake in that long list of genealogies."[41]

Some Blacks who could not read rationalized that since they could not read the Bible, God spoke to them directly, which made their message more authentic and original since it came directly from the source. "De Master teach we poor colored folk in dat way," proclaimed one elderly freedwoman, "for he hasn't education, and we can't read the blessed word for ourselves." Some believed if they knew Jesus in their heart, they knew the whole Bible and it was no longer necessary for them to read it. In South Carolina, several formerly enslaved maintained that they recognized verses read to them from the Bible because they had previously been revealed to them by the Holy Ghost during their experience in slavery. They believed that slavery, which denied them the opportunity to read, made it necessary for God to make special dispensations for the revelation of the word to them by direct inspiration from the Holy Spirit. These Blacks asserted that "The letter knows, but the Spirit makes alive."[42]

At the organizing General Conference of the C. M. E. church in 1870, one of the most contentious debates was over the education requirement for its ministers, who were just five years removed from slavery. One of the strongest arguments against a literacy requirement came from Anderson Jackson of Alabama. He insisted that "it isn't for us brethren, to measure out a man by book, and say who God shall call and whom he shan't. My father, sir, didn't know A from B, and yet by his preaching hundreds yes thousands—was converted. Scores of 'em in heaven, now, white as well as black."[43] Thus, it was argued that a person need not read the author's book in order to know the author.

THE SILVER BLUFF AWAKENING

The mass conversions of Africans to Christianity occurred during the First Great Awakening (1730–1780), accompanied by soul-stirring, call-and-response preaching.[44] One of the most important instances of the mass conversion of the enslaved population occurred on the plantation of Hugh and Jonathan Bryan in South Carolina, where George Whitefield achieved remarkable success ministering to both Blacks and Whites. After lamenting the physical conditions of the slaves while visiting the Bryan Good Hope Plantation in 1740, Whitefield expressed an interest in converting the slaves. The Bryan family's openness to Whitefield's interest led to the Bryan plantation becoming an important early nurturing ground for African-American religious and educational development. The opportunity for cognitive growth was attractive to the Blacks as well as the chance to be converted. The relatively supportive environment of the Bryan Good Hope Plantation resulted in one of the first Black Baptist churches and schools, which was inspired by revivalist preachers who found large gatherings of the enslaved eager for an expansion of their life opportunities.[45]

The Bryan Plantation was an incubator for the independent Black church movement and the training ground for the early leaders of the African-American religious experience. The focus on "new birth" during the Great Awakening provided a common ground for Blacks and Whites, rich and poor, to be recognized as part of God's elect and to be received as saints in the Body of Christ. The outcome of the gospel proclaimed on the Bryan Plantation was not the emancipation of the slaves but an affirmation of their humanity in the imago Dei. The Blacks were denied racial equality and they were maintained in slavery; however, they were permitted a somewhat more humane existence as the Bryan family at least acknowledged that their slaves had souls worth saving.

The latter half of the eighteenth century saw the emergence of a cadre of extraordinarily talented Black ministers and the awakening of the oratorical genius of Black preachers. Silver Bluff, South Carolina, was one of the fertile "watering holes" for Black preachers and independent churches that sprang up around the Savannah River from the Silver Bluff area to Savannah and back to Augusta on the west side of the river. Silver Bluff was the starting for the first major growth spurt of organized Black churches in America. In addition, the movement at Silver Bluff influenced the growth of churches in Canada, Jamaica, and Africa. George Galphin, a Scotsman, settled in Silver Bluff, where he built a successful trading business with the nation of Creek Indians. The trade of deerskin with the Native Americans was essential to the viability of the economy of the Carolinas. It became the primary source of commerce between the English and the people of South Carolina. During the first half of the eighteenth century, slaveholders often preferred African men and Native American women to serve respectively as the field slaves and house slaves. As a result Black men sometimes married Native American women and the Black men thereby became members of the wives' clan and citizens of their respective nations. However, by 1708, the number of Indians available for enslavement in the Carolinas was only about half that of the Africans.[46]

George Galphin became the primary land owner and the wealthiest man in Silver Bluff. He took pride in his new home. He used his enormous resources to develop and expand his plantation. In White society, Galphin was considered a "gentleman of distinguished talents and great liberality." He was the most successful businessman in the region, with extensive trade connections and influence with several Indian Nations. He was also married to four wives: one Black, one Native American, and two White.

The town of Silver Bluff became a celebrated place, with monuments, Indian Council mounts, terraces, fortresses, and remnants of the camps of the Spaniards, who had come hoping to find silver. In addition to these features, Silver Bluff has the distinction of being cited most often as the birthplace of the Black church in America. C. Eric Lincoln and Lawrence Mamiya made the following observation: "The oldest church in [our] study was Silver Bluff Baptist Church of Beech Island, South Carolina, which on the cornerstone claimed a founding date of 1750. It is usually regarded as the first known Black church." Also, the scholar Albert Raboteau made the same observation. He wrote, "The distinction of being the first separate Black church in the South (and north) belonged to the Baptist Church founded between 1773 and 1775 in Silver Bluff, South Carolina across the Savannah River from Georgia. The significance of Silver Bluff Church lies not only in its chronological priority but its reproductive role as the mother of Baptist Missions and schools across the African Diaspora."[47]

In considering the importance of the Silver Bluff Church, we must recognize the inspired leadership that emerged from that congregation. The early Black preachers out of Silver Bluff initiated the expansion and growth of Baptist Missions; their influence even became international. The story of Black church leadership began when George Galphin consented for Wait Palmer, a White evangelist, to preach to his slaves. Many slaveholders were reluctant to allow Northern Whites to preach to their slaves as they were afraid that they might incite rebellion, but Palmer was able to convince Galphin to allow him to preach. When Palmer came to the plantation a large crowd of slaves assembled at the Galphin Mill for worship. Eight people were converted, and they became the charter members of the Silver Bluff Church. The church was organized and the owner of the plantation and Palmer appointed David George as the first pastor. George began with a small congregation of slaves.[48]

David George was born in Virginia in 1743. Both of his parents had been born in Africa, but they were enslaved and brought to America. At the age of 19 he escaped from enslavement as the plantation slave master was most cruel to him, his mother and his siblings. He described this scenario in his autobiographical reflections:

> My oldest sister was called Patti; I have seen her several times so whipped that her back has been a corruption, as though it would rot. My brother Dick ran away, but they caught him and brought him home.... Then they hung him up to a cherry tree, quite naked, except for his breeches.... After he received 500 lashes, or more, they washed his back with salt water.... I also have been whipped many times on my naked skin, and sometimes till the blood has run down over my waist band; but the

greatest grief I had was to see them whip my mother, and to hear her, on her knees, begging for mercy.[49]

After escaping slavery, George found a Native American settlement where he worked as a servant for an Indian chief. Later he eventually migrated to Silver Bluff, South Carolina. He had an insatiable hunger for freedom and self-improvement as he taught himself to read, and he also helped many other Blacks to become literate. David George and George Liele became acquainted when they were both enslaved in Virginia. George Liele was later sold into slavery in Georgia. When George came to South Carolina, he heard his lifelong friend preach and Liele became his spiritual mentor. Liele taught him how to pray and George was a fast learner. When Wait Palmer came to Silver Bluff to preach at the Galphin plantation, George was one of the eight who converted. The biographer Grant Gordon maintains: "This gives George the distinction of being the first Black Baptist pastor in an all-Black Baptist congregation in North America."[50]

The charter members of the first African-American congregation were David George, his wife, Jesse Galphin or Peter, and five other unnamed Blacks. David George and Jesse Galphin were the first pastors and later they were supported by George Liele, who at that time was enslaved by Henry Sharpe. Sharpe was a deacon at the Buckhead Creek Church. During the War for Independence, Sharpe abandoned his plantation and fought against the rebellious American colonists, thereby freeing his slave George Liele. After attaining his freedom, Liele joined the Silver Bluff Church and supported the ministry of David George.[51]

In the years leading up to the Revolutionary War from 1773 to 1775, George and Liele preached and served together at the Silver Bluff Baptist Church. The church increased its membership from eight to more than thirty. When the British soldiers came to coastal Georgia and South Carolina, George and his fledgling membership took the opportunity to flee to Yamacraw, near Savannah. The transplanted congregation became the nucleus for the birth of the independent Black church movement in Savannah. George and his congregation joined the work that Liele had already begun in Yamacraw. After the British occupied Savannah, the slaveholders fled and the enslaved Africans abandoned their plantations and joined with the British by the hundreds. Liele seized upon the opportunity to preach and minister to these refugees. He departed from the Tybee River and assembled his congregation of refugees in nearby Savannah.[52]

As the war progressed it became clear to David George that the colonists would be victorious in the conflict and he decided to flee from the slavers and resettle in Nova Scotia. In Canada, George continued his missionary work by preaching the gospel to large crowds of Blacks who had fled persecution and slavery in the United States. Before departing Canada, after years of ministry, George planted the Shelbourne Baptist Church. In 1792, George and his friend John Marrant migrated to Sierra Leone as a part of the colonization efforts supported by Prince Hall, the prominent Methodist minister and founder of Black Freemasonry. In addition to founding Black Masonry, Hall is remembered for his advocacy of an African-American migration and colonization movement as he grew to believe that Blacks would never be treated equally by Whites in America. In his later years, George never lost his passion for spreading the gospel, and he became an international missionary spreading the gospel in Africa. In order to augment his efforts to establish the Baptist denomination in Africa, George visited England, the birthplace of the Baptists in the early seventeenth century. He was warmly received by the English Baptists and they were eager to learn firsthand about the Black Baptist preachers and churches in Africa and America. The British were impressed with George's resourcefulness and the Reverend John Rippon acknowledged his talents. Rippon assured his colleagues that he believed George to be the best man without exception to establish Baptist churches in Sierra Leone.[53]

While the Revolutionary War raged on, both sides made overtures to the enslaved Blacks along the following lines: "If our side wins, we will free you in return for your services," said the colonists. "Fight on our side and when we put down the rebellion, you will be free," said the British. Some Blacks responded to the appeals of both sides, but when the conflict was over neither the newly independent Americans nor the defeated British chose to honor their promises to the Blacks. David George led several thousand African-American men who had joined the British army during the Revolutionary War to Nova Scotia at the close of the war. But, the hostile climate in Canada motivated George and hundreds of Black men to later leave North America and return to Africa.[54]

When George immigrated with the Loyalists to Canada, he was accompanied by 30,000–35,000 Whites and Blacks. The British had promised free passage and provisions to all Loyalists. The Whites received the promised provisions, but the Blacks did not, and they made do with very little. After much suffering, sickness and hardship due to the harsh winter weather, George and his Black compatriots were permitted to settle in the Shelbourne province. Shelbourne was an undesirable and undeveloped wilderness at this time, and they did not have sufficient supplies to fully support themselves.[55]

In spite of harsh circumstances, George continued to preach the gospel with great zeal and passion, and his conversions helped to stabilize the fledging Black community. He initiated outdoor crusades, which attracted large numbers of both Blacks and Whites. People flocked to hear him preach every evening. George struggled to preach the gospel under the most adverse conditions and his tenacity caught the attention of Governor Parr, who gave him one-quarter acre of land and six months' provision of food. By the summer of 1784, the membership of his congregation had increased to more than 50. George founded the first church for Blacks in Canada and became the first pastor. The planting of this church preceded the activation of the Underground Railroad north of the border by 30 years.[56]

THE AGE OF THE HEROIC PREACHERS 1750–1800

After the departure of David George, the growth and development of the church in Savannah must be credited to George Liele. At the close of the Revolutionary War from 1777–1782, Liele nurtured the remnant of believers who remained in Savannah. The ravages of the war had left the small flock in great disarray. Liele was an effective pastor who brought hope to a people on the brink of despair. He baptized many new converts into the faith, one of whom, Andrew Bryan, was destined to continue the work that he had begun.[57]

George Liele had been born a slave in Virginia. He was separated from his devout Christian parents and sold to the slave-owner Henry Sharpe.

He took the surname of Sharpe at times. In Bartow County, Georgia, the Reverend Matthew Moore, pastor of the church at which Henry Sharpe was a deacon, took Liele into his church and baptized him. Henry Sharpe was killed fighting for the British during the war and so Liele went free. However, some of the Sharpe heirs questioned his manumission and Liele was thrown into prison. After he was able to produce papers proving his manumission, he was set free. Reverend Moore quickly discerned that Liele had ministerial gifts and he encouraged him to exercise them. Liele began to preach and evangelize among the Blacks and Whites on the plantations along the Savannah River. For almost three years he traveled down the river as far as Brampton, a plantation belonging to Jonathan Bryan, and he preached to a large gathering of Blacks there as he was received by the Bryan family. Also, he extended his evangelistic work to Yamacraw near Savannah, where he eventually formed a small congregation.[58]

In 1782 when the British army evacuated Savannah, Liele realized his freedom was in jeopardy, and upon the advice of Colonel Kirkland of the British army, who had befriended him, he left the country for the island of Jamaica.[59] Shortly after his arrival, the energetic Liele built the First Baptist Church of Jamaica and eventually baptized more than 400 free and enslaved Blacks on the island. Providentially, the ship that Liele boarded for Jamaica from Georgia was detained at the mouth of the Savannah River, near Tybee Island, for several weeks owing to stormy weather. While detained on Tybee Island he went to the city to preach and evangelize the local population. In the process he converted and baptized Andrew Bryan, his wife Hannah, Kate Hogg, and Hagar Simpson, all of whom were enslaved by the Bryan family. Andrew Bryan and the other converts became the nucleus of the congregation that would continue the work and cultivate the seeds planted by David George and George Liele.[60]

Andrew Bryan (1737–1812) built upon the rich legacy of Liele along with the other Yamacraw converts. A few months after his baptism, Bryan began to exhort and evangelize both Blacks and Whites. He preached and held service on the Bryan Brampton plantation near the city of Savannah. Bryan was rapidly becoming an effective preacher and pastor, which attracted the support of Blacks and some Whites. The ground on which Bryan assembled his congregation belonged to Edward Duron, who embraced Bryan's ministry, and he permitted him and his congregation to erect a small building for their services. Most of the Whites of Savannah gave little attention to the activities of Bryan when he was evangelizing as an open-air preacher. But when Bryan and his followers decided to erect a church building, a great deal of jealousy and hatred was aroused among some of the Whites. With strong determination and great faith, Bryan struggled to implement his vision of erecting a church building for his congregation. Bryan befriended a White plantation owner who permitted him to build a small structure on a plot of land. Despite the resistance, Bryan led his followers into their modest church home. In retaliation for Bryan's defiance, he and a number of his followers were beaten in the public square in the heart of the city of Savannah by a mob of Whites. With his clothes saturated with his own blood, Bryan lifted his hand and addressed his persecutors: "If you would stop me from preaching, cut off my head! For I am willing not only to be whipped, but would freely suffer death for the cause of Lord Jesus." Only then was the mob shamed into dispersing.[61] After the public beating, Bryan's adversaries then brought legal charges, accusing him and his supporters of planning a slave revolt. The slaves and their leader were tried in court, found guilty, and put in prison, and their church meeting house was destroyed. Jonathan Bryan, who enslaved Andrew Bryan, then secured the release of prisoners and gave them permission to hold services at the Brampton Rice Barn just outside of Savannah.

On one occasion, while worshipping at the barn, one of the Whites who had beaten Bryan came to eavesdrop on the worship service. The man was shocked however when he heard Bryan praying for his forgiveness and Bryan's prayer became the man's testimony throughout the city of Savannah. Thus history once again repeated itself as "the blood of the martyr [became] the seed of the church;" because of the faith, humility and courage exhibited by Bryan, he won widespread support from the people of Savannah. White sympathizers petitioned Chief Justice Osbourne of the State Court asking that Bryan and his followers receive legal protection. The provisions included that Blacks be free to worship from sunup to sundown on Sundays, but they were prohibited from worshipping during the week because of objections from the slave-owners.

In order to establish Andrew Bryan as the official pastor of the congregation he had built, Jonathan Bryan had his White minister, Abraham Marshall, and Jesse Peter, a charter member of the Silver Bluff Church, conduct the baptism of 45 converts and officially install Andrew Bryan as the pastor of the First African Baptist Church. In the aftermath of the death of Jonathan Bryan, his son William Bryan granted Andrew Bryan permission to purchase his freedom, which he did. Bryan was very enterprising and hardworking in business as well as in the ministry. In addition to his running a church, he operated a profitable hauling business. Also, William Bryan used his influence to convince several of his friends to sell Andrew Bryan's congregation a lot in the heart of the city in order to build a new structure for the First African Baptist Church. Andrew Bryan lived well into his 70s, and he died a well-respected, wealthy, and free man.

While Andrew Bryan was evangelizing, organizing and building a church and a strong religious community in Savannah, Jesse Peter and some of the charter members of the Silver Bluff Church returned home after the Revolutionary War. Unlike David George and George Liele, who joined with the British, Peter and his followers supported the colonists. Jesse Peter had strong ties to the Silver Bluff community. He may have been the biological son of the slave-owner George Galphin. Jesse Peter also used the name Jesse Galphin and was thought to have been the son of one of Galphin's African mistresses. After returning to Silver Bluff, Peter became the resident pastor of the Silver Bluff Church. The Silver Bluff Church was also assisted by Abraham Marshall, the White Baptist pastor from Coker, Georgia. In a letter dated May, 1, 1793, Marshall referred to Peter and his followers: "I am intimately acquainted with Jess Galphin; he lives thirty miles below Augusta. He is a Negro servant of Mr. Galphin, who, to his praise be it spoken, treats him with respect." At the time that this letter was written, which also praised the charity and work of Jesse Peter, the Silver Bluff Church was reported to have 60 members.[62]

For some reason the pastures looked greener across the Savannah River, and Peter moved his congregation to Augusta, Georgia. Jesse Peter brought his talents, energy, and devotion to building a church and viable faith community in Augusta. Peter came to Augusta with recognition and good standing within the fledgling independent Black church movement. He had almost single-handedly planted, nurtured, and developed the first independent Black church in Augusta. He was heralded as "a black preacher of respectable talents, and amiable character." He had long tenure as the successful pastor of the First African Baptist Church of Augusta. The name was later changed to the Springfield Baptist Church.[63]

It was the Springfield Baptist Church that gave birth to Morehouse College in 1867. Also, this historic church gave birth to the now disbanded Georgia Education Association, which fought hostile opposition to build public schools for Black children during the era of Jim Crow.[64] The great legacy of the Silver Bluff Church is that it nurtured the first beginnings of institutionalized religious practices among African Americans that would become the foundation of their communities.

The Silver Bluff Church was the starting point for many great eighteenth century Black preachers. The list of exemplary sons of Silver Bluff would not be complete without Henry Francis. Before moving across the river to Augusta, Jesse Peter converted Henry Francis. Soon after his conversion, he was called to preach while he was still enslaved. Francis had a White mother and Native American father. His freedom was purchased by some of his White friends. Those who purchased his freedom wanted to see him use his talents to lead the local Black community. Francis was deeply committed to his ministry and he advanced very rapidly. He moved to Savannah and became an apprentice under the Reverend Andrew Bryan at the First African Baptist Church. However, when Francis was ordained, his ordination sermon was preached by his first pastor, Jesse Peter, who was his minister at Silver Bluff.

Savannah was becoming a thriving seaport town, and the First African Baptist Church was growing. The church sent out two of its most promising young ministers, Henry Francis and Henry C. Cunningham to plant new congregations. Henry Francis, a son of the Silver Bluff Church, was called to the Ogeeche African Baptist Church in 1803. A year earlier, Henry C. Cunningham had established the Second African Baptist Church in the city of Savannah.[65]

This era of the heroic Black preachers was not confined to the southern United States however. In Philadelphia, Richard Allen would establish the first independent Black denomination. And by the opening of the twentieth century, W. E. B. DuBois would proclaim that the A.M.E. Church was, "the greatest Negro institution in the world." Richard Allen was born into slavery on February 14, 1760, and enslaved by Benjamin Chew, a Philadelphia lawyer. In 1767 there was a decline in Chew's practice, and he sold the Allen family—father, mother and all four children—to a slaver named Stokely Sturgis, who owned a plantation near Dover, Delaware. Allen was forced to work on that plantation until the age of 20. Allen wrote that Stokely encouraged his slaves to learn to read and write as well as attend church. Allen was exposed to the Methodist circuit riders who frequently preached to Blacks on the plantations. After hearing the revivalist Garrettson, Allen was converted. On one occasion the slave-owner Stokely attended one of Garrettson's crusades, at which the preacher denounced slavery as sinful and incompatible with the Gospel. Stokely was moved by the sermon but not enough to set his captives free. He offered Allen and his brother the opportunity to buy their freedom for $2,000. The prospect of freedom exhilarated Allen and he enthusiastically worked extra jobs as a day laborer and brick maker to make enough money to buy his freedom.[66]

After Allen purchased his freedom, he joined a Methodist society and became more acquainted with the Methodist program. As a free man, Allen worked in a brickyard for 50 cents per month. When he was not working in the brickyard, he was working in the vineyard preaching the gospel.[67]

Richard Allen demonstrated great tenacity and determination to preach the gospel despite many impediments along the way. His ministry was interrupted for a period when he was stricken with pleurisy. During this period he established a close friendship with a White Methodist evangelist named Benjamin Abbot. Allen's enthusiasm and indefatigable efforts as preacher caught the eye of some of the Methodist leaders. When he was not preaching, he was laboring in the brickyard or culling wood in the New Jersey forests. He traveled by foot preaching the gospel from East New Jersey to Pennsylvania, and the excessive walking afflicted Allen's feet with many blisters and sores.[68]

Richard Allen and Harry Hosier were the only African Americans present at the historic organizing of the General Conference of Methodism in America. These two Black preachers were present in the Lovely Lane Church in Baltimore, Maryland, in 1784, when the General Conference welcomed Thomas Coke, Richard Whatcoat, and Thomas Vasey, who had just been sent to America by the founder of Methodism, John Wesley.[69]

Richard Allen was licensed as an itinerant exhorter in the Methodist Church, but he never received any compensation for his work. He took work slaughtering cows and found odd jobs to make a living. The presiding elder in charge of the St. George's Church sent Allen to preach and hold class meetings for the Black members of that church. Some of the White members of the predominantly White church were then incited to jealousy as they witnessed a Black man assuming a leadership role among the 42 Blacks who belonged to the church. Allen proposed the creation of a worship place specifically for the Blacks, but he was rebuffed. The Africans attempted to start their own prayer meeting but the church hierarchy prohibited such gatherings because of the opposition from the White members.[70] The Black members of St. George's Church began to chafe under such mistreatment.

On a Sunday morning in November of 1787, Richard Allen, Absalom Jones, and several other Black members were determined to engage in prayer at the altar of St. George's Church. There was a scuffle, whereupon they were pulled up from their knees by the White trustees of the church. They were told, "You must get up—you must not kneel here." The Reverend Absalom Jones replied, "Wait until prayer is over." One of the trustees responded, "No, you must get up now or I will call for aid and force you away." Upon being forced to stop praying, Richard Allen and Absalom Jones led the walkout of the Black members from the church. Allen later expressed that the White members would "no longer be plagued with us in the church." Thus, concluded this seminal event in the development of the Black independent church movement.[71]

The living conditions for free Blacks in the North were not much better than the conditions of enslaved Blacks in the South. Many Blacks in the North had a semblance of freedom, but as a practical matter, they had few economic opportunities and they were often discriminated against and mistreated. Freedom without adequate housing or food was a precarious existence indeed. While Allen and his cohorts were protesting their mistreatment in the House of the Lord, free Blacks in Philadelphia were galvanizing the community in the City of Brotherly Love as they formed the Free African Society. The Society, which was established without a religious attachment, was organized on April 12, 1787. The Society was started in a private home as a mutual aid and benevolent society and was organized to improve living conditions within the Black community. Although the society did not have a specific religious affiliation, it did embrace Wesleyan methods for organization and discipline. Absalom Jones and Richard Allen took on the role of patriarchs, and Sarah Allen, the wife of Richard Allen, became the matriarch of the society. Other than independent Black churches, the Free African Society provided some of the first evidence of independent, organized, economic and social coopera-tion among Blacks in the United States.[72]

The Free African Society served to bring Blacks together in their com-mon interests and provided a training ground for the early Black Methodist leaders. Allen was supportive of the Society, but it did not fulfill his passion for preaching the gospel. His ultimate goal and ambition was to organize a church. Some of Allen's followers who joined his exodus from St. George's Church were inclined to join the Episcopal Church, which did seem more welcoming.[73] However, Allen was adamantly against the idea, because he believed that Methodism was more compatible to the needs of the people. He stated emphatically:

> I informed them that I would not be anything but a Methodist. I was
> born and awakened under them. The Methodists were the first people to
> bring glad tidings to the colored people. I feel thankful that I have ever
> heard a Methodist preacher. All the other denominations preached so
> high flown that we were not able to comprehend their doctrine. I am of
> the opinion that reading sermons will never prove as beneficial to colored
> people as spiritual or extempore preaching.[74]

Yet Allen was presented with a predicament. On the one hand he wanted to continue preaching and evangelizing using the Methodist doctrine, but he and other Blacks were clearly not respected or viewed as fully-fledged members of the White Methodist church. He resolved this predicament by summoning the faith and courage to initiate an independent Methodist denomination. The majority of the members of the Free African Society were reluctant to join Allen in the uncharted waters of a new independent Black-led church, and they remained with the White-dominated Episcopal churches. Richard Allen was offered the opportunity to become the first Black Episcopal pastor in America. He refused the offer and the denomination chose Allen's cohort, Absalom Jones, instead to become the pastor of the St. Thomas Episcopal Church. The Free African Society had provided Allen and Jones with the opportunity to develop leadership skills and to become successful organizers and pastors.[75]

Richard Allen took on the awesome challenge of organizing an independent church for Black people at a time when most of them were in chattel slavery and the degrading treatment of Blacks was a social norm in America. The unpretentious beginning of the African Methodist Episcopal (A.M.E.) Church took place in a rented storefront in Philadelphia. Allen found the support of sympathetic Whites in his efforts and befriended Robert Ralston, who helped him solicit money in order to build a church. Yet, the idea of building a Black independent Methodist church was vehemently opposed by the parent body of Methodism. The presiding elder of the Philadelphia district, John McClaskey, threatened to expel Allen from the Methodist denomination if he did not refrain from using the Methodist name in his solicitation of money. Allen did not allow those threats to deter his efforts. In 1793, he bought an old frame building that had been a blacksmith shop and he had it hauled to Sixth and Lombard Streets, a plot of land Allen had purchased with his own money.[76]

On July 29, 1794, Bishop Francis Asbury, the first American Methodist Bishop, preached the dedication sermon at the historic Mother Bethel A.M.E. Church. Allen's struggle for independence and complete freedom did not come easy. When Blacks were members of White-controlled churches, they were marginalized, and yet Whites were reluctant to give them the freedom to organize their own independent churches. While Allen had organized and built Mother Bethel, the parent body of the Methodist Church attempted to place onerous restrictions on the newly independent Black church by issuing the following edicts: (1) The Mother Bethel Church must continue in union with the Methodist Episcopal Church and under the supervision and authority of the White bishop in all church affairs except in the right to church property. (2) No one was to be admitted into the classes or as members except "descendants of the African race in order that they would be the only ones eligible to vote." The early stages of independence for Mother Bethel were more in theory than in practice because the pastor was still appointed by the White Methodists and the property was held by the trustees of the St. George's Church.[77]

The restrictions placed on the Black Methodists were obviously meant to perpetuate White domination, and this was bound to conflict with the aspirations of the Blacks over the long term. Allen struggled with the idea of making a clean break from the White Methodists for more than a decade. To control the property and the activities that went on in the church, the Presiding Elder demanded the keys to the church as well as the financial records. Also, the Black church members were prohibited from holding meetings in their own church. They were further required to pay an annual assessment of $600, which entitled them to the privilege of receiving a White supply pastor who would preach a grand total of five times per year.[78]

The determination of the Methodists to impede the progress of the Black church was only equaled by Allen's determination to successfully develop an independent Black church. The White Presiding Elder John Emory circulated a letter stating that the Black church members who followed Allen had been expelled from the Methodist connection and were no longer recognized as members. To counter any further growth of the movement led by Allen, the White Methodists organized a Black congregation near Allen's Mother Bethel Church, called Zoar Methodist Episcopal Church, which today is regarded as the oldest predominantly Black United Methodist congregation. The White Methodists even went as far as to encourage Mother Bethel's members to join the nearby Zoar Church in an effort to ruin Allen. The Presiding Elder insisted on going to Mother Bethel one Sunday with the intention of directing the congregants to transfer their memberships to Zoar. However, as the Presiding Elder approached the pulpit, he was told that he was not welcome. And when he attempted to mount the pulpit anyway his path was physically blocked by the Black preachers under Allen's leadership who were already there.[79]

Allen's resolve eventually led some members of the White churches to relent. The Presiding Elder Robert Birch applied to the Supreme Court for a writ of mandamus and the court ruled in Allen's favor to use the Methodist name for an independent Black church. Richard Allen responded with great relief, saying, "By the providence of God we were delivered." Despite the mistreatment he and his compatriots suffered, Richard Allen maintained friendship with some of the White Methodists. On June 11, 1799, Allen was ordained by Bishop Francis Asbury as the first African-American minister in the Methodist Episcopal Church.[80]

One of the great misconceptions of American history is that racial segregation originated in the South. Quite to the contrary, it was in the North where Whites first developed an elaborate system of regulations for the control of "free" Blacks and for the strict social separation of the races. This was because of the presence of so many free Blacks in the North, whereas in the South until the end of the Civil War, Southerners had no need to concern themselves too much with such social regulations, as their total subjugation of Blacks in slavery and otherwise was clear. In particular, White churches led the way in protecting White social domination over Blacks as the experience of Allen and his compatriots attests. Blacks in other cities throughout the North were also experiencing discrimination and mistreatment. But the success of Allen and his compatriots would serve as an example for other Blacks.

Eventually, Allen realized that the dignity and self-respect of his church, his people, and himself required complete independence from the White church. Allen seized the day and called an organizing conference of the A. M. E. denomination on April 9, 1816. Delegates came to the historic conference from Baltimore, Philadelphia, and Delaware to establish the first independent Black denomination in America.

The chairperson of the General Conference was Daniel Coker of Baltimore. Richard Allen, Jr., son of Richard Allen, Sr., who was only 14 at the time, was elected secretary, as he was one of the few there who was able to read and write. Stephen Hall, a delegate from Baltimore and the only attorney at the conference, presented the following resolution for the formation of the A.M.E. denomination:

Bishop Richard Allen (1760–1831)

That the people of Philadelphia, Baltimore and all other places, who should unite with them, shall become one body under the name and style African Methodist Episcopal Church of the United States and the book of Discipline of the Methodist Episcopal Church be adopted except that portion related to the presiding elder.[81]

On April 9, the organizing General Conference elected Richard Allen and Daniel Coker as the first bishops. Perhaps for politically strategic reasons, Allen was absent from the conference when he was elected. Upon his return he thanked the delegates for their trust in him, but he then dramatically offered his resignation stating that he did not feel that the denomination had the resources to support two bishops. He then called upon the delegates to decide who the one bishop should be. On April 11, 1816, Allen was consecrated as bishop by Absalom Jones, the Reverend Bishop White of Pennsylvania and several others. Richard Allen became a towering figure in the church and society. The A.M.E. Church in the nineteenth century experienced phenomenal growth and expansion. Sarah Allen joined her husband in nurturing the church and spurring its development into a prominent religious body.

Harry Hosier was a contemporary of Richard Allen and both had the distinction of being the only two African Americans present at the organizing General Conference of the Methodist Episcopal Church of America. Hosier was a pioneering Black Methodist preacher whose rhetorical skills are legendary. He is considered by some to be the first African American to achieve celebrity status. The Negro History Bulletin noted "Black Harry as a national figure and a companion of Bishop Francis Asbury who took care of the Bishop's horses and took turns in the pulpit." He was designated as "Black Harry" because it was indicative of his persona, which was described as being "very black with keen eyes and possessing great vocabulary in his voice." His strong voice was complemented by a quick mind, a photographic memory, and an eloquent flow of oratory. "Black Harry" never learned to read or write, but with his phenomenal memory he was able to quote word for word long passages of scripture that he heard others recite.[82] His innate ability surpassed that of most of his counterparts, Black or White. Hosier rose to prominence based on his talent and ability as opposed to family connections or privileged social status. On one occasion in Wilmington, Delaware, an overflowing crowd gathered to hear Bishop Asbury, and those who could not get into the church stood on the outside to listen to Hosier's sermon. One of the crowd on the outside thought that it was Bishop Asbury preaching as he remarked: "If all Methodist preachers can preach like the Bishop, we should like to be a constant hearer." Someone replied, "That was not the bishop but the bishop's servant that you heard." And the man in the crowd exclaimed, "If such be the servant, what must the master be like." Many prominent people sang the praises of Hosier. Dr. Benjamin Rush, a member of the Continental Congress and one of the signers of the Declaration of Independence called Hosier "the greatest orator in America." Rush echoed the sentiment of Dr. Sargent, who called Hosier the greatest "national orator he ever heard." Thomas Coke, the second bishop elected to the Methodist Episcopal Church of America said simply that Hosier was "the best preacher in the world." Hosier preached at the Adams chapel in Fairfax, Virginia. His sermon was titled "The Barren Fig Tree," and in 1781 it became the first sermon by an African American to be published.[83]

Harry Hosier was born in slavery in Fayetteville, North Carolina, around 1750. As records were irregularly kept about the enslaved, we do not know who his parents were or how he received his name. Although he never attained a level of independent action as a pastor in his own right like Allen, Hosier was still an important figure in the founding and development of American Methodism. Unfortunately, Hosier was also used as part of the Methodist efforts to undermine Allen with the Zoar Methodist Episcopal Church. He was never ordained, but he was the first Black preacher to be licensed in American Methodism. The extraordinarily talented Hosier died on April 30, 1806, and on his tombstone is engraved "Here lies the African Wonder."[84]

THE HISTORICAL ROLE OF WOMEN
IN THE BLACK CHURCH

In traditional African cultures women were not relegated to subordinate roles in society or religion. Indeed, from ancient times, most African culture groups maintained matrilineal systems of determining ancestry; that is, inheritance and family lineage were traced through the female ancestors. This was significant, since it meant that access to wealth and social status was more often dependent on one's mother than on one's father. Therefore, in order to secure social harmony and well-being the men had to learn to cooperate and work together with the women rather than seeking to subdue them. Also, royal lineage was traditionally traced through the female line, and a man could not hope to sit on the throne of an African kingdom unless he was born of the right mother or was able to marry the right woman. And there were even a few African societies that were matriarchal as well as matrilineal, worshipping God the Mother instead of God the Father. Of course these circumstances were greatly altered and in many cases completely changed after the invasions, enslavements, and colonization by Arabs and later by Europeans who came into Africa and imposed their patriarchal social structures.[85]

Enslaved Africans were introduced to sexism among other things when they were brought to the Americas. Unlike immigrants to America, the Africans were forcibly prohibited from maintaining their former cultural practices. They lost almost all of the material signs and symbols of their previous cultural identity, purpose, and calling. European Christianity played a central role in the process of eradicating traditional African religion and culture. Lincoln and Mamiya observed that the White church denominations in America preached and practiced the admonition of the Apostle Paul, which called on "wives to obey their husbands and slaves to obey their masters." The women were to be silent in church. The genesis of the male domination of leadership roles in the Black church took place within the circumstances of a wholesale adoption of European customs by the early church fathers, without sufficient comprehension of the impact of such behaviors on the community, and in the absence of a critical analysis of the values and psychological motivations underlying these customs.

The scholar Cheikh Anta Diop has described how women played a vital role in traditional African societies. They had high profile positions in society as priestesses, queens, and spirit mediums. Women were usually the chief custodians of the magical arts, or witchcraft, and they were often seen to have the capacity to mediate between the spirit realm and the material world. The natural psychic ability of the women was generally considered to be superior to that demonstrated by the men. In African religion and society, female deities were of equal status to male deities in power and esteem. Traditional African societies strongly embraced the mother-right or the organization of social structures based on the sacredness of motherhood as the means by which God sends humans into the world. To not have a child in the ancient world was often considered to be a curse.[86]

The skill and ability of midwives made their work sacred in African societies. These women not only delivered babies but they also accumulated much knowledge about using healing herbs and other therapeutic practices which made them healers and spiritual leaders in the community. African women traditionally were considered to have a special relationship with nature, which sometimes allowed them to regulate the forces of nature. For example, the queen of the Luvedu people of Africa not only served as the political head of state but was also the chief representative of the divine, she was considered to have the power to make rain, and even her changes in mood might induce alterations in the weather. The scholar Geoffrey Parrinder relates that among Africans: "Women may be priestesses and frequently they are as prominent as the men in the conduct of religious affairs. The psychic ability of women has received recognition and scope to a much greater degree in African Religion than they have in Islam or Christianity where women are still barred from the priesthood."[87] The Afro-Caribbean and Afro-Latin religions emerged in the New World in the aftermath of the slave trade. In these religions, the status of women was often considerably higher than in Eurocentric Christianity. Religious traditions like the Vodou of Haiti, the Santeria of Cuba, the Shango of Grenada and Trinidad, the Obeah of Jamaica, and the Candomblé and Umbanda of Brazil, women have played strong leadership roles since the beginning.

It seems that the Africans found it much easier to synthesize their traditional practices with the Roman Catholic religion, which included a host of saints and iconic images, but they had much more difficulty with the Protestant denominations. And this is indicative of the fact that the general format of iconography and symbolic displays used in the Roman Catholic Church is historically much closer to the African roots of Christianity than that of any of the various Protestant denominations. In the United States where Protestant Christianity dominated, the influence of African religious practices survived but in a more subdued and sublimated way. The beads, stones, and spiritual charms in Santeria, Shango, and Candomblé were all compatible with the saints and relics prevalent in Catholicism. For example, it was a relatively simple matter to correlate the worship of a Yoruba Orisha like Yemaya or the Vodoun Loa Erzulie with the veneration of the Virgin Mary. The Roman Catholics embraced the role of Christ, Mary, guardian angels, and patron saints as intercessory agents with God the Father in Heaven. And this cosmological, organizational scheme was similar to the African idea of the High God or the Supreme God, in which there would be human interactions with lesser gods who were involved in the daily affairs of the people while the Supreme God remained benevolent and providential but relatively distant from the affairs of man. In Cuba, Orunmila, the god of divination, is called by the name of the Catholic Saint Francis. There is a divinity in Haitian Vodou, Damballah Wedo, that was symbolized as a serpent, and this was correlated with the serpent of Moses in the Book of Exodus. Such correspondences also made the Catholics less likely than their

Protestant counterparts to press for the complete eradication of African religious practices. In New Orleans, which is heavily influenced by the French Catholic and Haitian traditions, the cult of Marie Laveau stems from a family lineage including the mother and daughter who exerted strong influence over the religious beliefs and practices of both Blacks and Whites. These women continued their African practice of healing by prescribing herbs and roots as medicines, and assisting at childbirths as midwives, and they engaged in fortune-telling via ecstatic trances. There was also an elderly Black woman by the name of Maum Katie, of the Sea Islands, who lived to be over 100 years old. She was considered to be a "spiritual mother" or a prophetess and she exercised a tremendous influence over her many spiritual children.[88]

During the 1970s at the Russell Memorial Christian Methodist Episcopal Church in Durham, North Carolina there was a local female pastor, Mother Essie Faucette, who served the church. Many of the members of the church looked upon her as a healer, spiritual advisor, and prophetess. Mother Faucette, as she was affectionately known, had a pervasive influence in the local community and in the church. Many of the church members would respond positively to any suggestion that she had.

In the African tradition, there was no impediment to women as spiritual leaders or women preachers. American slaveholders considered the women to be primarily sources of free labor and breeders for more free labor; they were property not human beings. Contrary to the traditional African practice of clearly defining and carefully balancing the roles of men and women, the enslaved Africans were desexualized, since in slavery the only distinguishing feature between a male slave and a female slave was the ability to become pregnant. If the female slave was not one of the slaveholder's concubines, then she was expected to work and to produce just as much as the male slaves.

After the African traditional practices were systematically suppressed, slave masters began to impress upon their slaves their Western Christianity, which excluded women from the vocation of the ministry. As the fledgling Black churches and denominations began to lay down their own written documents containing specific doctrines and codes of conduct, they adopted almost verbatim the beliefs, rules, practices, polity, institutional structure, and patriarchal customs of their White counterparts. Thus, the Black Baptist churches copied the White Baptists and the Black Methodist denominations copied the White Methodists. The leaders of the independent Black churches and their congregations were quite determined to have their own churches. They did make some adjustments to the doctrine they had received in order to suit their unique circumstances, and they also modified the style of worship to be more suitable to African sensibilities. But they made no comprehensive critique of the theological and sociological implications of imitating the forms and practices of their oppressors. The early church fathers apparently failed to perceive the inherent contradiction of attempting to make their brand of Christianity basically a replica of Eurocentric Christianity only without the Whites.

The role of women in the Black church has also been complicated by the historical exclusion of Black males from significant roles in American society outside of the churches. The peculiar institution of slavery deranged gender roles for Blacks. Women were put in the position to become more independent socially while the men were often forced into dependency because of prevailing circumstances. Black women often trained their daughters to be independent and their sons to be dependent in order to protect them from the brutality meted out to Black men who attempted to assert their manhood. For centuries, Black men in America have been victims of a system that was designed to suppress and obliterate their sense of confidence, self-reliance, and mature manhood. Until the 1960s it was not unusual for a Black man to be called a boy regardless of his biological age. Thus, preaching became one of the few avenues for social status and recognition for Black men.

The call to preach gave Black men instant visibility, recognition, and status. Preaching gave men a title that set them apart from the general population and provided an often elusive sense of self-worth and self-esteem. Consequently, there was a tendency for Black men to want to reserve the position of church pastor for themselves, not wanting to have to compete with their women for one of the few prestigious positions available to them. Also, there were many women who supported this exclusive role for the men. Some women believed it was important to have at least a few Black men of recognized social status in the community. During the days of segregation and an openly declared White supremacy regime, many Black women thought it was strategically important to help cultivate and encourage Black manhood.

The social dynamics of African-American culture have always had a strong underlying tendency toward the formation of matrifocal social structures. The Black church was no exception to this tendency, although the position of those who brought the Word and served as the titular heads of the churches was reserved for the men. Women often administered church affairs in the background and exerted great influence in organizing and maintaining the activities of the churches through various missionary societies, women's auxiliary boards, and so forth. As women of my mother's generation were apt to say, "It's ok for the men to have the title, as long as we are the ones who really run it." If the call to preach was the only available route for some semblance of identity and status for Black men, the inclusion of women would diminish even this tenuous hold on manhood.

There were women who preached in secret on the plantations, but no Black women prior to the late nineteenth century were ordained as preachers or made church pastors. Women did, however, play roles as exhorters, teachers, evangelists, missionaries, religious writers and influential wives of pastors.

During the spiritual revivals of the Great Awakenings in the eighteenth and nineteenth centuries, when there was an emphasis on personal salvation and experiential religion, women, both Black and White, had more freedom to express themselves and exercise their spiritual gifts. The Second Great Awakening ushered in an era of social reform, abolition, perfectionism, universal salvation, and appeals for a more egalitarian social order.[89] The new pietism enabled women to testify and witness publicly in church about their encounters with the Lord, and they were no longer relegated to a role of being seen but not heard in the church.

In 1889, the Philadelphia Quakers posthumously published the story of a former slave woman from Maryland who was called only Elizabeth in a pamphlet titled, "Elizabeth, A Colored Minister of the Gospel Born in Slavery." Elizabeth began to preach at the age of 30, and she was threatened once with arrest by the officials in the Commonwealth of Virginia for preaching without a license. When asked if she was ordained, Elizabeth answered, "Not by the commission of men's hands; if the Lord has ordained me, I need nothing better." She was released.[90]

The first woman on record to challenge the restrictions against women preachers in a Black denomination was Jarena Lee (1783–1857). She was probably born free in Cape May, New Jersey. Jarena Lee worked as a house servant in homes close to the Pennsylvania border. She had a number of religious experiences including spiritual visions and subsequently she heard the call to preach at the age of 24. In 1809, she approached the pastor of the newly established Bethel African Methodist Episcopal Church in Philadelphia, the Reverend Richard Allen, and sought a license from him to preach. Allen was not opposed to women leading prayer meetings and serving the communion tables as stewardesses but he refused to consider female pastors and would not issue her a license. Nonetheless, Jerena Lee was determined to carry out her calling, and she proceeded to preach anyway without a license. In 1811, she married an A.M.E. minister, the Reverend Joseph Lee, pastor of the society at Snow Hill. A year after the A.M.E. Church was officially established as an independent connectional denomination, Mrs. Lee again sought license to preach the gospel from the newly-elected Bishop Richard Allen. Allen responded by referring to the fact that it was against Methodist Church policy to include female preachers, so he could not therefore ordain her. However, he did approve her to lead prayer meetings and to be an exhorter. Allen recognized her gifts and he invited her to speak before his pastors at connectional meetings. The Reverend Jarena Lee was never officially recognized as a fully-ordained minister by her denomination; nevertheless, she might still be considered "self-ordained," as she described herself, as the first female preacher in the A.M.E. denomination.[91]

Unlike Jarena Lee, other women left behind the stifling impediments to progress in the Black churches and turned to White denominations that were open to women preachers. Rebecca Cox Jackson (1795–1871) experienced a profound spiritual awakening and she was called to preach. Her newfound calling was not supported by her brother, who was a leading minister in the Bethel A.M.E. Church, or by her husband because she would become, "a woman a leading men."[92]

Another important early female preacher was Amanda Berry Smith

(1837–1915). She was a former slave who became a wife, mother, washer-woman, evangelist, and international missionary. She was a strong advo-cate of holiness and she become associated with the Shouting Methodists. Smith was highly talented as both a singer and speaker. She did some missionary work in Africa; unfortunately, however, her view of the customs and religious practices of the indigenous people was primarily shaped by Eurocentric values. Toward the twilight of her career Smith worked with orphans, and she opened the Amanda Smith Industrial Orphan Home for Colored Children in Harvey, Illinois, in 1899. [93]

The African Methodist Episcopal Zion Church became the first Methodist denomination in the United States to ordain women in 1894 at the Second Ecumenical Conference. Bishop James Walker Hood defended the right of women to be elected delegates to the General Conference of the denomination. He said that, "There is one Methodist Episcopal Church that guarantees to women all rights in common with men." On May 20, 1894, Bishop Hood ordained Mrs. Julia A. Forte, who was also a missionary, as a deacon.[94]

Chapter 4 – The Conversion of Enslaved Africans

DISCUSSION & REVIEW QUESTIONS

1. How did the rationale Europeans used for their enslavement of Africans change over time?

2. When did large numbers of African Americans first become interested in Christianity and why?

3. Describe and explain the reasons why women were excluded from becoming church pastors in the early Black churches? Compare and contrast the difference in the role of women in traditional African societies with the role of women in the Black church.

4. What does Lucius H. Holsey's experience indicate about the value that enslaved African Americans placed on literacy?

CHAPTER 5

The Black Church and Black Reconstruction

THE EMERGENCE OF INDEPENDENT BLACK CHURCHES AND PREACHERS

General William Tecumseh Sherman launched a massive Union invasion of the Confederacy early in 1864. In July and August of 1864 he engaged in one of the most noted campaigns in military history through north Georgia's Kennesaw Mountains as his troops crushed the forces of the Confederacy. This campaign was a prelude to his famous march "from Atlanta to the sea." Atlanta was a major supply and distribution center for the Confederacy. It was widely believed by Union generals that the fall of the "gateway of the South" would ensure a victorious outcome for the Civil War. On the eve of Sherman's attack on Atlanta, he telegraphed General Bullock, describing the importance of the Union's campaign against the hub of the South. He relayed that in addition to having a military success, the capture of Atlanta by the Union Army would ensure the reelection of Abraham Lincoln in the November election. Also, although mostly overlooked, Sherman's march to the sea initiated a process in which Black churches would begin to play the role of the central organizing institutions in their respective communities during the Reconstruction period and thereafter. Until that time Black churches in the South were almost all directly under the supervision and control of their White counterparts.[1]

While north of Atlanta, General Sherman captured the town of Marietta, and in the process Zion Baptist Church was freed from the control of that city's First Baptist Church. The relationship between the two churches began when an enslaved woman named Dicey was permitted to join the First Baptist Church in 1836. Other slaves soon followed her lead, including Ephraim Rucker, who aspired to preach and pastor his own people. While the Blacks were members of the White church, Rucker emerged as their spiritual leader. His influence with the Blacks aroused the suspicion of some of the White members. On a number of occasions Rucker was severely whipped for leading slaves in unauthorized prayer meetings. Like many Black men who aspired to preach, Rucker was accused of being a troublemaker.[2]

During the years when the Zion Baptist Church was an appendage to First Baptist Church, the members longed for an independent church and a pastor of their own. Each time the Blacks petitioned for autonomy and independence they were met with strong opposition. After the first two years of the Civil War, most of the able-bodied White men of the First Baptist Church had enlisted in the Confederate Army. With the White membership depleted, the congregants were soon outnumbered by the Black membership. A White woman, who only supported Blacks worshipping from the church balcony, adamantly objected to any notion of religious independence for the slaves because they would be "just getting carried away. Why, you people can't be quiet in church."[3]

The Blacks' quest for a church of their own came to fruition when General Sherman captured Marietta in June of 1864. The general turned First Baptist Church into a hospital to care for his wounded soldiers, effectively releasing Zion Baptist Church from White control. Rucker realized the significance of the moment and began to organize his congregation. The First Baptist Church granted letters of demission to the Blacks, including 66 females and 23 males, so that they could start their own church. The historic Zion Baptist Church was officially organized on April 8, 1866.[4]

In the aftermath of Sherman's devastating destruction of businesses, homes, schools, and churches throughout Atlanta, Black churches emerged as beacons of hope and bases for community organization. During the burning of Atlanta, Sherman intentionally preserved the Big Bethel A.M.E. Church whose members originally started out in the Union Church, Atlanta's first White congregation. Blacks who had been members of the White church became the charter members of Big Bethel. They struggled for their religious freedom and worked ardently to build their own church in downtown Atlanta on Auburn Avenue. Big Bethel went on to become the cultural womb of significant institutions in the Black community of Atlanta. The first African-American public school, the Gate City Colored School was born and housed in Big Bethel. Also, Morris Brown College was conceived and delivered within the hallowed halls of Big Bethel.[5]

Fueled by the decisive defeat of the Confederates in Atlanta, Sherman moved east of the city to Stone Mountain, Georgia. There he liberated the Blacks and their Bethesda Baptist Church from control of the First Baptist Church. The Blacks honored Sherman by naming their neighborhood Shermantown.[6] From Stone Mountain it was on to the handsome hamlet of Covington. Here Sherman continued his campaign of delivering Blacks from the tyranny of slaveholders and their churches from the control of White churches. The Bethlehem Baptist Church (originally known as Bethlehem Baptist) was an appendage of First Baptist Church.[7] The Black membership in the church more often than not exceeded the White membership.[8]

When the White Methodists erected a new church in Stone Mountain, they donated their wooden building to the Blacks of the Bethlehem Baptist Church, and it was moved to the east side of Dried Indian Creek. After the pastorate of the Reverend T. Baker, the Reverend A.D. Williams, the maternal grandfather of Martin Luther King, Jr., became pastor. This began a long and storied legacy of Baptist preachers in the King family. The Bethlehem Church was also served by the Reverend Joel King, the brother of Martin Luther King, Jr.'s father, from 1935 to 1941.[9]

Owing to the large number of Black members, the church held a special Sunday afternoon service for them, conducted by the White minister. The Blacks desired to have their own preachers; they wanted to worship in their own way, and occasionally they found ways of expressing their dissatisfaction with White control of their religious services. For more than thirty years the Black members applied for licenses to preach and to form a church of their own, but the Whites steadfastly refused. During slavery, Whites were often suspicious and even paranoid when it came to the congregation of Blacks outside of their supervision.

The arrival of General Sherman was welcomed by the Blacks, not only because it delivered them from physical bondage but also because it meant their spiritual deliverance as well. After Sherman freed their church, they held their first service in a small house near the central depot, with the Reverend Henry Fresh conducting services. Soon the crowds became so large that a log hut was built where Bethlehem Baptist now stands and it was designated years ago as the "Colored Baptist Church." A formerly enslaved man, Toney Baker, who had been ordained by the White pastor of the First Baptist Church, became the first pastor of the "Colored Baptist Church," where he served for 46 years.[10]

Sherman's encounter with the Black congregations along the way from the north Georgia mountains to the port city of Savannah left him with a favorable impression of the Blacks. Also, he was impressed with the formerly enslaved people's insatiable desire for freedom as they abandoned plantations in large numbers following the march of the Union Army. While in Covington, Georgia, Sherman greeted an elderly gray-bearded Black man and asked him if he understood the progress of the war. The elderly gentleman replied that he had been looking for an angel of the Lord ever since he was knee high. He told the general that slavery was the cause of the war and that the Union's success would free the slaves. The freedmen were eager to abandon the plantations and follow Sherman and the Union Army. Follow to what they knew not, but they saw the defeat of their former slave masters and they were ready to become a part of this new reality which would surely be more positive than the old one. Sherman discouraged the former slaves from following. His army survived by foraging off of the land, taking food and supplies wherever they could be found. He did not want to be responsible for the care of thousands of ex-slaves, as they would eat food and consume supplies needed by his men.[11]

By the time the Union troops reached the outskirts of Savannah, the news of Sherman's torching of Atlanta had already reached the city. The business and civic leaders of Savannah came together in hopes of saving their city. The city leaders greeted Sherman just outside of Savannah to offer their surrender in hopes of averting the fate that befell Atlanta. Without firing a shot the Union gained control of Savannah on December 21, 1864. A wealthy merchant, Charles Green, offered Sherman the use of his mansion.[12]

It appears to be both providential and poetic that Savannah was the place to formally initiate the emancipation of the enslaved. Savannah was on the Atlantic Ocean, and it was one of the ports at which enslaved Africans were first brought into America. Also, the Savannah area was the region of the birthplace of the independent Black church movement and the institutional life of the Black community. The people of that region had benefited from the pioneering influences of George Liele, Andrew Bryan, and Andrew Marshall, whose sacrifices laid the foundations for Black religious institutions. Immediately after Sherman's arrival in Savannah, William Campbell, pastor of the First African Baptist Church, organized a small cadre of religious leaders and requested an appointment to meet with General Sherman in order to discuss the implementation of the Emancipation. General Sherman and Edwin Stanton, the Secretary of War, arranged to meet with 20 Black ministers and religious leaders at Sherman's mansion headquarters on January 12, 1865. Less than a week out of slavery, these twenty religious leaders provided a notable road map for the development of African-American communities going forward.[13]

Secretary of War, Stanton was sent to Savannah by Abraham Lincoln to find out from the former slaves how best to proceed. The meeting would allow Stanton to gain some insight into the caliber of character and temperament of these people who figured prominently in the postwar plans. Although all the 20 leaders had been enslaved, they were by no means ill-prepared for the opportunity that history had provided. They were all literate and they had all played leadership roles in the Black churches. On average they could boast of more than 14 years experience in ministry, and four of them had ministered for 20 or more years. This was indeed a remarkable profile of leadership experience for a group of people who were generally denied access to education and who had been unable to openly develop the cultural practices of their African ancestors which were subject to systematic suppression. Their drive, determination, creativity, and innate ability compensated for their lack of formal education. The majority of this cadre of Black leaders received training and leadership experience from the First, Second, and Third African Baptist Churches.[14]

Among the Black religious leaders was William Bentley who was the senior pastor of Andrew's Chapel, which had a congregation of 360 members and church property worth about $20,000. He had 20 years' experience in ministry and was widely respected in the community. Also, there was James Lynch who had been born in Baltimore, Maryland; he represented the A.M.E. Church and was assigned to evangelize the South. Before the leaders arrived at Sherman's headquarters, they had met and organized themselves in order to maximize the chances for a positive outcome. They designated the 67-year-old Reverend Garrison Frazier, a minister of 35 years, as their spokesperson. He was a native of North Carolina, where he worked until he saved enough money to purchase the freedom of his wife and himself. As free persons, he and his wife moved to Georgia where he was ordained to preach, but his poor health prevented him from pastoring a congregation.

After the twenty leaders had assembled, Stanton proceeded with a question-and-answer session. The Secretary of War asked them to state their understanding in regard to acts of Congress and President Lincoln's Emancipation Proclamation concerning the condition of colored people in the rebel states. Reverend Frazier responded thusly:

> So far as I understand President Lincoln's proclamation to the Rebellious States, it is, that if they would lay down their arms and submit to the laws of the United States before the first of January, 1863, all should be well; but if they did not, then all the slaves in the Rebel States should be free henceforth and forever. That is what I understand.[15]

When Stanton asked the group of Black religious leaders how they thought their people could best take care of themselves and how the government could assist in maintaining their freedom, the spokesperson gave the following answer:

> The way we can best take care of ourselves is to have land, and turn it and till it by our own labor that is, by the labor of the women and children and old men; and we can maintain ourselves and have something to spare. And to assist the government, the young men should enlist in the service of the Government, and serve in such manner as they may be wanted. The Rebels told us that they piled them up and made batteries of them and sold them to Cuba; but we don't believe that.[16]

After Pharaoh's Emancipation of the Hebrews, those former slaves immediately separated themselves from their former slave masters and oppressors. However, unlike the Hebrews in Exodus, the emancipated African Americans would remain bound to the same land and in the presence of their agitated former slave masters. The Secretary of War addressed this issue by asking the group whether they would rather live scattered [integrated] among Whites or in colonies by themselves. Reverend Frazier replied:

> I would prefer to live by ourselves, for there is a prejudice against us in the South that will take years to get over; but I do not know that I can answer for my brethren. [Mr. Lynch was the only dissenter from Frazier's proposal. All of the other Black religious leaders present, being questioned one by one answered that they agreed with Brother Frazier. The divergent view of Lynch likely reflects his roots in Baltimore on the Mason-Dixon Line while all of the others were native to the Deep South.][17]

The charge of the inherent inferiority of the Negro was the most potent accusation leveled by those who opposed the emancipation of the slaves. Also, the pro-slavery argument questioned whether or not the Blacks had the intelligence or the character needed for full citizenship in America. In response to these rationales, Secretary Stanton wanted to know whether the Blacks had the cognitive ability to understand the cause of the Civil War and its outcome and their new responsibilities as citizens. He asked whether Blacks had sufficient intelligence and feelings of loyalty to the United States and the ability to understand their responsibility to support and respect the side of the federal government. Reverend Frazier gave a terse affirmation to the intellectual capacity of Blacks. He then gave an insightful response that both demonstrated that capacity and further revealed that the Blacks had a keen awareness of their conditions and those forces operating for and against their interests:

> I think you will find there are thousands that are willing to make any sacrifice to assist the Government of the United States while there are also many that are willing to take up arms. I do not suppose there are a

dozen men that are opposed to the Government. I understand as the war, that the South is the aggressor. President Lincoln was elected President by a majority of the United States, which guaranteed him the right of holding the office and exercising that right over the whole United States. The South without knowing what he would do rebelled. The war was commenced by the Rebels before he came into office. The object of the war was not at first to give the slaves their freedom, but the sole object of the war was first to bring the rebellious states back into the Union and their loyalty to the laws of the United States. Afterward, knowing the value set on the slaves by the Rebels, the President thought that his proclamation would stimulate them to lay down their arms, reduce them to obedience and help to bring back the Rebel States; and their not doing so has now made the freedom of the slaves a part of the war. It is my opinion that there is not a man in the city that could be started to help the Rebels one inch for that would be suicide. There were two Black men who left with the Rebels because they had taken an active part for the Rebels, and thought something might befall them if they stayed behind; but there is not another man. If the prayers that have gone up for the Union Army could be read out, you would not get through them for two weeks.[18]

The Secretary asked the Black leaders a battery of other questions focusing on the sentiment and feeling of Blacks in general about the Union, the willingness of young Black men to enlist in the Union Army, and the most effective way for them to recruit Black soldiers. These religious leaders responded to Stanton's questions in such a way as to unequivocally assure the Secretary that the Blacks were prepared to move forward. The leaders further assured Stanton that the nature of their ministries in serving the people put them in position of knowing the pulse of the community. The leaders reminded Stanton and Sherman of the thousands of slaves who abandoned the plantations to follow the Union Army as indicative of their understanding of the war and its consequences. The Black religious leaders offered to take the initiative in recruiting young Black men for the Union Army. Reverend Frazier recommended that the U.S. Congress suspend compulsory recruitment of Black soldiers and empower the Black religious leaders with the responsibility of enlisting young Black men.

This meeting was historic for a number of reasons, the most important of which is that it represented the egression of leadership of the Black church and Black preachers. Such leadership had already begun to emerge, as it was Black churches and Black preachers who first organized and stood up for the interests of African Americans. Four days after the historic meeting, General Sherman issued Special Field Orders, No. 15, which set aside a large region of coastal land, stretching from Charleston, S.C., to northern Florida, "for the settlement of Negroes now made free by the acts of war and the proclamation of the President of the United States." Each family would be allotted "forty acres of tillable ground … in the possession of which land the military authorities will afford them protection, until such time as they can protect themselves, or until the Congress shall regulate their title."[19]

Thus, the Black church and the Black preachers began a long and historic legacy of working with government officials and sometimes against them on behalf of the Black community. Long before Black politicians, political scientists, and pundits, Black preachers were policy makers, organizers and advisors. Sherman and Stanton were surprised at the sophistication and intelligence exhibited by these religious leaders, who were only a few days removed from slavery. Certainly, their presentation disabused Sherman and Stanton of any notions that Blacks were inherently inferior or incapable of citizenship. In Stanton's evaluation of the meeting, he reported that the response was so profound that he could not have received a better response if he had been speaking with the President's cabinet.

These Black religious leaders vindicated the character and intelligence of the freedmen. Their responses to Stanton's questions were proof enough that African Americans had the capacity, if given the chance, to become productive and responsible citizens. The leaders also encouraged Sherman to provide the Black community with some reassurance and a clear explanation of the emancipation by addressing the Black community on the steps of the Second African Baptist Church.

Special Field Order 15 set aside the cities of Beaufort, Hilton Head, Savannah, Fernandina, St. Augustine, and Jacksonville, along with surrounding areas, as land that was to be exclusively for the settlement of Blacks. The order provided for each Black family to be allotted land and protection. The importance of this event, although mostly overlooked by current historians, cannot be overstated. The Black leaders and the White governmental officials of that time clearly intended for Blacks to develop themselves economically and socially, and they further understood that material resources were required for such an undertaking.[20]

General Rufus Saxton was in charge of supervising the resettlement of Negroes on the land and by the end of June 1865 more than 40,000 freedmen had moved onto their new farms. There was great enthusiasm among the Blacks as they looked forward to freedom and an improved quality of life. But, this movement toward independence and social uplift for Blacks would be aborted before it could be firmly established. Abraham Lincoln was assassinated and his successor, Andrew Johnson, in August of 1865 issued orders of pardon and restoration for the slaveholders and property owners of those lands. Thus, the freedmen were turned off of the land, some at the point of a bayonet. Although Congress passed legislation granting the evicted Blacks an option to purchase other government-owned land in the South, most of these recently freed slaves were instead compelled by pressing economic circumstances to go back to work for their former slave masters. The Reconstruction period would come to a tragic conclusion after beginning with great hopes for real democracy in America.[21] The failure of the government to fully implement Special Field Orders, No. 15 and to provide Black people with the means to develop their own communities left the United States with a legacy of racial injustice that it has yet to fully resolve. Returning the ex-slaves to conditions near what they had experienced in servitude and under the oppressive regime of the very same people who had just been defeated in war was yet another monstrous injustice done to Black people. The reversal of Special Field Orders, No. 15 was the first in a long string of broken promises made to Blacks. The Emancipation Proclamation freed the slaves but ignored the Blacks.

The period following emancipation from 1865 to 1877 is called Reconstruction. Reconstruction originally referred to a political process by which the defeated southern states, which had rebelled and seceded from the Union would be reinstated as part of the United States of America. But, beyond the political process, there were important social and religious implications to the Reconstruction period. The Southerners had been thoroughly routed, and any hopes for a Confederacy were completely smashed. Yet the racist attitudes and prejudice of most White Southerners were unabated. They continued to treat Blacks with wanton disrespect as they viewed them as subordinate, regardless of age or educational status, and they considered Blacks in general as resources available for exploitation.

THE SOUTH AS A FIELD OF MISSION

During Reconstruction, various political, commercial, and religious institutions sought to influence, manipulate, and exploit the conditions in the South. Politically, at least on paper, Black men in the South had acquired the right to vote. But such rights would later be curtailed with poll taxes, literacy tests, and intimidation. Thus, White men were able to perpetuate their control and domination of the political process and economic resources in the South. Some Whites pretended to befriend Blacks in hopes of garnering their votes and manipulating the political process. These people became known as scalawags. As Blacks learned of the treachery and duplicity of the scalawags, they turned to White northerners. Some of these White northerners had descended upon the South in order to take advantage of the disorder in the aftermath of the Civil War for economic gain, and they were known as carpetbaggers. The Blacks also gained the attention of White churches based both in the North and the South as the churches competed for Black converts.[22]

All the mainline denominations in the United States divided over the contentious issue of slavery in the years prior to the Civil War. After the schisms over slavery, the religious conversion and training of slaves was left to the southern branch of the various denominations, as northern missionaries and abolitionists were generally not welcome in the South. But during the Reconstruction era, northerners interpreted the outcome of the Civil War as a divine dispensation opening the gates of the South to northern evangelists, preachers, and teachers in order to educate, convert, and save the downtrodden former slaves.

The southern Methodists, Baptists, and Presbyterians were the most committed and most successful in evangelizing among the slaves. Prior to the war, the denomination with the largest slave membership was the

Methodist Episcopal Church, South, which had separated from the northern Methodists over the issue of slavery in 1844. After the Civil War and the defeat of the South, the northern Methodists sent missionaries to the South to convert and reclaim both Whites and Blacks. All the Methodists, including the Methodist Episcopal Church, the African Methodist Episcopal Church, and the African Methodist Episcopal Zion Church viewed the South as a mission field where they had an opportunity to add to their existing membership roles.[24]

Blacks took full advantage of the occasion of freedom as they sought to build and maintain their own religious and educational institutions. After the Civil War, there was a massive withdrawal from White churches and White denominations. Throughout the South, during Reconstruction, Blacks pooled their resources to purchase land and to erect churches. The mass defection of Blacks from White churches redrew the religious map. On the eve of the Civil War, 42,000 Blacks worshipped in South Carolina's White Methodist churches. By 1870, only 600 remained. In Cleveland County, North Carolina, there were 200 Blacks reported as members of White churches in 1860, but only 10 in 1867 and not a single one five years later. Overall, two-thirds of the Black members of the Methodist churches in the South exercised their newfound freedom by leaving the White denomination. The mass defections did not cease until the Black members of Methodist Episcopal Church, South, were assured of the transfer of property to an independent Colored Methodist Episcopal (C.M.E.) Church.[25]

Both northern White and Black missionaries from the various denominations made efforts to convert the freedmen. However, in some ways they proved no more successful than the White Southerners in making converts. Social, cultural, and regional differences proved to be a barrier for many of the northerners. There was also a general condescension toward the unlettered southern Blacks. Many northern missionaries denounced the tradition of slave preaching and worship, which emphasized shouting, dancing and demonstrative expression. They advocated a religion of the head rather than the heart, and they intended to suppress religious dancing, shouting, foot stomping and hand clapping. Most northerners came with cultural biases, and only a few listened long enough to appreciate the grammatically imprecise yet profound words of wisdom from southern Blacks and the remarkable effectiveness of the story-telling sermonizing of Black preachers.[26]

The Black denomination that wielded the most influence both before and after the war was the A.M.E. Church. The size of the overall membership in the A.M.E. Church was less than that of the Baptists, but the episcopal structure of the A.M.E. denomination facilitated better organization, more effective use of resources, and the capacity to speak with a unified voice on various issues. The A.M.E. Church helped to initiate the independent Black church movement, and it grew rapidly over the years. During the final days of the Civil War, the Reverend James Lynch "crossed the Rubicon" as he referred to the Potomac River in 1861, and followed Black troops and civilians preaching everywhere he went. The day after Sherman took Savannah, Lynch converted the Andrews Methodist Chapel over to the African Methodist Episcopal Church as the White minister had fled the city. This began the competition for converts that would continue throughout the Reconstruction period.[27]

Southern Blacks overwhelmingly preferred to worship among other Blacks and under the ministerial leadership supplied by those of their own race. The African Methodist Episcopal Church and the Black Baptist churches gained the advantage over the White denominations in winning Black converts. The A.M.E. Church had originated in the North more than 50 years prior to Reconstruction. The A.M.E.s were also better organized and more successful than the A.M.E. Zion Church. About a third of Black Methodists retained a relationship with the White Methodists until they organized their own independent denomination. It was originally known as the Colored Methodist Episcopal Church and became the Christian Methodist Episcopal Church in 1954.[28]

Besides gaining control of their churches and establishing historically Black colleges and universities, Blacks were often able to reconstitute their families. They established the tradition of family reunions as they literally reunified their families by seeking out and finding those family members who had been sold off into slavery. Also, it was during this time that Black state legislators in North Carolina established the first free and open-to-all public schools.[29]

BLACK PREACHERS AS POLITICAL LEADERS
DURING RECONSTRUCTION

The Black church was the first social institution owned and administered by African Americans. In many ways the Black church has been the cultural womb of the Black community, giving birth to schools, hospitals, and banks and providing a forum for social and political issues. The churches also served as ecclesiastical courthouses adjudicating family disputes, promoting moral values, and monitoring the community for illicit behavior.[30]

Given the central role of the Black church in Black communities, it was inevitable that Black preachers would play a prominent role in the political arena during Reconstruction. Charles H. Pearce, who was an office holder during Reconstruction in Florida as well as an A.M.E. minister, commented that it was "impossible" to separate religion from politics. Black ministers quickly grasped that the interests of the ministry and politics coincided when it came to the well-being of their communities. The Black ministers were often the best-prepared and most-respected members of their communities, and they often played the roles of mayor, state representative, senator, and even governor during the "mystic years" of the Reconstruction period. In all, more than one hundred Black preachers served as elected officials during Reconstruction.[31]

Henry McNeal Turner was born in South Carolina on May 1, 1834. He went on to become one of the most influential ministers of the period and one of the most courageous to embrace political involvement. Unlike most of the Black ministers of his generation in the South, he was never a slave. His mother was an African princess, and according to custom, the British refrained from enslaving African royalty. The British policy of not enslaving African royalty was not so much due to respect for the Africans. It was yet another scheme to corrupt and disarm the leaders by giving them a false sense of entitlement and privilege, making them less likely to oppose the wholesale exploitation of the masses of people they were supposed to be leading. Nevertheless, while growing up in Abbeville, South Carolina, Turner worked in a cotton field. After his father's death, to help support his family, he became an apprentice to a blacksmith. He was also employed for a time as an errand boy for a lawyer. While employed by the lawyer, Turner learned to read and write. He was licensed to preach in the Methodist Episcopal Church, South, in 1853 in Georgia. One of his most notable converts was Lucius H. Holsey, an early bishop of the C.M.E. Church and one of the founders of Paine College. In 1858 Turner joined the A.M.E. Church. He was appointed to the Baltimore-Washington area, and outside of the restrictive environs of the Deep South, he seized the opportunity to study Latin, Greek, and Hebrew at Trinity College in Baltimore. In 1862 at the height of the Civil War, he was assigned to the Israel A.M.E. Church in Washington, D.C. He immediately involved himself in the politics of the war. He publicly called for President Lincoln to free the slaves, and he predicted that the Union would lose the war without Black soldiers. As a consequence of his outspoken stance, his church was threatened with being burned to the ground. Nevertheless, he remained steadfast in his position and his determination and tenacity soon bore fruit. The war indeed turned badly for the North, and Lincoln and his advisors soon realized that the inclusion of Black troops would give a much needed boost to their war effort. Turner organized a regiment of Black soldiers and Lincoln commissioned him to be their chaplain with a rank of major. After the Civil War, President Andrew Johnson renewed Turner's appointment in the Regular Army, and he assigned the nation's first African-American chaplain to work with the Freedmen's Bureau in Macon, Georgia.[32]

Georgia was familiar ground for Turner and he got off to a quick start in his new assignment. Turner preached a message of liberation and resistance to oppressed Blacks, and this greatly disturbed many Whites. He was threatened and driven out of Macon in 1865, but he returned in 1866 with the same zeal and passion for freedom and the uplift of his people. He chided the freedmen for their attachment to a subservient status as he promoted racial pride and unity. He even called on Blacks to worship God in their own image, as to do otherwise, he relayed, would be unworthy of real men:

> We have as much right biblically and otherwise to believe that God is a Negro, as you buckra or white people have to believe that God is a fine looking, symmetrical and ornamented white man. For the bulk of you and

all the fool Negroes of the country believe that God is a white-skinned, blue-eyed, straight-haired projected nose, compressed lipped, finely robed white gentleman sitting upon a throne some where in heaven. Every race of people since time began who have attempted to describe their God by words or by painting or carving or by any form or figure have conveyed the idea that the God who made them and shaped their destinies was symbolized in themselves, and why should not the Negro believe that he resembles God as much as other people? This is one of the reasons we favor African emigration, or Negro naturalization, wherever we can find a domain, for, as long as we remain among the whites the Negro will believe that the devil is Black and that he (the Negro) favors the devil, and that God is white and that he (the Negro) bears no resemblance to him, and the effect of such sentiment is contemptuous and degrading and one half of the Negro will be trying to get white and the other half will spend their days in trying to be white men's scullions in order to please the whites.[33]

Turner was an outspoken cultural critic who admonished both Blacks and Whites to improve their social conditions. Once while speaking to an integrated audience in Greensboro, Georgia, he urged Black men to keep their women away from White men. Some of the White men in the audience drew their guns, but because the Black men were also armed, the Whites backed down without a fight. Turner did not believe that Blacks should remain defenseless in the face of brutal oppression. After he became a bishop in the A.M.E. Church, he continued his staunch advocacy of community development and self-defense for Blacks. At one church meeting he laid two revolvers atop his Bible and declared, "My life depends on the word of God and these guns."[34]

Turner was one of the most prominent African Americans of his era. His keen intellect and incisive oratory helped to inspire the Black community during a period of great transition and upheaval. He was also the consummate preacher/politician. He was elected to the Georgia Constitutional Convention, which convened in 1867 and 1868. The Black representatives were major contributors to writing the new state constitution, and it was Black votes that enacted it, as 80 percent of Blacks voted for the new constitution but only 12 percent of the Whites did so. He was then elected to the Georgia House of Representatives, where he introduced bills to establish eight-hour work days and prohibiting Jim Crow seating on public carriers. Also, he supported universal public education. Surprisingly, while in the legislature he pushed for the pardon of Jefferson Davis, the former President of the Confederacy. The Black legislators did much to strike political compromises with their White counterparts, but their hopes for an era of racial reconciliation would not be realized. Before long, the White legislators turned on the Blacks and had them expelled from the Georgia House of Representatives. This incensed Turner and his views turned to more radical approaches to resolving racial conflicts for Blacks.

In the 1870s, many White and Black churches were swept up by a zeal and enthusiasm to send missionaries to Africa. John Wesley Gilbert (1865–1923) was an African-American missionary who graduated from Paine College and later from Brown University as a classical scholar. He pioneered in archeological work in Greece, and he became Paine College's first Black faculty member. In 1911, Gilbert traveled as a C.M.E. missionary to the Belgian Congo (now the Democratic Republic of the Congo) in Central Africa. Also, Henry McNeal Turner embraced missionary efforts to Africa and even supported efforts toward the resettlement of Blacks to Africa. William H. Heard, an A.M.E. minister born in Elbert County in 1850, raised funds for the back-to-Africa initiative before he was elected bishop.[35]

Richard Harvey Cain (1825–1887) continued the precedent set by the 20 religious leaders in 1865 as he engaged in Reconstruction politics. Cain was a native of Ohio, and he was nurtured in the Methodist Episcopal Church. He became disenchanted with that church and later joined the A. M. E. Church, attending its denominational school at Wilberforce University. In 1862, he was transferred to the New York Conference, where he was ordained deacon by Bishop Daniel Payne. Cain was sent by his denomination to South Carolina at the close of the Civil War to seek new converts among the freedmen. He was appointed to "revivalize" and reorganize Emmanuel Church, which had been closed by Whites since 1822, after the Denmark Vesey slave revolt. At the time it was closed, the church had 3,000 members, but their pastor, Morris Brown, was run out of town by a White mob that accused him of being an accomplice to Vesey.[36]

In keeping with expectations of Black ministers during Reconstruction, Cain was drawn into the vortex of politics. In June of 1865, Blacks from South Carolina were represented at the National Union convention in Baltimore. After this convention refused to address issues of importance to the Black community, the Blacks met at the Zion Church in Charleston and denounced the mistreatment they received at the National Union Convention. The church gave Cain immediate visibility, and he was chosen to give an important speech at the Colored People's Convention held at the Zion Church. Cain's brilliant presentation at the convention earned him leadership recognition beyond the walls of the church. In 1866, he was elected as the editor of the *South Carolina Leader*, the first Black newspaper in that state. He served in a similar capacity for the *Missionary Recorder*.[37]

Similar to many Black ministers across the South, Cain's connection with the church provided a political base for launching a career in politics. In 1868, Cain was the leading delegate to the Constitutional Convention for the State of South Carolina, at which he initiated a drive to institute universal male suffrage for the first time in that state. Also, recognizing that freedom without land and resources was a delusion, he championed the campaign to obtain land for the freed men. He reminded the convention of the popular slogan "forty acres and a mule" for every Black man, symbolizing the passionate desire to own the very land they and their forbears had worked so hard on for the benefit of others.[38]

Both Turner and Cain effectively used their churches to expand their ministries so that they could not only address the needs of their congregations but could also address needs of the community at large. Cain's political influence and success eventually extended to the state and national levels. He was elected to represent Charleston in the state Senate, and in 1872 he was elected to the U.S. House of Representatives. He did not stand for reelection in 1874, but he was reelected in 1876. At this session of Congress, he introduced bills calling for money from the sale of land to be set aside for education. He also supported women's suffrage and advocated for trade and a steamship line between the United States and Liberia.

At the end of Reconstruction, when Blacks were expelled from political offices, Cain left South Carolina. He was elected as the fourteenth bishop of the A.M.E. Church and assigned to their districts in Louisiana and Texas. He was one of the founders of Paul Quinn College in Waco, Texas, and took a leave from his episcopal duties to serve as that college's second president. In 1880, he returned to his Episcopal duties and presided over conferences in New York, New Jersey, New England, and Philadelphia. When we consider the achievements of Cain and Turner, we observe two of the brightest lights among the many Black preachers who helped to lead their communities out of slavery.[39]

Ending slavery was the highest priority for northern Blacks. They were deeply concerned about the plight of their brothers and sisters in the South, not least of all because almost all of them had relatives south of the Mason-Dixon Line. Jonathan C. Gibbs (1827?–1874), a clergyman born in Philadelphia, was one of the strongest advocates for Blacks in the South. He turned from Methodism to Presbyterianism while attending Dartmouth College. After only two years of studying at Princeton, he was called to a Black Presbyterian congregation in Troy, New York, where Nathan Ford, the president of Dartmouth, preached his installation sermon. In the 1850s, Gibbs moved to Philadelphia, where he became active in the Negro Convention Movement, which provided a national platform for Black leadership to advocate for their communities, protest slavery and eventually support the Union Army.[40]

The missionary fever that had swept the leadership of the northern White Methodists and the A.M.E.s after the war, also affected Presbyterians. Gibbs was sent south to open schools and win converts for the Presbyterian Church. He began his work in South Carolina. He was introduced to politics by attending the Colored People's Convention which convened in Charleston in 1865. He moved back and forth between North Carolina and South Carolina working with the Freedmen's Bureau before settling in Florida in 1868. In Florida, Gibbs was elected to the 1868 Constitutional Convention, and he served as Secretary of State from 1868 to 1873 and as the Superintendent of Public Instruction from 1873 to 1874.[41]

Gibbs's achievements in the area of education caused the scholar W. E. B. DuBois to give him his highest marks. DuBois credited him for establishing the Florida Public School System. Gibbs authored and helped to pass the bill that made educational opportunities available for the first time to all classes of people in the state of Florida. His keen intellect and stately demeanor made him one of the most respected leaders in the state of Florida during Reconstruction. In 1874, Gibbs was attracting a great deal of public support in a bid to represent Florida in the United States Congress when he mysteriously died. It was believed by many Blacks that he had been poisoned, as many Whites resented the level of authority and respect that he had achieved.[42]

The church, education, and politics were closely related throughout the Reconstruction period for Blacks. Achievements in the fields of education and politics would not have been possible without the leadership of Black ministers. And many Black ministers were keen on developing the capacity of their communities through education and politics. Francis Louis Cardozo (1837–1903) was a successful minister, educator, and politician during the Reconstruction Era. He was born to free parents on February 1, 1837, in South Carolina. He studied at the University of Glasgow in Scotland and later entered the ministry. He served as the Secretary of State for the state of South Carolina in 1870 and planned a statewide public school system. Also, he served as the principal of Avery Normal Institute and eventually as professor of Latin at Howard University.[43]

Black preachers across the country led the first great mass movement for free and open-to-all public education, north and south. The genesis of the modern concept of public education originated with Black ministers, who saw education as the chief means of uplift and development for their people. Beyond public schools many Black ministers were also interested in building private church-related educational institutions. The impetus toward educational development for Blacks came out of the Black church, which served as the platform, funding source, and support mechanism for many Black colleges and universities. The uniqueness of the African-American community in Atlanta, Georgia, is largely due to the presence of the Atlanta University Center, a group of religiously affiliated schools that were begun by Blacks after the Civil War.[44]

The northern-based American Missionary Association (A.M.A.) sent White missionaries to introduce New England educational ideals into the southern Black schools and churches. The A.M.A. was one of the first organizations to respond when Sherman called for relief supplies to assist the Freedmen following his capture of Savannah. The goal of the A.M.A. was to come south and build Congregational churches and a school by every church to thus provide Blacks with a classical New England brand of education. Their strong denominational stand, however, insisting on a cold, unresponsive, and unemotional worship service, did not appeal to many Blacks. The First Congregational and the Friendship Baptist Churches were competing to win the souls of Atlanta's Black elite. The First Congregational Church of Atlanta was organized in 1867. It was the most integrated church in Georgia. By 1891, the congregation consisted of 351 members, mostly teachers and students from Atlanta University and the city's growing Black elite. About the same time of the founding of the Congregational Church in Atlanta, the A.M.A. planted the First Congregational Church of Savannah.[45]

THE DETERMINATION AND DRIVE TO ESTABLISH INDEPENDENT BLACK CHURCHES

The importance of the independent Black church movement with its genesis in Silver Bluff can hardly be overstated. The Silver Bluff Church initiated the independent Black church movement, which then contributed greatly to helping African Americans establish some sense of identity, raise their collective self-esteem and develop the organizational mechanisms necessary to survive the often harsh realities of being Black in America. The churches saved African Americans from the demoralizing prospects of having to completely rely on Whites for resources, financing, organizational structure, discipline, and leadership. In short, the independent Black church movement emerged as a result of the struggle to hold on to a sense of dignity and self-worth in the face of enslavement, degradation, and humiliation. The churches thus became the first (and continue to be the most important) institutions owned and controlled by Black people. The Black church has long been the pivotal training ground for developing political leadership, musical talent, rhetorical skills, and business acumen in the African-American community.[46]

The independent Black church movement, which manifested itself on the Bryan Plantation, had previously come forth as the Invisible Institution, hidden in the bush harbors and thickets beyond the prying eyes and ears of the slaveholders. But the origins of the Invisible Institution lay beyond the shores of America. The Black church and the Black Preacher became the transformed vehicles of the various traditional African spiritual systems that helped African Americans survive the horror of the Middle Passage, the process of natal separation, slavery, and the spiritual and cultural holocaust inflicted on them. Consequently, the Black preacher has the longest and most storied tenure of leadership in the African-American community. No other profession can claim the level of influence or a heritage that stretches back to the very beginning of the African-American experience.[47] The Black church became the cultural womb of the African-American community and the center of all institutional activities for Black people until the end of segregation. Near the end of the nineteenth century, W.E.B. DuBois recognized the Black church "as the only social institution of Negroes which started in the African forest and survived slavery under the leadership of the priests and after emancipation became the center of Negroes' social life."[48]

After slavery, southern White churches sought to maintain control over the religious affairs of their former slaves and to prevent the influence of the northerners, thus ensuring their political and economic domination in the South. However, they would soon discover that direct control of Black religious expression would not be possible. The Freedmen's determination and drive to build their own independent churches illustrate two key points about African Americans of that era: (1) contrary to the view of some historians, Black people were not enamored of their former slave masters and they sought to establish their independence from them as soon as it became clear that there was an opening to do so and (2) overwhelmingly, the formerly enslaved Africans had more confidence and faith in their own ministers, religious expressions and their traditional view of the divinity than they did in White churches. The Freedmen were frequently adamant and insistent about having their own ministers and churches. The Protestant Episcopal Church of Alabama gave up trying to evangelize Blacks because "the ex-slaves would take neither their politics nor their religion from their former owners."[49] Also, the development and growth of independent Black churches was a potent testimony against the argument that African Americans were inherently inferior and incapable of governing themselves. The proliferation of Black independent churches showed a willingness of the freedmen to make sacrifices to achieve collective goals. With limited resources, African Americans pooled their finances and improvised until they could construct a House of the Lord. The humble beginnings of many Black churches were in such places as the basement of White churches, boxcars, tobacco warehouses, carpenter and blacksmiths' shops, and individual homes. For example, in Richmond, Virginia, the Rising Mount Zion Baptist Church began with a prayer meeting held in a woman's home.[50]

The spontaneity and resourcefulness of the freedmen was matched only by their determination to establish independent churches. In Thomasville, Georgia, in 1865, the Black members of the Methodist Church decided to withdraw from the White church, and they petitioned the White church in order to purchase the praise house in which they had been worshipping with them. The White church offered to sell the property at an exorbitant price which the Black members rejected, and the Blacks further insisted that as they were two-thirds of the church membership they were therefore entitled to two-thirds of the church building.[51]

Most of the Black preachers who inspired the independent Black church movement were unlettered with no formal educational background. They derived their confidence and leadership ability from the "power and irresistible call to preach" and desire to minister to the people. The first A.M.E. Church conference in Savannah was in 1866, when Blacks were only one year removed from slavery and almost none of them knew how to read or write. They had to get young White boys and poor White men to act as secretaries for their Quarterly Conference. They struggled to achieve literacy and to build great churches and to organize their communities around their churches. And their efforts quickly paid off as they found ways to expand and develop their churches and communities.[52]

Finally, Black preachers sometimes paid the price in blood for their efforts to organize and uplift their people. Many politically active Black preachers were persecuted and a few were killed for their efforts. Politically active Black preachers did not confine their ministries to the four walls of the churches and the members of their own congregations. The entire community was their parish. They were in a real sense the whole community's preacher or "community preachers." Black communities looked to Black preachers for leadership. The local Black churches were meeting places for political rallies, social justice campaigns, and economic development initiatives. Racial justice was often high on the agendas of these churches during and immediately following Reconstruction. Of course such courageous efforts were bound to lead to confrontation with racist Whites.

A formerly enslaved Black man from Gainesville, Alabama, Richard Burke, was called to preach in 1870. He expanded his ministry and served in the State Legislature as a Representative of Sumter County. He was noted for his peaceful and conciliatory demeanor. Yet he was shot to death by a White mob when they attempted to break up a political rally he was attending. As the vicious mob approached, Burke stood up and denounced them. He addressed them as, "cowardly sons-of-bitches; you go back" and he exhorted the Black men to load their guns and fight to the last man.[53] The Black church was also the place where the Emancipation Proclamation was commemorated, a tradition that has continued in some churches until the present era. At one of the first such services, the Reverend William Thornton of Hampton Virginia was speaking in his hometown on January 1, 1866, when he was murdered by a White man. The perpetrator declared, "We hope the time will come that these Yankees will be away from here, and then we will settle with you preachers."[54]

Community involvement and social development have characterized the evolution of Black preachers and their ministries from the time of the historic meeting of the 20 Black religious leaders with Stanton and Sherman. In the Old Testament, prophets are often identified with the reigning monarch at the time of their prophesying. Isaiah is associated with King Uzziah and King Hezekiah, Moses with Pharoah, and Amos with Jeroboam II. The careers of the kings and the prophets paralleled each other. The relationships between the kings and the prophets defined their respective legacies. During Reconstruction, the Black church and many Black preachers arose to recapture the Old Testament model and, as with the ancient prophets, they felt called to speak truth to power on behalf of God's people.

Chapter 5 – The Black Church and Black Reconstruction

DISCUSSION & REVIEW QUESTIONS

1. Why did Secretary Stanton and General Sherman believe that religious leaders would be helpful in facilitating the emancipation and the development of the African-American community?

2. After the Civil War, even those Blacks who remained within predominantly White denominations often insisted on having their own churches and ministers. Why was it of the utmost importance for Blacks to establish independent churches?

3. Why did Bishop Henry McNeil Turner believe that it was detrimental for Black people to worship the image of a White God?

4. What are the legacies of Emancipation, Black Reconstruction, and the betrayal of Reconstruction that we can still observe today?

CHAPTER 6

The Struggle in the Wilderness

THE EMERGENCE OF COLOR CONSCIOUSNESS AND ELITISM AMONG AFRICAN AMERICANS: BACKGROUND TO THE *PLESSY V. FERGUSON* TRAVESTY

The division of the enslaved Africans into house servants and field hands gave birth to elitism and classism among African Americans. Generally speaking, the lighter-skinned Blacks, large numbers of whom were the result of sexual unions forced upon African women by White men, were assigned to do the domestic work in and around the master's mansion, while the more generously pigmented Blacks were relegated to the laborious work of the plantation in the fields. Consequently, house servants began to feel privileged and superior in status relative to their field-hand brothers and sisters. Even prior to emancipation in southern cities such as New Orleans and Charleston, there emerged a peculiar system of color-caste hierarchy and color-conscious determinations of social status in which light-skinned Blacks escaped some of the more intense racial prejudices and persecutions that the Whites inflicted upon the more generously pigmented Blacks. Occasionally, some mulattos, who had appearances more closely approximating the phenotypical pattern of Europeans, were permitted to go to restaurants, saloons and theaters which were forbidden to other African-Americans.[1]

The unique history of New Orleans led to the emergence of a curious set of ethnic classifications among African Americans. The Creoles were related to French men who had earlier settled in Louisiana and who then had numerous children with African women. Some of those who were the result of such unions considered themselves mulattos, or mixed, and there were further breakdowns determined by the supposed amount of "white blood" they possessed. Quadroons were supposedly three-quarters white or only one-forth black, while octoroons considered themselves to have seven-eighths white blood or a mere one-eighth black.[2] The Creoles and mulattos generally thought themselves to be not only different but also superior to the rest of those Blacks who had more heavily pigmented skin tones. They often chose not to associate, socialize, or cohabit with their brethren who were not as close to whiteness as they thought themselves to be, a circumstance that gave rise to much jealousy and resentment. This arrangement of racial classification was nominally supported by Whites, as it left Blacks divided and politically impotent. Also, Whites still treated the Creoles, mulattos, quadroons, and octoroons, as second-class citizens and lumped them in along with the other Blacks whenever they found it convenient to do so.[3] Many of those who adopted these peculiar designations of race based upon an imagined possession of "white blood" prior to the twentieth century can be at least partially excused for their ignorance and erroneousness as they labored under the most trying of circumstances. But even today, apparently satisfied with ignorance, a few people cling to such prejudices and preferences despite the revelation of the African origins of all human blood, white and otherwise, which renders such a classification scheme an absurdity. Human values and perceptions of self-worth are rooted in our sense of collective historical identity; excusing the rape and abuse of one's ancestors in preference for those who perpetrated the abuses is a sign of psychological and spiritual deficits.

At any rate, the Creoles of New Orleans became the colored elites, and as such they avoided social contact with the other Blacks of that city. Creoles lived downtown in the fourth, fifth, sixth, and seventh wards. Their neighbors were Jewish, German, and other Whites, who in turn, distanced themselves from the Creoles, whom they considered beneath them as Negroes or Black. Instead of a broadminded strategy of establishing a closer bond socially and politically with the larger Black population, the Creoles tended to withdraw into a world of their own, rejected by the Whites and contemptuous of other Blacks. They created a society that accentuated the differences between themselves and other African Americans.[4]

The elite Blacks or mulattos of the post-Reconstruction era, who considered themselves genetically superior to other Blacks, accepted an in-between social status, not fully White yet desperately trying to differentiate themselves from the Black masses. Many aspired to one day be accepted and assimilated completely into White society. Some had convinced themselves that by virtue of their lighter skins, conversion to Christianity and acceptance of the "civilizing" influences of Europe, they would one day be accepted as full-fledged members of White society. However, in the 1890s the Whites throughout the South begin to adopt legislation that codified racial discrimination and subjugation of Blacks and other people of color. In 1890 the Louisiana legislature passed a separate coach bill that required Blacks, including mulattos, to ride on train cars different from those of Whites. Many other Jim Crow laws, legalizing racial segregation, soon followed. Much to their dismay, the mulattos found themselves relegated beneath the Whites as colored and often not distinguished from other Blacks.[5] Some of the mulatto leaders soon realized that their dream of full assimilation was turning into a fantasy and their perception of a select social status and privilege for themselves was viewed as a farce by Whites and Blacks alike.

In response to the legislative enactment of laws that upheld White supremacy without any respect to a special status for mulattos, the Creoles organized a citizens committee, including Senator Henry Demas, the first Black elected to the Louisiana Senate. Senator Demas spoke to his Senate colleagues on behalf of the Creoles:

> Owing to the intermingling of races, it is frequently a difficult matter of determining from the standpoint of color, the white from the Negro. Would it not be unjust, I ask, to relegate the class to a coach occupied by those much inferior to them in life, and by thus doing, humiliate a people accustomed to better surroundings? It would force them to associate with the worst class of Negro element and be an unmerited rebuke upon the Colored man of finer sensibilities.[6]

To continue their efforts to be accepted and assimilated into the White race, the Creoles of New Orleans staged a legal challenge to the doctrine of separate train cars for Whites and Blacks on the railroads. The Whites had concocted the doctrine of "separate but equal" by which they meant to justify segregation in public accommodations, claiming that

Blacks received equal although separate facilities. In actual practice, the segregation laws were a means of perpetuating White social, economic, and political domination by denying access to resources and privileges for Blacks. The mulatto citizens committee selected Homer Plessy to test the constitutionality of the segregation laws. Tragically, in their blindness, the mulatto leaders offered a challenge to the doctrine of separate but equal, not in order to gain more opportunity for all Blacks but instead in hopes of gaining access to Whites-only areas for themselves.[7]

On June 7, 1892, Plessy entered the New Orleans station of East Louisiana Railway and bought a first-class ticket to Covington, Louisiana, a small town near Mississippi. Plessy took a seat in a coach that had signs posted designating it as an area for White passengers only. Upon being made aware of his presence, the White conductor ordered Plessy to vacate his seat and move to a coach assigned for persons of color. When Plessy refused to obey the orders to move, a policeman was called and he was arrested and imprisoned in the parish jail of New Orleans. His sponsors were expecting his arrest and they immediately arranged for his release on bail.[8]

Plessy and his fellow Creoles wanted to expose the absurdity of the law, which made the railroad conductor "the autocrat of caste, armed with the power of state, to decide which passengers were white and which were not using his eyes to measure racial purity."[9] As many Creoles were of such complexion that they could "pass" for White or there was little discernable difference between them and the general population of Whites, they hoped to show that it was unreasonable to attempt to enforce arbitrary designations of race. The jurist assigned by the state to hear Plessy's case was Judge John Ferguson, who ruled that "the foul odors of blacks in close quarters" made the law "a reasonable exercise of the state's police powers to protect the health safety, welfare, and morals of the public."[10] Plessy's attorney argued that the law and the doctrine of separate but equal imposed a "badge of servitude" on Plessy and other mulattos with Black ancestry, and deprived them of the privileges and immunities of citizenship. After the Louisiana courts upheld Plessy's conviction for violating the law, the case was appealed to the Supreme Court of the United States. In 1896 Supreme Court Judge Henry Brown wrote for all but one of his colleagues in upholding the Louisiana Jim Crow laws. The precedent that the Supreme Court used for this decision was the practice of school segregation in Boston, Massachusetts. In 1849 the Massachusetts Supreme Court in the case of *Robert v. City of Boston* found that segregation was in the best interest of all children and that the prejudices of both Blacks and Whites were not created by law and therefore could not be changed by law.[11]

The Supreme Court's decision, which found that the doctrine of separate but equal was consistent with the United States Constitution was at once both a devastating blow to the aspirations of the elites and a clear signal that de facto White supremacy was not permitted to be challenged in the courts. The decision destroyed any remaining illusions that the mulatto elites may have had concerning wholesale acceptance and assimilation within White society. These circumstances had far-reaching consequences for the social development of African Americans. With the modifications of time and sentiments, the mulatto elites would morph into the emerging Black elites. And there was also a greater impact on race relations and the fortunes of African Americans in general, as the practice of discriminating against Blacks in public accommodations was now legally protected. Thus, public schools, playgrounds, restrooms, graveyards, swimming pools, and even Bibles in the courtroom were segregated throughout the South. The term used for these practices was segregation but that term is somewhat deceptive, as it obscures the fact that Blacks were not only given separate facilities but fewer facilities, fewer resources, and fewer opportunities. White children in public schools received new textbooks, uniforms, and equipment, while the Black students were the recipients of what had been used by the Whites. Black students were frequently forced to walk up to ten miles to school or to move in with neighbors while Whites were provided with buses to transport them to and from school. The only "equal" in the doctrine of separate but equal seems to have been with the collection of taxes, with Blacks being required to pay the same proportion of their incomes in taxes as Whites in order to support a system that gave them far less in return.[12]

The elite White southern families, their past rooted in plantation slaveholding, had a long and dreadful history of political and social oppression. Besides slaveholding, their historical accomplishments included the decimation of indigenous populations, instigation of the Mexican-American War and secession from the Union. In part to furbish up their image as well as that of the South in general, social leaders in Atlanta hosted the Atlanta Cotton States and International Exposition in 1895. The event was organized with the hope of showcasing some strides that had been made in race relations. Changing the image of the South, from a retrograde backwater steeped in brutal mistreatment of Blacks to a setting appropriate for modern business and industry was important to many southern leaders. John D. Rockefeller, Henry Mellon, and J. Pierpont Morgan had just organized the southern railroad system. The Southerners hoped to lure more people like Rockefeller, Mellon, and Morgan into doing business in the South.[13]

The convention planners chose Booker T. Washington to represent the Negroes and their cause. Their first and only choice was a native southerner, a former slave, an educational visionary, and an opportunistic accomodationist on racial matters. Although born a slave, by the age of thirty-nine Washington had established himself as one of the foremost educators of the South by building the Tuskegee Institute. Washington delivered his speech at the Atlanta Exposition on September 18, 1895, and that one speech made him both the most famous Black man in America as well as the most influential. Washington gave a speech in which he surrendered any claims Blacks had to equal and just treatment under the law. He gave the businessmen a vision in which Blacks would willingly play the role of serfs or peons as they worked to develop themselves to be worthy one day of acceptance into civil society. When Washington finished speaking, the Governor of Georgia stepped up to the podium to shake his hands and the crowd gave him a thunderous applause. Washington had given the southern White businessmen exactly the message that they most wanted to hear. After his speech Washington became an instant "spokesman for the Blacks" for the Whites. The *Atlanta Constitution* reported: "The whole speech is a platform upon which blacks and whites can stand with full justice to each other." Washington became an uncrowned king of the Blacks. Indeed, for some years afterwards, no Black person was granted access to substantial resources or assistance by the White establishment without Washington's blessing. Washington's speech helped to allay the anxiety and fears of Whites, but it did little to address the real needs and concerns of Blacks. The attitude and behavior of Washington and other accomodation-ists helped to set the stage for more vigorous grassroots protests in the decades to come as it was becoming clear to the Black masses that their most prominent "leaders" were generally not up to the task of organizing a serious liberation movement.[14]

The doctrine of White supremacy held that Blacks were inferior and undesirable in every way in comparison to Whites. Images of Blacks as unintelligent, lazy, and prone to immoral behavior were common. But by developing their own churches, schools, fraternities, sororities, and busi-nesses, Blacks began to foster an image of themselves as resourceful sur-vivors. The *Plessy* decision attempted to forever confine Blacks to the role of a subservient race, unworthy of the best that society has to offer. But the reality of the creativity and genius of Black people still remained to confront the lies. The success of the Blacks, despite oppressive conditions, would occasionally outshine that of some of their White counterparts in various places including the Tulsa, Oklahoma "Black Wall Street" and Sweet Auburn Avenue in Atlanta.[15]

The *Plessy* decision also marked the failure of mulatto elitism and the end to organized efforts of the mulattos to escape into the White race. Out of frustration some began to embrace notions of Black Nationalism or sep-aratism which had long been championed by other race leaders. In 1899, the elitist and apologist for slavery, L.H. Holsey, bishop of the C.M.E. Church, announced in a speech his support for the separation of the races. Holsey suggested that Oklahoma or New Mexico and possibly other states out West be designated for settlement by African Americans which would then be governed by them. But the calls for Black Nationalism among the elites were mostly just a momentary reaction, as there was still considerable desire for assimilation into White society.[16]

The Black elites were also incensed by the efforts of Booker T. Washington, as his proposals left them with neither the hope of assimilation nor the opportunity to advance on their own. W.E.B. DuBois' classic liter-ary treatise, *The Souls of Black Folks* was in part a response to Washington's Atlanta Exposition Address.[17] DuBois recognized the pervasive and corrupting influence of the Washington regime. He called Tuskegee the "capital of the Negro nation."[18] In a deceptive scheme to appear progressive, southern White businessmen and politicians along with northerners including Theodore Roosevelt, had embraced Washington and promoted his leadership of the Blacks.

DuBois countered Washington's teaching on racial issues by projecting the destiny of the Black race to be placed in the hands of an elite Black leadership, which he called the talented tenth. He was proposing that an intellectual elite of well-educated Black men and women take on leadership of the race. By their gifts and graces they would then instruct and guide the people leading them toward higher civilization. DuBois galvanized supporters who embraced his philosophy. In June of 1905, he issued a call for a select group of Black men to meet in the vicinity of Buffalo, New York. Twenty-nine men assembled with DuBois in a small hotel on the Canadian side of the Niagara River to formally organize the Niagara Movement and to oppose the accomodationist agenda of Booker T. Washington. They countered Washington by proposing universal suffrage, abolition of segregation, social equality, and recognition of the highest academic training for all races. At this meeting they fashioned the framework for a permanent national movement, eventually giving birth to the National Association for the Advancement of Colored People (NAACP) in 1910. Thus, the Black elites had come full circle, as they now determined to lead a protest movement against a social order into which their highest aspiration was to gain acceptance.[21]

FROM SLAVERY TO PEONAGE IN THE POST-RECONSTRUCTION SOUTH

When juxtaposed against the dreadfulness of chattel slavery and the precariousness of the post-Reconstruction period, the mere survival of any semblance at all of community and family life among African Americans can be seen as something of a miracle. Emancipation freed the Blacks from servitude to the plantation slaveholders but left them still beholden to a vicious system of White supremacy with discriminatory Jim Crow laws and ruthless economic exploitation. After Reconstruction, Blacks were left with little or no legal protections and few provisions to begin making a decent living for themselves; the Emancipation Proclamation was a declaration that lacked substantive means for enforcement or implementation. Thus the people were left with no jobs, no land, and no shelter. Both regimes, one of plantation slaveholding and the other of the Jim Crow South, were designed and maintained to enforce a system of White supremacy with Blacks assigned to the bottom of the racial hierarchy, providing cheap and even slave labor to fuel the American economy. After emancipation, the formerly enslaved were still considered by most Whites to be inherently inferior and incapable of being anything other than a servant class of people. There were no resources systematically provided that would have permitted the formerly enslaved people to en masse become self-reliant, productive citizens, although many strived to become so even without such provisions.[22]

The Emancipation Proclamation ended 244 years of chattel slavery (360 years if we count from the first arrival of enslaved Africans to the island of Hispaniola). But chattel slavery was replaced by the peonage system, which turned out to be just as bad as slavery. This new enslavement was a web of deceit, exploitation and oppression that was entrenched throughout the South until World War II. Peonage was a system of terror in which countless thousands of Black men were arrested, often under the flimsiest pretext of an offense, required to pay exorbitant fines that they could not afford, and then sold out to work for corporations as a means of paying off the fines. State legislatures across the South enacted "black codes," a set of laws designed to intimidate Blacks and support the peonage system and make legally permissible the arbitrary arrests and excessive fines. With no means to pay these contrived debts, prisoners were sold and forced to become laborers in coal mines, lumber camps, railroads, and plantations.[23]

The enactment of vagrancy laws was one of the schemes used by the White Southerners in their development of the peonage system. These laws effectively made almost all Black Southerners fair game to become peons or to have any capricious, fraudulent or fictitious charges brought against them, as the laws required all Blacks to have a job. This meant they had to take any job that came along or face imprisonment and forced labor. Many were simply captured or kidnapped and the authorities did not even bother with a rationale. The prisoners were just forced into involuntary servitude. Forty-five years after emancipation, one thousand Black men worked in a coal mine on the edge of Birmingham near Pratt City, Alabama. These men had mostly been arrested on frivolous charges and the state of Alabama leased them to U.S. Steel to work in the mine. And it was the state, not the prisoners, that was compensated for their labor. The men at the mine were arbitrarily whipped or imprisoned, and they worked without compensation for the benefit of Whites long after emancipation.[24]

Like chattel slavery itself, the peonage system mitigated against the development of strong Black families and communities. The system doomed families to perpetual poverty, ignorance, and poor health, conditions that continue to plague African Americans in large numbers until the present time. Black men who attempted to be responsible husbands and fathers and provide protection and support for their families were frequently driven away from their families. White plantation owners would then have an affidavit notarized which stated that the father was out of the county and the mother was unable to support the children. These children were then made the plantation owner's legal apprentices until the age of 21, thus being forced into involuntary servitude.[25]

In order to implement this demonic web of lies, exploitation, and oppression, various devices including sharecropping, contract leasing, and tenant farming, the black codes were employed. This system was enforced by police brutality, mob beatings, and lynching. Indeed, lynching was much more prevalent after emancipation than before. The post-Reconstruction period saw a reign of terror unleashed. The public spectacle of lynching was intended to intimidate, especially the men, so that Black people would be compliant to the system which abused and oppressed them. Henry McNeal Turner observed, "Until we are free from the menace of lynching … we are destined to be a devastated people. Lynching was bad not only for the victims but the environment as well. It damaged the entire culture; it poisoned the shallow well of good feeling between the races."[26]

THE GREAT MIGRATION AND THE INITIATION OF THE CIVIL RIGHTS MOVEMENT

The Civil Rights Movement was initiated at the beginning of the twentieth century when Blacks began their silent but determined protest against lynching, Jim Crow, peonage, poor schools, disenfranchisement and deprivation. The Great Migration was one of the defining events of the twentieth century. The Great Migration became the Exodus of the African-American experience, though unlike the Hebrews of the Old Testament, their release from their oppressors did not occur immediately after their release from slavery. Black ministers encouraged the people and often acted as liaisons with the White power structure, but unlike Moses there was no single appointed leader. One migrant observed, "We have no leader to trust but the God overhead of us." In New Orleans, a prospective migrant summed it up when he said, "Every black man is his own Moses."[27] The biblical story of the Exodus resonated with the Black migrants from the South. The migrants had attended Black churches where they heard the Bible stories read and preached, and they were inspired by themes such as new opportunities in a promised land as they began to move north and west. They identified with the promise that God made to Abraham that He would make them a great nation, and they would be His chosen people.

Although lacking a centralized leadership, the people were nonetheless able to work together and cooperate effectively in this movement, as they mostly shared similar cultural values and historical experiences. They shared a deep sense of spirituality bequeathed from their African ancestors, a broad understanding that they were an oppressed people, and a strong desire to better their condition. They were motivated to leave the South because they were robbed of their labor and they sought refuge from beatings and lynching in southern cities. Black Southerners lived in a perpetual state of fear and trembling. They never knew what would happen from one moment to the next. At any time an incident might occur that could incite the madness of the Whites to engage in some new aggression or outrage. A columnist in the *Savannah News* wrote, "There is scarcely a Negro mother who does not live in dread and fear that her husband or son may come in unfriendly contact with some white person as to bring the lynchers … which may result in wiping out her entire family."[28]

There was a direct correlation between the mistreatment of Blacks and their zeal to leave the South. The *Atlanta Constitution* reported that "the heaviest migration of Negroes has been from counties from which there have been the worst outbreaks against the Blacks. A mass migration from Greene County followed a lynching in 1920." In contrast, relatively few Blacks migrated from Dougherty County, where lynching was rare. The Social Action Committee reported to the A.M.E. Annual Conference convening in Atlanta in 1919 that, "lynching and mob violence … have sent from us in the last three or four years more than a million … and they continue to go."[29]

Southern Whites were mostly hypocritical and sometimes delusional in their response to the labor crises caused by the Black migration. The former slaveholders pretended they had alternative labor forces available which would be superior to the Blacks. However, they were largely unsuccessful at replacing the Black labor force, although they did try with immigrants from China and Europe. The Whites sometimes resorted to the tactic of threatening the Blacks in order to get them to stay in the South. Apparently, some Whites had begun to believe their own myth. They had defended slavery on the grounds that Blacks were happy-go-lucky and content with living in perpetual servitude. Many Whites had difficulty accepting that Blacks would rise up and leave of their own accord. They felt there must be some outside propaganda that was influencing the Blacks. Henry Grady, the noted White journalist and orator who promoted notions of the "New South" after the Civil War, held that "Negroes were peaceable and harmless except when inflamed by troublemakers."[30] Some Whites charged that the Black-owned newspaper, the *Chicago Defender*, was one of the culprits and was an "outside agitator." *The Defender* was founded by an ex-Georgian, Robert Sengstacke Abbot, who was born on St. Simon Island in 1870. After working for the *Savannah News* for a few years, Abbott relocated to Chicago and founded the *Chicago Defender* in 1905. The newspaper championed Black causes and was particularly adept at exposing the horror of lynching in the South. The popularity of the paper was broad throughout African-American communities as its circulation reached 230,000. The publication was an anathema to White Southerners, and when traveling to Savannah, Georgia, to visit his grandmother, Abbott would use a fictitious name. His stepfather was a prominent Congregationalist minister, John H. H. Sengstacke of Woodville, Illinois.

The *Macon Telegraph* was one of the first to sound the alarm to the state of the economic danger of the Great Migration. "Everybody seems to be asleep about what is going on under our nose, that is, everybody but those farmers who have wakened up one morning and found every male Negro over 21 gone—to Cleveland, to Pittsburg, to Chicago, to Indianapolis."[34] The Central Georgia Railroad became so desperate for laborers that they hired Black women to lay cross ties because of the shortage of Black men. W.E.B. DuBois gleefully reported in 1919 that "white women of some of Georgia's first families had to do field work."[31]

Law officers increased their harassment of Blacks trying to leave the South. They patrolled railroad stations, and confiscated tickets of Blacks waiting for "freedom bound" trains. In 1916 the Macon police forced one thousand Blacks off a special train bound for Michigan. Post-emancipation Black life was as cheap after slavery as it was before. In 1916, a Black worker was killed near Macon for moving from one White landlord's property to another's. James Waters was lynched near Dublin after he served notice that he was going to leave the farm where he had been working for several years. It was still the case throughout the South, de facto if not de jure, that Blacks had no rights that a White man was bound to respect. In 1936 a White farmer who believed that three Black men were preparing to leave his farm had them lynched.[32]

The Great Migration was a crucial event in the struggle for civil rights in the post-emancipation era. White leaders in Atlanta conferred with the Black leaders to address the labor problem caused by migration. In July of 1923, the Black leaders pointed out to the Whites that the Great Migration, which was crippling the southern economy, was related to the unjust treatment of the Blacks. In response to this insight, James Peter, President of Georgia's Bankers Association, urged better wages, schools, and treatment of Blacks by law officers. Booker T. Washington's successor at the Tuskegee Institute, Robert Russa Moton, said in 1923 that the migration had cost Georgia alone $27 million. To change this situation,

Moton admonished the Whites to improve the economic and living conditions of those Blacks who yet remained in the South. Historians Carter G. Woodson and Nell Painter both concurred that to some degree conditions were indeed improved for Blacks who remained in the South in the wake of the Great Migration. Whites had begrudgingly begun to acknowledge that Blacks could effectively protest their mistreatment as well as do harm to the southern economy by simply leaving.[33]

Usually for small-minded and self-serving reasons, Black leaders including preachers in the South mostly attempted to dissuade Blacks from leaving. The exodus had not only an adverse effect on the southern economy for the Whites but also an adverse affect on Black businesses and churches in the South. But the efforts to dissuade the people were met overwhelmingly with deaf ears; the people instinctively knew better. The Black masses demonstrated a tenacious commitment to finding a better life for themselves and their families in the urban areas of the North and out West. The people, especially the poor and downtrodden, knew an opportunity when they saw one, and they were determined to seek refuge in the "New Jerusalem" of northern cities. Between 1916 and 1919, Robert Horton, a Black barber in Hattiesburg, Mississippi, organized a migration club and recruited nearly 40 men and women to migrate to Chicago. The migrants included Horton and his family, and once they settled in Chicago, they recruited other relatives and friends to come north. When the Blacks arrived in Chicago they assisted and looked out for one another. This illustrates that the Great Migration was mostly a people's movement and was not initiated by established organizations or recognized leaders. A Black preacher from Mississippi observed, "The leaders of the race are powerless to prevent Black Southerners from migrating to northern cities. They [the leaders] had nothing to do with it, and indeed, all of them, for obvious reasons, are opposed to the exodus."[34]

The north was not without problems, but in comparison to the conditions experienced in the South it was far more desirable. Liberation themes resonated with the migrants. In one incident as a train reached the middle of the Ohio River Bridge, the migrants stopped their watches and knelt to offer prayers of thanks. They celebrated their deliverance by singing "I done come out of the land of Egypt with good news."[35] But, after arriving in northern cities, migrants did not find the new surroundings to be a panacea for all their problems. The new arrivals were confronted with poor housing and frequent job discrimination. Also, they were not welcomed by many of the Black social elites of the North, who were embarrassed to be associated with the rude manners, thick accents, and rustic decorum of their southern cousins. Even many of the northern Blacks who had been born in the South were sometimes hard-pressed to be welcoming to the new arrivals.[36]

The intra-racial tensions were also evident in many northern churches. Southerners found the churches of the North to be larger, wealthier, and better organized. But, they also seemed less personal and overly class conscious. One northern postal worker in Chicago made the following comment about the worship decorum of the southern Blacks: "No wonder white people laugh at colored people and their peculiar way of worshipping. I don't believe in shouting. I like a church that is quiet. I just can't appreciate clowning in any church."[37]

It was not unusual for mainline, status-conscious Black churches to distance themselves from any semblance of holiness and Pentecostalism, which are associated with shouting and demonstrative and participatory worship practices. For example, the historic Second Baptist Church in Los Angeles, California, rejected Mrs. Julia Hutchins and a small band of her followers who had embraced the beliefs and practices of holiness. Hutchins and her followers withdrew from the church and founded their own holiness church. One of the members of her group, Mrs. Neely Terry, asked Pastor Hutchins to invite Elder William Seymour from Houston, Texas, to come and preach to their fledgling congregation about the beliefs of holiness. Pastor Hutchins agreed to the request and invited Seymour. Seymour came to Los Angeles, but once he began to preach on his interpretation of holiness, Hutchins and many of the members were dumbfounded by his declaration that speaking in tongues was evidence of receiving the baptism of the Holy Ghost.[38] He was rejected by Hutchins and most of her members. Seymour left the small congregation in an uproar, and when he returned to the church to preach his next sermon, he found the doors padlocked. There were two couples of the church, Mr. and Mrs. Richard Asberry and Mr. And Mrs. Edward Lee, who were receptive to his message, and they gave the stranded preacher refuge in their homes.

Edward Lee had some health challenges and so on April 9, 1906, he invited Seymour to his home to pray for his healing and for baptism by the Holy Spirit. Seymour prayed for Lee's deliverance and within minutes after his physical healing, Lee was engulfed by the Spirit, and he evidenced this by speaking in tongues. This act of evidently miraculous healing was the key to Seymour's evangelistic success, as soon large crowds were attracted to the home to hear him preach. The news of Lee's healing spread throughout the neighborhoods of Los Angeles like wildfire. Seymour was preaching in homes to overflowing crowds, and on April 12, 1906, he himself received baptism of the Holy Ghost and he too began speaking in tongues. These healing services ignited a spiritual awakening that attracted a diverse crowd of people from all nationalities.[39]

A building which had formerly housed the First A.M.E. Church and was later converted into a livery stable at 312 Asuza Street became available, and Seymour and his followers rented the building which seated 750. Thus, like the birth of Jesus, modern-day Pentecostalism was born in a stable. The spirit of the Asuza Street Revival lasted for one thousand days; people would gather at 10 A.M. and they would stay to 3 A.M. And they kept coming each morning, seven days a week. Ultimately, the revival reached people in more than 50 nations and touched every continent.

In 1907, Charles H. Mason, founder of the Church of God in Christ (C.O.G.I.C.), attended the Asuza Street Revival and he too received baptism of the Holy Spirit and the gift of glossolalia. Charles Mason and Charles Jones had been instrumental in planting the Church of God in Christ in Tennessee, Mississippi, and Arkansas. Both Mason and Jones grew up and were called to preach in the Baptist church, but the Baptists rejected their teachings and beliefs about holiness. They were excommunicated and barred from preaching in Baptist churches throughout the region.[40]

Mason and Jones continued to preach and teach of holiness from courthouse steps, in cotton gins, and in open fields. During a meeting in a cotton gin in Lexington, Mississippi, the service was interrupted with gunfire and several people were wounded.[41] But after Mason returned from the Asuza Street Revival and began speaking in tongues, Charles Jones left the Church of God in Christ and founded the Church of God (Holiness) because he did not believe in the practice of speaking in tongues.[42]

Bishop C.H. Mason
(1862—1961)

The Asuza Street Revival, which began with a small group of unassuming African Americans, may one day be regarded as the beginning of the Third Great Awakening in America. The modern Charismatic and Pentecostal movements can be traced to the Asuza Street Revival and the efforts of the self-educated preaching genius William Seymour. The work of Bishop Mason and the C.O.G.I.C. was invigorated by the Asuza Street Revival. As African Americans migrated from the South in large numbers to go to the cities of the North, the Midwest, and out West, Bishop Mason had the foresight to send appointed bishops and elders along with them to the areas where the migrants settled, and this greatly helped to expand the C.O.G.I.C. presence. These transplanted shepherds organized new congregations and rented store fronts that would become churches. Bishop Mason's evangelistic strategy laid the foundation for the phenomenal growth experienced by the C.O.G.I.C. in the later part of the twentieth century. This is particularly instructive as several of the more well-established Black denominations declined to follow Mason's strategy, not wanting to be too closely associated with the impoverished field hands and domestic workers migrating from the South, and many of these churches have faced stagnant and declining congregations in recent years. Also, the predominantly White Assemblies of God denomination has roots in the Asuza Street Revival, as several of the early pastors in the Assemblies of God received their ordination from Bishop Mason. They then split from the predominantly Black churches in 1914.

The origins of the storefront churches can be found in the negative response of northern Blacks to the Black migrants from the South. Blacks from the South felt uncomfortable in many cases in the northern churches, and they longed to establish their own churches in which they could worship more freely. Lacking the resources to build stand-alone church buildings they adapted storefront locations to their needs. It was in storefront churches that the migrants found a welcoming atmosphere as well as opportunities to meet old friends and to make new ones. The smaller storefront churches also offered more opportunities for greater involvement in operating and administering church affairs. They wanted to be more than "bench members" who warmed the pews and contributed to the offering plates but were unwelcome and unwanted in the administration of church affairs. For the Black masses the church had long been the most important place to obtain leadership positions, recognition and social capital. A lowly dishwasher in a restaurant during the work week might be the highly appreciated and favorite soloist in the choir during worship services, a $5-per-day construction worker could become the prestigious chairman of the deacon board in the church, and the housemaid who worked for wealthy Whites Monday through Friday could become the respected president of the missionary society at her church on Sunday morning.[43]

The storefront churches proliferated in northern cities as they served a vital function in helping the migrants to adjust to the northern metropolis. These churches enabled Blacks to preserve their traditional style of worship. Here they found spiritual and social encouragement and support with people who shared a similar background. Sometimes in storefront churches the congregants expressed a preference for their traditions by singing the favorite African-American spiritual, "Give Me That Ol' Time Religion."[44]

There were only a few noteworthy established Black churches in the North that reached out to welcome the migrants and initiate programs to serve their specific needs. Starting in 1914 Blacks began to migrate to Detroit in large numbers. The Second Baptist Church and its pastor,

Robert L. Bradley started self-help and social-welfare programs, including training classes in sewing, cooking, and millinery. They also provided information on employment opportunities and recreational activities. Unlike most of the other established churches in Detroit, Second Baptist never shunned migrants from the South. During the peak of migration, a hospitality committee from Second Baptist Church met every train arriving in Detroit from the South to greet the people and offer assistance. The outreach ministry of the church included providing shelter for the homeless and an educational institution staffed with 18 teachers to give classes in basic education and industrial training. By 1933, the church had made a substantial investment of time, effort, and thousands of dollars into serving the needs of the new arrivals from the South. Bethel A.M.E. Church in Detroit was also actively involved in assisting the migrants. The church members established the Bethel Benefit Association, which paid $3 a week to members who lost their employment owing to illness, and an additional $75 death benefit to the family members of the deceased. The association required $0.25 per month dues and a $0.50 membership fee. Not surprisingly, Black churches were the birthplaces of various Black banks and insurance companies. In 1936, Bethel opened its own credit union, and the nurses of the church organized a nurses guild that provided free medical services to the church membership and the general community. The oldest Black church in Detroit was the St. Matthew's Episcopal Church. Its membership was made up of many of the Black social elites, and they were not inclined to look to migrants as potential members. Nevertheless, St. Matthew's did offer some support and assistance to the incoming migrants.[45]

Henry Ford, through the Ford Motor Company, was the largest employer of Black workers in Detroit. He made an alliance with some of the leading Black pastors of the city to recruit migrants to work in his factories. His efforts were not exactly altruistic; Ford sought a strategic means of countering the influence of the trade unions with the White workers, and the Blacks seemed to be the perfect foil. In 1918, Ford arranged to meet Reverend Bradley of Second Baptist Church to solicit his help in recruiting those Blacks with good character and good work ethics. The influx of large numbers of migrants not only of Blacks from the South but also of Europeans increased the levels of competition for employment and racial tensions soon began to surface. Ford asked Bradley to help "manage" the situation, defusing tensions among the Blacks, and he would then hire the "good Negro workers." This arrangement, which was also followed by other churches, promoted a sort of corporate paternalism between the Black churches of Detroit and Henry Ford. Ford was adamantly antilabor and he used the Black migrants and Black churches in Detroit to impede the progress of the labor unions.[46]

A few of the Black ministers were able to curry favor with the Ford family, and they used this advantage to secure jobs and other perks of influence. The ministers and churches that recruited employees for Ford's factories were rewarded with generous contributions, and their status in the African-American community was often enhanced. Ford and his wife annually visited a few African-American churches and made substantial contributions.[47]

A decade prior to the rise of industrial unionism in the United States in the mid-1930s, Henry Ford, through a cadre of Black ministers, had drawn much of the African-American community of Detroit into a state of political and economic dependency. With the emergence of trade unions and the demand for fairer working conditions and wages, Black ministers and churches had to decide whether or not to support the movement for social justice for the working class or to remain co-opted by Ford's paternalistic regime.

The economic necessities of factory-based mass production created a voracious appetite for sources of manpower and labor, which helped to fuel the mass migration of Blacks from the South. This migration meant that for the first time in the history of America, the Black population would eventually become predominantly urban rather than rural with the largest proportion of them being northerners, not southerners. The following consequences would ensue: (1) the weakening and partial collapse of the oppressive race relations that had emerged in the South following chattel slavery and Reconstruction; (2) a greater participation by Blacks in the national economy and politics; (3) increased recognition and appreciation for African-American culture; (4) and forcing social and political leaders of the nation to confront the racial oppression of Blacks.[48]

From the birth of America through the mid-twentieth century, African Americans were the answer to the Whites' desire for cheap and exploitable labor. Both slavery and the post-emancipation period found the South dependent on keeping Blacks in their place, which mostly meant working on rural plantations. At the beginning of the twentieth century, mass production in the industrial plants of the North created a demand for cheap labor in that sector as well. The Great Migration served the needs of the White businessmen in the North as well as the Blacks who migrated. Henry Ford and other White businessmen used Black ministers to recruit "respectable Negroes." Many Black churches of the North became in effect, employment agencies, screening their congregants for reliable workers. And many Black ministers were professionally and financially empowered by such machinations. But it came at a price. The traditional "prophetic voice" of the Black churches was often silenced, and the stage was set for widespread corruption and abuse of the prestige and influence of churches.[49]

THE EMERGENCE OF NONCONFORMISTS, RADICALS, AND MILITANTS IN THE AFRICAN-AMERICAN RELIGIOUS EXPERIENCE

After a brief period of time in their new homes, the Black migrants often began to feel alienated, displaced and without a sense of belonging. Those who felt the most marginalized shared the lamentations of the prophet Jeremiah: "The harvest is past, the summer is ended, and we are not saved." The frustrated migrants found themselves still in search of deliverance, frequently discriminated against, and often rejected by those Blacks already established in the North. The accommodationist mindset that had taken hold in some of the more prominent Black churches made the churches useless with regard to addressing the real and pressing needs of the masses. Some Black ministers became puppets of the White establishment, and they provided no meaningful leadership toward trying to improve the conditions of the people. The widespread alienation and rejection provided fertile ground for charismatic mystics and religious visionaries who recruited for their sects and organizations. The appeal of these new religions was enhanced by the ongoing racial tensions in northern cities. Housing and job discrimination along with incidents of police brutality intensified the larger the Black populations became.[50]

Nonconformists, those who decline to follow prevailing customs, opinions, or social standards, can nonetheless play a critical role in society. They may point out the flaws and shortcomings of a social order that are overlooked or ignored by most. Nonconformists might be an annoyance to the civil authorities, but they often address needs in society that are otherwise unmet, and they can speak openly about issues that are not adequately handled by established social institutions. Any social order that hopes to endure over the long term, must occasionally renew and reinvigorate itself. It has often been the case that after a time the ideas and rhetoric of those outsiders, the nonconformists, once rejected by the establishment, become the organizing principles for a new social transformation. Occasionally in history we find instances in which those who were once labeled as cranks, radicals, and troublemakers in a previous age become heralded as precocious seers in a following period.

Marcus Mosiah Garvey arrived in New York City from the island of Jamaica in 1916. He was impressed with the work of Booker T. Washington at the Tuskegee Institute and he hoped to meet him. However, Washington died before that was possible. A charismatic figure who spoke and wrote eloquently, Garvey was one of the most inspiring and determined "race men." Although not a religious leader, Garvey nevertheless inspired a religious-like fervor among some adherents; people were enthused to find a leader who was genuinely and single-mindedly devoted to the interests of African humanity. He was affectionately called the "Negro Moses" by his followers, and he mainly appealed to working-class and poor Blacks. He attracted many followers in New York, and they helped to build the largest nonreligious mass movement of Blacks in history, which eventually spread throughout the Americas, Europe, and Africa. Garvey was one of the first to formulate self-determined programs in an attempt to address the challenges facing African humanity on a global scale. Like Henry Highland Garnet and others who over half a century earlier had advocated a program of emigration to Africa and Henry McNeil Turner after him, Garvey also advocated emigration for Blacks away from their oppressors and a "back to Africa" movement in which those who had knowledge and skills would return to the Motherland in order to help secure its liberty from colonialism and assist with Africa's development. Garvey's step onto the stage of history at the turn of the century was dramatic not only because of his flair for theatrical displays and his promotion of an uncompromising doctrine of racial uplift but also because of who he was not. Garvey did not have the university training of DuBois and he lacked an esteemed family background. And not insignificantly, he neglected to exhibit anything close to the preferred skin tone of the social elite. A man black in color as well as in consciousness asserting himself unapologetically as a leader of his people, and refusing deference to those who had presumed themselves to be his social betters, was a proposition of shocking audaciousness in an era of openly proclaimed White superiority. Garvey shattered a debilitating psychological image of Black people as he defiantly challenged social mores of that day. His grand parades and conventions, along with his inspirational literature and speeches, evoked a spirited response from the masses to the prospect of autonomous racial development. And as such, the Garveyite movement was infuriating to the elites, White and Black. In the end, Garvey's sometimes hastily conceived programs were easily foiled by conmen and government agents. He was deported from the United States on trumped up charges, but his ability to galvanize large numbers of Black people did not go unnoticed. In posture and style if not also in ideology, Garvey's leadership anticipated the later rise to prominence of other Black men without the approved credentials, including the leaders of the Nation of Islam, various anticolonial African-liberation movements' leaders, and many of the grass roots leaders in the Civil Rights and Black Power movements.[51]

The social conditions and racial milieu of the 1920s and 1930s helped give birth to Father Divine's Peace Mission. Father Divine was born as George Baker (1880–1965) on Hutchinson Island on the Savannah River in Georgia. He migrated to Baltimore in 1899, where he worked as a yard man and preached whenever the opportunity presented itself. In 1914, Baker and a few of his disciples returned to his home state of Georgia. After arriving in Valdosta, Baker bestowed divinity upon himself and claimed to be God. Baker was a street preacher and he was charged with being a public menace because of the clamor made during his preaching. In order to avoid commitment to a state mental hospital, Father Divine and his disciples returned to the North and settled in New York City. He started his own church and married one of his followers, Penniniah. Divine's peace missions were appealing to many Blacks because of his ability to accumulate wealth and his courage to speak his mind to those in power. By and large, Blacks continued to find themselves mistreated and degraded, and they were impressed with anyone who could "beat the system." He also endeared himself to the masses by providing shelter for the homeless and free meals for the poor. Also, a few wealthy Whites came under his influence, as they were impressed by his preaching, and they joined his congregation, becoming generous contributors. He also recruited Blacks from Harlem to work for rich Whites in Long Island.[52]

In 1930, Baker changed his name to Father Divine and there was an incident in which his mystical powers were apparently vindicated. Father Divine and some of his followers were arrested and imprisoned for disorderly conduct. Four days later in the midst of the trial proceedings, the court judge dropped dead of a heart attack. When told of the incident, Father Divine said from his jail cell, "I hated to do it." After he was released from prison, Divine received a hero's welcome at Rockland Palace in Harlem. Harlem was ripe for a new messiah, because the Great Depression left the Black masses without jobs or much hope. Black churches had largely adopted the disposition of social clubs with little outreach, insufficient moral courage to address social injustices, and no prophetic vision.[53]

Charles Manuel "Sweet Daddy" Grace (1881–1960) had an appeal similar to that of Father Divine. Grace was born on Cape Verde Island to a Black mother and a Portuguese father. Daddy Grace, as he was called, was no less charismatic than Father Divine, and he was even more flamboyant in his appearance and mannerisms. Grace migrated to New Bedford, Massachusetts, where he held odd jobs as a cook, a dishwasher, and a machine salesman. In New Bedford, he became a spiritual icon and founded the House of Prayer for All People in 1921. He was able to effectively address the spiritual and physical needs of his devotees. He provided for the needs of the poor and impressed many in the middle class with entrepreneurial ventures like the selling of Daddy Grace lotion, toothpaste, and hair products. Daddy Grace augmented his claim to divine status by telling his followers that he possessed the love of God and that God gave him His attributes so that God could take a much needed vacation.[54]

The charismatic leaders such as Daddy Grace and Father Divine, as well as most mainline churches, failed to address the injustices of a racist society and the need for racial solidarity and resistance in the face of the spiritual and cultural holocausts to which African Americans had been subjected. To step into this gap, there emerged race-based movements, including the Moorish Science Temple, the Garveyite Movement and the Nation of Islam.

In 1930, W.D. Fard appeared in Detroit peddling silk and African arts and raincoats. He also spoke publicly, praising the religion of Islam and demonizing Christianity. As Fard peddled from house to house, he also lectured to the people about not eating pork and warned Blacks against trusting in the "blue-eyed devils." Many Blacks in Detroit were impressed with Fard's message and his fearlessness. They were attracted to the anti-White message in particular because the behavior of most Whites they knew seemed to fit the description. Elijah Muhammad (1897–1975), who earlier had been associated with Garvey's movement, joined with Fard and carried his work on after Fard mysteriously disappeared. Elijah built a small following that would eventually receive worldwide attention after the emergence of Malcom X. Malcom X (El-Hajj Malik El-Shabazz) was one of the most forceful and brilliant orators of the twentieth century. His fiery rhetoric helped to give Blacks of the 1960s a greater sense of their own capacity to courageously confront the difficulties they faced.[55]

During the period of the Great Migrations, F.S. Cherry, sometime before World War I, founded the Church of the Living God, the Pillar of Truth for All Nations (Black Hebrews), and Timothy Drew founded the Moorish Science Temple of America. Drew later changed his name to Noble Drew Ali. He maintained that Blacks would not find deliverance until they discovered their original name. He taught those who embraced his teachings that African Americans should be called Asiatic or Moors. His converts built temples in Pittsburg, Detroit, Chicago, and in the South. His followers praised their spiritual leader for delivering them from the curse of European domination. After leaving the Deep South, Cherry traveled all over the world as a seaman. The global exposure enabled Cherry to read and speak Hebrew. He modeled his teachings after the Old Testament and Judaism. The devotees who embraced his movement were called Black Jews. Cherry admonished his followers not to eat pork and to adhere to the Jewish dietary restrictions. He had nothing positive to say about mainline churches and Black preachers, even going so far as to label preachers "damn fools, wild beasts, vultures." He consistently taught that Jesus was Black and frequently at his worship services he would pull out an image depicting a White Jesus, show it to those gathered and shout, "Who in the hell is this?" The crowd would respond, "Jesus." And he would reply, "That's a damn lie!"[56]

The radical movements outside of the religious mainstream grew as racial tensions flared in northern cities. These movements flourished as they served needs and spoke to aspirations that were not being met by the established churches. No aspect of the African-American experience can be completely disassociated from Black Nationalism. Black Nationalism is the principle that holds that African Americans must strive to build and maintain a "nation within a nation"—their own religious institutions, businesses, and civil organizations that promote the interests and welfare of Black communities, if they are to survive and prosper. Black preachers and religious leaders have consistently advocated various forms of Black Nationalism from the time of Richard Allen's Free African Society in Philadelphia to the latest efforts in various churches to form credit unions, build senior citizens' homes, and open community centers. Prominent proponents of Black Nationalism included the Anglican minister Alexander Crummell, and the Presbyterian pastor Henry Highland Garnett, along with Bishop Henry McNeal Turner. Turner was the first prominent African-American religious leader on record to openly support the concept of a Black God. [57]

THE RISE OF GRASSROOTS PROTESTS LEADING TO THE *BROWN V. BOARD OF EDUCATION* SUPREME COURT DECISION

The Supreme Court abolished segregation and by inference racial sub-jugation in public schools almost one hundred years after the Civil War had been fought ending slavery. The decision paved the way for a more complete legal emancipation of African Americans. The *Brown v. Board of Education* decision was authored by Earl Warren, the recently appointed Chief Justice, and it declared the doctrine of separate but equal to be unconstitutional. The decision also helped to set the stage for further pro-tests and push for civil rights, including the Montgomery Bus Boycott. The Montgomery Bus Boycott and the Great Migrations would prove to be the key events in inspiring the movements for Civil Rights and greater Black participation in the political and economic institutions of the nation.[58]

The NAACP provided the most significant legal expertise in the struggle against "separate but equal." The role of prominent leaders in the NAACP has been celebrated and well publicized. Much less appreciated is the considerable contribution of Black ministers and churches to the suc-cess of the case. In fact, it was the efforts of Black ministers that initiated the protests and grassroots struggles against Jim Crow, which would even-tually lead to court challenges and the *Brown* decision. While lawyers and public spokesmen grabbed the headlines and the attention, it was left to a few courageous and unheralded people to face the most intense assaults and indignities of the system of oppression. It is seldom recognized that the person who initiated the protests that culminated in the *Brown* deci-sion was an A.M.E. minister and school teacher, the Reverend Joseph A. DeLaine of Summerton, South Carolina.[59]

While the lore and legend of the NAACP emphasizes names such as W.E.B. DuBois, William English Walling, William Monroe Trotter, Joel Elias Spingarn (who turned out to be a traitorous government spy), Thurgood Marshall, and others, it was actually local leaders and especially ministers who made the efforts of that organization substantive. In local communities, on the grassroots level, the efforts toward civil rights often came from Black ministers and their churches, some of whom were also associated with the NAACP. In addition to providing much of the local leadership, the churches also served as the locations for branch meetings and places to galvanize public support for various efforts. In many communities the NAACP became synonymous with local churches and their pastors.[60]

During the summer of 1947 DeLaine attended a mid-day chapel service where he heard the Reverend James M. Hinton, who both managed the Black-owned Pilgrim Health and Life Insurance Company and served as president of the local NAACP chapter. Hinton was uncompromising in speaking out against racial injustices, and he inspired many people, including DeLaine.[61]

After hearing Hinton's sermon, a fire was ignited in DeLaine, and he was spurred to take action. Hinton's address radically altered DeLaine's perception of the role of the church in society. In his chapel message, Hinton focused on the power of education as a catalyst for change to liberate Blacks from the iron hand of oppression. He accused White South Carolinians of opposing the education of Blacks because they knew that education was the key to better jobs, more opportunities, and a higher quality of life. Hinton challenged the faculty and student body by denouncing the public schools provided for Blacks as a disgrace, with their leaking roofs and coal stoves that would engulf whole rooms in smoke. He also pointed out that while there were no school buses for Blacks, Whites could expect transportation to and from school. He called the disparity in teacher salaries between White teachers and Black teachers criminal.

This thought-provoking message resonated with DeLaine. Hinton's chapel talk had ignited a drive to pursue freedom for his people that would remain with him for the rest of his life. When DeLaine returned to the Pine Grove Circuit, where he was pastor, he returned to his wife and two children as a changed man. The Black community in that area was located near the Santee River, and there was seasonal flooding in which the roads to the Negro schools were often flooded out. As a result, the Black children sometimes had to travel to school in row boats and many were discouraged from attempting to go at all. Reverend DeLaine and Pastor Richburg, another local A.M.E. pastor, decided to take leadership in addressing the flooding problem. The ministers and some of their members requested a meeting with the local school superintendent to air their grievances. After the meeting, the response of the school officials was not encouraging, but DeLaine and his cohorts were determined, so they wrote a petition to the state superintendant of schools in Columbia, South Carolina. The state officials refused to hear the case, claiming that it was a local matter to be decided by local officials. Undaunted, Reverend DeLaine then wrote to the Attorney General of the United States in an effort to seek redress for his community. The response from the federal level was the same as that of the state officials and the Attorney General considered that the matter was to be handled by local officials.[62]

After exhausting his appeals to government officials, DeLaine turned to Reverend Hinton for further advice. Hinton had wanted to launch a court case against public school systems on the grounds that they were using taxpayers' money—all taxpayers Black and White—in order to provide adequate transportation for White children only. DeLaine arranged to meet with Hinton and a young Howard University–trained civil rights attorney, Harold R. Boulware. DeLaine had recruited as plaintiff, Levi Pearson, a highly-regarded farmer, who had three children attending Scott's Branch High School. The prospective plaintiff had a reputation for being courageous in the face of injustice and mistreatment. On behalf of the plaintiff, Boulware filed charges against the Clarendon County school board, claiming that the three children of Levi Pearson were discriminated against, as they were not provided with equal access to transportation and they were refused the same services as White children.[63]

Although Boulware delivered legal petitions to both the local school board and the state board of education, the White school officials responded with their characteristic disregard for the concerns of Blacks. Months passed and there was no response to the petition. The plaintiffs soon realized that they were in for a long and arduous fight against an obstinate foe. It was the churches that served as bases of strength and encouragement for the prolonged struggle. On March 16, 1948, Boulware filed a suit in the United States District Court against the local school board for refusing to provide transportation thereby causing the plaintiffs' children to suffer irreparable harm. Also, the suit asked the courts to issue a permanent injunction "forever restraining and enjoining the defendants …

The Reverend J. A. DeLaine, Sr. (1898–1974)

from making a distinction on account of race or color" in providing bus service to school children.[64]

Reverend DeLaine and other ministers mobilized and informed the community to remain vigilant in the support of the children. It was the Black preachers who rallied the people to the cause, and the response of the people inspired a sense that they could ultimately win. However, the opposition was also determined to continue their regime of discrimination. Scoundrels when faced with their misdeeds inevitably turn to violence, as they have no claim to reason, and predictably that was the case in Clarendon, South Carolina.[65]

The Clarendon school case had excited the Blacks and infuriated the Whites of South Carolina. Reverend DeLaine was fired from his teaching job and he faced constant threats of bodily harm. A few days before the case was to be heard in district court, the plaintiffs were informed that their property was not located in the school district where his children were attending school so the case was disqualified on a technicality. After the Pearson case was thwarted, DeLaine lamented, "I think that's when my hair turned white." What was disappointing to the Blacks was greeted with elation by the Whites. Some expressed their jubilation by proclaiming that, "our niggers don't even know where they live."[66]

In March of 1949, DeLaine called for a strategy meeting in Columbia, South Carolina, along with top state officials of the NAACP and the leading legal strategist, Thurgood Marshall. Marshall advised DeLaine and his supporters to expand the plaintiffs to twenty and to broaden their grievances by asking not only for equal treatment with bus transportation but in everything else as well: equal buses, equal teachers' salaries, equal student-teacher ratios, equal school supplies, and equal facilities. Reverend Hinton had challenged DeLaine to find a single plaintiff; now Marshall was sending him back to find twenty qualified and courageous plaintiffs. Their minds set on a just cause, DeLaine and his followers eagerly went out to complete the task.[67]

Reverend DeLaine along with the Reverend J. A. Seals returned to Clarendon and immediately organized a series of mass meetings around the county in various churches. These mass meetings, along with others held around the country in various communities at different times were critical to the success of the civil rights struggle. These gatherings energized, inspired, and electrified the crowds while sharing important information needed to support the struggle. At one mass meeting, Reverend DeLaine mounted the pulpit to exhort the people saying, "My mind is made up and there is no turning back. There is a fire here and no amount of water is gonna put it out." The Clarendon County movement attracted support from other communities from surrounding states as they sought to take up the cause of liberation.[68]

It was through the mass meetings, usually held at Black churches, that parents were recruited to become plaintiffs. The Whites threatened the Blacks with loss of jobs if they signed up to become plaintiffs or if they became involved in the movement. This made many parents hesitant and fearful. They rightly understood that they would face reprisals from the Whites upon whom many of them depended for jobs and housing. And there were also stooges among the Blacks who would inform the Whites about the mobilizations and organization efforts within the community. The Whites put the word out that whoever signed up to be a plaintiff would become a "homeless hero." Nevertheless, after eight long months of visiting parents, conducting mass meetings, and saying fervent prayers, DeLaine had twenty plaintiffs to report back to Thurgood Marshall.

Twenty courageous Black parents put their livelihoods and lives on the line by signing up to petition the United States government for equal educational opportunities for their sons and daughters. Their stand for justice was buttressed by the Black community and their churches.[69]

The class action suit was listed under the name of Harry Briggs, the first name of the plaintiffs by alphabetical order. Briggs was respected in the community as a hard-working man from a reputable family. He was 34 years old and had five children. He was the unpretentious son of a sharecropper. Except for the time he spent in the United States Navy, Briggs had spent his entire life in Summerton. He had been employed for 14 years at the town's only service station. He was the handy man who pumped gas, lubricated engines, and repaired tires. He also was one of the best-informed persons regarding local issues in town, as most everyone, Black and White, sooner or later came through the service station. He consistently made his family a priority in his decision-making. Prior to his involvement in the suit he had obtained a small loan from the Summerton Bank, which he used to buy a small plot of land from Reverend DeLaine near the Scott's Branch School. He built his home near the school so that his children would be in walking distance. Briggs's strong character and solid reputation emboldened other parents to sign up as plaintiffs for the law suit.

The community leaders and pastors made the petitioners aware of the consequences of the decision they were making. Briggs anticipated that he and his family would be the object of the anger and hatred from some in the White community. After it became public that Briggs had signed the petition, his boss and other Whites in town began to pressure him to remove his name. The Whites accused the Black ministers of misleading the petitioners. When Briggs was asked if he knew what he was doing, he responded with a resounding, "Yes, I'm doing it for my children." Shortly before Christmas, Briggs's longtime employer gave him a carton of cigarettes and told him, "Harry, I want me a boy and I can pay him less." By signing the petition and refusing to back down when pressured, Briggs was exercising his manhood, always a risky proposition for Black men in America. The demonstration of Black manhood was an anathema to White Southerners, and Black men who did so became prime candidates for losing their jobs, their homes and sometimes their lives.

Briggs's decision also impacted his family. Briggs's wife was a chambermaid at the local motel and her employer asked her to persuade her husband to remove his name from the petition. In response to her employer, she said that her husband was old enough to have a mind of his own and that she was not going to tell him otherwise. The Briggs family, like many others, never wavered or second-guessed the merit of their cause: "We figured anything to better the children's condition was worth it." Those plaintiffs who suffered economic hardships as a result of reprisals were supported by the churches and community with financial assistance. The entire community banded together as a mutual aid society, as there was the realization that whatever happened to the plaintiffs affected them all.[70]

Although the White community leaders accused Reverend DeLaine of being a troublemaker and rabble-rouser, the Blacks were not deceived. The religious leaders in the Black community had taken care to articulate the rationale for their cause, and they laid out a case that addressed the real needs and concerns of the people. The churches were the principal instruments for keeping people informed and motivated. Reverend Richburg exhorted his followers to never give up: "You're just like mules. You don't know your own strength." The ministers threatened to expand the protest with a boycott of the White businesses in town.[71]

Those ministers who became involved in rallying and organizing the community did so at risk to themselves and often with little outside support. DeLaine had a reputation of being agreeable and easy to get along with and community activism seemed out of character for him. Nevertheless, he grew into the role and resolved to see this fight through to the end. An open letter that DeLaine composed and circulated within the community is representative of the rhetoric and illustrations used to make the case to the people:

> Is this the price free men must pay in a free country for wanting their children trained as capable and respectable American citizens?... Shouldn't officials employ the dignity, foresight, and intelligence in at least, the honest effort to correct outstanding evil?... Is it a credit for Summerton to wear the name of (?) persecuting segments of its citizens? Shall we suffer endless persecution just because we want our children

raised in a wholesome atmosphere? What some of us have suffered is nothing short of Nazi persecution.[72]

Reverend DeLaine's involvement expanded his view of the nature and mission of the church. He recognized that the church is responsible for the community beyond the walls of the church building. He also recognized the liberation potential inherent in Black churches.

The more he became engaged in the community, the more he saw the church as an agent of progressive social change and reform. African-American churches have a history that pre-dates legalized family life for African Americans. These churches provided the first and most significant sense of community solidarity, social uplift and political and educational opportunity. At the time of Reverend DeLaine's ministry, pastors were still highly regarded in most African-American communities. Yet, it must also be noted that the leadership of DeLaine and other ministers involved in the Clarendon movement was exceptional. Most Black religious leaders were conservative and cautious to a fault. They were eager to retain a status of prominence in the community, but they were timid in the face of injustices perpetrated by the White establishment.

The conversion of DeLaine to the cause of social justice required both faith and courage on his part, but it was also in keeping with a longstanding tradition in Black churches. Reverend Hinton's challenge at the Allen University chapel became his Damascus Road experience. DeLaine made his sermon preparations a priority. He sought to make his interpretations of scripture relevant and applicable to what people were experiencing in their everyday lives. He literally believed that faith without works is dead. Also, the time was right and the community was prepared for a change. The people had just gone through the Depression and World War II. Black men who had been drafted into the military had become exposed to various nations and peoples in which they found themselves treated better than they were in their homeland. They also found that they could fight for freedoms abroad that they were denied at home.

The price of standing against injustice can be costly indeed.[73] DeLaine reinforced his rhetoric with action and thus raised the ire of the White establishment. His wife and both of his sisters lost their teaching jobs because of his stand. He was sued for libel and denied credit by the local bank. And his home was burned to the ground while the local firemen stood by watching as though they were at a campfire. In Lake City, South Carolina, DeLaine's church was burned to the ground. The persecution continued when on the night of October 10, 1955, the DeLaine family was awakened by gunshots being fired into their home. In an effort to defend his family, the preacher took up arms and fired back. He then fled with his family driving at top speed over country roads until they reached North Carolina. Another one of his churches was burned down soon afterward. In addition, he was charged with felonious assault with a deadly weapon for firing back at those who had attacked his family. The state of South Carolina issued a warrant for his arrest and extradition to be returned to the state. He became a fugitive from White injustice and fled to New York. The events of Clarendon came to the attention of Brooklyn Dodger stars Jackie Robinson and Roy Campanella. They sent letters to the governor of New York urging him not to sign letters of extradition returning DeLaine to South Carolina. The baseball greats used their celebrity to expose the persecution of DeLaine.[74]

The long struggle taught Reverend DeLaine that the *Brown* decision would not be a panacea for the deep-seated racial issues affecting American society. DeLaine and the people of Clarendon County started a struggle against unjust treatment and for more access to resources and opportunities for their children. The fight was changed by the elites, namely Thurgood Marshall and the national leadership of the NAACP, into a fight for integration which translated into more privileges in the dominant institutions for themselves, and this was not the original intent of the local activists who initiated the struggle.[75] The Supreme Court decision did not change the attitudes of White racists toward Blacks. On the local level Whites continued to make the law, interpret the law, and enforce the law as they saw fit. The Clarendon County school case had helped to bring down the regime of legalized segregation in public schools but 20 years later, the strict separation of the races remained as entrenched as ever. Most White parents sent their children to private schools rather than to public schools with Black children. In 1967, the Clarendon County public schools had an enrollment of over three thousand with just one student being White. The

Brown decision, which proclaimed that racial segregation was unlawful and unconstitutional, did little to actually end racial discrimination. But, the decision did help to invigorate a whole new phase of the Civil Rights Movement. This movement would encounter reluctant clerks at voter registration offices, gun-toting drivers enforcing segregation on buses, and thuggish local policemen. By the thousands, civil rights foot soldiers would challenge segregation throughout the South, risking life and limb. The struggle moved from the courts to the streets, and again the Black church would play a central role in the movement toward justice.

Chapter 6 – The Struggle in the Wilderness

DISCUSSION & REVIEW QUESTIONS

1. What were the factors that led to the Great Migrations? How did the Great Migrations change the outlook of African Americans?

2. How did the Plessy decision change the outlook and efforts of the Black elites?

3. What factors led to Black ministers becoming leaders in the Civil Rights Movement?

4. Describe Reverend DeLaine's struggle and its importance in the school desegregation fight.

CHAPTER 7

The Civil Rights Movement as an Outgrowth of the Black Church

THE MONTGOMERY BUS BOYCOTT—THE EMPOWERMENT OF A MOVEMENT AND THE COMING OF A LEADER

It has been observed that much like John the Baptist, who was the forerunner to prepare the way for Christ, the Reverend Vernon Johns, predecessor of Martin Luther King, Jr. at Dexter Avenue Baptist Church, made a powerful impact that helped to prepare the stage for his successor. Johns may not have eaten locusts and wild honey, but his style, much like John the Baptist's demeanor, was quite unorthodox. At the age of three, Vernon Johns began declaring the gospel while standing on a stump in his native home of Prince Edward County, Virginia. At the age of seven Johns was kicked in the face by a mule. The injury scarred his left cheek, damaged his eyesight, and left him with an eyelid twitch for the rest of his life. He learned to compensate for this infirmity by committing scripture and sermons to memory.[1]

King and his predecessor Johns were both the sons of families with long traditions of producing Baptist preachers. Also, they had both received formal theological training for the ministry. Johns was educated at Virginia Union, Oberlin, and Virginia Seminary in Lynchburg. Prior to accepting the call to the Dexter Avenue Baptist Church, he had served as the pastor of historic churches in Lynchburg and Charleston, West Virginia. By the time he arrived at Dexter Avenue Baptist Church, Vernon Johns was a nationally acclaimed preacher. He was the first African American to have a sermon appear in *Best Sermons*, an annual volume of sermons featuring homilies delivered by some of America's most eloquent

preachers. Although he was widely respected for delivering powerful sermons, as a pastor Vernon's leadership style was brusque and heavy-handed.
His oratorical skills earned him the opportunity to serve at several premier
historical churches. However, his mannerisms and behavior outside the
pulpit sometimes shocked and unsettled the congregations. Thus most of
his appointments to churches were tenures of short duration.[2]

Dexter Avenue Baptist Church had a membership composed mostly
of the social elites in the Montgomery Black community. Church members included college professors, successful lawyers, businessmen, and
high-profile community leaders. Johns, however, gave little attention to
elitist social sensibilities. Reverend Johns embarrassed the refined and
dignified church members of Dexter by dressing in farmer overalls while
going about selling watermelons and collard greens from the back of a
pickup. He further antagonized the local White establishment by protesting discrimination on the city buses. Johns would board the buses and then
encourage the Blacks who had gotten on to walk off. He upset both the
Black elites and the White authorities by preaching sermons with such
topics as "It's Safe to Murder Negroes in Montgomery," "Money Answers
All Things," and "When the Rapist Is White." After a few years Johns had
more detractors than supporters at his church. The church trustees cut off
the utilities to the parsonage where he lived in order to drive him out. They
then voted to oust him from the church, and in doing so they paved the
way for Martin Luther King, Jr.[3]

When Dr. Martin Luther King, Jr., came to Montgomery, Alabama,
to assume the pastorate of the Dexter Avenue Baptist Church, he did not
come with an intention or preconceived notion to start or lead a movement
for social justice. He did possess several outstanding qualities, including
high scholastic achievement, a powerful baritone speaking voice and a
family legacy of producing significant preachers, including his grandfather and father. But, his background was safely middle class and there
was nothing to suggest that he might risk life and limb on behalf of the
masses of Black people. He got caught up by the zeitgeist, or spirit of the
moment, and that spirit transformed him into a leader and provided him
with a leadership platform that the people most needed at the time of his
arrival. The decisive moment of history was on his side. The same month

and year that King arrived in Montgomery, the United States Supreme Court handed down the widely heralded school desegregation decision in *Brown v. Board of Education*. The civil rights struggle sought to obtain the rights of citizenship for African Americans already guaranteed by the fourteenth Amendment to the U.S. Constitution but which were inconsistently recognized and often disregarded in practice. This struggle began with the collapse of Black Reconstruction and the imposition of Jim Crow and a White supremacy regime in the South. African Americans protested and resisted in numerous ways, from writing letters to filing lawsuits to appealing for federal protection to just getting up and leaving the South. In Martin Luther King, Jr., the movement found a leader with the courage, determination, and formal training to make him a most capable representative of the cause before the national leaders, before international audiences, and on the streets of the Jim Crow south before the people who made it all happen.[4]

The Brown decision invigorated the movement toward justice, as it was at least a hopeful sign that after the many long years of heartache and hardship there was finally going to be some sense of justice for African Americans. It was symbolically a repudiation of the infamous *Plessy* decision which had been the signal to White racists that it was constitutionally acceptable to crush the hopes of Blacks for social equality. Of course the *Brown* decision did not result simply because of the judicious insights of the nine Supreme Court Justices; the decision came after many years of struggle and hardship with many setbacks. After more than two centuries of slavery, the abortion of Black Reconstruction and more than fifty years of legalized segregation and open discrimination against Blacks, African Americans were once again hopeful that their change had finally come and that American justice, freedom, and equality would become more than just words on a piece of paper.

But what Blacks saw as a beacon of hope, most White Southerners viewed with contempt, and they considered the decision to be an omen of regional catastrophe should the *Brown* decision actually be enacted. There was still deep hostility for any notion of Blacks entering the exclusive social realms of White privilege, prestige, and power. Southern Whites from cities as large as Atlanta to those as small as Cowpens, South Carolina, denounced the sweeping ruling that would put Black and White children together in the same public classrooms. From Virginia to Texas, Whites mobilized to organize opposition and in every way possible impede implementation of the decision. In the immediate aftermath of the announcement of the Supreme Court's ruling, crosses, homes, and churches were burned in those places inhabited by Blacks.

King arrived in Montgomery on the eve of the brutal murder of Emmitt Till in Mississippi. Emmett Till was just 14 years old when he traveled south from Chicago to visit relatives in Greenwood, Mississippi. The mutilated body of Till had been badly beaten and tossed into a lake with a 70 pound cotton gin tied around the neck by barbed wire. This dastardly act was carried out by three bloodthirsty White men on one sweltering summer night in August. The Klansmen brutalized the boy because they had heard a rumor that he dared to whistle at a White woman. The men were brought to trial but set free. One sympathizer at the trial commented, "Why all the fuss over a dead nigger?" Mamie Till, Emmett Till's mother, had the courage and wisdom to bring the body of Till back to Chicago, where she insisted on an open-casket funeral for her son. She wanted the whole world to witness what had been done to her son, to see what southern "justice" looked like. The ghastly sight of Till's disfigured body evoked a sense of outrage and indignation among African Americans across the nation. In a sense, Till's murder became a sacrifice, the shedding of an innocent child's blood, that spurred the movement onward. Rosa Parks would cite the murder of Emmett Till as one of the motivating factors for her courageous act that fateful day when she set off the Montgomery Bus Boycott.[5]

As White opposition to the *Brown* decision escalated, some of the Black leaders in Montgomery viewed the situation with some optimism, as they were well prepared for action. It was not Martin Luther King, Jr., who set up the organizational structures, acclimated the minds of the people to the need for resistance, or designed the tactics necessary for a successful boycott; those things had already been prepared by others.

Mrs. Jo Ann Robinson was a community activist who had moved to Montgomery a few years earlier to teach English at the Alabama State College. Immediately after arriving in the community, she joined the Women's Political Council (WPC). Like King, upon arriving in Montgomery, Mrs. Robinson immediately took up the struggle for justice. In 1949 she had an incident on a city bus in Montgomery as she was en route to the airport to visit relatives in Cleveland, Ohio. She sat toward the front of the bus, but she was taken aback when the driver angrily ordered her to the rear. Mrs. Robinson was then convinced to put the problem of segregated buses on the agenda of the WPC. Upon returning to Montgomery, she promptly called a meeting of the WPC to address the segregation policy on city buses. She quickly discovered that her encounter with the bus driver was not an isolated incident, as many Black women had experienced similar humiliating experiences. This mistreatment of Blacks, and particularly the women, was an egregious affront to many, but the Black leadership, including the well-educated elite and the church ministers, mostly looked the other way. Nevertheless, at this time Robinson and other Black leaders began contemplating, discussing, and planning a citywide bus boycott.[6]

Four days after the Brown decision was announced, Mrs. Robinson sent a letter to the mayor, insisting that the bus situation be improved. She reminded the White city officials that Blacks constituted the majority ridership of their buses. There was already widespread sentiment in the community that something needed to be done about the degrading treatment on the buses. But, Mrs. Robinson's threat of a boycott was not supported by a unified front of Black community leaders. There was only a small cadre of progressive leaders who consistently supported taking legal action. On March 2, 1955, an incident occurred that agitated the festering wound of racist humiliation and galvanized the sentiment in the community. A 15-year-old high school student, Claudette Colvin, refused to give up her seat to allow a newly boarding White passenger to be seated. A police officer dragged Colvin from the bus. Word of this incident quickly spread throughout the Black neighborhoods.[7]

Robinson and several other community leaders thought that this was the incident needed to finally move toward an all-out protest against the city bus company. However, this was not to be. The move toward freedom was thwarted by Colvin's supposed imperfections and by a lack of nerve among Black leaders in Montgomery. Colvin had been charged not only with violating the city ordinance regarding bus seating and the state law upholding segregation, but also with resisting arrest and assault and battery. Then rumors began to spread in the Black community that the teenager was two or three months pregnant. She was unmarried, and unwed mothers in the heart of the sanctimonious Bible Belt were looked upon with great disdain at that time. Many of the Black leaders saw this as their chance to stay on the stool of do-nothing, and they declared that she was an unacceptable litigant for a civil rights test case.[8]

A few months prior to Dr. King's arrival in Montgomery, the Reverend T. J. Jemison, pastor of the Mount Zion First Baptist Church in Baton Rouge, had initiated a mass boycott against segregated buses in that city. In June of 1953, Jemison and several of his ministerial cohorts took to the airways and appealed to the Blacks of the city to refrain from riding the segregated buses. Rev. Jemison reported that the boycott was 100 percent effective. There were a few people who did not get the message and rode to work on the buses the next morning. But, by that afternoon not a single Black passenger could be spotted on any bus. "Nobody rode the bus during our strike. There were about eight people who didn't hear the call that night [on the radio] and they rode to work. But, in the afternoon there was nobody riding the bus. For ten days not a Negro rode the bus."[9] Nothing breeds success like success, and it was the success of the Baton Rouge Bus Boycott that spurred other protests against segregation across the South, including in Montgomery. Both King and the Reverend Ralph D. Abernathy, who would join with him in the Montgomery movement, were well aware of the successful Baton Rouge effort, and they sought the advice and counsel of Reverend Jemison.

After completing his graduate studies at Boston University, King decided to return to the South in order to initiate his professional career. In response to the world-shaking *Brown* decree, King thought it was, "an auspicious time to be going home to the South, a time when good things seem to happen there." When Dr. King came to Montgomery, Blacks in that city and throughout the South were already mobilizing and organizing against segregation. The *Brown* decision had precipitated a season of contention and intensified underlying tensions that had always been just beneath the surface. The Blacks were reacting with renewed hope, pressing toward social justice, while the Whites reacted mostly with resentment and defiance. By the spring of 1955, a deep unrest was smoldering in the Black community of Montgomery, Alabama.[10]

The city buses of Montgomery proved to be an excellent target for the efforts to bring down segregation for several reasons, including: (1) Blacks were the majority ridership, about 75 percent of the total, and providing most of the operating revenue, they could financially cripple the bus company if they acted in concert; (2) almost everyone in the Black community rode the buses sooner or later, so that situation was familiar to all; and, (3) desegregation of city buses had already been accomplished in Baton Rouge, so this was not something outside of the realm of conceivability or possibility.[11] The situation was rife with abuses and begging for a change. All of the drivers for the city buses were White men, many of whom clearly had no respect or regard for their Black riders. Some of these drivers made a habit of going out of their way to be insulting and demeaning. They would call people apes, black cows, and niggers. And Black women were often singled out for such mistreatment. The experience of riding a bus in Montgomery was dehumanizing and degrading for all Blacks from the beginning of the journey to the end. Blacks were required to pay the bus fare at the front of the bus, and then to get off the bus in order to reboard through the back door. It was not unusual for drivers to intentionally drive off before a passenger could get to the back door and reboard. Once a Black rider succeeded in getting on the bus, the degrading treatment continued, as they were prohibited from sitting in the first four rows, which were reserved for Whites as indicated by a "Whites Only" sign. If more Whites entered the bus than could be accommodated in the first four seats, Blacks were required to relinquish their seats to White passengers as they moved further back, or if there were no more seats, they would simply have to stand. If the situation was such that the Black passenger found the unreserved seats (Black section) full and the reserved seats (White section) empty, she would still have to stand in the aisle, gazing at the empty seats in the front of the bus. A Montgomery city ordinance enforced the seating policy and those who violated the ordinance faced fines or jail.[12]

The unjust law had been sporadically tested, and Blacks in pool halls, barber shops, beauty salons, churches, and social clubs had often discussed the idea of a massive citywide bus boycott. It was on Friday morning, December 2, 1954, that Dr. King received a call from community activist Edgar Daniel Nixon (1899–1987). Nixon exclaimed, "We got it. We got our case!" E.D. Nixon was one of the most respected leaders of the Black community of Montgomery. He held an office in the A. Philip Randolph Brotherhood of Sleeping Car Porters, and he was also a prominent figure in the local and state branches of the NAACP. Nixon had long considered ways in which Blacks might counter their mistreatment on Montgomery city buses. He realized that segregation on the buses was one of the most visible examples of racial degradation in the city, and he actively looked for incidents through which the legality of the city ordinance could be challenged. With great excitement Nixon recounted to Dr. King what had just happened to Rosa Parks.[13]

Parks was a tailor's assistant in a downtown department store, and after leaving work, she boarded the city bus at the court square and took a seat behind the section reserved for Whites. When the bus filled to capacity, the driver ordered Parks to stand so that a White man could be seated. Mrs. Parks refused and she explained that her feet were tired and hurting. The driver threatened to call the police. "Go ahead and call them," she replied. "Let the cops come; I'm not moving."[14]

Two police officers took Rosa Parks down to the police station, where she was booked for violating the city ordinance. She made a phone call to Nixon and he immediately went to the police station and posted her bond. When Nixon learned of the official charges against Parks, he was beside himself. "We can go all the way to the Supreme Court with this." And surely Black Montgomery would rally behind Mrs. Parks, for she was an outstanding citizen. She was known for her honesty and integrity. She was well-respected in the community and she served as the secretary for the local branch of the NAACP.[15]

In some sense King was lured into the movement by Nixon, who needed assistance in launching a massive citywide boycott of the buses and he knew that the key to mobilizing the community was through the churches with the aid of sympathetic ministers. In their conversation, Nixon suggested that the organizing meeting for the protest be held at King's church, to which King agreed. Some seventy leaders assembled in the basement of the Dexter Avenue Baptist Church. The Reverend Ray L. Bennett, president of the Interdenominational Alliance, was selected to preside over the meeting. However, Bennett had a domineering and truculent approach toward the other leaders, which prompted many of them to get up and leave the meeting early. The situation deteriorated to the point that the Reverend Ralph David Abernathy had to take charge of the meeting. And Abernathy is credited with saving the day. Abernathy had a more affable personality and a good sense of humor. He had a natural gift for diffusing contentious situations, which would turn out to be a great asset in the days to come. Abernathy quickly became one of Dr. King's closest friends and confidants.[16]

After Abernathy took the floor to address the gathering, he insisted that all the people present have an opportunity to speak and give their perspectives. Jo Ann Robinson rose to speak strongly in favor of a boycott and what it would mean for the community. She called for the boycott to begin on Monday morning and for a mass meeting to be held that Monday evening. The community leaders agreed with Robinson's proposal. The Black leadership finally found a show of solidarity as even those leaders who were more cautious and ambivalent about a protest movement decided not to be left out and they too supported the boycott. This plan gave them only two days to mobilize and get the word out for the planned boycott on Monday. The mass meeting was to take place at the Holt Street Baptist Church. The leaders wanted the mass meeting so that they could assess the sentiments of the people and determine whether the community would support extending the boycott beyond Monday.[17]

To make preparations, King and Abernathy remained at Dexter that evening in order to mimeograph informational leaflets announcing the boycott on Monday. Early Saturday morning the distribution began, with about two hundred or so volunteers going door-to-door to give out the leaflets. The Reverend W.F. Powell headed up a taxi committee, which arranged an agreement with Black taxicab drivers to transport riders on that Monday for only ten cents, the standard bus fare at the time. On that Saturday evening, King and Abernathy made pastoral visits to various nightclubs in the community in order to spread the news about the upcoming boycott.[18]

E.D. Nixon called Joe Azbell, a sympathetic White reporter with the *Montgomery Advertiser* and alerted him to their plans, encouraging him to write a story for the local newspaper. On that Sunday morning, as Nixon had hoped, the local paper featured as its headline, "Negro Groups Ready Boycott of City Bus Lines." Also, the article reported that Monday's boycott would be followed by a community mass meeting at the Holt Street Baptist Church. The story advanced the cause of the movement and helped to spread the word. The newspaper story also informed members of the White community of the initiative.[19]

The boycott was originally to be under the direction of the Interdenominational Alliance led by Reverend Bennett. But, owing to less than effective leadership and the desire to maintain community solidarity, it soon became apparent that some new organizational structure would need to take responsibility for the effort. There was no desire to unceremoniously push Reverend Bennett aside, so to assuage any ill feelings, the meeting to set up a new organization to oversee the activities of the boycott was called at Bennett's church, the Mount Zion A.M.E. Zion Church, which also happened to be the home church of Rosa Parks. This meeting of these eighteen Black leaders at the Mount Zion A.M.E. Zion Church was on the eve of the first day of the boycott. When the presiding officer called for the name of a person to serve as presiding officer of this new organization, Rufus Lewis, a member of Dexter Avenue Baptist Church, recommended his pastor, Dr. Martin Luther King, Jr. His motion was immediately seconded, and King became the first president of the Montgomery Improvement Association.[20]

Years prior to the arrival of King, the Black leaders of Montgomery already knew what needed to be done. And Black ministers through the organizational bases of their churches dominated the leadership of the community. However, overactive egos, grandstanding, jealousies and infighting amongst the ministers and other leaders hampered their efforts. On the one hand, members of the Black leadership were concerned about one leader gaining more attention and recognition than the others. On the other hand, there was some trepidation about stepping out in front of a movement for social justice and then becoming a target of the White backlash, which was certain to follow against any protest effort. Some feared that the boycott would fail, and they pushed King as a sacrificial lamb. King was new on the scene in Montgomery. He was young, only 26 years old at the time, and relatively inexperienced. In a sense he was the perfect choice to serve as front man for the protest movement. He was a fresh face, so there had not been sufficient time for other leaders to build up resentments and jealousies against him, and given his educational and family background, he seemed respectable enough to garner wide support in the community. E. D. Nixon made the following assessment of King's unique position: "King had not been in the city long enough to be spoiled by the politicians—the city fathers had not gotten their hands on him. So many ministers accept hand-outs and they owe their soul."[21] King did not owe the local White people anything. Some also saw King's ascension to leadership as a compromise between two factions—one led by Nixon, who was a leader of the "masses" (the manually skilled, lower wage earners), and the other represented by Rufus Lewis, a leader of the "classes" (the professionally trained, higher income earners).[22]

In the final analysis, King's leadership was of great importance, though not indispensable to the movement. The movement started without him and it would have continued without him had he not emerged. It is entirely possible that absent King's presence, some other Black minister would have emerged as a unifying leader during those challenging but hopeful times. As eloquent and talented as King was, he was not singularly or primarily responsible for the successes of the civil rights years; it was a mass movement arising from a historical tradition, not a distinctive personality that released African Americans from the clutches of an openly declared regime of White supremacy. And it is the spirit of a people, not the peculiarities of personality that makes for truly magnificent and lasting achievements. In recent years, now that King is safely dead, many have engaged in the hero worship and adulation of a shallow and one-dimensional image of the man; he has been reduced to snippets from a single speech. And some Black politicians, intellectuals, and various opinion leaders have helped to promote the glamorized media image of the Reverend Martin Luther King, Jr., as celebrating an image is far easier than pushing for policies of substantive change or engaging in genuine struggle on behalf of the people, which would constitute a much more befitting tribute.

After the election of King, the Black leaders then began a discussion of the strategy and course of the boycott that they had just initiated. Some of the more cautious and conciliatory leaders wanted to call for a moratorium after one day of boycotting so as not to antagonize the Whites. However, most of the leaders favored continuing the boycott until they could extract concessions from the city. After a lengthy discussion, they decided to present the options to the people at the Monday evening mass meeting. One minister reported to the group that photographers would be at the rally, and this made a number of the ministers decline to volunteer to address the rally, not wanting to be publicly identified with the boycott. Nixon, a layman, then got up and scolded the Black preachers saying, "Somebody in this thing has got to get faith. I am just ashamed of you. You said that God has called you to lead the people and now you are afraid and gone to pieces because the man tells you that the newspaper men will be here and your picture might come out in the paper. Somebody has got to get hurt in this thing and if you preachers are not leaders, then we have to pray that God will send us more leaders." Having been duly reprimanded for their spinelessness, the ministers renewed their courage, and it was then decided that a committee would draw up a resolution supported by the collective body to be presented to the people. If the people were enthusiastic in their support, the protest would continue, but if there was not sufficient enthusiasm, the leadership would contemplate next steps.[23]

Although many were hopeful, nobody really knew how the community would respond on the first day of the boycott. Early Monday morning it soon became apparent that there was widespread compliance by the Black community with the proposition advanced by the Black leaders. Then later that evening a crowd of thousands entered the church for the 7 P.M. mass meeting. The people filled the aisles and the narthex of the church and by the time the meeting got started, four to five thousand people stood reverently outside, listening attentively to the meeting over loudspeakers.

The people were more than enthusiastic; they were uplifted, excited, and highly energized. There was a massive outpouring of support from the people as they finally perceived that their cause, a just and rightful cause, was to be addressed. Those fortunate enough to get inside sang hymns and spirituals and prayed until the meeting started. The mass meeting had the ambiance of a powerful revival service. The meeting used the same tunes and rhythms that the people were used to in Sunday morning services. The hymns played included "Onward Christian Soldiers" and "Leaning on the Everlasting Arms." After a fervent prayer and appropriate scripture readings, an erudite young minister, who only just a short while ago had arrived in the city, was called to present the most important speech of his fledgling career.[24]

Without consciously intending to do so, in King's first mass meeting address, he set out the agenda and the paradigm for the modern Civil Rights Movement. He spoke extemporaneously, as he opened his remarks by saying, "We're here this evening for serious business." He went on to outline the rationale for protesting, which was to obtain the rights of citizenship already guaranteed by constitutional law. King explained, "We are here in a general sense because first and foremost, we are American citizens and we are determined to acquire our citizenship to the fullness of its meaning. We are also here because of our deep belief that democracy transformed from the paper to thick action is the greatest form of government on earth." King focused on the promises, principles, and ideals of the American government, which were often incompatible with its practices. He echoed what the Swedish sociologist Gunnar Myrdal had pointed out about American democracy less than a decade earlier. Also, King attempted to reassure the people that their protest was just and their cause righteous. He indicated that their protest actions were not destructive but in reality constructive, an attempt to correct the injustices to which they had been subjected.[25]

As King continued his speech, he set forth the strategy and methods for social change that he would later use in civil rights campaigns in Albany, Birmingham, and Selma. He told his followers in his first address as a civil rights leader that their actions must be guided by the deepest principles of the Christian faith. Love was to be the regulating ideal and he recited the Christian admonition "Love your enemies." The call to "love your enemies" was a call not to reward wrongdoing as misinterpreted by some critics but to expose wrongdoing, overcome evil, and dispel hatred by doing good and behaving with kindness. King also made it clear to the people that if they failed to follow these practices, their efforts would be futile and meaningless.

King concluded his remarks by reminding those at the mass meeting that they were rewriting history and that their actions would be judged by their children and their children's children. He said emphatically, "If you will protest courageously, and yet with dignity and Christian love, when history books are written in future generations, the historians will have to pause and say "There lived a great people—a black people—who injected a new meaning and dignity into the veins of history and civilization. This is our challenge and our overwhelming responsibility."[26] This speech set the tone and the theme for nonviolent civil rights struggles across the country for the next decade.

After King's address, Reverend Abernathy moved to the podium. He listed demands that the Montgomery Improvement Association would present to the city officials. The first demand was that the Negroes must be treated courteously by the drivers. Second, all passengers must be seated on a first-come, first-served basis, with Negroes seated from the back forward with Whites from the front backward. The third demand was that Negro drivers should be employed by the bus company on all predominantly Negro routes. And, finally, it was stated that until these demands were met, Blacks in Montgomery would decline to ride the city buses. As support for the motion was called for, the crowd stood in unison, waving their hands and letting out cheers and shouts of joy, which could be heard both within the church and from those standing outside.[27]

The overwhelming majority of the people, both the masses and the classes, held together and stopped riding the buses for 381 days. It was a great collective struggle, perhaps the finest moment in the entire history of Africans in America. The Baton Rouge Bus Boycott had been an excellent example, but it lasted only ten days, not long enough for a major outpouring of the transformative spirit of unity and cooperation. For once, the entire Black community came together in support of the common good and to defend their honor as a people. For 381 days there was an epiphany in which Black people spontaneously and frequently gave one another support and encouragement. Each giving according to ability and each receiving according to need was put into actual practice, becoming more than a theoretical proposition. The whole community held together through what was an awesome and challenging task. People made sacrifices for the common good in the form of time and resources. They readily suffered inconveniences in support of a worthy cause. They formed car pools to get to and from work, and they walked for miles when they had to. Those with cars would drive around to pick up and transport walkers. Elderly Black men and women, some of whom could barely walk, inspired teenagers and youngsters to join in the movement.[28] On one occasion an elderly woman was walking from work to one of the Monday night mass meetings. Someone called out to the old lady, "Why don't you ride the bus?" She replied, "I'd rather walk in dignity than ride in shame." Even the Black vagabonds and street toughs got involved. Some of the more hardheaded and recalcitrant members of the community had decided to continue riding the buses anyway, contrary to the overwhelming sentiment of the people. Several of the leaders organized a few of the street toughs to go around to the homes of these wayward souls and knock on their doors just to let them know that the community was displeased. This tactic worked wonders. Some Whites threatened the leaders of the movement with bodily harm, many people were fired from their jobs, and White hooligans made various efforts to intimidate the Blacks, but the people were undeterred.[29]

The people's struggle and sacrifice were not in vain. On November 13, 1956, the Supreme Court ruled that "Alabama's state and local laws requiring segregation on buses are unconstitutional." After that ruling came down, King expressed the sentiments of many when he said, "At this moment my heart began to throb with an inexpressible joy. The darkest hour of our struggle had indeed proved to be the first hour of victory."[30]

Dr. King convened a mass meeting on November 14, 1956, to celebrate the momentous occasion. He had to engage two different churches on both sides of the city in order to accommodate the masses of people who wished to share in the celebration. Some eight thousand people crowded in and around the churches. The spirit was high from the beginning of the opening hymn to the benediction. The evening scripture was read by the Reverend Robert Graetz, the first White minister who came out in support of the boycott. He read Paul's famous letter to Corinthians: "Though I have all faith, so that I could remove mountains, and have not love, I am nothing.... Love suffereth long, and is kind." As he spoke, people were shouting and cheering and waving handkerchiefs as if they knew that they had come of age, that they had won a new sense of dignity. This struggle started in the Church with an initiating mass meeting, and it ended in the church with a celebratory mass meeting. King felt vindicated and he was jubilant. "Only a people who had struggled to love in the midst of bitter conflict could have reacted in this fashion. I knew then that nonviolence for all of its difficulties had won a way into our hearts," he said.[31]

A White news reporter approached Reverend Abernathy and inquired about what he thought might be the inappropriate behavior of the congregation. He asked, "Isn't it a little peculiar for people to interrupt scripture in that way?" "Yes it is," Abernathy replied, "Just as it is peculiar for people to walk in the snow and rain when there are empty buses available; just as it is peculiar for people to pray for those who persecute them; just as it is peculiar for the southern Negro to stand up and look a white man in the face as an equal."[32]

The efforts of the Black community in Montgomery during their bus boycott breathed new life into the movement for social justice and inspired a new generation of social activists throughout the nation. The success of the Blacks in Montgomery inspired Black ministers across the South to take up the fight for freedom. Local groups embraced nonviolence as a philosophy and as a strategic means of protest. For example, in early January of 1956, seventy-two Blacks, mostly students from Xavier University in New Orleans, were jailed for protesting segregation on the city buses. Like most of the civil rights initiatives that were springing up throughout the South, this protest was led by a local Black minister, the Reverend A.L. Davis, who chaired the Interdenominational Ministerial Alliance of that city. With the support of various churches and educational institutions, the New Orleans community continued their protests until the buses were finally desegregated in 1958.[33]

African Americans found a new sense of empowerment and purpose, which arose from people coming together in a spirit of unity for a just cause. Just five months after the Montgomery Bus Boycott began, the Reverend C.K. Steel mobilized a massive bus boycott in Tallahassee, Florida. The spark that ignited the protest in Tallahassee occurred in May of 1956 when two women students from Florida A&M University followed the example of Rosa Parks and refused to give up their seats to Whites. The Black churches and ministers rallied around them and organized a protest campaign initiated by the college students.[34]

In Tallahassee, the strategy of nonviolence was used in the same way it had been used in Montgomery. Carrying out difficult and trying tasks with an unshakable faith that God would see them through and enduring hardships without forsaking a loving spirit have been key elements in the ethos and culture of African Americans since they started their sojourn in America under the yoke of human bondage. Faith in the sustaining powers of God and a hopeful outlook that transcends material conditions are the psychological cornerstones of the Black church and the African-American spiritual tradition. Thus it is no surprise that in Tallahassee and in civil rights struggles throughout the nation, many Blacks readily adopted the philosophy and tactic of nonviolence. In the 1960s, there were frequent spontaneous outbreaks of acts of violence and eruption of riots in response to the numerous outrages perpetrated by the police or to other repressions from the White establishment. These acts, however, were disorganized, and they accomplished little beyond the devastation of already economically distressed neighborhoods. It was the implementation of disciplined nonviolent civil disobedience tactics which proved to be remarkably successful at drawing attention to oppressive conditions while inspiring a sense of moral indignation in the people, and these actions were taken often against the full force and resource advantages of local, state, and federal agencies.

The nonviolent approach and the appeal to moral conscience arose from the Black church tradition; they were not transplants from Gandhi or Indian philosophy. With all due respect to Martin Luther King, Jr., and his crediting of Gandhi as an inspiration, Black people never would have accepted the nonviolent approach and appeals to remain on the moral high ground in their struggle in such large numbers had they not already been familiar with a tactic that was embedded in the philosophy and culture of their churches. It was relatively easy for the nonviolent approach to be adopted as a disciplined form of mass protests by the Blacks of that era because of this familiarity.[35] There is an unfortunate tendency among African Americans, a people subjected to a 300-year systematic attempt to suppress and debase their cultural heritage, to look for validation of their own insights, innovations, and historical achievements among other people who had little or nothing to do with them, and to seek approval even from those who express sentiments antagonistic to their social aspirations. Under the brutality of White supremacy, people have learned, and perhaps too well, how to dissemble and deliver conciliatory reports, no matter how preposterous, in deference to White authority. Long before Gandhi or King, the Black church was preaching and teaching of the transformative powers of faith and love and expressing a philosophy of nonviolent resistance to oppression. This can readily be observed in the examples of Andrew Bryan, George Liele, and Richard Allen, among others. The *ahimsa* teachings of the Jain tradition are indeed quite profound, but no less profound has been the capacity of African Americans to transcend some of the most intense forms of oppression the world has ever known through their spirituals, inspired gospel preaching, and Holy Ghost shouts, giving new meaning to Christian love as they resisted racist subjugation without succumbing to blind hatred. It was no foreign philosophy or the assistance of a few nice White people which brought African Americans through slavery and segregation. It was their own faith, courage, creative genius, spirituality, and wisdom that saved the day. Forbearance in the face of violent oppression and dehumanization is much more deeply ingrained in the African-American tradition than it has ever been in Hindu India with its monstrous caste system. Besides, some of Gandhi's writings and actions were racist and disrespectful toward African people.[36] Gandhi was just as much an Indian nationalist as he ever was the philosophical idealist, and he saw nonviolent tactics as a useful way to drive the British from his homeland. Gandhi is also widely viewed with disdain by the native Blacks of India and the outcast Dalit people, who found him to be condescending and supportive of the awful discriminatory practices of the Hindu caste hierarchy.[37]

The boycott by the Black community in Tallahassee put the buses out of business. This struggle was concurrent with the struggle in Montgomery and the Tallahassee leaders decided to continue the boycott until the Supreme Court ruled on the case from Montgomery; and after the decision came down Blacks resumed riding the newly integrated buses. The outcome in Tallahassee was the same as in Montgomery, which was the same as had been in Baton Rouge. These successes caught the imagination of Black people and there was a great hopefulness that the promises of America would finally be extended to them.

CONFRONTING THE PHILISTINES—THE STRUGGLE TO BRING SOCIAL JUSTICE TO BIRMINGHAM

Birmingham, Alabama, was a much larger city than either Tallahassee or Montgomery. Its population in the mid 1950s exceeded 300,000, of which Blacks comprised at least half. Segregation was deeply entrenched in the fabric of the city, which was aptly named "Bombingham" by the Blacks owing to the not infrequent fire bombings of Black homes and churches.[38]

For the Blacks of Birmingham, racial subjugation was the determining factor for everything in their lives. Wherever they lived, worked, went to school, ate, or entertained themselves, there were constant reminders of their inferior social status. Everything was determined according to the dictates of a regime of White racial domination. When Dr. King came to Birmingham in the early 1960s, he called it the most segregated city in America.

Prior to being outlawed, the leading organization in the drive for equality, justice and freedom was the Birmingham NAACP, and the Birmingham branch was the southern regional headquarters for that organization. Locally, there were 58 chapters with a total membership of about 14,000, and of course Black churches constituted the strongest bases of support for this organization. In June of 1956, the Alabama state legislature voted to outlaw the NAACP throughout the state.[39] This action triggered the effort to form a new civil rights group to fill the void. The membership chairman of the now outlawed NAACP was Reverend Fred Shuttlesworth, and he would prove to be champion for his people second to none. He had been a keen observer of the civil rights struggles taking place in Montgomery and Tallahassee, and the success of these movements moved Reverend Shuttlesworth to convene a mass meeting in order to discuss the formation of a local civil rights organization to replace the NAACP. The Civil Rights struggle was a divine imperative for Shuttlesworth. On the afternoon of May 17, 1954, he saw the newspaper headlines as he walked near the federal courthouse in downtown

Birmingham. He later reflected on the incident and compared it to "getting religion." He said this was second only to what he felt on the day his soul was saved. Reverend Shuttlesworth was well aware of the impact of the Brown decision. He realized that the decision provided the legal opportunity for Blacks to push further and faster in fulfilling the promises of the Constitution. Yet he also knew that there was still much work to be done before achieving social equality.[40]

It was at the mass meeting called by Shuttlesworth that the Alabama Christian Movement for Human Rights was organized. The leaders of this new organization hoped that it would be able to replace the now defunct state NAACP. The leadership of this new organization was again dominated by Black ministers. Reverend Shuttlesworth was elected president. Like civil rights organizations and activities in most other southern cities, the organization was an outgrowth of Black churches, and it was dependent on them for financial support, meeting halls, volunteers, and leadership.[41]

Birmingham was to the Black Civil Rights movement what the Philistines were to the Children of Israel in the Old Testament. The White racists in Birmingham would be among the most formidable and symbolically the most important foes that the movement would face. The White power structure in Birmingham maintained a thorough and vicious system of segregation, and they would supply some of the most intense resistance to social justice seen throughout the 1960s. But the heroism of Shuttlesworth and others would prove equal to the task. Reverend Shuttlesworth was considered by friend and foe alike to be one of the most courageous and incorruptible leaders in the Civil Rights Movement.

The White resistance was led by the Commissioner of Public Safety, Eugene "Bull" Connor and buttressed by Governor John Patterson and later George Wallace, who succeeded Patterson as the Governor of Alabama. Their efforts were joined by vigilante groups including the Ku Klux Klan and the White Citizens' Councils. Black political disenfranchisement, lack of educational opportunities, and economic exploitation were central to an agenda of White supremacy in the South. And this agenda was imposed and secured by various efforts of intimidation, lynching, arbitrary arrests, and police harassment, along with the firebombing of the homes and churches of those who resisted. The Birmingham White power structure controlled, co-opted, and manipulated the Black middle class, including many of the Black ministers. They did so by throwing off a few crumbs in exchange for passivity and feckless leadership of the Black masses. Most of the Black leaders in Birmingham were publicly accommodating toward the establishment, and White businessmen gave them modest favors like deals on clothing and cars in order to keep them in line. In retrospect, the outlawing of the NAACP was a serious tactical error by the Whites. This act created a vacuum and removed some of the more indecisive leaders. Into this vacuum stepped a new generation of more courageous and progressive-minded leaders. The new leadership was independent of the old regime and they felt free to publicly address the needs of the masses.[42]

By the 1950s, Birmingham's system of White domination and racial segregation was so well established that for most White citizens it was beyond question. Its members felt their legal position was impenetrable and airtight, with precedents going back to the 1896 *Plessy v. Ferguson* Supreme Court decision. Many believed that their "Southern way of life" was unassailable. And it was the Reverend Fred Shuttlesworth who was called to Birmingham to take on the task of leading a struggle against the most entrenched forces of segregation. Birmingham had rightly earned the reputation as the seat of violent racist resistance to civil rights for Blacks. It was also in Birmingham that the civil rights struggle would find a character, Eugene "Bull" Connor, who was practically a caricature of the White racist southern sheriff. He would become the perfect foil for the efforts of Shuttlesworth in taking on injustice; Connor would be the implacable antagonist, Shuttlesworth the heroic protagonist. Both Connor and Shuttlesworth were deeply committed to their beliefs, even to the point of obstinacy. Connor was committed enough to brutalize, maim, and hurl racist insults; Shuttlesworth was committed enough to withstand beatings and imprisonment and to declare his rightful manhood through it all. Birmingham was noted for producing steel, and it has been noted that the hard, unbending nature of this metal could be found in the personalities of both Connor and Shuttlesworth. Shuttlesworth's audacity and tenacity set the tone for the movement in Birmingham, and his devotion made him the unquestioned leader in the eyes of the local people. He provided the character and the vision that, supported by

the spirit of the people, guided the movement through the most difficult
moments of the struggle.[43]

From the very outset of their confrontation, Connor, materially at least,
had the upper hand. He had at his disposal a large police force, vicious attack
dogs, electric cattle prods, the White Citizens' Councils, the KKK, and a
southern White culture solidified by racism. Yet, Shuttlesworth repeatedly
outmaneuvered and embarrassed Connor. Shuttlesworth goaded Connor
into making a public spectacle of himself, confronting the racist policeman,
who true to his byname, could not help charging in. Although facing great
difficulty, Shuttlesworth was able to mobilize the masses in the Black community and win enthusiastic and committed supporters for the effort. After
President Kennedy responded to the outrages and protests in Birmingham
during a national address, Shuttlesworth urged him to do more than deliver
empty rhetoric: "The new frontier is trying to catch up with the Negro
frontier, unless the President moves with dispatch, vigor and a degree of
dedication, Negroes will be demonstrating in every nook and cranny of
the nation—North, East and West."[44] To build a movement in a place like
Birmingham, where racial inequality was so deeply entrenched, he felt it
was necessary for the leader to lead from the front lines and accept the same
hardships as those who were the followers. A strong civil rights supporter,
Glenn Smiley made the following remarks about Shuttlesworth's bravery:

> Once he told me, after he had been chain whipped by going into a
> White group that chased him ... that "It doesn't make any difference;
> I'm afraid of neither man nor devil." And I said, 'Fred don't ever ask me
> to go with you on a project because if you're not afraid on occasions,
> and there's plenty to be afraid of out here, I don't want to be around
> you'.... Now Martin [King] and these other guys just wouldn't allow
> their fears to govern their actions. Now this is courage. This is bravery.
> Not Shuttlesworth. I think Shuttlesworth, his bravery is in defiance of
> possible consequences. But that's the way he is. He is strong willed, a
> strong character person, and directed.[45]

C.K. Steel, the leader of the movement in Tallahassee made the following assessment of his colleague in Birmingham.

See nothing was happening in Birmingham, but they had outlawed the NAACP in Birmingham, and so Fred said, "We've got to do something." And all of the bigwigs said, "Now Fred's going crazy, he's trying to whip him up some, you know." But Fred persisted. Because he persisted, he finally got it off the ground. I expect that the Birmingham Movement remained strong longer than almost any movement in the south that I know of.[46]

It would be Shuttlesworth and the Birmingham Movement that would rescue King and the Southern Christian Leadership Conference from their crushing defeat in Albany, Georgia. The Birmingham Civil Rights Movement helped lead to the 1964 Civil Rights Bill, and the success of the movement set the stage for the Selma campaign, which then precipitated the historic 1965 Voting Rights Act.

Courtesy of Birmingham Civil Rights Institute

The Reverend Fred Shuttlesworth

By this time, King had attained an international stature and towering presence wherever he went, but the movement in Birmingham was still guided by the energetic personality and spirit of Shuttlesworth. The scholar Aldon Morris noted that Shuttlesworth did not have a single event like Montgomery to precipitate widespread moral outrage; thus he chose to take direct and confrontational action, his charisma and personal courage being his primary weapons. Dr. King and Reverend Steele approached the struggle in a different manner. Their leadership was initiated by crucial events that were conducive to mobilizing large numbers of people into direct-action movements.

The Alabama Christian Movement for Human Rights was unapologetically Black run and operated. Unlike the Montgomery Improvement Association and most of the other local civil rights organizations, the movement in Birmingham did not receive financial support from outsiders or White-controlled foundations. The Birmingham movement was sustained financially by local Black churches and donations from the community. Members and supporters of the movement would solicit weekly contributions from their friends and church members who did not attend the meetings. Mr. Ocie Thompson, a steel mill worker, was a member at the church at which I pastored in Birmingham, and he was an ardent supporter of the local civil rights movement. Of his own accord Mr. Thompson would go out and raise hundreds of dollars each week for the movement by soliciting donations. The ministers who presided over the mass meetings were gifted at moving the people with oratory, not the least of which included appeals for donations. These donations would then be used to bail the protestors out of jail, pay for legal assistance when needed, support those who had lost jobs, and provide for the travel and lodging of activists and organizers. The songs and soulfulness of the choirs was often matched in enthusiasm by the joyful expressions of those in the congregation. And perhaps owing to the deadly seriousness of the times, these services frequently became spirit-filled, and many were overcome with an outpouring of emotions to the point where there were some totally unexpected occurrences. The city of Birmingham assigned a police detective to monitor the mass meetings and to report to authorities what took place. The fervor and spirit of the mass meetings was such that on several occasions I witnessed detectives moved to tears and even walk down the center aisle of the sanctuary to put money in the collection plate.[47]

Reverend Shuttlesworth and those who followed him constituted the leading phalanx of the Birmingham Movement; they had the inspiration and courage to step into one of the most fearful struggles to take place during the civil rights era. Shuttlesworth was totally committed to destroying Jim Crow, even to the point of making the ultimate sacrifice. Perhaps his most potent weapon was his fearlessness in the face of death. The importance of restoring a sense of honor to Black people via the destruction of segregation trumped even the importance of living. In his own words, Shuttlesworth explains his commitment: "I tried to get killed in Birmingham." His position was: "When you organize to fight segregation that means you can never be still. We gonna wipe it out or it's gonna wipe us out. Somebody may have to die." He took seriously and personally the words Christ spoke when He said, "Whoever will lose his life for my sake shall find it."[48] Shuttlesworth literally considered himself to be a soldier for Christ. His reckless courage was not only incomprehensible to Connor but to many Blacks as well. The bold initiatives of Shuttlesworth and his cadre not only antagonized the White community but also divided the Black community. The Black community was basically separated into two factions—those who supported Shuttlesworth and thought he could do no wrong, and those who opposed him thinking he was always wrong.

Those pastors who did not support the movement were often ridiculed by the movement's supporters. It was widely understood that many ministers were paid off and otherwise co-opted by the White power structure. There were even civil rights advocates who threatened to boycott some of the anti-Movement pastors. This contentiousness was the source of great controversy in some congregations, and it stimulated much debate.

The Civil Rights Movement in Birmingham revolved around Reverend Shuttlesworth, and the Black elites detested this arrangement, his leadership style, and what he symbolized. Many of the more conservative elements in the community, those who did not want to antagonize the White power structure, including most businessmen, along with most educational and civic leaders, viewed Shuttlesworth with disdain. They felt that he disregarded social graces and the opinions of others, which he did since more often than not those graces and opinions tended to uphold the status quo. They thought his leadership style was crude, uncouth and dictatorial, and especially so since he declined to listen to them. The Black bourgeoisie leadership ridiculed the Black masses who followed Shuttlesworth, calling them "Shuttle-lites." Wyatt T. Walker gave the following assessment of Shuttlesworth and his leadership: "His activities were a reproach to the more timid African-American clergy and professionals. Fred intimidated the vast majority of clergy in Birmingham who had been cowed by segregation. He made the elite feel uncomfortable around him."[49]

Overwhelmingly, Black professionals, including most businessmen, doctors, lawyers, entertainers, college professors, school teachers and administrators, stayed a safe distance away from the trenches of the civil rights battles. But, there were notable exceptions. One of Shuttlesworth's most able defenders was Lucinda Robey, a public school principal. She was an active participant in the Alabama Christian Movement for Human Rights from its inception. She publicly defended Shuttlesworth against criticisms launched against him by her professional peers. It was the consensus among the middle-class professionals that civil rights for Black people were simply not worth putting their own jobs and personal safety in jeopardy. The status quo was tolerable to them as long as they got a few perks here and there. The medical doctor James T. Montgomery and the dentist John W. Nixon were the only Black physicians actively involved in the Birmingham Movement. Montgomery reported that the Black professionals were afraid; they did not want to lose their jobs or social status, so they refused to embrace a struggle for justice. James Armstrong, a barber and foot soldier in the movement, provided the following insight about Black middle-class professionals: "They were just waiting for somebody else to shake the tree so they could get the grapes." The Birmingham Black elite learned to temper their public criticisms of Shuttlesworth because of his popularity and because they did not want to be identified as Uncle Toms. Many of the middle-class Blacks were just like the Sadducees during the time of Christ. They did not care for the oppressors any more than did Shuttlesworth, but they were nevertheless willing to accommodate oppression in order to retain a few economic allowances.[50]

The scholar Andrew Manis has noted the distinct contrast between the approaches of King and Shuttlesworth to the civil rights struggles; both wanted to achieve the same goals, but Shuttlesworth was more provocative and uncompromising, while King was more the conciliator. Unlike King who came from a middle-class background, Shuttlesworth emerged from a relatively impoverished rural working class family. Whereas King received seminary training and graduate studies at highly respected White universities and his orations would be sprinkled with quotes from some European philosophers or theologians, Shuttlesworth's training came from all-Black segregated schools in Alabama, and he was not enamored with White theologians. There were no influential White advisors, mentors, or counselors for Shuttlesworth. His sense of identity had not been substantially modified by the dominant culture. Shuttlesworth always identified with the poor and working class Black Southerners and they always responded positively to him as one of their own. There were many critics and detractors from the Black middle class who disagreed with Shuttlesworth's audacious and uncompromising approach to attacking Jim Crow. However, his courage and heroic style resonated with many in the community who were disappointed with the indecisiveness of Black bourgeoisie leadership. Jonathan MacPherson, an activist professor at Birmingham's Miles College, contended that Shuttlesworth's followers "just loved the man because he could articulate the innermost feelings of the rank and file...."[51]

GATHERING OF THE MASSES—THE SPIRITUAL POWER BASE OF THE MOVEMENT

I began working at Miles College while also serving as the pastor of Metropolitan C.M.E. Church in the fall of 1963. I found the church membership to be almost equally divided between those who supported Civil Rights protest activities and those who preferred not to be involved. Those who opposed direct action claimed to do so for various reasons, but mostly they were satisfied with the sublime serenity of mindless passivity—passivity toward White injustice, that is, but definitely not toward those involved in efforts to overcome the injustice. The older members were more conservative in their attitudes and much less likely to be involved in the movement than the younger members.

The Alabama Christian Movement for Human Rights held mass meetings each Monday night, rotating at various churches. When I arrived at Metropolitan, the members had barred such meetings from taking place at the church. I decided to openly embrace the movement, and I directed the church officers to open the doors of the church for the Monday night mass meetings. I was able to win over majority support from the church members, but there remained strong opposition among some.

Middle-class and professional Blacks who would later reap the lion's share of the financial rewards from newly-opened business and career advancement opportunities usually kept at a safe distance. In all honesty, most Black churches and most Black leaders were spectators during the height of the struggle for civil rights and social justice in Birmingham. Now that the civil rights battles are over, many have belatedly attached themselves to the heroism of that movement. The Civil Rights Movement emerged out of the fundamental guiding spirit of the Black church, but it absolutely did not emerge out of each and every single one of the churches. Of the more than 400 Black churches in and around Birmingham at that time, only 60 were actively involved in the fight, and only the faithful few, about 15 percent, were willing to provide shelter in the time of a storm.[52]

The ecumenical nature of the mass meetings was very important since this tended to defuse inter-church rivalries. In fact in the 1950s and 1960s many churches still strongly adhered to policies that barred worshipping together with congregations that were of a different denomination. The mass meetings contributed much to breaking down these denominational barriers. Black people came together for a common cause, the greater good of the community, and this effort transcended denominations and the pursuit of more narrowly focused agendas. The mass meetings became the focal point for inspiring a sense of greater possibilities and asserting the humanity of Black people. The meetings offered the people a chance to express what was on their hearts but had been too often repressed.[53] As one observer stated, the meetings helped the people "to give vent to what they had felt so long."

The mass meetings would begin in the evenings with an informal praise service. These services were usually led by laymen who were deacons or church officers, and they led the people in congregational singing, prayers, and testimonials. The formal service would begin when the ministers mounted the pulpit and the movement choir assembled in the choir stand. At this point, one of the ministers would rise to preside over the service as worship leader. The other ministers were called upon to share in the service with prayers and scripture readings. Next, there would be inspirational and encouraging short speeches delivered by various ministers, and these would be interspersed with freedom songs from the movement choir. The musicians would often improvise or create lyrics for familiar tunes that would then serve as freedom songs. In the struggle for freedom the movement choirs gave a potent majestic voice to freedom, and by singing, they helped to strengthen the courage of the people. One of the popular songs of that time was "Ninety-Nine and a Half Won't Do," which was inspired by the struggles of the people and composed to inspire the people even more. But all of these events were actually preliminary activities and a buildup for the main event, which would be the presentation of the featured speaker for the evening. During 1963 when I first went to Birmingham, the featured speaker was almost always either Fred Shuttlesworth or Martin Luther King, Jr. And both of them represented their respective civil rights organizations, the Alabama Christian Movement for Human Rights and the Southern Christian Leadership Conference.[54]

The mass meetings in Black churches were the structural pillars, providing the spiritual foundations of whatever successes were achieved by the movement. It was at the mass meetings more than anywhere else that hearts and minds were girded for rightful struggle. It was not uncommon for the magnificent spontaneous spirituality of the people to take hold in these gatherings, completely transforming the planned order of worship. The people encouraged the leaders to bravely lead on, and the leaders were inspired to give their very best efforts.

African-American culture is rich with charismatic appeals, theatrical displays and the enthusiastic responses of the crowd. But the capacity to organize and lead in the midst of difficult and challenging circumstances requires more than charisma or theatrics. I was quite fortunate to have had

the opportunity to meet and closely interact with several of the outstanding community leaders of that time, including King and Shuttlesworth. I
also had the chance to encounter Malcolm X on a number of occasions.
In my experience I found that there were several qualities that seemed
most beneficial toward obtaining a high degree of respect and cooperation
from the masses, including: (1) sufficient charisma to capture and hold the
attention of people; (2) a genuine concern for their welfare; (3) a willingness to sometimes dispense with social etiquette and be open and honest
with them; (4) enough moral scruples not to take advantage of them; (5)
the intelligence and confidence to organize, strategize and plan actions
against powerful interests; and, (6) most importantly a willingness to take
responsibility for the collective as reflected in the capacity to courageously
submit to the possibilities of personal hurt, harm, and losses, physically or
financially, in support of the greater good of the community. Would-be
leaders of the struggle who were in it more for their own aggrandizement
than for the uplift and protection of the people could not long endure the
pressures brought to bear in the absence of support from the people.

I was, for example, deeply involved in the Birmingham Movement
when the White establishment decided to move against me. One evening,
a White police officer was sent to my home with the instructions to impress
upon me that the appropriate time had come for my family and me to leave
the city of Birmingham permanently. As soon as I saw the policeman at
my door, I surmised what his purpose was. Nevertheless, I invited him
inside and we spoke cordially for a few moments. While we were speaking
some of the local men who would drink liquor and play dice in an alleyway
behind my church saw the patrol car in front of my home. Although none
of these fellows ever attended church, they nevertheless considered me to
be their "pastor," as I would occasionally converse with them about various
affairs. I also considered them to be a part of my "extended community
parish," even though I knew none of them would ever put a dime in the
collection plate. We would also open the doors of the church to perform
funerals and other services on their behalf as needed. Thus, upon observing
the patrol car, the men then called this matter to the attention of others
in the community, as they were quite concerned about my welfare. Before
long, a fairly large crowd of people had assembled on the front lawn of

my home. When the police officer got ready to leave, he looked outside the door and saw the none-too-friendly looking crowd. He then turned to me and asked if I would please walk with him to his car. Thus, the man who had been sent to my home in order to intimidate me found the tables completely turned, and this was due only to the genuine respect I had won from many of the people in that community.

BLACK POWER EMERGES OUT OF THE MOVEMENT

Mississippi was a hotbed of ferocious opposition to civil rights during the movement. In the summer of 1966, James Meredith took up the struggle as he endangered his life in order to integrate the University of Mississippi. He was determined to show the obstinate state of Mississippi that Blacks were no longer to be cowed by the heavy hand of White oppression, so he decided to march from Memphis, Tennessee, to Jackson, Mississippi, in order to support voter registration. Just inside the Mississippi line, outside of Memphis, an unemployed White man rose from the bushes and shot Meredith in the back. Meredith was hospitalized. When King heard of this incident, he summoned other civil rights leaders to rally the troops so that they could continue the march that Meredith had started. King understood that it was important not to back down in the face of racist brutality, but instead to use such incidents to further the cause of the movement. Both the Student Nonviolent Coordinating Committee (SNCC) and the Congress for Racial Equality (CORE), respectively under the leadership of Stokely Carmichael (Kwame Ture) and Floyd McKissick, responded to the call to continue the "James Meredith March Against Fear." They would resume the march through the state of Mississippi from the very spot on Highway 51 at which Meredith was shot.[55]

The members of CORE and SNCC were generally much younger than the followers of King. And the new generation of activists was impatient and much more inclined toward militant confrontation than their elders. During this march, many of the youth expressed dissatisfaction with nonviolence as a philosophy and a way of life rather than simply a tactic. They were also displeased with what they saw as the more conciliatory nature of the older civil rights leadership. When the old guard started to sing, "We

Shall Overcome," they were upbraided by the youngsters who considered "overcoming" to be much too tame, and they asserted, the words should be changed to "we shall overrun." It was now clear that there was a sharp philosophical difference between King's nonviolent approach and the more militant approach of Carmichael and McKissick. And then Willie Ricks (Mukasa Dada) uttered the startling phrase "Black Power," conceptually overturning the established order and signaling the awakening of a new generation. SNCC seized the opportunity to promote their more radical agenda, and during the march they began boldly shouting a new chant calling for Black Power.[56]

The young people took advantage of the march to promote a posture of an uncompromising militancy and the immediate empowerment of Black people. King and the older leaders were at first taken aback by this uprising; they were somewhat agitated by the youngsters and were concerned that such behavior might chase away their White supporters. Yet King also learned to see their approach, this "marvelous new militancy," as a vital element in an evolving new awareness. The energy and enthusiasm of the youth helped to propel the movement forward through some of the most difficult circumstances. The older leaders focused on removing the barriers of segregation and appeals for equitable treatment, while the younger leaders realized that there must also be a focus on establishing a strong collective identity among Blacks and racial solidarity—a glaring omission from King's nonviolent philosophy. King and the other civil rights leaders seemed not to realize that bringing together people of different colors, shapes and sizes in order to obtain an "interracial gathering" in and of itself proves nothing; indeed, such pursuits often represent the height of superficiality. There is no automatic virtue in variety. An effective program to address the overall interests and needs of the Black community implies that a definitive sense of community awareness and self-determination has already been achieved. Absent such awareness, bringing together an interracial or multiethnic group for something more than displaying a colorful mosaic is most unlikely to create change. Far more likely is a continuance of the same oppressive status quo but under the guise of racial inclusion and diversity. The exercise of communal will and the full realization of self-determination absolutely require that some activities be planned, initiated, and carried out by those within the community as an organic expression of the community, without reference to input from others, even if in some cases outside assistance might make things less burdensome. As a people, we are indebted to Stokely Carmichael, Floyd McKissick, Angela Davis, Willie Ricks, and others for turning our attention toward an empowering reassessment of our own values and sense of self-worth.

The Black Power movement would help to establish Black Studies programs at universities across the nation, and the scholars in these programs would began a dynamic discourse on the history, life, and culture of African Americans, and they have helped to produce a comprehensive literature countering the many racist characterizations of Africa and African people. The Black Power Movement can also be credited with helping to accelerate Black political and social empowerment, especially in large metropolitan areas. There is also a debt owed by the Black Power Movement (which was linked with the Black Nationalist Movement and helped to inspire the Afrocentric perspective) to the Civil Rights Movement, and by extension, the Black church, and this must not be overlooked. It was in the churches that the early civil rights leaders first mobilized the people and gave them a new sense of possibility. The Black Power advocates would later take that energy and spirit and help achieve substantive gains in the economic and political arenas.

Black theology can be connected to the Black Power and Civil Rights Movements. Professor James Cone and a number of scholars and clergymen began to realize that struggles of African Americans called for a new conceptualization of themselves in their relationship to the divine that was radically different from the theology provided by Eurocentric Christianity. Charles B. Copher, the distinguished professor of Old Testament at the Interdenominational Theological Center (ITC) in Atlanta, pioneered scholarly research on Blacks in the Bible. Also, he was a prime mover for the inclusion of African-American experiences in the curriculum study for theological education. At Howard University in 1970, Copher delineated five requisites for the infusion of the Black religious experience into theological education, including: 1) reclamation of Black heritage, 2) development of appreciation and pride in that heritage, 3) knowledge of liberation skills, 4) liberation of Whites from their ignorance of Blacks, and 5) an analysis of the Black religious experience to discern its total liberating potential for Blacks and Whites. Gayraud S. Wilmore, who was professor of church history, became an influential voice at this time in advocacy of Black theological perspectives. The emergence of Black Theology helped to inspire the Liberation Theology movements which took hold in Latin America and other parts of the globe.

Albert B. Cleage, Jr. (Jaramogi Abebe Agyeman) had already founded the Central Congregational Church in 1953 to serve the disadvantaged and poor. He then sought to institutionalize the political, economic, and cultural praxis of Black Christian Nationalism. Cleage discerned that the worship of a blond-haired, blue-eyed Jesus effectively maintained a psychological disposition of inferiority and subservience among Blacks. He replaced the impotent White Jesus with a revolutionary Black Messiah who was sent to rebuild the Black nation and liberate the people from exploitation by the White gentile world. In 1968, Cleage formed the Shrine of the Black Madonna in Detroit. He denounced American Christianity for preaching and promoting a White messiah incapable of delivering the people from oppression. In response to what Cleage called the false messiah, he wrote and published a series of powerful sermons embracing a "revolutionary Black Messiah." In 1973, students from Detroit who had been influenced by the teachings of Cleage came to the Atlanta University Center. These students eventually organized a local temple of the Pan African Orthodox Christian Church under Cleage's leadership.[57]

The Black Power Movement of the 1960s is also related to the neo-Pentecostalism movement that took hold in many mainline Black churches during the 1980s and 1990s. In large numbers, middle-class and college-educated Blacks began to embrace more demonstrative styles of worship, which many of their parents had previously ridiculed and thought overly emotional. However, the new generation did not feel constrained by the old social restrictions; they had a new sense of identity prompted by Black Power that did not need validation by conventional religious practices. Neo-Pentecostalism gave many declining mainline churches a new lease on life. Praise became the focus in their worship services. Black Power and Black theology helped to give this wave of neo-Pentecostalism the conceptual framework and inspired confidence to decisively break with the more conservative and restrictive practices that had systematically suppressed traditional African expressions and beliefs. The fastest growing and most vibrant mainline churches became those which embraced and celebrated shouting or spirit possession, baptism of the Holy Spirit, religious dancing, faith healing, and the laying on of hands. Black Power addressed the Black identity crisis and helped the people to become more comfortable with their own culture and way of doing things, more at peace with just being themselves. According to C. Eric Lincoln: "Ironically, the white Church in America is the principal *raison d'être* for the Black Church, for just as the white Church permitted and tolerated the Negro Church, it made the Black Church necessary for a new generation of Black people who refuse to be "Negroes" and who were not impressed by whatever it means to be white."[58]

From the point of the Meredith March onward, Black militants and the civil rights leadership would move mostly in different directions, and the youngsters would often express harsh criticism of their more conservative elders. Many in the Black Power Movement would deliver scorching critiques of Christian churches, their complicity in slavery and racist exploitation programs, and the accommodating posture of many Black ministers. And many of these criticisms were rightly deserved, for too many Black churches and too many ministers had lost their way and become compliant with the system of oppression. Black ministers were sometimes rightly ridiculed for their complacency, corruption, and subservience. Of particular concern was the image of a blond-haired, blue-eyed White Jesus which often adorned churches and homes in the Black community. This image was of course a historical fallacy and it has tended to insidiously promote notions of White supremacy and Black inferiority in the minds of Black people. Yet, the critiques often failed to differentiate between Eurocentric Christianity and the adaption thereof, which was created to fill the cultural void for African Americans. In their eagerness to push for change, some of the critics did not give sufficient consideration to the humanity of people who sometimes made mistakes as they struggled against many hardships in a strange and often hostile land. The real value and deeper meaning of any spiritual tradition is found in its capacity to evoke the collective will to endure hardships and overcome difficult conditions, and not in the various forms adopted to facilitate transitory presentations.

The churches set up by enslaved and formerly enslaved Africans were limited but still effective vehicles for nurturing the vital sense of collective identity. And even imperfect people can sometimes accomplish extraordinary things. The independent Black church movement was not expected, conceived, or planned by Whites, and its emergence was at first fiercely resisted by the White denominations. They relented only after it became apparent that independent Black churches were going to be formed anyway. In the absence of the cultural and spiritual accomplishments of their enslaved ancestors, what other authentic foundations might African Americans call upon? Despite its shortcomings and weaknesses, the Black church still gave the people a semblance of community and facilitated expressions of hope during their most trying times, and this must not be disregarded or forgotten. How is it possible to claim such great love for the people and to fight forthrightly for their liberation, but yet be dismissive and disrespectful of their ancestral and spiritual heritage, offering only negative commentary about the cultural foundation historically embraced by the overwhelming majority of them? Failure to seriously consider the spirituality of the people is more characteristic of the materialistic Western mindset than reflective of traditional African approaches to life. And those with no appreciation for the spiritual aspirations of the people, their strivings to come to terms with ultimate reality, are those who have not yet become acquainted with the genuine character of the people. We may search far and wide on every continent, study the sacred teachings of every faith, contemplate every philosophical rendering, and become conversant with all the economic theories that the world has to offer, but if we never find that sublimity and deepest meaning already present in our own history and heritage, our searches will all prove to be empty and vain, always ending in disappointment and dismay. The whole world will become a better and more beautiful place once we discover the goodness and beauty that we already have. And besides, what wisdom traditions run deeper, what accumulated human experience is greater, and what spirituality more vibrant than that demonstrated in the Black experience? If we are unable to find the wisdom and guidance in the traditions and experiences of Black people sufficient to formulate resolutions for the difficulties they confront, then it means that either our efforts are lacking or that such resolutions cannot be obtained by human effort. Alas, some of the Black Power leaders, radicals, and militants turned out to be just as corruptible and full of hypocrisy as they accused Black ministers and churches of being. Too often these militants would engage in vainglorious chest-thumping exercises devoid of substance and disconnected from the practical needs of the people. As it turned out, wearing African clothing and jewelry, giving the Black power salute, or making loud statements lambasting the "White man" were poor indicators of real commitment to the struggle.

THE SOUTHERN CHRISTIAN LEADERSHIP CONFERENCE—THE BLACK CHURCH AS THE INSTITUTIONAL CENTER OF THE MOVEMENT

The SCLC would provide an organizational framework for further Civil Rights advances, and it was plainly an outgrowth the Black church. The culture, rhetoric, and spirit of the Black church permeated the movement for social justice in the South. The Black church served as the institutional

Children at the Mourners' Bench (see Glossary)

center of the modern Civil Rights Movement, as the churches provided a platform to announce and promote a restoration of human dignity and social justice for African Americans. It was not academia or labor unions or fraternal lodges, but it was the Black church that had cultivated and prepared a cadre of ministers skilled in the art of mobilizing, motivating, and managing the Black masses toward a higher cause.[59]

The independent base of the Black church provided a safe haven for holding meetings to plan and strategize next steps in the movement. It was in the churches that the people gathered to worship and collectively commit themselves to struggle for social justice. The Black church supplied the Civil Rights Movement with the evocative rhetoric and rhythms to generate the uplifting enthusiasm needed to wage a successful fight. The rich culture of songs, testimony, oratory, sermons, and prayers spoke to the needs and the longings of a materially dispossessed but spiritually empowered people.

The Black church was born as a protest movement. Since its inception it has demonstrated a capacity for providing leadership to meet the challenges of the day. W.E.B. DuBois once remarked that the Black church was "overworked" because it was the place in the Black community that had to provide political organization, economic development, educational opportunity, socialization processes, a civil rights agenda, artistic expression, leadership training, and literary activities, among other things. The Black church is unique in that it was organized and developed as an outlet and platform for those who were deemed unworthy and incapable of social development. The problem of being Black in America had been presented. The Black church attempted to provide a resolution to that problem.

The success and high profile of the Montgomery experience inspired ministers, activists, and ordinary people to organize and take up the fight for justice. The SCLC allowed the ministers to pool their resources in the struggle for civil rights. Montgomery had demonstrated that the Black church could unleash a great transforming power if it would only be true to its mission, its magnificent heritage, and its illustrious tradition. A half century prior to the Montgomery Bus Boycott, W.E.B. DuBois had acknowledged the genius of the Black preacher when he wrote: "The [Black] preacher is the most unique personality developed by the Negro on American soil. A leader, a politician, an orator, a "boss," an intriguer, an idealist—the combination of a certain adroitness with deep-seated earnestness, of tact with consummate ability gave him his preeminence and helped him to maintain it."[60]

In 1960, the Reverend Wyatt T. Walker was hired to be the executive director of the SCLC. Walker had already demonstrated leadership ability, as he had built a strong grassroots chapter of the SCLC in Virginia. In 1958, the White leaders of Petersburg, Virginia, elected to close their public schools in an effort to circumvent integration. Walker responded by leading a successful prayer vigil protesting the closing of the public schools. His efforts got the attention of Dr. King and other civil rights activists. It should be remembered that at this point in the movement, when leading a protest effort against segregation, one was by no means certain of success or safety. There were many arrests and beatings, jobs were lost, homes were lost, and lives were lost. Intimidation and surveillance of protesters was widespread by both government agencies and White vigilante groups. A leader who could effectively organize people, courageously withstand the pressures applied by the White establishment, and then articulately represent the cause was considered a great asset, as there were many who tried and failed. Walker had excellent administrative skills, and this would prove helpful for the efforts of the SCLC.[61]

Walker made a determined effort to cultivate the support of the churches. He was able to convince many ministers and church officers of the responsibility they have for the people. Walker understood that the church was an essential presence and the strategic key to victory in the movement. He made the following observations: (1) churches are located in practically every community; (2) the churches' membership meets regularly, usually each Sunday and often several times per week; (3) the churches are committed to the idea of serving the basic needs of people and having a general concern for their problems; (4) church membership cuts across age, economic, educational, class and geographic lines in the community; (5) churches have the resources and techniques for motivating people to volunteer for altruistic service; (6) Black preachers have the capacity to adjust their schedules more easily than persons of other professions; and, (7) churches remain relatively stable and free of the narrow and divisive handcuffs that frequently afflict other types of organizations in the Black community.[62]

The Black church provided the SCLC with charismatic leadership, institutional structure, a mass base of support and financial resources. Joseph Lowery, one of the founding members of the SCLC, maintained that the Civil Rights Movement was really the Black church in disguise. It was the Black church realizing its potential for progressive social action as churches came together across denominational and geographical lines. Joseph Lowery noted that, "[the SCLC] was really the black church, that's what it was. It was the black church coming alive. It was the black church coming together across denominational and geographical lines."[63]

Without knowing it, the Black church had become a training ground for civil rights activism. The churches not only taught that Christian love conquered hate, they also developed programs for putting this philosophy into actual practice. Black preachers appealed to the people by invoking the teachings of Jesus from the Sermon on the Mount. Proclaiming love for everyone, even for their oppressors, allowed the Blacks to assert a kind of moral superiority over their enemies, a stunning turn of events in the history of America. Black preachers and civil rights activists stirred up a moral force among the people by their willingness to move forth boldly sacrificing their bodies and livelihoods. Today such tactics may no longer be viable, but we should never lose sight of the fact that the history of African Americans indicates the capacity to arouse a moral authority that can be a pathway to empowerment and have influence over temporal affairs. Moral authority, properly cultivated and spiritually endowed, can be invoked with no less potency than the influences of militancy or political authority.

Martin Luther King, Jr., became the paramount leader of the movement and he grew into the role. His political and social consciousness expanded as he traveled around the country and witnessed the plight of the people. King was well connected with the faith community of his time. He was the rare leader who was able to attract the respect of both the masses and the classes. King's classical formal training earned him the respect of academia. And he was as comfortable in a poolroom as he was in the pulpit exhorting the people to join the movement and to struggle for justice. His oratorical acumen and personal charisma captured the attention and respect of ministers—the lettered and the unlettered. King was heralded as an outstanding orator, but this was no less true of any number of other Black preachers. The oratorical tradition, which is not always distinguishable from the grand rhythmical music and dance traditions among Africans, runs deep in the Black community, as can be observed from the ennobled griots of West Africa to the great abolitionist orators of the pre-Civil War period to the rapping poets of today's youth culture. Indeed, it has been the attainment of skill in the oral tradition even above literary achievement that has been the hallmark of excellence and accomplishment in Black culture. In the hands of an experienced practitioner, words and rhetoric become much more than simple vehicles of communication; they are raised to the level of an art form and can invoke a spiritual awareness. An orator who can command attention and move his audience can have great influence, and this has often translated into political and social capital.

Writing the "Letter from a Birmingham Jail" was a planned event, but the seed for such a project was planted many years earlier as King heard his father and many other preachers tell the story of the great Apostle Paul and his letter from the Philippi jail. So, like Paul of Tarsus, King set out to pen a letter that would outline the universal meaning of the struggle for freedom. Sometimes scribbling on the margins of the newspaper in which the White clergymen's letter had appeared in the Birmingham News, he responded to their charge that the demonstrations were "unwise and untimely."[64] His response was reflective of some of the philosophical and theological principles that he learned in various academic settings. But, the basic themes of the letter—what justice means to the oppressed and the underlying moral interconnectedness of life—he had already learned in Sunday School, in the church services listening to Black teachers and preachers, and from observing the experiences of Black people struggling to live meaningful lives in the midst of racist oppression.

When Dr. King delivered his farewell address in Memphis, the speech was filled with images and metaphors reflecting the intellectual and spiritual profundities of the Black church. He was to speak at the Mason Temple, the historic church named in honor of Bishop Charles H. Mason, founder of the Church of God in Christ. It was a stormy evening, with tornado warnings, and there was anticipation of a sparse gathering for this particular mass meeting. King was quite fatigued so Reverend Abernathy, as he had done so many times before, was sent out to speak in his place. But, when Abernathy arrived, he could sense an anticipation from the crowd that he would not be able to meet. These people had braved howling winds, pouring rains, and tornado warnings for one reason. Abernathy called his friend and relayed, "Your people are here and you ought to come and talk to them. They didn't come to hear Abernathy. They came tonight in this storm to hear King."[65] Dr. King responded positively to Abernathy's call and he headed for Mason Temple. The content of King's last oration reflected what he had learned in the Black church. He did speak of the Greek philosophers Plato, Aristotle, and Socrates, of whom he had learned during his matriculations at Morehouse, Crozier, and Boston University. But, his primary theme was delivered using metaphors often employed in the Black churches. In his melodious baritone voice, King declared to the crowd:

> Well, I don't know what will happen now. We've got some difficult days ahead. But, it doesn't matter with me now. Because I've been to the mountaintop. And I don't mind. Like anybody, I would like to live a long life. Longevity has its place. But, I'm not concerned about that now. I just want to do God's will. And He has allowed me to go up to the mountain. And I've looked over. And I've seen the Promised Land. I may not get there with you. But I want you to know tonight, that we, as a people will get to the Promised Land. And I'm happy tonight. I'm not worried about anything. I'm not fearing any man…. Mine eyes have seen the glory of the coming of the Lord.[66]

King's valedictory message was a prophetic vision, a surge of hope and inspiration for his people using the cultivated capacity to move the masses and the rhetorical skills that had been honed and perfected in the Black church.

Chapter 7 – The Civil Rights Movement

DISCUSSION & REVIEW QUESTIONS

1. What were the factors that led to the success of the bus boycotts?

2. What was the importance of the mass meetings?

3. What factors made Birmingham a critical battleground for civil rights?

4. Describe and explain how civil rights protests were organized? How were people mobilized? How was money raised and what was was it used for? What were some of the basic strategies and tactics used by civil rights organizers? What strategies and tactics were used by the supporters of White supremacy?

CHAPTER 8

Conclusions

THE PEOPLE WERE BURDENED WITH A GREAT OPPRESSION...

The African-American experience is the encounter of a people with circumstances in which they have had to struggle, at times desperately so, in order to maintain a sense of dignity, sanity, and humanity. The Black church has been one of the determining factors throughout this struggle. One cannot even begin to understand or have any real regard for African Americans if one does not appreciate the history of their churches; for it is the churches that have been there since the beginning, giving hope to the people and encouraging their best instincts when no other way was provided. It was the Black church and Black preachers who were the frontline defenders of the humanity of the people when there were no Black politicians, lawyers, businessmen, labor leaders, journalists, or university professors to call upon. The Black preacher has the longest tenure of professional leadership in the Black community.

The Black church gave birth to the leaders and organizations that would attempt to breathe new life into the unsaved soul of America. Since America's founding included the extermination of Native Americans and the enslavement of Africans by the millions, the moral authority of White Churches and temporal institutions was rendered impotent as they largely supported or remained silent on such activities. By enslaving Africans physically, Europeans enslaved themselves morally and spiritually. One cannot dehumanize other people and simultaneously preserve one's own humanity. It now appears that as a group, White folks, the global collective of those people of European descent, are all but hopelessly addicted to the ill-gotten gains bought with human degradation while repeatedly lunging for the mirage of security in material things. From continental genocide and mass enslavement to stealing the mineral wealth of "underdeveloped" countries, from engaging in unprovoked warfare, to perpetrating massive fraud in the financial markets—they just cannot seem to help themselves. No amount of tokenism, pretentious gestures, empty apologies, or superficial adjustments can substitute for completely dismantling the regimes of oppression, recompense for the abused, and the dispensation of justice for wrongdoing, all of which must precede any kind of meaningful reconciliation. The most prolific criminal propensity in recorded history will not be redirected by mere pleasing rhetoric. Pronouncements of the dawning of a new age of postracial internationalism is only a pathetic attempt to lock in the ill-gotten gains of the elite and to lock out the masses of the dispossessed by disarming their rightful claims for justice and equity. Those who call for unity and oneness in the absence of morality and justice are delusional.

Of course, White people are not singularly responsible for oppression and exploitation in the world, practices sadly all too common among all races and ethnicities. But White people have excelled at the practice. White power elites in Europe and America have achieved an unprecedented and unparalleled global dominance and preeminence via relentless pursuit of exploitation regimes. They have used whiteness as a passport to privilege all over the world.[1] We are witnesses today to a modern world largely shaped by Europeans and Americans, a world that is characterized by frequent acts of naked aggression, ruthless economic exploitation, and mindless mass consumption, a world in which people of all races and nationalities are losing their compassion for others, and thus their humanity. The social elites of practically every nation have followed the negative example of pervasive corruption, greed, and systematic oppression of the masses. But the bold pretensions of these oppressive regimes are in the end nugatory, and every attempt at averting the inevitable will utterly fail; the coming hour of reckoning and retribution will be terrible and mighty indeed.

The latest devious scheme concocted by those who deviate and connive is to promote the notion that the struggle for justice is now an anachronism, as they disparage and mock all attempts to build upon and celebrate the achievements of the Civil Rights and Black Power Movements. But any successful group of people is so in part because they have successfully engendered a collective historical consciousness, and this must be so for African Americans as well. The Black freedom struggles of the sixties were informed by the Great Migrations, anti-lynching campaigns, and the Garveyite movement of the twenties and thirties, and those movements benefited from the legacy of the Black confidence asserted during Black Reconstruction, which itself was indebted to the spirit that prompted the slave rebellions and to the seeds of resistance sown during the transformative religious experiences in the clandestine bush harbors. Those who have been historically oppressed and exploited will decisively overcome that condition only in a concerted effort and collective movement.

From the days of enslavement, the Black church has been that place where the people could recapture their dignity and self-worth and hear a positive message of hope and liberation even while living in utter despair. Through their sermons and exhortations, early Black preachers identified the plight of the Hebrew Israelites in the Old Testament with their own struggle, and they helped the people understand that the same God who delivered Israel was also able to liberate them. Much of recent scholarship has tended to marginalize the role of the Black church in the Civil Rights Movement. Besides being grossly inaccurate, such perspectives tend to obscure the potential that these churches still have to transform our communities. It was the Black church, more than any other institution, that became the platform for proclaiming a truly liberating theology of overcoming even the most horrific trials and tribulations by an irrepressible faith in the goodness of God.

How did it happen? How did it occur that a people despised for their color the world over, abused and ill-treated in the worst of ways and with no army or political doctrine in support of their interests, nevertheless could rise up out of chattel slavery with any amount of dignity and confidence, and in mass movement overcome the dehumanizing restrictions of segregation to proclaim a new paradigm of social uplift and hope for humanity? Ultimately, the people require more than a new political ideology, greater access to economic resources, improved academic training, or a military victory over their enemies, since obtaining such things in the absence of moral uplift would leave them still wanting; the people must be healed and made whole physically and spiritually. The necessary political and economic liberation of the people shall be obtained, but only secondary to a realization of the magnificent spiritual presence and power that has always been there, struggling along with them since they first arrived in chains on the shores of America; it is their spirituality that capacitates their endurance, inspires their creativity, and envisions their deliverance even through the most difficult of tribulations. Though covered with the filth of a 400-year-long blasphemous deluge, our spirituality impels us onward; it will not allow us to settle for a debased image of self, a caricature of civilized living and the truncated potential of human life.

The African-American story, this great sojourn in a strange land, has seen its share of losses as well as triumphs. Many ministers and churches have turned a blind eye to injustice and a deaf ear to the call of the ancestors for vindication. Too many Black churches have been super-conservative, reacting negatively to any changes which seem inconvenient or challenging. Too many ministers and church leaders have held on to their titles and positions for way too long, denying opportunities for growth and leadership development among younger generations. And then there are the charismatic conmen, pulpit pickpockets, hustling religious sentiments for every dime they can get and preying upon the gullible and those easily led astray. But these are not serious people; they are nowhere to be found once the real work of the church is evoked. Some Black preachers have taken the position that the ministry should not involve politics, in effect proposing that churches should be the captive rather than the conscience of society. Perhaps they have forgotten and maybe they never did realize that at its very initiation with the "invisible institution," the formation of the Black church had far-reaching political implications just as sure as it had spiritual ones. Any claim to holiness that excuses the oppression of the people is a sham. Such attitudes represent a loss of the sense of true purpose, meaning, and identity of the Black preachers. And this behavior is always a liability to the community, since history waits on no one. We are too often caught unawares, hurriedly reacting to circumstances to which we should have had the foresight to proactively manage years earlier. Corruption, materialism, and servile orientations toward oppression have left too many of our churches and communities morally voiceless in the face of deepening crises. The churches exist for the benefit of the people, not the other way around, and if the people are not redeemed, then the mission of the church has failed.

History takes no prisoners. Those caught off guard by outdated notions and empty rituals are left in the dust by the inexorable march of time. And yet there are elements of our tradition that are timeless. Among those elements is the inspired capacity to invoke the presence of the ancestors and the presence of the Supreme Being, even while being subject to the most terrible injustices and in the face of seemingly insurmountable odds. Our forbearers beseeched the divine, but not to destroy their enemies or to remove their burdens, as they already knew that without struggle there is no progress and that those who struggle for righteousness sake are assured of the ultimate triumph. But they called upon the divine to be with them as they passed through their valleys of the shadow of death. Properly understood, the "invisible institution" was a rebellion against every level of slavery and oppression. When the White slaveholders were attempting to force our ancestors to accept a status as less than human, they called upon the presence of the Holy Ghost to say otherwise, to effectively trump evil with good. We must return to those immortal elements of our tradition that lift us up to be more than soul-less thrill-seekers unable to find the wisdom and courage to address the pressing concerns of our communities.

Disconnected from the source, can any be saved? Disconnected from the source, we become like the flower cut from the vine, withering and tossed about with every rushing wind. Our connection to the source is mediated always via our collective consciousness—our sense of community, shared history and ancestral heritage. And in maintaining its integrity, collective consciousness necessarily rests upon a foundation of cultivated moral values, the broad observance of public decency, and an abiding civility and mutual respect among community members. Our connection to the source supplies the strength and power to ultimately overcome all manner of adversity. It was their connection to the source, their desire to maintain a communal identity, and their sanity that inspired our ancestors and led them to form the Black church, a way out of no way, enabling them to survive by empowering them to spiritually transcend the evils of American chattel slavery. And it is up to us to renew our covenant with our ancestors and our commitment to social justice in order to fulfill the true mission of the church.

It is not enough to call for the oppressed to exercise personal responsibility without addressing the adverse conditions that breed destructive behaviors. The oppressed do not need to be corrected; they need to be relieved of oppression. Once the people are relieved of that crushing burden, perspectives, values, and behaviors will be dramatically transformed—in many cases even without further intervention. The most meaningful way toward uplift for the people is to resolutely engage in collective efforts of resistance against the tyrannical regimes of neo-colonial exploitation, the insanity of mindless mass consumption, and the impositions of an unspiritual mentality. And in any case, accountability starts at the top, if it begins at all. To enforce rules, regulations, penalties, and "accountability" upon the masses while privileged "leaders" are permitted to act with impunity is to demonstrate the very definition of oppression.

The ground of our being will countenance arising of the just and the unjust alike, but it is the just alone who shall ultimately be fulfilled. Nations gorged with the blood of the millions slaughtered have severed their linkage to the source; having built empires of lies and monuments to deceit, there are those who cannot tell the truth, because they have no truth to tell. The wicked and the worldly-wise do not know it, but the faithful surely do, that evil is but a means to mature the righteous, and the self-destruction of those who resort to wrongdoing is inevitable. It is only those people, the disinherited who profited not from a world awash in the evils of oppression and materialism, who can lead humanity out of the spiral of death and destruction. When we recapture our deeper sense of self, and reaffirm our spiritual heritage, we shall free ourselves from the pessimistic, depressing, debasing, limiting, and uninspiring materialistic outlook that has been adopted in the wake of long centuries of heartache and sorrow. Acculturation into an immoral and unjust social order will lead to somewhere other than deliverance. It is the presence of mind to draw a clear distinction between ourselves and those who would oppress, the courage to resist oppression, and the faith to renounce those practices that reduce the morals of our community which are the keys to opening the doorway to a meaningful future. Are we to struggle and persevere for righteousness sake or are we to acquiesce? We must choose, and our choice has definite consequences; for the destiny of the oppressors is not interchangeable with that of those who resist.

AND SO GOD CALLED THEM TO PREACH TO THE PEOPLE

The Black preacher has of course played a vital role in this drama which we call the African-American experience. Sometimes heroes, occasionally sell-outs, always figures of prominence in the community, Black ministers have made their mark on American history and have helped to transform American Christianity into a more inclusive experience. It has been as Black preachers, despite the many failings and imperfections of those who would preach, that African-American men have most often assumed the critical role of exemplars of Black manhood, though this fact is rarely recognized. The call to preach was the call to instant recognition and leadership in the Black community.

Throughout the history of America, Black manhood has been under a relentless and vicious assault. Perhaps owing to subconscious fears of genetic annihilation as suggested by the psychiatrist Francess Cress Welsing or perhaps for some other reason, White men have historically focused the most hateful vindictiveness on Black men. The mere presence of the Black man has been a threat because the realization of his heritage has the potential to cut the heart out of White supremacy. This can be seen in the lynchings, beatings, unjust imprisonment, job discrimination, police executions, and other forms of suppression. It would seem that the system of White supremacy, if it required nothing else, absolutely required the emasculation of Black manhood. Men have historically expressed themselves as providers and protectors of their families. But, in chattel slavery and the peonage system that followed, this role was made precarious if not impossible for many Black men. Slavery effectively reversed the traditional roles of Black males and females by leaving Black women to be more socially assertive and imposing a more dependent role for the men. Those Black men who dared to stand and oppose injustice or attempted to defend their families, their communities, and their dignity have been subject to the most horrific brutality besides loss of livelihood and homes. When Malcolm X and Martin Luther King, Jr., decided to stand up and be men anyhow, come what may, assassination became necessary in order to maintain the political-economy of America.

In the face of this pervasive suppression of Black manhood, there arose the courageous Black preachers—those preachers who found the wisdom and strength not only to give the people the word of hope, the word of resistance, and the Word of God, but who would also put themselves at risk to help bring liberty to their people. In this discussion, we do not mean to belittle or ignore the role of Black women as preachers and ministers, many of whom have made significant contributions in their own right; without the women there would be no Black church. But, the psychological landscape of America has provided outlets for femininity and Black womanhood that it has denied to the men. Possibly, as some scholars suggest, this was strategic, a plan all along to separate and create hostility between the genders.

It would be the ministry, however, and the call to preach more than any other vocation, that would provide an avenue for the expression of manhood that had otherwise been denied to Black men. The Black preacher like no other has been there to serve the needs of the whole community. Black men have sometimes been warriors, fighting in every war this country has fought. But save, perhaps, those who fought on the side of the Union during the Civil War, they have never fought explicitly in the interest of their own people. Thus, the warrior role was not a real avenue for the expression of Black manhood. There is also the field of athletic endeavor in which men have traditionally demonstrated their physical prowess and vitality in competition with others. Black men have brilliantly demonstrated their gifts in this arena, but until the 1950s they were barred from doing so on the main stages of American society. And the White man has never questioned the physical prowess of Black men; it has been the mind and morals of Black men that have been repeatedly maligned. The centerpiece of the argument used to justify slavery and segregation was the inherent mental and moral inferiority of Black men. Athleticism, while a significant expression of talent and ability, falls well short of the highest and most noble expressions of manhood.

Some Black men have accomplished great deeds as scholar activists, mastering the educational system of America, correcting the defaming characterizations of racist scholarship and defending the honor of the people. But it is not the scholar who has always been there in the times of greatest need. The scholar is not the one called upon when someone falls ill in the middle of the night, when the children have no clothes to wear, or when people are being put out of their homes. In order for a man to be a man in the highest sense of the word, he must serve by providing some level of guidance and leadership to his people. And this leadership, if it is to be authentic and not a fraud must arise organically from the people; it must be definitively in the interest and in the image of the people who are so led.

The highest expressions of Black manhood can be found only when Black men are striving to lead their own communities toward the inter-related aims of justice, righteousness and real prosperity. This has con-stituted the supreme challenge for Black men in America as they have faced overwhelming, relentless and withering racist hostility. It is no acci-dent that the most potent and efficacious leadership of the masses comes always from those who find themselves spiritually impelled to lead. And so a select few—Andrew Bryan, Richard Allen, Henry Highland Garnet, Henry McNeal Turner, Martin Luther King, Jr., and Fred Shuttlesworth, among others—have been provided by history with the opportunity to rise up in struggle to meet this challenge, that even when the powers and principalities of this world had decreed that for them there should be no way, they supplied the leadership for a dispossessed people to make a way out of no way.

Notes

Chapter 1: Our Mother

1. John G. Jackson, *Introduction to African Civilizations* (New York: Kensington Publishing Corp., 1994), 66-67; Cain Hope Felder, ed., *The Original Heritage Study Bible* (Nashville: The James C. Winston Publishing Company, 1993), ix. The word *negro* specifies the color black in Portuguese and Spanish. The historian Yusef ben-Jochannan has suggested that *Alkebu-lan,* which means "mother of humankind," was the first name used by Africans to designate that continent which is their historical homeland. Yosef ben-Jochannan, *African Origins of Major Western Religions* (New York: Alkebulan Books, 1970), 1. The Blacks is one of the oldest names historically applied to African people, although it is perhaps a less formal name than the designation of Africans. Our use of Blacks as a proper name when referring to people of African descent is in keeping with the given historical identification. The descriptive black is used in some cases to simply denote skin color. People have distinctive skin colors, but they have much more besides. People also have shared histories, family lineages, and cultural backgrounds along with skin color as a related attribute. There are many different skin tones apparent among people of African descent, and it is important not to confuse global patterns with specific representations thereof. The fundamental frequency of skin tone demonstrated by African people does not preclude variations spanning the entire orbit of human colorations. Indeed we find that black bodies emit all other colorations both electromagnetically and genetically.

Were we to sever the Africans from that skin color characteristic as some would now have us to do, they might no longer be recognizable. Africans were Black long before they were African as indicated by the terms Ethiopia and Kemet, both of which predate the term Africa. The Greeks began referring to Africans as "burnt face people" or Ethiopians when they were still under the influences of the Ancient Egyptians, who had the habit of calling their country Kemet, "The Black Land," represented hieroglyphically with a burnt piece of wood followed by images of people. Also, the Ancient Sumerians, who preceded the Ancient Greeks and the Romans, named themselves the "black heads" thereby signaling their African heritage. (Runoko Rashidi, "More Light on Sumer, Elam and India," Ivan Van Sertima, ed., *The African Presence in Early Asia* [Transaction Publishers: New Brunswick, NJ, 1987], 162–171.) The presence of the Blacks antedates the conceptualization of the races, and that land mass called Africa has always been known as the homeland of the Blacks. We would do well to bear in mind the words of historian Chancellor Williams from his challenging study, *The Destruction of Black Civilization*: "An African is a member of the black race, and from time immemorial he was known as such by all peoples of the world.... [Africans are] essentially one people, one 'race' if you please, the African race. In ancient times 'African' and 'Ethiopian' meant the same thing: A Black. This of course was before the Caucasians began to reorder the earth to suit themselves and found it necessary to stake their birthright over the Land of the Blacks. In line with this, some Western historians have recently wondered where the Africans came from!" (*The Destruction of Black Civilization: Great Issues of a Race from 4500 B.C. to 2000 A.D.* [Chicago: Third Press, 1987], 31.) Lastly, we note that the use of the appellative Black can invoke a sense of commonality that readily transcends differences by geographic region, language, culture group association and historical era in a way that other names may not—a useful property when undertaking the holistic consideration of these people.

2. Colin McEvedy, *The Penguin Atlas of African History* (New York: Penguin Books, 1980), 8–34; J.D. Fage, *The Cambridge History of Africa Vol 1* (New York: University Press, 1982), 9–11, W.E.B. DuBois, *Africa, Its Geography, People and Products* and *Africa, Its Place in the Modern History* (New York: Kto Press, 1930), 1. The geographical size of the African continent is three to four times larger than Europe and twice the size of North America. The Mother Continent is second in size to Asia, and since time immemorial it has been considered a land of inexhaustible resources. Africa has linguistic and cultural ties with Western Asia or the Near East including Palestine, the Arabian Peninsula, and India, as Africans settled that part of the world in deep antiquity. Africa is separated from Europe by the Mediterranean Sea.

Richard E. Leakey and Roger Lewin, *Origins* (New York: E.P. Dutton, 1977), 7–15.

3. "Search for Adam and Eve," *Newsweek*, January 11, 1988; J.D. Fage, *The Cambridge History of Africa, Vol. 1* (New York: Cambridge University Press, 1982), 24–27.

4. Ivan Van Sertima, ed. *Great African Thinkers: Cheikh Anta Diop* (New Brunswick, NJ: The State University, 1986), 34–42. The authors Richard Leaky and Roger Lewin also found humanities origins in the regions of central east Africa (Richard E. Leakey and Roger Lewin, *Origins*, 80–117).

5. Jun Z. Li, et al., "Worldwide Human Relationships Inferred from Genome-Wide Patterns of Variation," *Science*, Vol. 319. February 22, 2008. The authors of this research paper studied the genetic ancestry of persons from around the world. They report that their research found that "The relationship between

haplotype heterozygosity and geography was consistent with the hypothesis of a serial founder effect with a single origin in sub-Saharan Africa," i.e., an ultimate African ancestral origin for all of humanity. "New fossil evidence from Ethiopia shows that anatomically modern humans roamed Africa about 195,000 years ago—at least 35,000 years earlier than previously thought." *The Atlanta Journal-Constitution*, "35,000 Years Added to Age of Man," February 17, 2005.

6. "Search for Adam and Eve," *Newsweek*, January 11, 1988, 47.

7. Kevin Shillington, *History of Africa* (New York: St. Martin Press, 1995), 1–6.

8. Cheikh Anta Diop, *Civilization or Barbarism* (Nerw York: Lawrence Hill Books, 1991), 11–23. "Gene Mutation Might Explain Evolution of Some Skin Colors," *Atlanta Journal-Constitution*, Sunday, December 18, 2005. The skin of Europeans may have turned white after their ancestors migrated from Africa because of a single mutation among the 3 billion genetic "letters" that make up the human genome, according to the article.

It is interesting to note that medical agencies in the United States, particularly the Centers for Disease Control, are able to provide us with elaborate epidemiological statistics according to racial designations (see *National Vital Statistic Report*, any year). But alas, to date there is no definitive biomedical description of race (see Camara Jones, "'Race', Racism and the Practice of Epidemiology," *American Journal of Epidemiology*, Vol. 154, No. 4, 2001, 299–304). How is it then that medical authorities can be so certain in giving us epidemiological statistics using racial designations about which anthropologists, demographers, and sociologists are so confounded? Most scholars, writers, and media spokespersons have followed the current trend of using race as a descriptor without any political, social, or cultural implications. The racial designation "black" has become a catchall for reporting only negatives about such people; to say anything approving is mostly avoided. And so we are left with the farcical circumstance in which anything positive that occurs concerning Blacks is attributed to something other than themselves, while all negative occurrences can only be due to their own faults. Public discourse involving the subject of race has become filled with platitudes and non sequiturs, and discussion has at times descended into sheer asininity. Recently, the Pew Research Center published the results of a study that included a survey of African Americans in which they concluded that 37 percent of African Americans do not believe themselves to be members of a single race. That is, these astute researchers identified a distinct group of people, African Americans, whom they called so that they might conduct their survey. They then proceeded to ask these people whether they thought that African Americans ought not be considered a single race because they have some amount of diversity amongst them or whether instead African Americans might be a single race since they apparently do have enough commonality to permit a survey of them. No explanation of terms was given. Besides endeavoring to instigate confusion and doubt about the identity of Blacks, what on earth could any of this possibly mean? The statement "There is no single race of European Americans because one-third of them have recent African ancestry," may be confusing, even if factual, since we have both identified a single entity and simultaneously declared it to be a plurality. Certainly it can be said that Whites have some commonality and some diversity amongst them; diversity within an encompassing unity being an inherent property of all groupings. Such studies reveal a great deal about the researchers, but next to nothing about the subjects supposedly under research. It is not incumbent upon Blacks to abdicate their identity and heritage so that some other people can feel comfortable with whoever it is that they think they might be. If we must question people about their racial identity, then clearly the original people should be the last ones to be queried; how exactly all subsequent races materialized is the real mystery here. ("Optimism About Black Progress Declines: Blacks See Growing Values Gap Between Poor and Middle Class," *Pew Research Center Social and Demographic Trends Report*, November 13, 2007.)

9. The dating of early civilizations is subject to some interpretation. Different scholars use different criteria for determining the presence of civilization, such as the existence of writing scripts, construction of buildings, emergence of central governing authorities, evidence of advanced craftsmanship with crafted tools and pottery, and so forth. In any case, there is quite substantial evidence that early civil societies first emerged in Africa and later diffused out to Asia, Europe, and then the Americas. The domestication of animals and organized agriculture began in the Nile Valley below the first cataract, or in the region of Nubia, as far back as 18,000 years ago (Kevin Shillington, *The History of Africa* [New York: St. Martin's Press, 1995], 16). The earliest fixed date in history is 4,121 B.C.E. from the Ancient Egyptian Sothic calendar. There is also evidence that Nile Valley civilization was already advanced enough to build the Great Sphinx 7,000–9,000 years ago. (Charles Finch, "Nile Genesis: Continuity of Culture from the Great Lakes to the Delta," Ivan Van Sertima, ed., *Egypt Child of Africa* (New Brunswick, N. J., Transaction Publishers, 1995), 47, 51.) According to the historian Runoko Rashidi the Sumerians flourished in Mesopotamia from 3,000–1,750 B.C.E. (Runoko Rashidi, "More Light on Sumer, Elam and India," Ivan Van Sertima, ed. *African Presence in Early Asia* (Transaction Publishers: New Brunswick, NJ, 1987), 162. Wayne Chandler found that the greatest examples of ancient Indian architecture in Mohenjo-Darro and Harrapa occurred between 3,000 and 2,500 B.C.E. The author also states that this civilization arose out of earlier villages that were indigenous to that area as far back as 7,000 B.C.E. (Wayne B. Chandler, "Jewel in the

Lotus: The Ethiopian Presence in the Indus Valley Civilization," *African Presence in Early Asia*, ed. Ivan Van Sertima, Runoko Rashidi, 83.) Both Frank Snowden and Ivan Van Sertima maintained that in antiquity black was the color of preference. The Roman historian Pliny, described the Britons in the second century c.e. as having skin as black as Ethiopians. Also, records from China show that the first emperor of China, Fu-Hsi, was described as being "a wooly-haired Negro," and men with black skin dwelled there during the Shang Dynasty (1,766–1,100 B.C.E.) the first historic dynasty of China. (Ivan Van Sertima, *Egypt Child of Africa* [London: Transaction Publishers, 1994], 2, 122–123; and Frank M. Snowden, Jr., *Blacks in Antiquity* [Cambridge: Harvard University Press, 1970], 1–7.) It is well known that the dates of distinctly Greek and Roman civil societies are much more recent than any of the other aforementioned ancient cultures.

10. Bruce Bower, "Africa's Ancient Cultural Roots," *Science News*. Vol. 48, No. 23. December 2, 1995, 378.

11. Kevin Shillington, *History of Africa*, 9-10; Richard E. Leaky and Roger Lewin, *Origins*, 79–117.

12. Ibid., 14–16. Richard E. Leakey, *Origins* (New York: E.P. Hutton, 1977), 119. None of the other ancient cultures knew about iron in prehistoric times, and the evidence points to Africa as the origin of the use of iron in the world. Some scholars contend, however, that the Hittites of Western Asia were the first in historic times to develop a process that allowed for the widespread use of iron. Chancellor Williams argued that the Africans first developed a process of iron smelting but that it was jealously guarded by their secret societies, which constituted guilds, so that its spread among them was minimized. (See W.E.B. DuBois, *Africa Its Geography, People and Products* and *Africa, Its People in Modern History*, 3; Van Sertima, Ivan. (1984). *The Lost Sciences of Africa: An Overview*. Ed. Ivan Van Sertima [New Brunswick (U.S.A.): Transaction Books,1984], 7-26. Claudia Zaslavsky. *The Yoruba Number System*. Ed. Ivan Van Sertima [New Brunswick (U.S.A.): Transaction Books], 110- 126. *The Destruction of Black Civilization: Great Issues of a Race from 4500 B.C. to 2000 A.D.*, 132–133.)

13. Ben-Jochannan gives a description of the ancient Grand Lodge of Luxor, which he describes as the center of an extensive educational system in antiquity. He dates the temple Karnak back to 2685 B.C.E. (Y. A. ben-Jochannan, *Black Man of the Nile and His Family* [Baltimore: Black Classics Press, 1978], 313–338). George James gives an overview of the teachings propounded by the ancient Africans in their temples in *Stolen Legacy* (Chicago: *African American Image*s, 2001), 131–152.

14. Martin Bernal, *Black Athena: The Afroasiatic Roots of Classical Civilization, Vol. I: The Fabrication of Ancient Greece 1785–1985*, 22, 105–106, 108, 510.

15. Henry Louis Gates, *Wonders of the African World* (New York: Alfred A. Knopf), 1999, 27.

16. Yosef ben-Jochannan, *African Origins of the Major Western Religions*, XIX–XXVI.

17. Mircea Eliade, ed., Benjamin C. Ray, *Encyclopedia of Religion*, "The Dogon Creation Story," 24–40.

18. E.A. Wallis Budge, *Egyptian Religion* (New York: University Books, 1959), 89–103. Further parallels between the religious allegories of ancient Egypt and traditional Africa as compared to those of Christianity are extensively documented in Yosef ben-Jochannan's *African Origins of Major "Western" Religions* and *African Origin of the Major World Religions*, ed. Amon Saba Saakana (London: Karnak House, 1988).

19. Cain Hope Felder, ed., *The Original African Heritage Study Bible*, X.

20. Ibid., 3; Cheikh Anta Diop, *The African Origin of Civilization* (Westport: Lawrence Hill and Co., 1974), 24–28.

21. Felder, x.

22. Ibid., ix. Diop, *The African Origin of Civilization*, 7–9, 94–98. The Merneptah stele was discovered by Flinders Petrie in 1896. This ancient document written in Egyptian hieroglyphics is the oldest document with mention of Israel outside of the Hebrew Bible. The Merneptah stele is dated at 1200–1300 B.C.E.

23. Yosef A. ben-Jochannan, *Black Man on the Nile and His Family.* (Baltimore: Black Classics Press, 1978), 102–104, 237–240. There were Jews present in Ancient Egypt, but the record does not indicate that they were enslaved or forced to build any of the pyramids. It has now been fairly well established that the enslavement of Jews and their subsequent exodus as described in the Bible was not a historical event. The Ancient Egyptians built the pyramids mostly if not entirely by themselves, through the conscription of farmers for labor during the annual inundation period. There are archeological remains and numerous accounts indicating that the pyramid builders were compensated; some were skilled artisans and others were well trained administrators. (Morris Bierbrier, *The Tomb Builders of the Pharaohs* [New York: Charles Scribners Sons, 1982], 10–12.) The myth of the Exodus was used to foster a sense of national unity among the early Jews. In ancient Ethiopia, Jews were also present and there they were often among the ruling classes of society.

24. Frank M. Snowden, *Blacks in Antiquity*, 101–120; Kevin Shillington, *History of Africa*, 108–109.

25. Felder, 1820–1822, 1833–1840.

26. Ibid, 48. Yosef ben-Jochannan, *We the Black Jews,* Vols. I & II.

27. Harold Courlander, *A Treasury of African Folklore: The Oral Literature, Traditions, Myths, Legends, Epic Tales, Recollections, Wisdom, Sayings, and Humor of Africa* (New York: Crown, 1977), 203–205.

28. Ibid., 236–241.

29. Felder, 1828–1832.

30. Yosef ben-Jochannan, *African Origins of Major "Western Religions,"* 85–88.

31. Tertullian, *Prescription Against Heretics,* 89; Felder, 1829–1830.

32. Justin Martyr, *Dialogue with Tripplis the Few;* John McManners, *The Oxford History of Christianity,* 52–58; Frank M. Snowden, Jr., *Blacks in Antiquity: Ethiopians in the Greco-Roman Experience* (Cambridge: Harvard University Press), 1970, 207. In Justin's Apology XIV he states that the Logos (universal reason) was to be found in every man. Even the philosophers such as Heraclitis, Musonius and others had lived by seminal logos. However, the Logos common to all did not give full knowledge, for only a portion of the Logos was distributed. Thus, philosophy could not lead men to God, for it was dependent on man's reason, which was only partial. The way to God ultimately was not through a reasoning process, but through God's revelation which was the whole of Logos, and that became incarnate in Christ. (See Willis A. Shotwell, *The Biblical Exegesis of Justin Martyr* [London; S.P.C.K. , 1965], 2,3,6.) Von Campenhauser acknowledged Tertullian's African heritage when he described him by stating, "It is characteristically African to combine discipline with criticism and state of order with scorn and passion preferring self-suffering even to the point of rebellion, rather than blindly follow and obey." (See H. Von Campenhauser, *The Father of the Latin Church* [London: A. C. Black, 1964], 5.)

33. Tatian, *Address to the Greeks* (*Tatiani Oratio ad Graecos*) (New York: W. De Grufter, 1995) Tatian made an acerbic attack against the cultural hegemony of the Greeks. He accused them of promoting the notion that those people who did not speak Greek and who were not familiar with Greek culture were inferiors and barbarians. Yet, as he pointed out, the Greeks adopted much of what constituted their celebrated cultural achievement from these same barbarians.

34. Tertullian, *Apology XXXVI, L,* Justo L. Gonzalez, *The Story of Christianity (Vol. 1),* (New York: Harper Collins Publisher, 1984), 86; John Esposito, *The Oxford History of Islam* (New York: Oxford University Press, 1999), 481–484. Tertullian is the father of Western theology. He laid out the foundations for orthodox Christian theology ratified by the Council of Nicea (325 c.e.). He used his legal training to craft his systematic theology. In his treatise on the "Witnessing of the Soul," Tertullian maintained that the soul took the virtuous stand and concluded

that the soul is by nature Christian. Thus, it is not necessary for Christians to seek truth through philosophy because it is inherent in their nature.

35. Aarib Nukavecm, *The Didache* (New York: The Newman Press, 2003, vii). This document gives an account of the oral training for new converts that occurred during meetings in the early church. This ancient document recalls more about how Jewish Christians saw themselves and how they adapted their Judaism to accommodate gentiles than any book in Christian scripture. *The Didache* is older than the canonical gospels. It was not written by one author. It is the product of the oral tradition of storytelling arising from different communities.

36. David Chichester, "Christianity," *A Global History* (New York: Harper Collins, 2000), 12–42; Eugene G. Bewkes, *A Survey of Philosophy and Religion* (New York: Harper and Brothers Publishers, 1940), 131–156.

37. Henry Chadwick, *The Early Church* (New York: Penguin, 1967), 9–31; Justo L. Gonzalez, *The Story of Christianity*, 7–11.

38. Gonzalez, 7–11.

39. R. Joseph Hoffmann, *Celsus on the True Doctrine* (New York: Oxford University Press, 1989), 12–24, 35–45.

40. Margaret R. Miles, *The Word Made Flesh: A History of Christian Thought* (Malden, MA: Blackwell Publishing, 2005), 69, 70, 102–103; George Herring, *Introduction to the History of Christianity* (New York: New York University Press, 2006), 42–62.

41. Gonzalez, *The Story of Christianity* (Vol. 1), 40–41. Henry Bettenson and Chris Maunder, *Documents of the Christian Church* (New York: Oxford Press, 1999), 3–5.

42. H. A. Drake, *Constantine and the Bishops* (Baltimore: The Johns Hopkins Press, 2002), 198–211; Gonzalez, *The Story of Christianity*, 53.

43. Gonzalez, *The Story of Christianity*, 88–90. Drake, 212–230.

44. Gonzalez, 56; Chadwick, 220, 224.

45. Gonzalez, 88–90; Miles, 52–54.

46. Gonzalez, 88–90; Drake, 108.

47. McManners, 49, 64, 78, 85; Chadwick, 123–224; Drake, 214–215.

48. Some scholars doubt the approach of considering African cultures or African traditional religions in a comprehensive and holistic manner, or as expressive of stupendous, interrelated, evolving, collective historical patterns, an unfolding diachronic presence. And it is indeed the case that there are about 1,000 different indigenous culture groups and as many or more different languages and

dialects spoken throughout the continent, and even more across the Diaspora, each group with its own spiritual system, beliefs, and practices. It is true that Africans occasionally have political squabbles sometimes erupting in warfare; they have linguistic differences as well, some of them have obscure origins, and they widely comingle with other peoples. But much the same may also be said of other groups of people, including Europeans, Chinese, Jews, Indians, and Arabs. African culture groups are interrelated with large subgroups stretched across extended geographic regions sharing many perspectives and practices. The Kenyan scholar John S. Mbiti observed the following:

> Studies of African religious beliefs show that there are probably more similarities than differences.... As with material culture religious ideas and activities are exchanged when people come into contact with one another even though there is no organized missionary work of one group trying to proselytize another. This exchange of ideas is spontaneous and probably more noticeable in practical matters like rain making, combating magic and witchcraft and dealing with misfortunes. In such cases expert knowledge may be borrowed and later assimilated from neighboring peoples. Fundamental concepts like belief in God, existence of spirits, continuation of human life after death, magic and witchcraft seem to have been retained when one people may have split or branched off in course of the centuries, the new groups forming "tribes" of their own, which we now can recognize under the broad ethnic groupings of African peoples. This probably explains the fact of fundamental beliefs being found over wide stretches of Africa. Therefore, names for God, words for spirits, magic and medicine men are similar among many peoples.... (John S. Mbiti, *African Religions and Philosophy*, 134–135.)

There are underlying similar philosophical approaches, some historically related symbolisms and linguistic interrelatedness, a broadly shared outlook of deep respect for elders and family ties, an emphasis on the establishment of mutually beneficial communal relationships, complex patterns of rhythmic expression, and strong interest in the pursuit of specialized knowledge and skill in dealing with spiritual matters, among other things, which unite African traditions. (For further considerations of the underlying philosophical and cultural unity of African peoples, see Cheikh Anta Diop, *Civilization or Barbarism? An Authentic Anthropology*, 309–376; *The Cultural Unity of Black Africa: The Domains of Patriarchy and Matriarchy in Classical Antiquity*; and Jacob Caruthers' work *MDT NTR: Divine Speech, Historiographical Reflection of African Deep Thought from the Time of the Pharaohs to the Present*.)

Collective presence springs from a common ancestry and shared heritage which spiritually implies the possibility of a common ultimate destiny. Limiting ourselves to parochial concerns among African people is myopic, disconcerting, degrading, and unhelpful. We need not be dismayed or perplexed by so many differences; we should be respectful of the differences—local and regional—and then we can move beyond artificial limitation. In a holistic treatment we may consider African culture groups from the full range of perspectives: focusing on culture groups as separate entities or centering on interrelated regional subgroups or even viewing relationships in the context of the broad sweep of African cultures. It is no less possible to speak in generalized terms of African culture, history, and values than it is to speak of a European or Western culture, history, and heritage.

Throughout Africa the unity of life and an ultimate underlying oneness implied by the all-encompassing spiritual nature of things were not just interesting conjectures and idle speculations, but they historically have been reflected in widely practiced ways of living that stressed the value of community. The philosophy of the Zulus in southern Africa tells us "*umuntu ngumuntu ngabantu*," or that a person is a person only through other persons. This was reflected in the fact that in pre-colonial times Africans could often travel long distances over wide regions, safely and without the benefit of a monetary system, as strangers were generally welcomed and well treated. It was realized that human beings are social beings; individuals need other individuals in order to exist, to survive, and to find value in living. Individual achievement without a background and community of support from somewhere is an illusion of artful speech. The Bantu philosophical perspective of *ubuntu* which means "humanness" or "collective personhood" encourages the establishment of relationships built upon reciprocal dependencies by which people can successfully share a communal way of life and it is similar to other philosophical outlooks and practices found throughout Africa. (See Nomonde Masina, "Xhosa Practices of Unbuntu for South Africa," I. William Zartman, ed., *Traditional Cures for Modern Conflicts: African Conflict "Medicine"* [Boulder, CO: Lynne Rienner Publishers, 2000], 169–181.)

In African traditions there is generally no definitive demarcation between the physical and the spiritual. Spiritual entities were involved in every aspect of human life. Reality may be considered a kind of continuum between the two poles of the spirit world and the earthly realm, the visible and the invisible, with materiality being a condensed but transitory representation of the more permanent spiritual nature of things. Thus, as Mbiti relates, the Africans lived in a religious universe: "Wherever the African is, there is his religion: he carries it to the fields when he is sowing seeds or harvesting a new crop; he takes it with him to the beer party or to attend a funeral ceremony; and if he is educated, he takes religion with him to the examination room at school or in the university; if he is a politician, he takes it to the house of parliament." (John S. Mbiti, *African Religions and Philosophy*, 2.)

Understanding the primacy of the spiritual relative to the material in the traditional African view may also be helpful in an exegesis of the Nestorian and Arian controversies, as there were many in the African wing of the Church who had some difficulty with the conceptualization of the supreme deity in human form. The greatness of the spiritual and divine realities in the traditional African view involved these spiritual presences forever encompassing, transcending, supporting, and correcting the material world. Thus, it would not be possible for the Spirit or the Supreme God to ever fully incarnate or become completely reduced to any material body, although there would always be correspondences with the innumerable forms of the physical realm through the various spiritual agencies. In this sense materiality while at times enticing is also inevitably limited and corruptible, fugacious and relative, and as such it is found to be a peripheral and secondary reality or even a superficial representation of the indispensible spiritual essence. Material reality is the means, not the end. It is the Spirit which is eternal. It is the Spirit, never the material, which provides genuine enlightenment and righteous empowerment. Thus, it is important to gain insight and knowledge of spiritual affairs and establish a proper relationship with the immaterial essence of our being, the all-encompassing foundation of reality, as doing so implies the capacity to transcend and overcome impossibly difficult circumstances and to resolve seemingly insoluble entanglements. From this view then, any attempt to force fit the Spirit into a single body or to claim that the Spirit was born of a particular physical womb indicates a fundamental misconception of the nature of reality; the nature of the Spirit is to be unbounded by material conditionality. Attempting to particularize and materialize the Spirit in effect demotes and downgrades the supremacy of the Supreme Being.

49. Western materialism has been at the root of a cultural mindset that seems poised to pursue objectification and exploitation to destructive extremes. Anything and everything is objectified, detached from its natural setting, bought and sold if possible, and gratuitously used with little or no consideration of the moral consequences. In Western materialism there is an exaggeration of the importance of individuality and personal attributes at the expense of the value and sense of community. Although Westerners have written profusely about community, appropriate forms of governance, and spirituality, the history of Europe and European America demonstrates far more regard for predatory enterprises and relationships based on domination and exploitation than for peaceful cooperative efforts. (See Michael Bradley, *Ice Man Inheritance* [Toronto: Dorset Publishing Inc., 1978]; Marimba Ani, *Yurugu: An Afrikan-Centered Critique of European Cultural Thought and Behavior* [Washington, DC: Nkonimfo Publications, 1994], Walter Rodney, *How Europe Underdeveloped Africa* [Washington, DC: Howard

University Press, 1982]; and Frances Cress Welsing, *Isis Papers* [Chicago: Third World Press], 1-16, 193–208.) African psychologists have also given insightful descriptions of the materialistic Eurocentric perspective: "The alien (Euro-American) way of life assumed man to be first and foremost a material being in search of physical gratifications. Normative behavior is thus viewed in terms of the maximal gratification of one's material ambitions (variously referred to as achievement motivation, territorial dominance, political power, etc.) The exploitation of people and resources is considered of little consequence, in as much as the core of it all is believed to be dispensable material." (Na'im Akbar, *Akbar Papers in African Psychology* [Tallahassee, FL: Mind Productions, 2003], 23–24.) The dangers of a materialistic approach to living are addressed in all major religious systems. But, even religion and the concept of God can be objectified, turned into exploitable devices, made into political tools, or commoditized and then used to gratify one desire or another. This is suggested by Karl Marx's observation that "religion is the opiate of the people." And it should be noted that materialistic objectification in the sense described can also be applied to political ideologies as well as to religious practices. Political ideologies and economic theories, just like religions, can be used to self-delude or to seduce, manipulate, and mislead so that they too can sometimes constitute "opiates of the people," especially among those aspiring to intellectual pretensions. Materialism is not confined to the West and such views have long existed in African and Asian cultures as well. However, it is among Westerners that materialism has achieved a level of social preeminence and ruthless application which was not known to non-Western cultures prior to contact with Europeans.

50. Drake, 214–217.

51. Gonzalez, 156. The Circumcellions launched attacks against wealthy Catholic landowners. The Donatists represented Christians in the North African Church who broke away from Western Christianity.

52. Ibid., 123. Prior to the fourth century, Christians held as an ideal that there should be a universal church, one body with a single hierarchy, but in practice at this time Christians were mostly part of small disparate communities that were often persecuted. It was the conversion of Constantine that radically changed circumstances for early Christians. For the first time the Church became a recipient of the financial and military support of the imperial government. The emergence of Constantine marked the beginning of efforts by emperors and bishops to create a worldwide universal church with a hierarchical command structure strictly under their authority. (See David Brakke, *Athanasius and Asceticism*, 2.)

53. George Herring, *Introduction to the History of Christianity*, 50–55.

54. Gonzalez, 161.

55. The Nicean Council remains a source of great controversy and contention and some African scholars, including Yosef ben-Jochannan, have made various claims that it was at Nicea in 325 c.e. that certain teachings of the church were altered in order to obscure or displace the African origin of Christianity. Among those claims include the changing of the birthplace of Jesus Christ from a cave in Ethiopia to a manger in Bethlehem and the removal of all African saints from the list of the saints of the church. Our review of sources available to us does not corroborate those specific charges. It is well known, however, that church doctrine was reformulated at this conference and that some scriptures that had been used by earlier groups of Christians were removed from the canon.

56. John McManners, *The Oxford History of Christianity*, 56–57.

57. David Brakke, *Athanasius and Asceticism* (Baltimore: The Johns Hopkins University Press), 1–16. Monasticism, which has an African origin, embraced asceticism. The men who chose an ascetic lifestyle were called solitaries and the women were known as virgins. Both genders were expected to practice sexual renunciation. Their lifestyle set them apart from other Christians and they were a target of both consternation and adoration. Athanasius held up the example of the virgin women to support his theological position against Arianism. He maintained that the virgin women were a concrete example of the power of the incarnate Word, which supported orthodox views of the divinity of Christ. "What person ... taught about virginity and did not reason it to be impossible with the virtue to exist among human beings? Yet our Savior and King of all, Christ, so prevailed in his teaching about this that even children not yet of legal age promised virginity over and above the law." Athanasius argued that as "brides of Christ," virgins were proof positive of how humanity may be united with the divine Word. Their renunciation of sex decisively demonstrated that the incarnate Word had triumphed over death and the human soul's bondage to bodily passions. (See Brakke, *Athanasius and Asceticism*, 17.) Athanasius' emphasis on the "virgins" gave prominence to women in the Egyptian Christian Church. These women played significant roles in providing anti-Arian ammunition for those who supported the outcome of the Council of Nicea. Also, he used the title "brides of Christ" to make the secluded lifestyle seem natural and appropriate.

58. Chadwick, 150–151; Miles, 189–193. Athanasius was a strong advocate for the full divinity of Jesus. When asked by an Arianist, "How is the son equal to the Father?" Athanasius replied, "Like the sight of two eyes." He based his views of the full divinity of Christ as necessary for Christ to save humankind from the evil of death. It was Athanasius' contention that Christ entered human nature in order to achieve solidarity with the human race and thereby open the way for salvation.

59. Chadwick, 146–147.

60. Buell G. Gallagher, *Color and Conscience: The Irresistible Conflict* (New York: Harper and Brothers Publishers, 1946), 44.

61. Ben-Jochannan, *African Origins of the Major "Western Religions,"* 73–78.

62. Herring, 106–111.

63. Mbiti, xiii, 300.

Chapter 2: Christianity in Transition

1. Buell G. Gallagher, *Color and Conscience: The Irresistible Conflict* (New York: Harper and Brother Publishers, 1946), 44–45.

2. Ibid.

3. Ibid., 40–41.

4. Justo L. Gonzalez, *The Story of Christianity,* Vol. 1 (New York: Harper Collins Publisher, 1984), 138–143.

5. Ibid., 136–138.

6. According to the author Tamara Sonn, "The Quran does not abolish the institution of slavery. As in the Hebrew Bible, slavery was an integral part of the eco-system at the time the Quran was revealed." (Tamara Sonn, *A Brief History of Islam* [Malden, MA: Blackwell Publishing, 2004], 16.) Hugh Thomas also notes that initially both Christianity and Islam accepted slavery as part of the natural order of society. (Hugh Thomas, *The Slave Trade* [New York: Simon and Schuster, 1997], 36–37.) Chancellor Williams, H. A. McMichael, and Alfred J. Butler each give accounts of the Arab invasions and conquests of North Africa, and the resultant subjugation of the Africans who were already present. Thus, the abolition of slavery by the early practitioners of Islam would have required a complete overhaul of the economic and social system, something they apparently were not prepared to do as they spread their new religion in Africa primarily through military conquests. (Chancellor Williams, *Destruction of Black Civilization: Great Issues of a Race 4500 B.C. to 2000 A.D.* [Chicago: Third World Press, 1987], 150–156; H. A. McMichael, *A History of Arabs in the Sudan: And Some Account of the People Who Preceded Them and of the Tribes Inhabiting Darfur* [Cambridge University Press, 1922], 155–190; and, Alfred Butler, *The Arab Conquest of Egypt and The Last Thirty Years of Roman Domination* [Oxford, Clarendon Press, 1902].)

7. Carlos Moore, "Afro-Cubans and the Communist Revolution" in *African Presence in the Americas*, Carlos Moore, ed. (Trenton, NJ: African World Press, 1995), 204-209.

8. Chancellor Williams, *The Destruction of Black Civilization: Great Issues of a*

Race from 4500 B.C. to 2000 A.D. (Chicago: Third World Press, 1987), 150–156; Lamin Sanneh, *West African Christianity* (Maryknoll, New York: Orbis Books, 1983), 15–17. It should be noted that the religion of Islam shares many of the same historical and theological roots as Christianity and Judaism. And just as the case has been with Christianity, the religion of Islam has been used as a device to pursue political goals. Arab-centric Islam like Eurocentric Christianity has been affected by anti-Black racist sentiments, with those who identify themselves as Arab and Muslim continuing to persecute and enslave Africans in the nations of Sudan and Mauritania up to the present day.

9. Gallagher, 52–53. Western scholars sometimes identify the early church fathers of North Africa as Berbers as though that might separate them from their African heritage. The original people of North Africa were the same as the original people of the rest of the continent, who were the same as the original people of the planet. Frank Snowden provides documentary and archeological evidence relating ancient North Africans phenotypically to Africans throughout the rest of the continent. Chancellor Williams observes that the original Moors were Black and that over time that designation was assumed by other people who came from outside of Africa. The original Berbers may have also been Black, and the historian Runoko Rashidi reports that there remain some communities of Black Berbers present to the current day in North Africa. As more and more people from Europe and Asia settled on the Mediterranean coastline of North Africa the cultural character of the local populations began to change, and especially so after the Arab invasions.

Some scholars have characterized Ancient Egyptian civilization as a mulatto or a mixed-race culture and they have also applied such terms as Afroasiatic to people in the kingdom of ancient Axum. Indeed some of the founders of Axum did come from the Arabian Peninsula around 800 B.C.E. But, as Queen Makeda, who occupied the throne of Ethiopia circa 1000 B.C.E., also ruled part of the Arabian Peninsula, we are left with the likely event that many of those who came to establish the Axumite kingdom were of a similar cultural and racial background as the people they found already residing in that region of Ethiopia. Of course the commingling and cohabitation of human beings from various racial and ethnic backgrounds has been ongoing for many centuries. However, we must be careful when applying modern concepts of race and ethnicity to ancient peoples who had not yet developed such viewpoints. In particular, it is found that early migrants generally adopted the names and cultural values of the peoples in whose lands they settled; once migrants adopted the customs of their new homeland they were absorbed into the general population. Only when larger numbers of newcomers arrived, imposing their own traditions on the already established cultures, did there arise what we might call ethnic or racial tensions. Diop gives a detailed discussion of the commingling or confluence of racial or ethnic groups and he indicates that ethnic hostilities tend to increase once the concentration of immigrants settling in a new region exceeds 4–8 percent of the total population. (Cheikh Anta Diop, *Civilization or Barbarism? An Authentic Anthropology*, 123–128, 211–227.)

The notion that some people might be mulatto, or of "mixed blood," and belong to a separate racial class different from that of either of their parents, seems to be a more recent invention. The early civilizations of the Ancient Nile Valley were founded by Blacks, and there is evidence that the same is the case for the early civilizations of Western Asia and the Indus Kush Valley. Beginning around 3500 B.C.E. Asians and Whites from the Eurasian steppes began to steadily stream down into the Mesopotamian region of Western Asia and the Mediterranean coastline areas of Northern Africa. By 1500 B.C.E. there were full scale invasions from the North and the early Black civilizations collapsed under the pressures. The notion of mulattos or a mixed-race type does not seem to have been widely applied to human beings until much later with the rise of Arab hegemony over much of Western Asia and North Africa. The scholar Carlos Moore links the concept of "mulattoism" with the racial subjugation of Blacks. The mulatto identity has been used as a divide-and-conquer stratagem against African people at least since the time of the Arab ascendancy; the term mulatto may have originated with the Arab word *muwallad* which means "mixed ancestry." Prior to this time there were certainly programs of conquest, ethnic suppression and even genocide as can be found with the Hebrew invasions of Canaan circa 1300 B.C.E.–1400 B.C.E. and the persecutions of Cambyses in Egypt in 525 B.C.E. However, it is not until much later that the historical record clearly shows systematic programs perpetrated by imperialist invaders promoting racial distinctions and proclaiming the existence of a "mixed blood" or mulatto classification all with the aim of subduing indigenous populations.

10. Albert J. Raboteau, *Slave Religion: The "Invisible Institution" in the Antebellum South* (New York: Oxford University Press, 2004), 47; Joseph E. Harris, *Africans and Their History*, 5.

11. Harris, 48–49. There was great resistance within the African wing of the church to the imposition of Roman domination over their faith. Some of the Africans formulated theological doctrines supporting the traditional African view of divinity in response to the materialistic notions advanced by the Roman-dominated church. Gallagher observes that the Christological debates of the fourth and fifth centuries involved much more than differences of opinion about esoteric theological matters, but the arguments reflected deep socioeconomic, political, and ethnic divisions: "That these attitudes of universalism in the empire did not always appear to non-Hellenistic peoples as a shining invitation to equality is another matter. The cruder, less developed Germanic and Celtic peoples of Central and Northern Europe tended to be flattered by the universalism of

the empire, and to respond favorably to it. The more advanced peoples of Africa, Egypt and the Near East were not complimented in the same degree: they tended to resist the new doctrine, resenting the paternalism implicit in its use, preferring freedom and autonomy to the specious universalism of imperial control... The 'new race' notion of Christianity did not appeal to the peoples along the eastern and southern shores of the Mediterranean: to them it was a cloak of political imperialism and dominance.... [Constantine] sought to use, according to his own statement, 'the secret eye of thought' to achieve religious unity, while at the same moment using military force to achieve political unity." Gallagher continues: "It is commonly believed that the principal point of controversy between the centers of Rome and Constantinople, on one hand, and the churches in Egypt and Africa, on the other, was theological. In reality, both the Monophysite heresy in Egypt and Donatism in Africa were theological fronts for the fight against imperialism." Gallagher, 43–44, 49.

12. Ibid., 52–53. John Esposito, *The Oxford History of Islam* (New York: Oxford University Press, 1999), 309–317.

13. John G. Jackson, *Introduction to African Civilizations* (New York: Kensington Publishing Corp. 1994) 93–95; Harris, 39–40. For the well-informed and intellectually honest reader the question of the racial character and cultural affinity of the Ancient Egyptians has ceased to be a matter of serious debate. The racial or ethnic character of the Ancient Egyptians is no more in question than the racial origins of the Ancient Romans. The prodigious work of Cheikh Anta Diop and that of other scholars has been decisive. Ancient Egypt was basically a Black civilization. (See Diop, *The African Origin of Civilization: Myth or Reality* and *Civilization or Barbarism?: An Authentic Anthropology*.) Of course, in the aftermath of the European Slave Trade, modern Western scholarship has continued to make frantic efforts to rationalize why it must not be the case that civilization emerged in Africa and was brought forth by Africans. Even in the face of meticulously documented and rigorously tested scholarship indicating the African origins of civilization, some will make specious and misleading assertions that contradict the balance of the evidence or they simply ignore what they do not wish to address. Whatever happened to the dispassionate detachment of the scientific method and the discipline of objective standards for scholarship? Actually, subjective decision-making goes into every scientific or scholarly project from the moment a subject of study is chosen. Choosing to study or critique a given subject while forgoing others, determining what is relevant for an adequate description, prioritizing, categorizing, and drawing conclusions necessarily involve selection processes indicative of personal interests, motivations, insights, intuitions, and preferences. The description of a phenomenon is closely related to and often inseparable from its interpretation. They who believe themselves to be somehow completely detached

from the very subject they wish to investigate, unmoved by human passions and possessing a perspective impervious to all emotional reactions, believe in the most fantastic of fairytales. Fair-mindedness is tied to a willingness to listen and engage in mutually respectful discourse, and not so closely associated with the presumption of a superior capacity to know. In practice, assertions of objectivity often have little to do with fair-mindedness but instead frequently reflect the collective subjectivity or prevailing opinion of those who profess to know; a shielding of the status quo. The pronouncement of objectivity or the lack thereof has become a shibboleth for those who favor the current dominant power structure employed in the effort to discourage the dispossessed from applying their creativity and intelligence resolutely in their own best interests.

14. Diop further notes that while the Ancient Egyptians used the symbolic representation for the color black (kmt) to indicate their beneficial divinities, they used the symbol for the color red to represent malevolent deities including those gods which came from White nations. Ivan Van Sertima, *Great African Thinkers: Cheikh Anta Diop* (New Brunswick, NJ: The State University, 1986), 34–42, 46.

15. Ibid., 24–25.

16. Harris, 51–53.

17. Shillington, 68; Harris, 42–45; Esposito, 309–317.

18. Harris, 45 -51; Williams, 138, 156.

19. Sanneh, 5- 6; Frank M. Snowden, *Blacks in Antiquity: Ethiopians in the Greco-Roman Experience* (Cambridge: Harvard University Press, 1970), 214–215.

20. Harris, 50–51.

21. Ibid.

22. Ibid., 50.

23. *African Geography*, "Hewn from Rock; The Stone Churches of Tigray," Vol. 9, Number 8, September 2001, 49. When European researchers first located this series of rock churches carved from a stone mountain, they found ten churches, but three years later priests, scholars and explorers documented as many as 123 rock-hewn churches in Tigray. These churches represent a testimony to the strength and longevity of ancient Christianity in Ethiopia.

24. Ibid., 50.

25. Ibid., 56.

26. Harris, 53. Williams, 44–52.

27. Ibid., 53–63.

28. Snowden, 130–134. John G. Jackson, *Introduction to African Civilizations*

(New York: Kensington Publishing Corp. 1994) 148; Edward Mcnall Burns, Western Civilization (New York: W.W. Norton and Co., 1954), 188; G.P. Baker, *Hannibal* (New York: Barnes and Noble Inc., 1967), 2–6, 70, 72, 74–86; and, Dexter Hoyos, *Hannibal: Rome's Greatest* Enemy (Exeter, Devon U.K.: Exeter Press, 2008), 14–15.

29. Harris, *59, 75, 79.*

30. Kevin Shillington, *History of Africa*, 83–86. Jackson, 196–198.

31. Harris, 54, 65–66.

32. Ibid., 61.

33. Ibid., 62–63; Shillington, 103.

34. Shillington, 101–102.

35. Jackson, 213–218.

36. Jacob Carruthers, *MDW NTR: Divine Speech—A Historiographical Reflection of African Deep Thought from the Time of the Pharaohs to the Present* (London: Karnak House, 1995), 82–84.

37. Harris, 66, 115–121.

38. Raboteau, 15.

39. Ibid.

40. Ibid., 73.

Chapter 3: The European Slave Trade

1. Buell G. Gallagher, *Color and Conscience: The Irresistible Conflict* (New York: Harper and Brother Publishers, 1946), 52.

2. Ibid., 53–54.

3. Lamin Sanneh, *West African Christianity* (Maryknoll, New York: Orbis Books, 1983), 22–24.

4. All nations involved in the European Slave Trade embraced Christianity and they invoked God's blessings on their activities by giving holy names to the slave ships that transported enslaved Africans to America. This practice led to some searing ironies. On October 18, 1564, a large slave ship that had been christened the *Jesus* set sail leading a fleet of smaller vessels. Thus, the fleet of slave ships set off to capture and enslave Africans figuratively and symbolically under the direction of Jesus. (See George Francis Dow, *Slave Ships and Slaving* [Port Washington, N.Y.: Kennikat Press, 1969], 22.)

5. Daniel P. Mannix, *Black Cargoes: History of the Atlantic Slave Trade 1518–1865* (New York: Penguin Books, 1962), viii. Estimating the devastating impact of the European enslavement of Africans both in the Diaspora and on the Continent is challenging and contentious partly because the negative effects of slave trading continue to the present day. Modern Europe and European America were invigorated and remain wealthy, powerful, and dominant today in part because they literally sucked the life's blood out of Africa. W.E.B. DuBois observed that the slave trade changed the face of African life and deprived the Black race of hundreds of millions of human beings. (See W.E.B. DuBois, *Africa, Its Geography, People and Products* and also *Africa, Its Place in Modern History*, 7.) Historian Joseph E. Harris contended that whatever figure anyone uses in assessing the number of Africans involved in the European Slave Trade, it is no more an "educated guess." (See Joseph E. Harris, *The History of Africans and Their People*, 88, and for a graphic description of the horrors of the Middle Passage see John R. Spears' *The American Slave Trade: Its Origin, Growth and Suppression* [Williamstown, MA: Corner House,1970], 68–81.) It is not possible to know the exact number of Africans enslaved and murdered or the many who suffered and died from wounds and disease due to the enterprise of enslavement. Currently, most European scholars of the subject suggest a figure of 10–20 million for those transported to the Americas. However, even if we could obtain all the ship manifests and sales records to account for those Africans who survived the journey to the Americas, all would not be counted. There were unscrupulous characters among the slave ship captains who would purposely undercount the number of slaves captured so that they might profit from the sale of surplus captives. Furthermore, we would still have to account for the untold numbers killed in Africa during the process of capture and herding into the baracoons before being loaded onto slave ships. Also, the crossing of the Atlantic during the Middle Passage was a perilous journey, notorious for the numerous deaths that occurred. Deaths on slave ships averaged 15-20 percent of the slave cargo. These figures would then expand by several orders of magnitude if we went on to include those Africans whose lives were cut short due to the massive disruption of African civil societies during the period of the slave trade as millions were removed in order to become sources of labor for foreigners. In short, African-American and African scholars have tended to give a wide range of estimates of the number of those affected by the slave trade, from about 10 million to well over 100 million. And if we were to also consider the widespread Arab enslavements carried on for centuries throughout northern and eastern Africa, the numbers are expanded even more, perhaps doubling as we get a sense of the magnitude of the calamity which the European and Arab–led slave trades have wrought upon the people and cultures of Africa. (See Walter Rodney, *How Europe Underdeveloped Africa* [Washington, D.C.: Howard University Press,

1982], 96 and Basil Davidson, *The African Slave Trade* [Boston: Little, Brown, and Company, 1980], 95.)

6. Hugh Thomas, *The Slave Trade* (New York: Simon and Schuster, 1997), 153–155.

7. Ibid., 303–305.

8. Ibid., 128–149; Daniel P. Mannix, *Black Cargoes: A History of the Atlantic Slave Trade 1518–1865*, 19–20.

9. Gallagher, 52–53.

10. Mannix, 11; Basil Davidson, *The African Slave Trade* (Boston: Little, Brown, and Company, 1980), 101–106; Thomas, 71; John Thornton, *Africa and Africans in the Making of the Atlantic World, 1400–1800* (New York: Cambridge University Press, 1998), 21–27; John G. Jackson, *Introduction to African Civilizations* (New York: Kensington Publishing Corp. 1994), 199–220. Jackson's chapter on the "Golden Age of West Africa" gives a detailed description of the economic and political developments in that region just prior to the European Slave Trade.

11. Thomas, 51–67; Thornton, 66–71; Davidson, 28, 133–136; Mannix, 4.

12. Thomas, 108–111. Thomas notes: "Despite the developments in the Congo, Elmina remained the keystone of Portuguese activities in Africa. There was now a town beneath its walls: inhabited by half-Europeanized Africans, 'the Mina blacks', it became a self-governing republic at the disposal of the Portuguese governors." The British scholar Hugh Thomas gives a description of many aspects of the European slave trade. Thomas notes that from the beginning there was a concerted effort to coax Africans into adopting European cultural values: "There King Manuel of Portugal (the Fortunate) undertook to send missionaries and other clergy to Benin; 'and, when we see that you have embraced the teachings of Christianity', he said, 'there will be nothing in our realm with which we will not be glad to favor you, whether it be arms, or cannon, and all other weapons of war for use against your enemies.... These things we are not sending you now ... because the law of God forbids it.' Manuel also asked the oba to open his markets in order to allow trade to be carried on freely." (Thomas, 108.) Thomas further relates, "There had been a slave trade to Congo, and slaves in the kingdom, before the Portuguese arrived. But the Portuguese market transformed matters and caused an upheaval in the interior of Africa." (Thomas, 110.) Thomas also indicates the role Europeanized Africans frequently played in the slave trade: "First the slaves themselves were procured, almost always bought in the interior, by Luso-Africans— mulattoes of half-Portuguese, half-Angolan descent...." (Thomas, 367.) Sanneh also took note of the desire of Europeans to "take special care, to command that the sons of Blacks" be trained in the ways of Europe. Sanneh, 26.

13. Sanneh, 21.

14. Thomas, 410–414; Thornton, 154–161. Stanley Elkins has written extensively on the appalling conditions of the Middle Passage and the continuing adverse impact on the progeny of those Africans who experienced this event. "The Middle Passage was the first step toward deculturalization. It was a psychological shock from which they never recovered." Elkins correctly identifies the ultimate intention of the chattel enslavement process; however, he fails to perceive that the nefarious intention was never fully realized; African spirituality could not be extinguished and the recovery process is still under way. (See Stanley Elkins, *Slavery: A Problem in American Institution and Intellectual Life*, 2ⁿᵈ ed. (Chicago: University of Chicago Press, 1969), 103 -15.

15. Ibid., 400, 412, 417, 422–423.

16. Ibid., 424.

17. Ibid.

18. Ibid., 425–432.

19. Spears, 1978, 77–78.

20. Thomas, 307.

21. Ibid., 306–307.

22. Ibid., 308. The rationalization that prior to the arrival of Europeans Africans were uncivilized savages who benefited in some way from enslavement and colonization by Europeans has often been called upon in efforts to divert attention away from the sheer inhumanity of the endeavors. The scholar C.L.R. James addressed such rationalizations by observing the following:

...In the sixteenth century, Central Africa was a territory of peace and happy civilization. Traders travelled thousands of miles from one side of the continent to another without molestation. The tribal wars from which the European pirates claimed to deliver the people were mere sham fights; it was a great battle when half a dozen men were killed. It was on a peasantry in many respects superior to the serfs in large areas of Europe, that the slave trade fell. Tribal life was broken up and millions of detribalised Africans were let loose on one another. The unceasing destruction of crops led to cannibalism; the captive women became concubines and degraded the status of the wife. Tribes had to supply slaves or be sold as slaves themselves. Violence and ferocity became the necessities for survival. The stockades of grinning skulls, the human sacrifices, the selling of their own children as slaves, these horrors were the product of an intolerable pressure on African peoples, which became fiercer through the centuries as the demands of industry increased and the methods of coercion were perfected... (C.L.R. James, "The Atlantic Salve Trade and Slavery: Some Interpretations of Their Significance in the Development of the United States and the Western World," Floyd Hayes, ed., A Turbulent Voyage: Readings in African American Studies, (Collegiate Press: San Diego, 2000), 59.

23. Ibid., 309.

24. Ibid., 123.

25. Mary Berry and John Blassingame, *Long Memory: The Black Experience in America* (New York: Oxford University Press, 1982), 3–7. During the slave trade, European influence in Africa was disastrous for the Africans in many ways. John Newton, the hymn-writing slave ship captain, indicated as much in his descriptions of slave trading:

I verily believe, the far greater part of the wars in Africa, would cease; if Europeans would cease to tempt them, by offering goods for slaves. And though they do not bring legions into the field, their wars are bloody. I believe the captives reserved for sale, are far fewer than the slain. (John Newton. *Posthumous Works of the Late Reverend John Newton* [W.W. Woodward: Philadelphia, 1809], 245.)

Newton further observed that those Africans who traded with European slave traders received far less than what they expected. The Africans who collaborated were frequently cheated and often misled by their slave trading partners:

Accustomed thus to despise, insult, and injure the slaves on board, it may be expected that the conduct of many of our people to the natives, with whom they trade, is, as far as circumstances admit, very familiar... Every art is employed to deceive, and wrong them...Not an article that is capable of diminution or adulteration, is delivered genuine or entire. The spirits are lowered by water. False heads are put into kegs that contain the gunpowder; so that, though the keg appears large, there is no more powder in it, than in a much smaller. The linen and cotton cloths are opened, and two or three yards, according to the length of the piece, cut off, not from the end, but out of the middle, where it is not so easily noticed. The natives are cheated in the numbers, weight, measure or quality of what they purchase in every possible way. And by habit and emulation a marvelous dexterity is acquired in these practices. And thus the natives in their turn in proportion to their commerce with Europeans, and (I am sorry to add) particularly with the English, become jealous, insidious and vengeful. (John Newton. *Posthumous Works of the Late Reverend John Newton* [W.W. Woodward: Philadelphia, 1809], 240–241.)

26. Thomas, 113.

27. Ibid.

28. Chancellor Williams, *The Destruction of Black Civilization: Great Issues of a Race from 4500 B.C. to 2000 A.D.* (Chicago: Third Press, 1987), 276–289.

29. S. J. S. Cookey, *King Jaja of the Niger Delta, His Life and Times: 1821–1891* (London: UGR Publishing, 2005), 25–133.

30. Richard Kluger, Simple Justice (New York: Vintage Books, 1977), 27.

31. Abdias Do Nascimento, "The African Experience in Brazil," Carlos Moore, "Afro-Cubans and the Communist Revolution, Carlos Moore, ed., *African Presence in the Americas* (Trenton, NJ: African World Press, 1995), 97–117, 199-239.

32. Herbert G. Gutman, *The Black Family in Slavery and Freedom* (New York: Vintage Books, 1976), 317–319.

33. Frank J. Kingsberg, *An Appraisal of the Negro in Colonial South Carolina* (Philadelphia: Porcupine Press, 1975), 14.

34. Peter Wood, *It Was a Negro Taught Them: A New Look at African Labor in Early South Carolina, Journal of Asian and African Studies*, 9; 160–179.

35. Judith A. Carney, *The African Origin of Rice Cultivation in the Americas* (Cambridge, MA: Harvard University Press, 2001), 105. The knowledge of planting and cultivating rice which some enslaved Africans brought with them from their native lands allowed them a rare opportunity to gain some degree of leverage over their enslavers and to negotiate terms of their bondage. The White slavers' need for African labor but also African skills enhanced the status of some of the Blacks and allowed them to retain more elements of their African cultural heritage than was possible for most. During the eighteenth century Africans were perhaps the largest group of newcomers entering the Americas. Also, some Africans brought along with them extensive knowledge of healing herbs and remedies and they were particularly adept at treating infectious diseases. (See Faith Mitchell, *Hoodoo Medicine: Gullah Herbal Remedies* [Columbia: South Carolina, Summerhouse Press, 1999].)

Research and scholarship have yet to fully uncover and detail the full impact of African skill, technology, and agricultural know-how in America.

36. Ibid. 140; Daniel C. Littlefield, *Rice and Slaves* (Baton Rouge: Louisiana State University Press, 1981) 4–6.

37. Carney, 106.

38. Thomas, 258.

39. Ibid. 259.

40. Ibid. 298. Some Quakers were prominent in the slave trade in the eighteenth century in New England and Pennsylvania. Quaker slave traders frequently transported captured Africans from the West Indies to slave markets in America.

41. Ibid. 299; B.M. Smith, *Galtons of Birmingham*, Business History, 138.

42. Thomas, 302. In W.E. Minchinton's, "The Virginia Letters of Isaac Hobhouse," *Virginia Magazine of History and Biography* 66 (1958), 279.

43. Thomas, 302.

44. Ibid. 412–413.

45. Ibid. 438.

46. Ibid. 309.

47. Ibid. John Newton had already retired when he wrote the popular hymn "Amazing Grace."

48. Ibid. 311.

49. Love Henry Whelchel, *Hell Without Fire: Conversion in Slave Religion* (Nashville: Abingdon Press, 2002), 30; Thomas, 305.

50. Thomas, 298–305.

51. Ibid. 235–244.

52. Spears, 72–76.

Chapter 4: The Conversion of Enslaved Africans

1. Love Henry Whelchel, Jr., *Hell Without Fire: Conversion in Slave Religion* (Nashville: Abingdon Press, 2002), 34. Africans were among the earliest migrants to America after the "discovery" of Columbus. Africans arrived in large numbers, sometimes exceeding those of Europeans, during the early days of European colonial expansion in the Americas. However, these Africans were mostly brought over involuntarily and were denied the promise of freedom and new opportunities afforded European immigrants who came to America's shores.

2. Alexander X. Byrd, *Captives and Voyagers: Black Migrants Across the Eighteenth Century British Atlantic World* (Baton Rouge: Louisiana State University Press, 2008), 2–5. Byrd maintained that from "1630 to 1780, more than two and a half times as many Africans arrived in Great Britain's Atlantic possessions as did Europeans, and in the critical near century from 1700 to 1780, more than four times as many Africans as Europeans departed their homelands for British colonies."

3. John Thornton, *Africa and Africans in the Atlantic World, 1400–1800* (New York: Cambridge Press, 1998), 43–66. The study of the institution of slavery in the Americas is imperative if one wishes to understand the dynamics of the African-American experience and race relations in the Americas. The currently prevailing set of social relationships is based upon the central organizing principles of European cultural hegemony and white racial domination, factors that were firmly established during the slave trade. Blacks and other nonwhites may participate in the dominant social structures as long as they submit to the cultural standards and economic programs of the dominant group, and such standards and programs tend to maintain Blacks as a group in a weak and subordinate position. These relationships are primary shaping factors in our social environment and they affect education, health care, housing, job prospects, etc.—in short, every aspect of everyday life. (See Thomas C. Holt, *The Problem of Race in the 21ˢᵗ Century* [Cambridge, MA: Harvard University Press, 2002], 60–61.)

4. John Butler, *Awash in a Sea of Faith* (Cambridge, Mass.: Harvard University Press, 1990), 158–159.

5. Stanley Elkins has compared the enslaved Africans to Jews in concentration camps in Nazi Germany. Both the Jews and the Africans were psychically and physically traumatized by their captivity. Stanley M. Elkins, *Slavery: A Problem in American Institutional and Intellectual Life* (Chicago: University of Chicago Press, 1969), 103–15. Elkins' comparison is informative but we should also be note that, while American chattel slavery was not systematic mass murder, it was of longer duration and affected more people than the Nazi pogrom against the Jews. E. Franklin Frazier also offered an assessment of slavery's impact on African Americans: "Probably never before in history has a people been so nearly completely stripped of its social heritage as the Negroes who were brought to America. Other conquered races have continued to worship their household gods within the intimate circle of their kinsmen. Through the force of circumstances, they had to acquire a new language, adopt new habits of labor, and take over, however imperfectly, the folkways of the American environment. Their children's children have often recalled with skepticism the fragments of stories concerning Africa which have been preserved in their families. But, of the habits and

customs as well as the hopes and fears that characterized the life of their forbearers in Africa, nothing remains." (E. Franklin Frazier, *The Negro Family in the United States* [Chicago: University of Chicago Press, 1939], 23.) Frazier's evaluation correctly identifies many of the challenges and hardships faced by enslaved Africans, but his analysis demonstrates little insight otherwise. He was unable or unwilling to critique the actions of an oppressor in comparison to the reactions of the oppressed, leading him to make many overly negative, one-sided, and inaccurate characterizations. He failed to perceive that though often sublimated, African cultural sensibilities have continued to inform the various customs of African Americans and especially so in terms of religious practices.

6. Mechal Sobel, *Trabelin' on the Slave Journey to an Afro-Baptist Faith* (Princeton, NJ: Princeton University Press, 1988), 22–56.

7. Whelchel, 31.

8. Albert J. Raboteau, *Slave Religion: "The Invisible Institution" in the Antebellum South* (New York: Oxford University Press, 1978), 152. See H. Shelton Smith. *In His Image But...Racism in Southern Religion, 1780–1910.* Durham, N. C.: Duke University Press, 1972, 129–165.

9. Archives of Maryland, I: *Proceedings and Acts of the General Assembly of Maryland, January 1637, September 1664* (Baltimore: Maryland Historical Society, 1883), 526–27.

10. Whelchel, 32–33.

11. Ibid.

12. Ivan Van Sertima, *They Came Before Columbus* (New York: Random House, 1976); Lerone Benett, Jr., *Before the Mayflower: A History of Black America* (Chicago: Johnson Publishing Company, 1987), 4-10.

13. Richard Hofstader, *America at 1750: A Social Portrait* (New York: Alfred A. Knopf, 1971), 90. Although there was a systematic effort to suppress African cultural awareness among the enslaved, those efforts were never entirely successful. As the scholar Raboteau observes:

It is important to realize, however, that in the Americas the religions of Africans have not been merely preserved as "Africanisms" or archaic "retentions." The fact is that they have continued to develop as living traditions putting down new roots in new soil, bearing new fruit as unique hybrids of American origin. African styles of worship, forms of ritual, systems of belief, and fundamental perspectives have remained vital on this side of the Atlantic, not because they were preserved in a "pure" orthodoxy but because they were transformed. Adaptability, based upon respect for spiritual power wherever it originated, accounted for the openness of African religions to syncretism with other religious traditions and for the continuity of a distinctively African religious consciousness. At least in some areas of the Americas, the gods of Africa continued to live—in exile. (Raboteau, 4–5.)

14. Eugene D. Genovese, *Roll Jordan, Roll: The World the Slaves Made* (New York: Vintage Books, 1976), 1183–1184; Whelchel, 35. The African-American church is complex in its historical origins, development, and functions. This complexity is due to the multifarious societal and psychological shaping factors involved, the cultural crosscurrents at play, and the fact that Africans were forced to symbolize and sublimate rather than openly express many sentiments during slavery. Understanding symbolic references is important not only because certain images and words have been used to concurrently reveal and conceal certain information, but also because words are not the only way to convey significance and meaning among spiritual people. Unfortunately, some scholars have offered interpretations of the Black church experience in the absence of in-depth knowledge of the symbolic modalities communicated via rhetorical and ritualistic practices. Scholars have diverse views on the mission and contributions of the Black church. The views range from E. Franklin Frazier's assertion that the church basically played a compensatory function serving as a means to escape the harsh reality of life in America to the more positive assessments of the Black church held by Carter G. Woodson and Gayraud Wilmore. According to these scholars, the Black church has provided a liberating platform in a racist and hostile society. Joseph Washington maintained that the folk religion that Blacks inherited from White Christians who extolled the virtues of the next world and the afterlife was "otherworldly." According to Wilmore, the tenets of the "otherworldliness" in slave religion was nothing more than an interim strategy providing Blacks some relief from the conditions of chattel slavery, but they never gave up their commitment to freedom and human dignity. The religious practices among the enslaved were necessarily irregular and inconsistent. However, the basic themes of freedom, in this world or the next, the ultimate goodness of God, ecstatic conversion experiences, and the rhythmic soulfulness of demonstrative spirituality were ever present. The capacity of the religion of enslaved Africans to inspire physical resistance as well as spiritual transcendence can be witnessed in the experiences of Gabriel Prosser, Nat Turner, and Denmark Vesey, among others. Some scholars, like Peter Paris, have indicated that the social teachings of the Black church, including protest movements, emanating from the independent church tradition were based on the need for survival. Necessity dictated the prophetic pastoral vision of the Black church. The communal nature of African people permeates the inclusive

spirit of their churches. Black churches embody a spirit of community because the African cultural personality embraces community as the essential nature of humankind under the divinity. (Peter Paris, *The Social Teaching of the Black Church* [Philadelphia: Fortress Press, 1985], 12; Cornel West, *Prophecy Deliverance: An Afro-American Revolutionary Christianity* [Philadelphia: Westminster Press, 1982]. C. Eric Lincoln and his coauthor Lawrence Mamiya proposed a dialectical model that "holds polar opposite tensions, constantly shifting between the polarities in historical times. There is no Hegelian synthesis or ultimate solution in modern times." (C. Eric Lincoln and Lawrence Mamiya, *The Black Church in the African American Experience* [Durham: Duke University Press, 1990], 11.) Lincoln and Mamiya found that since the Black church has historically been the only accessible institution for Blacks and often the only means for communal expression, this institution has been variously pulled between six poles: priest/prophetess, otherworldly/this-worldly, universal/particular, communal/private, charismatic/bureaucratic, and secular/spiritual.

Since emergence from the Invisible Institution, there has been an underlying tension between seemingly contradictory impulses at the very heart of the Black church. On the one hand, there is the motivational factor of maintaining organizational cohesiveness and the overall sense of communal integrity permitting the development of a dynamic cultural presence. On the other hand, there has been an assimilationist urge, giving rise in some churches to an elitist tendency and various efforts to promote the adoption of "civilized religion" as opposed to the "heathenish" practices of worship fashioned by enslaved Africans. This urge has led some ministers and church officials to discourage shouting, hand-clapping, call and response, and other participatory and demonstrative worship practices. But it is those very practices that helped to preserve ancestral memory and thus allowed African Americans to forge a sense of community and maintain the values that empower their churches. Assimilation of the practices of the dominant culture does have value in that doing so can facilitate effective navigation of the prevailing social order. However, assimilation for many has not meant the strategic enculturation of selected social practices, but a wholesale adoption of such conduct and practices along with associated values resulting in the evisceration of traditional cultural sensibilities and abandonment of commitment to the community. Churches have the potential to serve as platforms for liberation and uplift, but church leadership can be corrupted and churches may become a means to smother and extinguish progressive impulses.

More recently we have seen this underlying tension played out during the resurgence of Pentecostalism and increasing emphasis on spirit-filled services. This has been especially the case in nondenominational churches and megachurches, which have seen the most growth over the past 20 years. However, contemporaneous to the Pentecostal movement arising in some churches we find that in many of those same churches there has also been the emergence of "prosperity gospel" teachings or "feel-good religion," which emphasizes materialistic acquisition, ostentatious display, and "worldly" success with a repudiation of the teachings of the "social gospel" or "do-good religion" which emphasizes struggles against injustices and the dangers of "worldliness" along with ministry to the "least of these." (For further discussion see Harry S. Stout and D. G. Hart, *New Direction in American Religious History* [New York: Oxford University Press, 1997], 423–427.)

15. Susan Hill Lindley, *"You Have Stepped Out of Your Place": A History of Women in Religion in America* (Louisville: Westminster John Knox, 1996), 174. The historian Sterling Stuckey gives an insightful exposition of how the enslaved Blacks continued to practice a modified traditional African spirituality via the ring shout during the slavery period. He shows that this practice in various guises and forms was widely practiced throughout the South as well as the North: "The majority of African Americans brought to North America to be enslaved were from the central and western areas of Africa—Congo-Angola, Nigeria, Dahomey, Togo, the Gold Coast, and Sierra Leone. In these areas an intimate part of religion and culture was movement in a ring during ceremonies honoring the ancestors. There is in fact substantial evidence for the importance of the ancestral function of the circle in West Africa, but the circle ritual imported by Africans from the Congo region was so powerful in its elaboration of a religious vision that it contributed disproportionately to the centrality of the circle in slavery.... The circle is linked to the most important of all African ceremonies, the burial ceremony." Stuckey continues: "Wherever in Africa the counterclockwise dance ceremony was performed—it was called the ring shout in North America—dancing and singing were directed to the ancestors and gods, the tempo and revolution of the circle quickened during the course of movement. The ring in which Africans sang and danced is key to understanding the means by which they achieved oneness in America." Sterling Stuckey, *Slave Culture: Nationalist Theory and the Foundations of Black America* (New York: Oxford University Press, 1987), 10, 12.

Shouting, which was associated with spirit possession among the early Africans in America, can still be experienced in many African-American congregations. Ecstatic conversion experiences and the call to preach are also related to the retention of an ancestral memory among the enslaved Blacks, which survived in the Americas as African spirituality adjusted to a new reality. Funerals and burial rituals were very important to enslaved Africans and for many, upon death, going to heaven was synonymous with going back to Africa.

The preacher presiding over the deceased, overseeing the ritual, assumes major responsibility for the fate of the deceased's spirit. The obligation of the occasion suggests a power beyond the grave for him and leads him to assume the role of the African priest over the burial mound. Thus, the divine-kingship function of mediating with the ancestors was reborn on the plantations of the South, as Africa was recalled on a level of precise symbolism. Slaves found objects in North America similar to the shells and close enough to the earthenware of West Africa to decorate the grave in an African manner. (Stuckey, 42.)

To this day one can find celebrations of "Homecoming" and references to the deceased as "going home" in Black churches. Of course, by this time, conscious association with the African ancestral heritage has been lost.

16. Carter G. Woodson, *The History of the Negro Church* (Washington, DC: Associated Publishers, 1921), 23.

17. Ibid., 22–39. The worship experience in the Black Church transcends emotional display, and cannot be confined to a rigid order of worship or a set liturgy. Worship involves complex cultural patterns of expression engaged to evoke a spiritual presence. The scholar Cheryl Sanders gives important insight on the nature of worship in the Black Church:

> Worship has fixed and fluid forms, rehearsed and unrehearsed, scripted and improvised, and prepared and spontaneous. To make matters more complex, it is clear that some forms and events in worship reflect both fixed and fluid elements at the same time. For example, the quintessential ecstatic expression in Sanctified worship is the shout, or holy dance which usually occurs as a spontaneous eruption into coordinated, choreographed movement. There are characteristic steps, motions, rhythms and syncopations associated with shouting. It is not a wild and random expression of kinetic energy. Rather, a culturally and aesthetically determined static structure sustains the expression of ecstasy in a definite, recognizable form, the existence of which may not be apparent to the casual or uninformed observer. Similarly, speaking in tongues may appear to be spontaneous and unrehearsed verbal expression, but, in reality the practice is evoked by "tarrying" or other repetitive patterns of activity designed to encourage tongues-speaking. Glossolalia is not the only ecstatic speech used in worship. The vocabulary of utterances spoken spontaneously is not random or undefined. There is a definite lexicon for intelligible ecstatic utterances in the sanctuary that may manifest cultural and regional variants but is, nevertheless, known to the group. Most of these terms can be found in the King James Bible with reference to the praise and attributes of God: "Hallelujah," "Amen," "Glory," "Holy," "Praise the Lord," "Yes," and "Thank You Jesus." In the ecstatic state the worshipper may repeat one or more of these expressions many times, in

a loud or subdued voice. (Cheryl J. Sanders, *Saints in Exile* [New York: Oxford University Press, 1996], 61.)

18. Robin Horton, "African Conversion," *Africa* 41 (April 1971), 94. During the Great Awakening many Whites began to embrace more demonstrative religious expressions. When Whites experienced the new birth, they experienced a religion of the heart, which made them shout, dance, and leap for joy. In Jonathan Edwards' Northampton, Massachusetts, where the Great Awakening originated in America, the religious fervor was contagious: "Many were not merely leaping for joy, they were falling into twenty-four hour trances, under a strong imagination that they were in heaven beholding glorious objects." (Sobel, 92.) From Northampton there were reports of jerking, fainting, and crying; Edwards, for one, wept during the whole of Whitfield's preaching at his church. (Sobel, 97, 102.)

19. Whelchel, 40; Samuel Davies, *The State Religion Among the Protestant Dissenters in Virginia* (Boston: S. Kneeland, 1751), 23. The Anglican Rector Thomas Bacon admonished slave masters in 1750 of their responsibility to bring literacy to their slaves: "We should make ... reading and studying the Holy Scriptures available ... to our children and servants. If the grown up slaves from confirmed habits of vice are hard to be reclaimed, the children surely are in our power and may be trained up in the way they should go, with rational hopes that when they are old, they will not depart from it." (Woodson, 24.)

20. Ibid., 42.

21. Cecil Cone, *Identity Crisis in Black Theology* (Nashville: African Methodist Episcopal Church, 2003), 54.

22. White missionaries, revivalists, and pious planters and teachers began the work of Christianizing the Blacks. But, it was the emergence of independent Black preachers that made Christianity viable among the Africans, enslaved and free. The leadership of these early preachers became the catalyst for the conversion process. This established them as mediators between the slave community and the slave masters, and this leadership role demanded that the preachers become literate. (Whelchel, 44.)

23. Carter G. Woodson, *The Education of the Negro Prior to 1861* (New York: G.P. Putnam's Son, 1915), 18; Henry W. Haynes, "Cotton Mather and His Slaves," *Proceedings of the American Antiquarian Society*, New Series, vol. 11 (Worchester: American Antiquarian Society, 1889), 194. Cotton Mather's essay, "The Negro Christianized" (Boston: B. Green, 1706) is a rare book only found in the Boston Public Library.

24. Raboteau, 240.

25. Frank J. Klingberg, *An Appraisal of the Negro in Colonial South Carolina* (Philadelphia: Porcupine Press, 1975), 8. Robert Stevens to the Society for the Propagation of the Gospel (n.d.) Goose Creek, S.C., in S.P.G. MSS (L.C. Trans.) A2, No 1.

26. Harry S. Stout and D.G. Hart, *New Generations in American Religious History* (New York: Oxford Press, 1997), 185–186.

27. Rawick, 1B, Georgia, Part 3, p. 97; Yetmon, p. 36; Raboteau, 239.

28. Raboteau, 240, Woodson, 221; Elizabeth Ware Preson, ed., *Letters from Port Royal (1862–1868)* (New York: Arno Press).

29. Frederick Douglass, *Life and Times of Frederick Douglass* (Hartford, CT: 1881), 75.

30. Janet Durstman Cornelius, *When I Can Read My Title Clear* (Columbia, SC: University of South Carolina Press, 1991), 2.

31. Whelchel, 51–52.

32. Cornelius, 77.

33. Whelchel, 48–49.

34. Ibid.

35. Ibid., 52.

36. Ibid. The first essay printed in America encouraging slave masters to teach the slaves to read was published by the Boston preacher Cotton Mather. Mather supported better treatment for the slaves and it has been reported that he even wanted the slave masters to "treat their servants not as brutes but as men." Of course this is a contradiction in terms as one cannot simultaneously hold someone in chattel slavery and yet consider them to have full and equal status as a human being. Cotton Mather, *The Negro Christianized* (Boston: Printed by B. Green, 1706), 3.

37. William H. Heard, *From Slavery to the Bishophric in the A.M.E. Church* (Philadelphia: AME Book Concern, 1924).

38. John Brothers Cade, *The Incomparable* (New York: Pagent Press, 1964), 5–6.

39. Cornelius, 17.

40. Heard, 31.

41. Raboteau, 241.

42. Ibid. 242.

43. *Christian Advocate* (Nashville), January 7, 1871; Othal H. Lakey, *The History of the C.M.E. Church* (Memphis: C.M.E. Publishing House, 1985), 207.

44. Whelchel, 53.

45. The Reverend George Whitefield and the Bryans were noted for evangelizing those enslaved on the Bryan plantation. (Gerhard Spieler, "Lowcountry Settlers Helped Area Slaves," *The Beaufort Gazette*, 28, July 1991, sec. C, p.71.)

46. Carter G. Woodson, *The History of the Negro Church* (Washington, DC: Associated Publishers, 1921), 41–44.

47. Albert J. Raboteau, 139; C. Eric Lincoln, H. Mamiya, *The Black Church in the African American Experience*, 24, 102, 137. Church historians have long recognized the seminal role and far-reaching influence of the Silver Bluff Church on the African American religious experience. David George and his fifty enslaved Black congregants made a decisive move to leave Silver Bluff for the promise of freedom in Savannah. George's outstanding pastoral leadership and the prospect for freedom made the Silver Bluff movement appealing to Blacks along the coast of Georgia. George's ministry in Savannah experienced phenomenal growth: "In Savannah the Silver Bluff congregants commingled with the Blacks in the city to nurture among the chaos of occupation a viable, living church." (Alexander X. Byrd, *Captives and Voyagers: Black Migrants Across the 18th Century British Atlantic World*, 162–163.) After the Revolutionary War, many members of the Silver Bluff independent Black church movement wanted to retain their freedom and they became Black British refugees, and some of them went on to accomplish even greater deeds after leaving America. Students of African American church history already know about the emigration of the preachers David George to Nova Scotia and Sierra Leone, and George Liele to Jamaica, but much less is known about the other congregants of the church who emigrated with them. Hannah Williams was one member who decided to return to London with the British. She requested a letter of recommendation from George Liele verifying her membership in good standing with the church. He wrote: "We do certify, that our beloved Sister Hannah Williams during the time she was a member of the church in Savannah until the vacuation, did walk as a faithful well-beloved Christian." (Byrd, 163) Hannah Williams gave voice to the origin the African-American Baptist tradition in the city of London which was the birthplace of the first Baptist denomination. Williams continued the work of spreading the influence of the church abroad. Also, there was Brother Amos, a product of the Silver Bluff movement, who left the Bahama Islands at the end of the war and founded a congregation in Providence, and by 1791 his church boasted three hundred members. In short, the Silver Bluff experience became the seed for the international growth of Black churches, especially in the Baptist tradition.

48. Walter H. Brooks, *A History of Negro Baptist Churches In America* (Washington DC: Press of Pendleton, 1910), 6.

49. Peter J. Paris, *David George: Paramount Ancestor of the Black Churches in the United States, Canada and Sierra Leone*, "Criterion," Winter, 1996, 3. Grant Gordon, *From Slavery to Freedom: The Life of David George, Pioneer Black Baptist Minister* (Hantsport, Nova Scotia: Lancelot Press, 1992).

50. Gordon, 30.

51. Brooks, 9.

52. Ibid.

53. Ibid. 17. Lewis Jordan, *Negro Baptist History U S.A., 1750–1930* (Nashville: The Sunday School Publishing Board, N.B.C.,1995), 49.

54. Ibid. 23.

55. Paris, 5.

56. Ibid.

57. Sobel, 188–189.

58. Brooks, 11–12.

59. James M. Simms, *The First Colored Baptist Church in North America* (Philadelphia: J.B. Lippincott, 1888), 14–15.

60. Ibid., 15

61. Andrew Billingsley, *Mighty Like a River* (New York: Oxford University Press, 1999), 60. Carter G. Woodson, *The History of the Negro Church* (Washington DC: Associated Publishers, 1921), 48.

62. Brooks, 25–26.

63. Ibid., 33–34.

64. Lincoln and Mamiya, 25.

65. DuBois, 1.

66. Richard Allen, *Life Experience and Gospel Labors of Rt. Rev. Richard Allen* (Nashville: Abingdon Press, 1983), 15–18; Allen, 17.

67. Ibid., 18–19.

68. Warren Thomas Smith, *Harry Hosier* (Nashville: The Upper Room, 1981), 30–3. Freeborn Garrettson, an early Methodist circuit rider, in his journal wrote about Hoosier's command of large crowds who came to hear the unlettered African preach and expound upon the gospel. Nathan Bang's *The Life of Rev. Freeborn Garrettson* (New York: T. Mason and G. Lane, 1839), 188–189.

69. Allen, 24.

70. Ibid., 24–25.

71. George A. Singleton, *The Romance of the A.M.E. Church* (New York: Exposition Press, 1952), 13. James Cone, *Black Theology and Black Power* (New York: Seabury Press, 1969), 95.

72. Richard Allen, *The Life Experience and Gospel Labors of the Rt. Rev. Richard Allen*, 22–25.

73. Ibid., 30.

74. Charles H. Wesley, *Richard Allen Apostle of Freedom* (Washington, D.C.: The Associated Publishers, Inc., 1935), 209–210.

75. Allen, 26.

76. Ibid., 81.

77. Singleton, 20–23; Woodson, 73–78. Daniel Payne, *History of the A.M.E. Church* (Nashville: Publishing House of the A.M.E. Sunday School Union, 1891), 3–12.

78. Ibid.

79. Ibid.

80. Ibid.

81. Singleton, 21–22. Carter G. Woodson, *The History of the Negro Church*, 73–78. Bishop Daniel Payne maintained that the independent Black church movement benefited African Americans and opened opportunities for Blacks to cultivate their own leadership and public institutions such as schools, churches, and fraternal organizations. Bishop Payne cited three main reasons for these developments: (1) Out of necessity Blacks were forced to use their own minds and develop their own resources to govern and support their churches. Before the separation Payne maintained that, "the colored man was a mere hearer." (2) The triumph and success of independent Black churches helped to dispel the notion that Blacks were inherently inferior and incapable of taking care of themselves and sustaining their own institutions without the aid of Whites. (3) The separate churches gave Blacks a chance to develop independent character and confidence, which would have never happened had they remained as ecclesiastical vassals of their White counterparts. The ecclesiastical organization of the A.M.E. Church was advanced through independent thought and action in nearly all states and parts of Canada. These circumstances in the A.M.E. Church and other churches inspired and nurtured a sense of autonomy in Black communities. The independent church movement helped to counter the charge that African Americans were inherently inferior and incapable of doing anything constructive on their own. (Daniel Payne, *History of the A.M.E. Church* [Nashville: Publishing House of the A.M.E. Sunday School Union, 1891], 9, 12.)

82. Warren Thomas Smith, *Harry Hosier* (Nashville: Upper Room, 1981), 5-30.

83. Ibid.

84. Ibid., 60.

85. African culture groups have developed different forms of social organization in response to varied circumstances including patrilineal and double descent patterns. Yet, as we move back through history the matriarchy looms ever larger among African social orders, with matrilineal patterns becoming predominant in ancient times. It should also be noted that though these societies may be considered mother-centric they were not based on female domination; motherhood was an achievement but not necessarily gender status. Diop compared differences between the development of civil societies in Africa and Ethiopia (which he called the Southern Cradle of Civilization) with civil societies in the Eurasian steppes (which he called the Northern Cradle of Civilization.) Whereas the northerners were nomadic, patriarchal and much more warlike in their affairs, the Africans tended to form agriculturally-based societies and matrilineal organizations and they were xenophilic. Diop reports that both social orders, the patriarchy of the North and the matrilineal systems of the South were instituted by the men and not the women. In the North the patriarchy was viewed as the best way to manage under harsh environmental conditions while in the South the men sought to strike a balance when they gave women the central role in family life, as they took the more prominent roles in government. Interestingly, Diop further notes that the cultivation of corn and millet was an innovation brought forth by Black women in ancient times as reflected in one of the stories about the goddess Isis, the Mystery of Isis and Osiris being in part a conceptualization of the agrarian and therefore matrilineal way of life. He goes on to state: "Among the Southern societies all that relates to the mother is sacred; her authority is so to speak, unlimited. She can choose a partner for her own child without previously consulting the interested party." Diop observes that in agricultural societies the dowry is usually presented to the women by the "economically less favored sex." He also found that the current conditions in Africa are heavily influenced by foreigners: "It is found that the present tendency of internal evolution of the African family is towards a patriarchy more or less attenuated by the matriarchal origins of society. We cannot emphasize too much the role played in this transformation by outside factors, such as the religions of Islam and Christianity and the secular presence of Europe in Africa." (Cheik Anta Diop, *The Cultural Unity of Black Africa: The Domains of Patriarchy and Matriarchy in Classical Antiquity* [Red Sea Press, 2000], 37, 52, 55, 125.)

86. Diop, *47–54, 57–64.* In matrilineal societies siblings were sometimes married, not for sexual cohabitation, but as a ritual act, to facilitate the orderly transfer

of property and rights among family members. Diop relates: "Marriage with a sister is a consequence of matrilineal law. It has already been seen that under an agricultural regime, the pivot of society is woman: all rights, political and otherwise, are transmitted by her, for she is the stable element, man being relatively mobile: he can travel, emigrate, etc., while the woman raises and feeds the children. It is normal therefore, that these latter owe everything to her and not to the man who, even in sedentary life, retains a certain nomadism. To begin with, in every clan it was the female element—and to her alone—that the bulk of any heritage was left. It seems that the need of avoiding quarrels about succession rights between cousins—that is to say, between the sons of brothers and sisters—led these, within the framework of the royal family, to perpetuate the example of the first couple, Isis and Osiris." (Diop, 53.) Lincoln and Mamiya also note that the central role of women in African religious institutions was brought to the Americas during the slave trade. (Lincoln and Mamiya, 7–10.)

87. Lincoln and Mamiya, 276–281; Geoffrey Parrinder, *African Traditional Religions* (New York: Harper and Row, 1976), 101; Raboteau, 75–80; Sobel, 49–50. John Mbiti, *African Religions and Philosophy* (New York: Anchor Books, 1969), 234.

88. Lincoln and Mamiya, 277.

89. Whelchel, 63. The scholar John W. Blassingame reports that, "Christian forms were so similar to African religious patterns that it was relatively easy for the early slaves to incorporate them with their traditional practices and beliefs. In America, Jehovah replaced the Creator, Jesus, the Holy Ghost, and the Saints replaced the lesser gods. The Africans preserved many of their sacred ceremonies in the conventional Christian ritual and ceremonies: songs, dances, feasts, festivals, funeral dirges, amulets, prayers, images, and priests. After a few generations, the slaves forgot the African deities represented by the Judeo-Christian gods, but in many other facets of their religious services they retained African elements." (John W. Blassingame, *The Slave Community: Plantation Life in the Ante-Bellum South* [Oxford University Press: New York, 1972], 19.) We would further note that the "African religious patterns" were similar to the "Christian forms" because historically the latter are derivative of the former.

90. Lincoln and Mamiya, *Elizabeth, A Colored Minister of the Gospel Born in Slavery*, 279.

91. Milton C. Sernett, *Afro-American Religious History* (Durham, NC: Duke University Press, 1985), 173. Lincoln and Mamiya, 280; Jean McMahon Humey, ed., *Gifts of Power: The Writings of Rebecca Jackson, Black Visionary, Shaker Eldress*.

92. Lincoln, C. Eric and Mamiya, 280.

93. Amanda Berry Smith, *The Story of the Lord's Dealings with Mrs. Amanda Smith, the Colored Evangelist Containing an Account of Her Life's Work of Faith and Her Travels in America, England, Ireland, Scotland, India and Africa, as an Independent Missionary* (Chicago: Meyer and Brother, 1893), 185–188. Lincoln and Mamiya, 285. The prominent and influential historical role of women in traditional African cultures is an underlying source of great creativity, resilience and strength for African people and not a sign of cultural deficiency. The history of African Americans has dictated that women be the backbone of the institutional life of the Black community, which is primarily represented by the Black church. One of the most dramatic changes taking place in the Black church today is the emerging presence of prominent female leadership. The increasing profile of Black women is augmented by a corpus of scholars and researchers who are providing new depth to the analysis and documentation of the African-American religious experience. Important research has been conducted by various scholars, including Lisa Allen, Margaret Aymer, Jacquelyn Grant, Cheryl Sanders, Delores Carpenter, Evelyn Brooks Higgenbotham, Anne E. Wimberly, Delores Williams, Cheryl Kirk-Duggan, Tumani Nyajeka, Maisha Handy, Carolyn McCrary, Evelyn Parker, and Katie Geneva Cannon. These scholars and others have explored the range of experience in the Black religious tradition and they have contributed to the growing recognition of the inherent Pentecostal tenets in the African spiritual cosmos. One of the leading womanist scholars, Jacquelyn Grant has noted the disabling contradiction of fighting racism while ignoring sexism in the church: "If the liberation of women is not proclaimed, the church's proclamation cannot be about divine liberation. If the church does not share in the liberation struggle of Black women, its liberation is not authentic." (Anthony B. Pinn, *The Black Church in the Post-Civil Rights Era* [Maryknoll, NY: Orbis Books, 2002], 131.) According to scholars Jualynne Dodson and Cheryl Townsend Gilkes, "The role of women in religion in America [has been an] extension of their individual sense of regeneration, release, redemption and spiritual liberation to a collective ethos of struggle for and with the black community." (Judith Weisenfeld, "On Jordan's Stormy Banks: Margins, Center and Bridges in African American Religious History," *New Directions in American Religious History* Harry S. Stout and D.G. Hart, eds. [New York: Oxford University Press, 1997], 428.) Also, Marsha Snulligan Haney has given important insights on Afrocentric approaches to Christianity and the nature of missionary work. It has also been observed that in the subtleties of Black church politics women have never been powerless, even when barred from the pulpit. Some scholars emphasize that the women in the Black church have a long history of asserting themselves through their majority numbers, their talent for organization, and their financial resources. In particular, Dodson points out that the women's

organizations in the A.M.E. Church are regularly consulted by bishops before any critical decisions are made including certain pastoral appointments, and thus women are able to exercise considerable influence over the affairs of the church whether as pastors or not.

94. Winthrop S. Hudson and John Carrigan, *Religion in America* (Upper Saddle River, NJ: 1992), 223. Susan Hill Lindley, *"You Have Stepped Out of Your Place": A History of Women in Religion in America* (Louisville: Westminster John Knox, 1996), 174.

Chapter 5: The Black Church and Black Reconstruction

1. William T. Sherman, *Memoirs of General William T. Sherman* (Bloomington: Indiana University Press, 1957), 96–99.

2. W.P. McClutchey, November 15, 1952, Wylie and Minerva McClatchey family papers, Georgia Department of Archives and History, Atlanta, Georgia, Andrew Billingsley, *Mighty Like a River: The Black Church and Social Reform*, (New York: Oxford University Press, 1999), 22–23.

3. *Marietta Daily Journal*, May 3, 1960. When Mother Dicey and other Blacks were allowed to join First Baptist Church of Marietta, Georgia, there were some Whites who raised the question as to whether Blacks had souls. Despite the dangers, the enslaved exhorter, Ephraim Rucker, was determined to proclaim the gospel regardless of the consequences. Once Rucker was brutally whipped, but despite the beating he resolved to lead the enslaved Blacks in a private prayer meeting, which was discovered, and he was whipped yet again even while the wounds from the first lashing were still healing.

4. Celestine Sibley, "Restoring Zion in Cobb County," *Atlanta Journal-Constitution*, September 25, 1985. Church attendance was often more appealing to the enslaved than to the slaveholders. The enslaved attended the First Baptist Church of Marietta in such large numbers that the church leaders considered extending the gallery or cutting open a window in the front of the church to accommodate the increased number of Blacks. Blacks eventually grew restless and eager to form their own church. Rucker Ephraim, property of the Dobbs family, petitioned to perform marriages to "persons of color." The church minutes indicate that the White members felt it was "inexpedient at the present time for Ephraim to marry persons of his own color," but they permitted him to preach in prayer meetings when called on by the watchman or slave overseer.

In 1855, the Black members of First Baptist petitioned the White members to allow them to organize their own church. For some reason, Rucker Ephraim, who had been a strong advocate of an independent church, asked the White pastor to drop the petition. This infuriated the Black church members, and they voted him out of the church on April 1, 1855; however, they restored his membership two months later.

In April 1856, the First Baptist Church convened a church conference to find out why the Blacks had boycotted communion on the previous Sunday. The Blacks stated in their response that "they did not feel prepared to take communion as their minds were rather frustrated about the alteration made relative to their occupying a portion of the altar and they thought they would wait until another time." The Blacks assured the church that "they did not think of rebelling against the church and were sorry the church thought so." *The Marietta Daily Journal*, Saturday, May 17, 1986, 7A1.

In May of 1856, First Baptist Church voted to grant the Blacks their request to secure their own place of worship, while the Whites would continue as members of the First Baptist Church. The White church was reluctant to relinquish control over the Black members. The church appointed a committee "to assist the black members in procuring a lot and drawing up rules by which they will be governed."

The Black congregation petitioned the White overseers and deacons for church officials of their own color, and this request was granted by the ordaining of Joshua, the property of Mrs. D.A. Campbell, and Richard, the property of the estate of Dr. S. Smith, as deacons. Also Rucker Ephraim was appointed to preach to the Black members.

In 1862, there were twice as many Black members as there were Whites. During the Civil War the disparity between the Black and White members increased because many White men enlisted in the Confederate Army, a circumstance that inadvertently gave the Blacks more freedom to govern themselves. During the war, First Baptist Church was used as a hospital, and the Blacks worshipped in a separate facility. At first they remained an appendage of the White church until the arrival of the Union General William T. Sherman, who literally set the captives free. (*The Marietta Daily Journal*, Saturday, May 17, 1968, 6A–8A.) On April 8, 1866, Zion Baptist Church was formally organized with Ephraim B. Rucker serving as the first pastor. Ruth W. Miller, First Family Memoirs (*A 150-Year History of First Baptist Church* [Marietta, Georgia, 1985], 27.)

5. Billingsley, 23; Gregory D. Coleman, *We're Heaven Bound* (Athens: C. of Georgia Press, 1992.) This book describes the illustrious history of Bethel A.M.E. Church, and the production of the plays which became major social events at the church on Sweet Auburn Avenue in Atlanta, Georgia. For a vivid description of the capture of Atlanta, see William T. Sherman, *Memoirs of General William T. Sherman*, Volume II, 96–136. The two pioneering Black churches in Atlanta

were the Bethel A.M.E. Church and Friendship Baptist Church; they respectively gave birth to Morris Brown College and Spelman College. These churches also laid down the economic foundations for a vibrant Black professional class in Atlanta. Both leased property to the Atlanta Board of Education to ensure that Black children would have public schools to attend. (Jerry John Thornberry, *The Development of Black Atlanta*, 167.)

6. Ibid. After being liberated from the control of the White church, the jubilant Blacks named their side of town Shermantown to honor the man who led the Union troops. (Cathy Tyler, "Church History Recorded," *The Daily News*, Stone Mountain, Georgia, January 31, 1992.)

7. Sara Louis Gray, *Baptist Heritage: Bethlehem Baptist Church of Christ, 1823– First Baptist Church, 1973* (Covington, Newton County, Georgia), 24.

8. Ibid. 25.

9. Billingsley, 23.

10. Gray, 25. Sara Louis Gray's history of Bethlehem Baptist Church noted the first enslaved male to join the White First Baptist Church. The enslaved was named Brother Glasgow, and he was the property of Mr. Mathew Smith. His membership was facilitated by a letter from the slave master and the first enslaved member by conversion or profession of faith was Celia, the property of Mr. Carey Wood. The professors of Oxford, which was not too far from the church, permitted their slaves to attend Bethlehem Baptist Church. An old enslaved preacher known as Brother Jerry was permitted to preach to the enslaved as long as it was done under White supervision. (Gray, 12.)

11. Sherman, 180–181.

12. Billingsley, 24.

13. Billingsley, 24; Ira Berlin, et al., *Free At Last: A Documentary History of Slavery, Freedom and the Civil War* (New York: The New Press, 1992), 310. After the emancipation, these religious leaders were well aware of the need for fostering a sense of community and the most formidable and effective institution that the formerly enslaved had developed was the independent Black churches—to which the freedmen now turned for leadership. The proliferation of newly independent Black churches was a natural consequence of emancipation. Immediately following the abolition of slavery, urban Blacks moved quickly to seize control of their own religious institutions. Reconstruction dictated a time for consolidation and transformation of religious and cultural institution for Blacks. The "Invisible Institution" of the rural south now emerged into the full light of day. Eric Foner, *Reconstruction America's Unfinished Revolution*, 1863–1877 (New York: Harper and Row Publishers, 1988), 88–90.

The emancipation freed the Blacks with a promise of material provisions, but that promise would not be fulfilled. And worse still, the defamatory image of Black people and trauma to their collective psyche was not addressed. The theological, anthropological, medical, and economic justifications for slavery and racism were developed and promoted by White clergy, physicians and university professors in the leading ecclesiastical and academic institutions of America and Europe. In the aftermath of the collapse of southern slaveholding those justifications were not rebutted. Indeed, arguments for the intellectual and moral inferiority of people of African descent continued well into the twentieth century, and they were not widely challenged until the 1960s. All of the mainline White denominations urged Blacks to remain within their folds but as subordinated members. White ministers and church officials continued to promote the inferior status of Blacks with segregated seating in churches and exclusion from church administration. (Foner, 89; H. Shelton Smith, *In His Image But: Racism in the Southern Religion (1780–1910)* (Durham: Duke University Press, 1972), 209–213.

14. Sherman, 243–252.

15. Ibid.

16. Ibid. These religious leaders who conferred with Stanton and Sherman were well aware of the fact that freedom without land left them in a vulnerable and destitute condition not much better than their previous condition of servitude. It was on the issue of land tenure that the real struggle for Black freedom would be won or lost. The freedmen sagaciously realized that gaining immediate control of their destiny hinged upon the ownership of land. Without land, they would have lives of dependency, subservience, and poverty. Donald L. Grant, *The Way it Was in the South: The Black Experience in Georgia* (Athens: University of Georgia Press, 1993), 93.

17. Billingsley, 23.

18. Ibid.

19. Ibid.

20. Ibid., 29. Vincent Harding, *There Is a River* (New York: Vintage Books, 1983), 258–276.

21. James M. McPherson, *The Negro's Civil War* (New York: Vintage Books, 1965), 300.

22. Willie Lee Rose, *Rehearsal for Reconstruction* (New York: Vintage Books, 1964), xiii. W.E.B. DuBois, *Black Reconstruction in America, 1860–1880* (New York: Atheneum, 1972), 3–16. DuBois provides an insightful study of one of the most fascinating periods in American history. He gives a meticulous interpretation of "twenty years of fateful history with especial reference to the efforts and

experiences of the Negroes themselves." DuBois attempted to correct a gross imbalance in telling the story of Reconstruction, as the works of White scholars had previously focused on presenting the side of the former slaveholders, and they largely ignored the story of those who were enslaved and oppressed. The thesis of this undervalued book is: "How black men coming to America in the sixteenth, seventeenth, eighteenth and nineteenth centuries became a central thread in the history of the United States, at once a challenge to its democracy and always an important part of its economic history and social development." (DuBois, 3.)

23. *Journal of the General Conference of the Methodist Episcopal Church, 1844,* 63, 64, 66, 143, 148; John N. Norwood, *The Schism in the Methodist Episcopal Church, 1844* (New York: Alfred, 1923). This book provides an account of the divisiveness over the question of slavery in the church.

24. *General Conference of the Methodist Episcopal Church Minutes 1868,* 373, 238, 241. Joel Williamson, *After Slavery: The Negro in South Carolina During Reconstruction 1866–1877* (Chapel Hill: The University of North Carolina Press, 1965), 180–181.

25. Othal H. Lakey, *The History of the C.M.E. Church* (Memphis: C.M.E. Publishing House, 1985), 179–182. Love Henry Whelchel, *Hell Without Fire,* 93–109.

26. Walter L. Fleming, *Documentary History of Reconstruction* (Cleveland, Ohio: The Arthur H. Clark Company, 1907), 233–234. Emory Stevens Burke, ed., *The History of American Methodism,* 3 vols. (Nashville: Abingdon Press, 1964), 11, 65–85. Robert Cruden; *The Negro in Reconstruction* (Englewood Cliffs: Prentice Hall, Inc., 1969), 36. *Testimony from Report of the Joint Committee on Reconstruction,* 1866, Parts II, III, and IV; Hunter Dickinson Farish, *The Circuit Riders Dismount* (Richmond: The Dietz Press, 1938), 174. Martin Luther King, Jr., would later speak of the folk wisdom expressed by southern Blacks as their "ungrammatical profundity." Stephen B. Oates, *Let the Trumpet Sound: The Life of Martin Luther King* (New York: Harper and Row, Publishers, 1982), 77.

27. Grant, 267.

28. Ibid.

29. DuBois, 637–699. "The first great mass movement for public education, at the expense of the state, in the South, came from Negroes. Prior to the Civil War there were advocates for better education in the South, but few had been listened to. Schools for indigents and paupers were supported, here and there, and more or less spasmodically. Some states had elaborate plans, but they were not carried out. Public education for all at public expense was, in the South, a Negro idea." (DuBois, 638.)

30. C. Eric Lincoln and Lawrence Mamiya, *The Black Church in the African American Experience*, 92–93.

31. Foner, 92–93.

32. Grant, 113–116, 267; Lakey, 263; Whelchel, 103.

33. Mary Frances Berry and John Blassingame, *Long Memory: The Black Experience in America* (New York: Oxford University Press, 1982), 108.

34. Grant, 112.

35. Ibid., 257.

36. Foner, 329, 426; Lincoln and Mamiya, 204, 217; George Brown Tindall, *South Carolina Negroes, 1877–1900* (Columbia: University of South Carolina Press, 1952), 14.

37. DuBois, 387; Alrutheus Ambus Taylor, *The Negro in South Carolina During Reconstruction* (New York: A.E.E. Press, 1924), 107.

38. Foner, 534.

39. Tindall, *South Carolina Negroes, 1877–1900*, (Columbia, SC: University of South Carolina Press),154–156; Rayford W. Logan and Michael R. Winston, *Dictionary of American Negro Biography* (New York: W.W. Norton and Company, 1982), 84–85.

40. Logan and Winston, 523; Foner, 352–353; DuBois, 449, 450, 594–595.

41. Ibid.

42. DuBois, 638.

43. Foner, 27, 426; DuBois, 393, 395; Criden, 88; Lerone Bennett, *Before the Mayflower: A History of Black America* (Chicago: Johnson Publishing Company, 1987), 231, 481; Logan and Winston, 89–90; Richard Bryant Drake, "The American Missionary Association and the Southern Negro, 1861–1888" (A Thesis: Emory University, 1957), 221.

44. DuBois, 637–667; Janet Duitsman Cornelius, *While I Can Read My Title Clear*, 85–104; Whelchel, 48–62; Raboteau, 96–150; Drake, 9, 31; Thornberry, 183, 140, 150. With gunfire at Fort Sumter signaling the beginning of the Civil War, a war to save the Union that was unintentionally transformed into a war to free the slaves, Northern abolitionists began to redirect their efforts toward protecting those Blacks who were seeking refuge in the Union Army from their former slaveholders. Several benevolent societies sprang up ostensibly to aid the Negro, and the foremost among these was the American Missionary Association (AMA). The AMA comprised erudite Northerners trained at leading northern universities such as Harvard, Yale and Princeton. These missionaries also went

to the South after the Civil War as they attempted to release the freedmen from the influences of the slaveholding South by indoctrinating them into the cultural hegemony of the White North. These Northern missionaries came south with a mission and a paternalistic attitude. They considered that the Blacks would now accept their leadership and direction in the churches and schools that would be set up for them. The administration and faculties at the schools established by the missionaries were primarily made of White Northerners. According to Thomas Chase, an AMA faculty member at Atlanta University, "It should be the policy of the AMA to make haste slowly in this direction and as a rule employ only such colored teachers and preachers as we make in our institutions and feel that we can trust and rely upon." (Richard Drake, 179–180.) The AMA missionary workers played a key role in cultivating cliquish dispositions among the Black elite in Atlanta. Influential AMA teachers such as Thomas Chase, Horace Bumstead, and Edmund Asa Ware had all attended Ivy League schools, and they wanted educators and ministers serving in Black churches and schools to receive the benefit of the elitist values which they espoused. Through their funding capacity, the AMA exercised effective control over a number of the colleges that were set up for Blacks, and they also financed the early development of the historic First Congregational Church, which was attended mostly by Black professionals. Indeed, as long as the church received AMA monies it accepted the appointment of White ministers. In 1894, the church became self-supporting and the members forthwith proceeded to vote for the appointment of a Black pastor.

The legacy of elitism cultivated among Blacks included the formation of exclusive social gatherings and Eurocentric-style worship services, which tended to limit both the growth of their churches and the extent of community services provided by those churches. (Jerry Thornberry, *The Development of Black Atlanta*, 180–181.) Henry L. Morehouse, president of the AMA stated without apology that the goal of the organization was to indoctrinate "America in the Negro," by which he meant the "American ideal of citizenship, of church membership, of family life, etc., incorporated in the Negro character." The goal of these White educators was to create White men and women inside black skins. [James M. McPherson, *The Abolitionist Legacy* (New Jersey: Princeton University Press, 1975), 184.] The historic Morehouse College in Atlanta is named in honor of Henry L. Morehouse, first president of the AMA. His philosophy and attitude about the role of the Negro and the purpose of education for Negroes speaks volumes about the original mission of Morehouse College and a number of other postbellum historically Black colleges and universities—to produce graduates who would seek to assimilate as far as possible into the larger society, and who would have no inclination whatsoever to develop autonomous agency in the interests of their own community.

45. Thornberry, 12, 1977, 154–156, 178–184.

46. Lincoln and Mamiya, 7–10.

47. W.E.B. DuBois, *The Negro Church* (Atlanta: The Atlanta University Press, 1903), 1–7.

48. Brooks, 29–32.

49. Edward Madal, *A Right to the Land: Essay on the Freedmen's Community* (Westport, Conn.: Greenwood Press, 1977), 77.

50. Ibid., 78.

51. Ibid.

52. Ibid., 79.

53. Ibid., 8.

54. *Report of the Joint Committee on Reconstruction*, 39th Congress, 1st Session, Vol. 11, 1:52–53.

Chapter 6: The Struggle in the Wilderness

1. Willard B. Gatewood, *Aristocrats of Color: The Black Elite 1880–1920* (Bloomington: Indiana University Press, 1993), 12. Ira Berlin, *Slaves Without Masters: The Free Negro in the Antebellum South* (New York: Pantheon Books, 1974); Marilyn Manhard, "Free People of Color in Mobile County, Alabama," M.A. thesis, University of South Alabama, 1986; C. Eric Lincoln and Lawrence Mamiya, *The Black Church in the African American Experience*, 8–9.

2. The terms quadroon and octoroon are usually defined in terms of the number of African ancestors. These terms emerged during the slave trade and the primary motive for using such terms was to place value on one's humanity by identifying proximity to "whiteness." Racial and ethnic classification schemes widely used in the Americas have always been based on an underlying preference for the phenotypical appearance and cultural values of Europeans. These terms represented a measure for moving closer to "whiteness" and thereby further away from "blackness." Gatewood gives a description of the color-conscious classification schemes of New Orleans. (Gatewood, 13, 87–88; Mary Church Terrell, *Diary*, January 18, 1915, 18; Terrell Papers.)

3. Gatewood, 82–84; Richard Kluger, *Simple Justice* (New York: Vintage Books, 1972), 73–83. The early European explorers who first made contact with the Africans in the fifteenth century placed great emphasis on describing the skin color of those Africans whom they encountered. They also gave accounts of various

cultural, religious, and linguistic differences, which they believed emanated from the generously pigmented complexion of the Africans. A well-defined contrast between black and white was already deeply ingrained in European consciousness and the encounter with Blacks ignited deep passions and emotions. The scholar Winthrop Jordan noted: "As described by the Oxford English Dictionary, the meaning Black before the sixteenth century included, 'Deeply stained with dirt; soiled, dirty, foul... Having dark or deadly purposes, malignant; pertaining to or involving death, deadly; baneful, disatrous, sinister... Foul, iniquitous, atrocious, horrible, wicked... Indicating disgrace, censure, liability to punishment, etc.' Black was an emotionally partisan color, the handmaid and symbol of baseness and a sign of danger and repulsion." The color white was associated with more positive qualities such as purity and virginity. Winthrop D. Jordan, *The White Man's Burden: Historical Origins of Racism in the United States* (London: Oxford University Press, 1974), 6. The Black Power Movement in the 1960s was in part a response to America's deep-seated color consciousness, which had left some Whites with a false sense of superiority and some Blacks with a false sense of inferiority. "For years the Negro has been taught ... that color is a sign of biological depravity, [and] that his being has been stamped with an indelible imprint of inferiority." Martin Luther King, Jr., *Where Do We Go from Here: Chaos or Community* (New York: Harper and Row Publishers, 1967), 38.

4. Gatewood, 82–84. Sterling Stuckey describes the instigated divide between free Blacks, who were mostly mulattos, and enslaved Blacks in Wilmington, North Carolina:

> While for free Negroes who had intimate social contact with slaves there was perhaps some sharing in a common culture, the majority of free Negroes were mulattoes with little or no contact with their brothers and sisters on the plantations. Not only were efforts made to keep slaves and free Negroes apart, for fear of political consequences of contact between the two groups, but the limitations of distance and the resulting modes of cultural expression available to free Negroes, considering their ignorance of African culture, appear to have greatly limited their cultural horizons in North Carolina. For them, however acute their sense of political realities, the cultural consequences of slavery, when not enriched by exposure to slaves in all-Negro churches or elsewhere, were disastrous. The oppression of blacks cast a shadow across the free Negroes' social relations with slaves, making ever more remote the possibility of their understanding the values in terms of which slaves organized their lives.
>
> It appears certain that the repression of free Negroes was such that near the bottom of the economic ladder, just above slaves, unprotected by

law and custom and generally scorned because of African ancestry, they found cultural concerns necessarily secondary, the struggle for survival pressing. Given their small numbers in Wilmington—no more than a few hundred at a given time in slavery—their sense of vulnerability must have been great and, therefore, unity among them more to be hoped for than realized. Besides, mulattoes constituted the great portion of free Negroes, and were less likely to identify with slaves, whether in Wilmington or on plantations, than free Negroes with dark skins. (Sterling Stuckey, *Slave Culture: Nationalist Theory and the Foundations of Black America* [New York: Oxford University Press, 1987], 110 -111.)

5. Ibid., 82–89. Hollis R. Lynch, *The Black Urban Condition: A Documentary History, 1866–1871* (New York: Thomas Y. Crowell Co., 1973), 58–59. Kluger, 72.

6. Gatewood, 85.

7. Kluger, 73.

8. Ibid.

9. Ibid., 74–83.

10. Ibid.

11. Ibid.

12. Ibid. Between 1870 and 1891, most railroad companies had a "whites only" first-class car but they also continued to offer accommodation to some elite usually light-skinned Blacks, some of whom could pass for White. In 1888, the Georgia Railroad Commission decided that it did not have proper jurisdiction over pullman cars. George Pullman, the manufacturer and leaser of the cars, refused to order segregated train cars. Blacks filed lawsuits against railroad companies which maintained segregation, and they sometimes won their cases. But, following the "separate but equal" ruling in the *Plessy v. Ferguson* (1896) decision, all efforts to resist segregation in public facilities in the South through legal means were effectively defused. The Georgia Legislature passed laws requiring segregated pullman cars in 1899. Prominent Georgians such as W.E.B. DuBois, Atlanta Congregational minister Henry H. Proctor and Gammon Seminary theologian John W.E. Bowen met with Governor Allen D. Candler to urge him to veto the bill, but to no avail.

The institutional life of the early Black church was closely related to development of educational institutions. This can be seen by occurrences in the vicinity of Augusta, Georgia, along the Savannah River at the end of the nineteenth century. The first school for Blacks in Augusta was founded by William Jefferson White and Richard C. Coulter (formerly enslaved), who opened the Augusta Baptist Institute at the Springfield Baptist Church. The school was moved from Augusta to Atlanta

NOTES

in 1879 and later became known as Morehouse College. When this private school moved to Atlanta, there was no school left for Black children. The Black citizens of Augusta used their political capital to push for a public school for their children, and the Richmond County School Board established Georgia's first public high school for Blacks. The school was named in honor of Atlanta University President Edmond Asa Ware. In 1897, with the advent of the "whites only" primary elections in Georgia and the decline of Black political clout, the school board decided to convert Ware High School into a primary school. The prominent and elite Black families of the community, the Cummings, Harpers, and Ladeveses, sued for equal treatment under the terms of *Plessy v. Ferguson*. They argued that no money could go to a White high school if there was not also a high school to serve the Blacks. The Whites countered that Blacks could attend one of their own private schools if they wished. The Augusta court case, *Cumming v. Richmond County Board of Education* was historic because it was the first time that the Supreme Court ruled on school segregation and it marks the beginning of the legal battles against school segregation. By siding with the Richmond County School Board, the court encouraged continued discrimination and sent the message that the focus of *Plessy v. Ferguson* should be on "separate" rather than "equal" education for Blacks.

13. Kluger, 69.

14. Ibid., 70–71.

15. The case of *Plessy v. Ferguson* set the tone and agenda for racial relationships in the South for the next fifty years. Gatewood notes: "[The decision] was a blow to [some] black Americans who still clung to notions of complete assimilation into White society and culture. The death of Frederick Douglass a year before the decision removed from the public discourse the most fearless and eloquent advocate for first-class citizenship and accommodations for blacks." (Gatewood, 302–303.) Booker T. Washington was promoted by Whites to replace the national voice of Douglass. Washington was born a slave in West Virginia. He believed his father, whom he never met, was White. He became an advocate for industrial education. His willingness to forgo efforts to obtain social equality with White America garnered the financial support of White businessmen. By winning the support of affluent and influential businessmen who supported his formula for race relations in which Blacks would remain subservient, Washington was able to wield enormous power over the distribution of funding from White philanthropic resources, especially involving higher education for Blacks. To ensure his own status and preeminent position among Blacks, and to put down rivals, he maintained an extensive network including publicity agents, informants, and detectives. He thus created what became known as the "Tuskegee Machine." Anyone who publicly challenged either his racial program or his personal prestige was at risk of

falling under the scrutiny and disapprobation of the Tuskegee Machine. (David S. Barry, *Forty Years in Washington* [Boston: Little Brown, 1924], 59–61; Samuel D. Smith, *The Negro in Congress, 1870–1901* [Chapel Hill: University of North Carolina Press, 1940], 27–38.)

16. Glen T. Eskew, *Black Elitism and the Failure of Paternalism in Postbellum Georgia: The Case of Bishop Lucius Henry Holsey, The Journal of Southern History*, Vol. LXIII, no. 4, November 1992, 658–659.

17. Donald L. Grant, *The Way It Was in the South: The Black Experience in Georgia* (Athens: University of Georgia Press), 190. At the dawn of the twentieth century the Black race was under attack; continental Africans were slaughtered by the thousands while in the process of being relieved of their autonomy by European imperialists, and Blacks throughout the Americas were oppressed under brutal regimes of racial domination. And the attack was not only physical. There was a psychological assault as well via the relentless propaganda spewing forth from White universities, churches, and mass media organs propagating an image of Blacks as a depraved and degenerate people. Thomas Dixon wrote *The Leopard's Spot* (1902) and *The Klansman* (1905). Both books were best sellers. The books celebrated the activities of the Ku Klux Klan and depicted White Southerners as victims of Black politicians during Reconstruction. The books portrayed Blacks as inherently inferior, incapable of rising above menial work, and Black men were presented as harboring uncontrollable lust for White women. Dixon's book gained popularity and it was made into a popular movie, *The Birth of a Nation*, which helped to stimulate the growth of the Klan. Expressing contempt for Blacks became a kind of rite of passage for many southern Whites.

18. Ibid., 46, 47.

19. DuBois, 1903, 203.

20. The end of slavery was in many ways more perplexing for the former slaveholders than for the formerly enslaved. Without their slave laborers, who had acquired expertise in the operation of farm equipment and the organization of work crews, agriculture, and related industries in the South, they were crippled. With emancipation, the question was not just what will happen to the oppressed, but also what will happen to the oppressors. The Union won the war but that had little effect on the attitudes and opinions of White Southerners toward Blacks. As for Blacks, a life of freedom without command of resources was hardly any better than enslavement.

Large numbers of Black men found few job opportunities, and they would travel about in search of odd jobs and food. They used empty freight trains as transportation. These men gathered around camp fires outside of small towns. They were often threatened by Whites, especially local Klansmen, many of whom were all too willing to carry out their threats. Black life has always been cheap in America, and the long, tragic story of lives devalued and casual carefree killings continues to be an ongoing saga. (See Douglass A. Blackmon, *Slavery by Another Name* [New York: Doubleday, 2008], 39.)

21. Blackmon, 6, 52–83. Alex Lichtenstein, *Twice the Work of Free Labor: The Political Economy of Convict Labor in the New South* (London: Verso, 1996), 48; William Andrew Todd, "Convict Lease System," *New Georgia Encyclopedia*, December 2005.

22. Blackmon, 2. Mary Ellen Curten, *Black Prisoners and Their World, Alabama, 1865–1900* (Charlottesville: University Press of Virginia, 2000), 48; (Van Woodward, *Reunion and Reaction* (New York: Little Brown, 1951); David W. Blight, *Race and Reunion: The Civil War in American Memory* (Cambridge: Howard University, 2001); Ethel Armes, *The Story of Coal and Iron in Alabama* (Birmingham Chamber of Commerce [1910]), 422.

23. Blackmon, 58–83. Blackmon gives a description of the emergence of sharecropping and peonage. Edward Payce, *The Origins of Southern Sharecropping* (Philadelphia: Temple University Press, 1993), 101.

24. Grant, 159.

25. Nell Irvin Painter, *Exodusters: Black Migration to Kansas after Reconstruction* (New York: Alfred A. Knopf, 1977), 188. Philosopher Alain Locke made the argument that the wave of Blacks migrating from the South to large cities of the East and Midwest was the genesis of "group self-expression and self-determination" among Blacks. The Great Migration was a grassroots movement without an established leadership. For many migrants, moving out of the South opened a whole new world of possibilities. Other scholars joined in the conversation and they gave voice to a new aesthetic and new self-confidence emerging from the "New Negro." In 1920, Emmett Scott published a comprehensive description of this phenomenon called *Negro Migration During the War*. Two years later, Carter G. Woodson, the father of African-American history, gave further elucidation in his pioneering textbook, *Negro in Our History*, as he wrote a chapter titled "The Migration of the Talented Tenth." In a most insightful essay, "New Negro," Locke links the migrations to the urban crucible and the urban crucible to the Harlem Renaissance and the Harlem Renaissance to the worldwide cultural awakening taking place during that time. Locke described the race as progressing through history in a direction that was toward the awakening of a "collective mind." Like the Jews, African people in the Americas and in Africa were beginning to acquire a sense of connectedness that transcended national boundaries. Locke observed that "the tide of Negro migration, northward and city-ward" was not "a blind flood started by the demands of war industry coupled with the shuttering off of foreign migration,

crop failures and lynchings"—these failed to fully explain the Great Migrations. "The boll-weevil nor the Ku Klux Klan is a basic factor." It was a "push" and a "pull" of segregation and jobs that unleashed the migration, but the ultimate driving force was a dramatic new stage in the psychology of African Americans—"a new dynamic phase, the buoyancy from within compensating for whatever pressure there may be of conditions from without." Locke concluded that the new "unique social experiment" was a commitment to become more American by becoming more Negro—"to build his Americanism on race values." David Levering Lewis, *W.E.B. DuBois*, 164–165, "The Negro Is Becoming Transformed." Alain Locke, "The New Negro," in Locke, ed. *The New Negro*, 6–7.

26. Grant, 291.

27. Ibid.

28. Ibid., 292, 266.

29. Ibid., 285.

30. Ibid., 292.

31. Ibid., 293.

32. Ibid., 296.

33. Grant, 286–296.

34. Richard W. Thomas, *Life for Us Is What We Make It* (Bloomington: Indiana University Press, 1992), 24; Painter, 108–134. Richard Hofstader has commented that "the U.S. was born in the country and has moved to the city." In 1890 more than 90 percent of the Black population resided in the rural south. The first three decades of the twentieth century witnessed a demographic shift of massive proportions mostly from the rural south to the urban north.

35. St. Clair Drake, Horace R. Cayton, *Black Metropolis: A Study of Negro Life in a Northern City*, Vol. 2 (New York: A Harbinger Book-Harcourt, Brace and World, Inc., 1945), 385–397.

36. Ibid.

37. Fred T. Corum and Rachel A. Harper Sizelove, "Like As of Fire," Newspaper from Asuza Street Worldwide Revival, Washington, DC: Middle Atlanta Regional Press, vii; Lincoln and Mamiya, 76–79; James B. Tinney and Stephen Short, eds. *In the Tradition of William J. Seymour* (Washington, D.C.: Spirit Press, 1978), 13.

38. Louis F. Morgan, "The Flame Still Burning," *Charisma* (Celebrating a Century of the Church of God in Christ), Vol. 33, Number 8207, 45–47. Douglas J. Nelson, "For Such a Time As This" (Ph.D. dissertation, University of Birmingham, England, 1981).

39. Corum and Harper Sizelove, vii.

40. Lincoln and Mamiya, 80.

41. Allowing for occasional exceptions and the sometimes ambiguous use of the terms, holiness and Pentecostalism may be described as follows: 1) The Holiness tradition emphasizes sanctification, biblical inerrancy, the Second Coming, and Baptism of the Holy Spirit. 2) Pentecostalism includes the same elements but places more emphasis on the importance of speaking in tongues and demonstrating the gifts of the Spirit as evidence of divine presence. Lincoln and Mamiya give a description of the Holiness and Pentecostal traditions. Lincoln and Mamiya, 76–79. *The Apostolic Faith,* "Pentecost Has Come," Los Angeles, September, 1906, Vol. 1, No. 1, 1.

42. Arthur Huff Fauset, *Black Gods of the Metropolis* (Philadelphia: University of Pennsylvania Press, 1944), 1; C. Eric Lincoln and Lawrence Mamiya, *The Black Church in the African American Experience,* 81. Seymour briefly attended classes in Houston, Texas, given by Charles F. Parham who was head of the Apostolic Faith movement. Some have proclaimed Parham to be one of the founders of modern Pentecostalism along with Seymour. Parham and others advocated holiness teachings, but the flame that ignited the mass Pentecostal movement began under the preaching of Elder Seymour in Los Angeles during the Asuza Street Revival, after the healing of Brother Lee. Due to his race, Seymour was denied a seat in the classroom, and he was obliged to sit out in the hallway while attending Parham's classes. The Asuza Street Revival was inclusive and Seymour and his followers did not see the need to racially subjugate any of the attendees.

Lincoln and Mamyia characterize the Black Methodist and Baptist denominations as separatists while stating that the Pentecostal churches like the Church of God in Christ began as part of an "interracial movement." (Lincoln and Mamiya, 76.) However, a review of the historical context in which these churches originated gives us a different view. The Black Baptist churches along with A.M.E. and A.M.E. Zion began prior to emancipation, not as separatist movements. They were separate because of the rejection and subjugation of Blacks perpetrated by the Whites at that time. The C.M.E. denomination developed in the immediate aftermath of the Civil War and emerged out of the racial politics of those turbulent times. It was perhaps providential that these institutions did develop independently as they gave African Americans some semblance of autonomous cultural and institutional development, opportunities to play leadership roles, and the chance to acquire property that they otherwise would not have had. Pentecostalism emerged well after the Civil War, and both Blacks and Whites were attracted to that movement, but there was no specific emphasis on interracial cooperation or social justice. The Whites who were part of the early Pentecostal movement were mostly poor and working-class people and they had much in common with the Blacks. However, the dictates of White racial domination and Black subordination were still very strong, and so the Whites eventually moved to form their own separate denominations even though they were generally welcomed among the Blacks.

43. Ibid.

44. Thomas, 2–3.

45. Ibid., 184.

46. Ibid., 274.

47. Ibid., 275.

48. Ibid.

49. James H. Cone, *Black Theology and Black Power* (New York: The Seabury Press, 1969), 113–115.

50. Arthur Huff Fauset, *Negro Religious Cults of the Urban North*, 1944), 41–51; Winthrop S. Hudson and John Corrigan, *Religion in America*, 340; Sydney E. Alstrom, *A Religious History of the American People* (New Haven: Yale University Press, 1972), 1066–1067, 1077. Prior to Martin Luther King, Jr., Marcus Garvey attracted the largest mass movement of Blacks in the United States. Garvey's organization was known as the Universal Negro Improvement Association (U.N.I.A.). Garvey founded the U.N.I.A. in his native Jamaica in 1914, with the motto and rallying call, "One God! One Aim! One Destiny!" His aim was to awaken a new consciousness in Blacks worldwide and redeem Africa for Africans at home and abroad. Between 1916 and 1923 he had phenomenal success in recruiting a large following. His appeal to the masses included stirring oratory, flashy military parades, and entrepreneurial ventures. Also, he was the founder of the African Orthodox Church, along with a militant Episcopal priest, George Alexander McGuire, who exhorted his parishioners to "forget the White God" and provided them with pictures of a Black Madonna and Child. Garvey's movement won the sympathy and goodwill of a number of Black pastors and churches at that time, especially in the urban north. In 1919, William Yancey Bell became the pastor of the William Institutional Christian Methodist Episcopal Church in Harlem. Bell was an erudite biblical scholar with a Ph.D. from Yale and he later became a bishop in his denomination. Bell delivered an unpublished speech titled, "The Christian Spirit In Race" at the headquarters of Garvey's organization, Liberty Hall on August 1, 1923. Marcus Garvey, *Message to the People: The Course of African Philosophy* (Dover, Ma.: The Majority Press, 1986), 163–189. Sydney E. Ahlstrom, *A Religious History of American People*, 1066.

51. Arthur Huff Fauset, *Black Gods of the Metropolis*, 52–55.

52. Ibid., 50.

53. Ibid., 23–30. Winthrop S. Hudson and John Corrigan, *Religion in America* (Upper Saddle River, NJ: Prentice Hall, 1999), 341–344; John W. Robinson, "A Song, a Shout, and a Prayer." In *The Black Experience in Religion*, C. Eric Lincoln, ed. (New York: Doubleday Press), 212–234.

54. C. Eric Lincoln, *The Black Muslim in America* (Trenton, N.J.: African World Press, 1994), 11–20. Alhstrom, 1067.

55. Fauset, 41–51.

56. Ibid.

57. Alhstrom, 1066–1070; Essien-Udom, E.U. *Black Nationalism: The Search for an Identity* (Chicago: University of Chicago Press, 1962) Albert B. Cleage, Jr. *The Black Messiah* (New York: Sheed and Ward, 1968). August Rudwick Meier, Broderick Elliot, Francis L. eds. *Black Protest Thought in the Twentieth Century*, 2nd ed. (Indianapolis: Bobbs-Merrill Co., 1971); Harold Cruse, *The Crisis of the Negro Intellectual* (New York: William Morrow and Company, Inc., 1967), 476–496. Permitting Eurocentric values and views to masquerade as universal qualities renders one's universe small indeed. Such views tend to delete most of world history and almost all of humanity prior to 1500. Under current circumstances, forsaking indigenous heritage for a pretense of universalism would seem to imply capitulation to superimposed Eurocentric conditionings, along with all of the blatant contradictions and insidious abnormalities.

On occasion it has been pointed out that Jesus was a Black man, as can readily be seen in the various images of the Black Madonna and Child found in cathedrals throughout Europe, those being the earliest representations of the Virgin and the Christ child. Notwithstanding the rationalizations to the contrary, such images are in fact indicative of the African roots of Christianity. (Danita R. Redd, "Black Madonnas of Europe: Diffusion of the African Isis," *African Presence in Early Europe*. Ivan Van Sertima ed. [New Brunswick, NJ: Journal of African Civilization, 1985], 108-133; Eloise McKinney-Johnson, "Egypt's Isis: The Original Black Madonna," *Black Women in Antiquity* [New Brunswick, NJ: Journal of African Civilization, 1987], 64–71.) To this observation some have retorted by proclaiming that, "color doesn't matter" or "in Christ there is no color." But such utterances more often than not represent attempts to evade unsettling historical realities, and may signify willingness to lie prostrate before the gods of materialism. If Christ in person was ever present on planet earth, then He had need of a physical appearance, which invariably entails specified skin coloration of one kind or another; that which can be seen is that which has a color, and if any color at all will do for Christ, then we might as well stick with the original. If the intent is to mimic every aspect of Eurocentric Christianity, then the raison d'être of Black churches vanishes, as people can readily get actual White religion as opposed to just an imitation by simply joining predominantly White churches. Black preachers might as well abandon their pulpits and urge their members to go join the congregations that they so much wish to emulate.

We further note that much the same can be said for prominent Black politicians, professionals, entertainers, and athletes, as well as historically Black colleges and universities, fraternal organizations, civic organizations, business enterprises and other organizations consisting predominantly of African Americans. Although they may not explicitly claim to do so, at their convenience, such persons and organizations will exploit African-American cultural expressions, the historical pathos, and the population base of Black people as they seek out corporate largess or government funding along with media recognition and legal protections all based upon their implicit representation of the African-American community of interests. Without genuine commitment to community, racial or ethnic identity becomes just another object of exploitation.

58. Mary Frances Berry and John Blassingame, *Long Memory: The Black Experience in America* (New York: Oxford University Press, 1982), 107–108; Gayraud S. Wilmore, *Black Religion and Black Radicalism* (Maryknoll, New York: Orbis Books, 1998), 125–156; August Meier, *Negro Thought in America, 1880–1915* (Ann Arbor: University of Michigan Press, 1971), 52–58; Alan Paton, "The Negro in America Today," *Collier Magazine* (October 15, 1954).

59. James Hinton, the South Carolina state leader of the NAACP, was looking for the right incident to launch a court case against the discriminatory public school bus policies in the state. The Reverend J. A. DeLaine approached a successful farmer, Levi Pearson, who had three children attending Scott's Branch High School nine miles from his farm. He convinced Pearson to file charges of racial discrimination against the Clarendon County School Board. Pearson involved his family and children even though he was aware of the difficulties and potential dangers. Reverend DeLaine arranged for a meeting in Columbia, SC, with Levi Pearson and Attorney Harold R. Boulware. The meeting of Rev. DeLaine along with Pearson and Boulware in Boulware's Columbia office on July 28, 1947, marked the initiation of a new phase of concerted and determined efforts that eventually led to the *Brown v. Board of Education* desegregation case.

60. Kluger, 13–14. The Reverend A.C. Redd, a C.M.E. pastor, took a leave of absence from his denomination in order to serve as the executive secretary of the state conference of the NAACP. Redd was successful in mobilizing ministers, college presidents and faculty members, school teachers and businessmen for the fight. Redd estimated that 85 percent of the college presidents in the state gave at least tacit support for the move against Jim Crow. *Minneapolis Sunday Tribune*, December 8, 1953.

61. Ibid.

62. Ibid.

63. Ibid., 15.

64. Ibid.

65. Ibid.

66. Ibid., 18.

67. Ibid.

68. Ibid., 19.

69. Ibid., 23.

70. Ibid., 24.

71. Ibid.

72. Ibid., 25.

73. The Reverend Joseph A. DeLaine, son of A.M.E. minister Henry Charles DeLaine, was an unsung foot soldier in the struggle against injustice in America. DeLaine's efforts made possible the landmark Brown case. Like many other Black ministers who took up a just cause on behalf of their people, DeLaine sometimes experienced some of the most intense faithlessness, narrow-minded resistance, double-dealing, and cravenness from his own church officials. Reverend DeLaine was an itinerant pastor with the A.M.E. Church and received appointments to minister to various congregations from his supervising prelate. It has been speculated that the White establishment pressured the bishop who supervised his region to uproot his family and then move them unceremoniously from place to place. When DeLaine was approached by the bishop about moving to Lake City, S.C., he said, "I don't want Lake City stewed, broiled, baked and fried." He was summoned to the bishop's office where he was told that the pastor whom the bishop had intended to send to church in Lake City had died. So the church in that area, St. James A.M.E. Church, needed his services as pastor. DeLaine tried to convince the bishop that it would not be an appropriate appointment for him. But the bishop insisted that his work in Summerton was done, as his life was threatened if he returned. DeLaine replied that Lake City was a haven for the KKK. "That is the place where years ago, the white people killed Mr. Baker (who was the local postmaster)." Baker's attackers had set his house on fire and shot him as he came out. The murderers of Baker went free, setting precedence in "southern justice" for the murders of Medgar Evers and Emmett Till. When DeLaine informed his church officers that the bishop was assigning him to another church, most of them agreed with the bishop. They argued that it was in DeLaine's best interest if he obeyed the bishop's orders. Thus, the church officers encouraged their courageous pastor to

leave the torment of Summerton for the hell of Lake City. Seeing that he had no support, the chagrined pastor informed his wife of their predicament. She bravely accepted the difficulties and remarked, "A man's wife is his strong fortress when she stands by him with fortitude in the hours of crises." (*A.M.E. Christian Recorder*, October 3, 1967; *A.M.E. Christian Recorder*, October 10, 1967.)

As DeLaine had expected, the KKK greeted his arrival in Lake City with a barrage of gunfire. DeLaine called the police, who declined to respond to the call. So the Black preacher took matters into his own hands, armed himself, and began firing back. In fear of injury to his family and himself, DeLaine finally packed up his family and fled. DeLaine was charged with felonious assault with a deadly weapon and was declared a fugitive from justice. In time, likely owing to unfavorable media attention, the governor of the state of South Carolina decided to drop the pursuit of DeLaine and simply commented, "Good riddance."

The fascinating story of the struggles and trials of Reverend DeLaine and his family deserve much more attention than they have received. It was more than clever legal arguments and dramatic speechifying which ultimately brought down Jim Crow. The most necessary work was done by those willing to sacrifice and struggle, sometimes at great cost, and most of these people received little attention and no financial rewards for their efforts. It was they who generated the moral force that carried the day. DeLaine was not a member of one of the elite cliques, and despite his heroic efforts, he was never welcomed into their circle. He could not even get a seat in the courtroom when the court was in session to hear the case that was initiated by his efforts. The headline of the *Afro American Newspaper* for December 20, 1952, read: "South Carolina Minister [DeLaine] Who Started School Case Can't Get Into Courtroom."

74. Marguerite DeLaine, F.S. Corbett, and Cecil J. Williams, *Image of America, Clarendon County* (Charleston: Arcade Publishing, 2002), 7-9; J.A. DeLaine, Jr., *Briggs V. Elliot, Clarendon County* (Pine Brook, NJ: O. Gona Press, 2002); Julie Magruder Lochbaum, *The Word Made Flesh: The Desegregation Leadership of Rev. J.A. Delaine* (Pine Brook, NJ: The O. Gona Press, 1999), 29–40.

75. The original name of the court case was the *Clarendon County Equal Education Opportunity and Facility Case* which was filed in the Eastern District of South Carolina, United States District Court Charleston Division in 1948. In an account he wrote of his experiences, titled "History Leading up to the United States Supreme Court Decision Outlawing Segregation in Public Schools," Reverend Delaine clearly relates that the original purpose of the lawsuit was to gain access to adequate resources for the education of Black children. The plaintiffs wanted equal teacher salaries, bus transportation, and adequate facilities, and originally the focus was not on integration. There was much dissatisfaction among local activists concerning the decision of the NAACP lawyers to change the focus

from equalization to integration. In order to counter charges of betrayal, Thurgood Marshall offered the following defense: "The decision to challenge segregation directly had been made not by a cabal of NAACP bigwigs behind closed doors, but by the national convention on the recommendation of the legal staff which had consulted with the presidents of the state conferences.... If we had not challenged the legality of the segregation system, and if we do not continue the challenge to segregated schools, we will get the same thing we have been getting all these years—separate but never equal." In effect Marshall admits that the change in strategy was prompted by the legal staff, and the local activists were then co-opted into following. But, this contortion of the original objective was vigorously questioned and never embraced by all. Would the masses have been moved to struggle against injustice if they realized that the effort would be redirected and used more for getting social privileges for elites than obtaining resources for their own families and communities? In 1951, Majorie MacKenzie, an attorney, wrote an editorial for the *Pittsburg Courier* picking apart Marshall and his staff for pushing integration rather than equalization. (Richard Kluger, *Simple Justice*, 515–525.)

Chapter 7: The Civil Rights Movement as an Outgrowth of the Black Church

1. Henry L. Gates, *African American Lives* (New York: Oxford University Press, 2004), 545–546.

2. Mary Frances Berry and John A. Blassingame, *Long Memory: The Black Experience in America* (New York: Oxford University Press, 1982), 344; Richard Kluger, 454–457.

3. David Lewis, *King: A Biography* (Chicago: University of Illinois Press, 1979), 46–48; Gates, 445; Samuel L. Grady, *Human Possibilities* (Washington, DC: Hoffman Press, 1977), xvi–xix.

4. E.D. Nixon, "How It All Started," *Liberation* (December, 1956), cited in William Robert Miller, *Martin Luther King: His Life, Martyrdom and Meaning for This World* (New York: Weybright and Farley, 1968), 36; David J. Garrow, *Bearing the Cross* (New York: Vintage Books, 1988), 14; Stephen B. Oates, *Let the Trumpet Sound: The Life of Martin Luther King* (New York: Harper and Row, Publishers, 1982), 50; Martin Luther King, Jr., *Stride Toward Freedom* (New York: Harper and Row, 1958), 34–35.

5. Oates, 62; Stewart Burns, *To the Mountain Top* (New York: Harper Collins, 2004), 9–11.

6. David Lewis, *King: A Biography*, 124; Oates, 14.

7. Oates, 15; August Meier and Elliot Rudwick, *Along the Color Line* (Urbana: University of Illinois Press, 1976), 365–366.

8. Oates, 15.

9. Aldon D. Morris, *The Origins of the Movement* (New York: Free Press, 1984), 18.

10. Lewis, 28–35, Oates, 46–51. Donald L. Grant, *The Way It Was* (Athens, GA: University of Georgia Press, 2001), 386–390.

11. Morris, 56.

12. Oates, 62–63.

13. Garrow, 18–19; Oates, 64–73; Lerone Bennet, Jr., *Before the Mayflower* (Chicago: Johnson Publishing Company, 1988), 378–379.

14. Oates, 64–65.

15. Ibid., 65; Garrow, 16–17.

16. Garrow, 19; Oates, 65.

17. Garrow, 19.

18. Ibid.

19. Ibid., 20.

20. Ibid., 20–22; Morris, 52. Morris notes that prior to the maturation of the Civil Rights movement with the Montgomery Bus Boycott, a surplus of fragmented civil rights organizations operated in Black communities across the South. For example, until the formation of the Montgomery Improvement Association, such organizations as various branches of the NAACP, the Inter Civic Council, and the Women's Political Action Council along with many others proliferated and attempted to address social issues in the community. But, their effectiveness was limited. There was not even a pretense of unity, and there were incessant power struggles along with a general lack of cooperation among the leaders. Many local organizations became little more than personal fiefdoms confining their political "organizing" to begging the White establishment for recognition and favors. This made it necessary for the formation of new and more progressive organizations in places such as Montgomery, Tallahassee, and Birmingham.

21. Oates, 68. Lewis, 57.

22. Ibid.

23. Ibid.; Garrow, 23; Morris, 51–63. For an in-depth discussion of King's ascension to leadership see Lawrence D. Reddick, *Crusade Without Violence: A Biography of Martin Luther King, Jr.* (New York: Praegar, 1970).

24. Burns, 25.

25. After his election to the presidency of the Montgomery Improvement Association, Dr. King walked onto the stage of world history as he spoke before his first mass meeting. From that moment until the time of his death about 13 years later, hardly a week went by when he did not speak before a gathered mass meeting somewhere across the country. From birth, church gatherings had been his second home. After all, King was a third-generation Baptist preacher. He was ordained to preach at age 19. For King, a life in the church was all but inevitable; as he himself said, "religion for me is life." Indeed, much the same could be said for most of African America in that era. Church mass meetings were a natural habitat for Black people. (Clayborne Carson, Ralph E. Luker, Penny A. Russell, and Peter Holloran, eds., *The Papers of Martin Luther King, Jr.* [Berkeley: University of California Press, 1992], Vol.1, 361–362. King, 86.) A *Pittsburg Courier* reporter observed: "When one sits in their mass meetings and hears them sing and pray and lift their voices to their God, you get the feeling that here is a boundless and ever growing faith in God that will not let these people lose their courage and their faith." (*Pittsburg Courier*, February, 1959).

26. King, 63.

27. King, 64. It appeared that he had spent his entire life preparing for the most important speech of his young career. The many years of burning the midnight oil in study and contemplation at Booker T. Washington High School, Morehouse College, Crozier Seminary, and Boston University provided the conceptual groundwork that allowed him to construct a compelling interpretation of the meaning and purpose of the times.

28. Burns, 32–33.

29. Oates, 76–77.

30. King, 160.

31. Ibid., 161.

32. Ibid.

33. Ibid., 162

34. Morris, 63.

35. Ibid., 51–76. Morris gives an insightful description of the emergence of civil rights campaigns throughout the South.

36. Ibid. Gandhi's role in South Africa is controversial. He served with the British military in South Africa and he publicly encouraged other Indians to join the British in their efforts to violently crush the Bambatha rebellion of the Zulu people, a campaign in which thousands of Zulus were slaughtered. At a public

speech in Bombay in 1896, Gandhi made the comment, "Ours is one continual struggle against a degradation sought to be inflicted upon us by the Europeans, who desire to degrade us to the level of the raw Kaffir, whose occupation is hunting, and whose sole ambition is to collect a certain number of cattle to buy a wife with and, then, pass his life in indolence and nakedness." (Mohandas K. Gandhi, *Collected Works of Mahatma Gandhi* II, 74.) Kaffir is a bigoted reference to Blacks. Although the caste system has been officially outlawed in India, many of the adherents of Hinduism still cling to the old prejudices, and the Dalit people continue to face widespread persecution and discrimination.

37. According to the Reverend W. J. Hodge: "Intellectual leaders like Dr. King used Gandhi's non-violent resistance as a justification for the tactics of the movement but gandhism as a philosophy and way of life is completely alien to the Negro and has nothing in common with the social heritage of the Negro. The black church, not Gandhi, gave birth to the movement, songs, spirituals and gospel hymns, the marchers sing when they engaged in civil rights protests." (White and Manis, 55–56). The effusive praise that King and other civil rights leaders heaped on Gandhi is most unfortunate, as it was quite unnecessary. Gandhi did nothing for them or for the movement, and their misguided extolment, seeking a validation for the struggle of the people outside of the experience of the people, now turns out to be something of an embarrassment. There is a preponderance of evidence indicating that Gandhi held anti-Black views and was not favorably disposed toward the cause of justice for Black people. The columnist Richard Grenier observed: "Since the great soul opposed South African discrimination against Indians, one would think he also opposed discrimination against black people. But, this is not so. While Gandhi fought furiously to have Indians recognized as loyal subjects of the British Empire, and to enjoy the full rights of Englishmen, he had no concern for blacks whatever. He joined the British forces to ruthlessly subdue the Zulu freedom uprising. It is speculated that these accusations have been deliberately omitted from much of the corpus of literature to Gandhi's hagiography." (Richard Grenier, *The Gandhi Nobody Knows* [Nashville: Thomas Nelson Publisher, 1983], 51–52.)

38. Morris, 68.

39. Morris, 68–73.

40. Morris, 68–76; White and Manis, 92–105; Joanne Grant, ed., Alabama Christian Movement for Human Rights, "People in Motion: The Story of the Birmingham Movement," in *Black Protest History Documents, and Analyses* (Greenwich, Conn.: Fawcett Books, 1968), 284–285.

41. Morris, 68–73.

42. Ibid.

43. White and Manis, 31–66. Shuttlesworth maintained that his struggle with opposition from lay leaders in the churches where he ministered helped prepare him to take a stand against George Wallace, Jim Clark, and Bull Connor. He found that dealing with sometimes obstinate and contrarian church officers trained the successful Black preacher to be as wise as a serpent, as diligent as a bumble bee and as peaceful as a dove. Skillful diplomacy plus willingness to compromise anchored by unwavering focus on rightful purpose proved to be a successful formula for navigating politics within the churches, and in other venues besides.

44. Ibid., 28.

45. Morris, 72.

46. Ibid., 73.

47. Police Commissioner Eugene "Bull" Connor assigned two or more detectives to attend each mass meeting. Using radio communications and transcriptions these detectives filed reports of which 169 remain covering the period from 1961 to 1963. These reports are included in the Bull Connor papers at the Birmingham Public Library Department of Archives and Manuscripts. "The police became more friendly as we went on. Some became our friends. They understood the movement.... When the police would go there (to ACMHR meeting) and be nice and get religion, Bull (Connor) would move them." (Col. Stone Johnson, 1998). I served as the Vice President for the ACMHR from 1963 through 1969. The movement met each Monday night after June 5, 1956, and when trouble was brewing, we met every night. The police had knowledge of our activities, but they were far from all-knowing; they did not attend all meetings. The available police reports do not list every gathering or all of the churches, activists and ministers who were involved. (Marjorie L. White, *A Walk to Freedom*, 27; Andrew M. Manis, *A Fire You Can't Put Out*, 94.)

48. Ibid., 59.

49. Ibid., 301–302.

50. Ibid., 302–303. Black professionals and intellectuals have long struggled with the meaning of empowerment as they seek social status and resources. Shuttlesworth was keenly aware of the serious class divide in the Black community concerning civil rights issues. The professional classes, then as now, were mostly oblivious of their ultimate dependence on the masses and the need to maintain some semblance of social cohesion and community solidarity: "Our professional people need to understand that the gap between the class[es] and the masses must be closed. The classes evolved up from the masses and where would you go and what would you do without the masses?" (White and Manis, 36–37.)

51. Ibid., 56–57. Miles College students were deeply involved in the Civil Rights movement in Birmingham along with its president and some faculty members. Askew, 195.

52. White and Manis, 26. The majority of Black churches and their respective leaderships have been open to involvement in social justice issues in only the most marginal and least challenging of ways. Contrary to the image of opulence and prestige exhibited by the mega churches, about 80 percent of Black churches are composed of small congregations of less than 500 members. Most of these churches have few resources and they serve mainly as conduits for social expression among working class people. Many of the churches, especially in rural areas, are based around a small group of families, and in the older churches some of the families have had continuous memberships going back generations as far as Emancipation. Such churches have provided a means of expression, social stability, and a support network in times of greatest need. Black churches are often roundly criticized for many shortcomings, real and imagined. But it is still the churches, more consistently than any other social institutions, that have helped to give the people a sense of place and identity. Most churches would not have been able to develop and sustain leaders who could mobilize and organize a mass movement. The larger and more prestigious churches have had resources and at times dynamic leadership, but the leaders and the members have more often than not lacked the will to become seriously involved in social justice issues, preferring instead the comforting illusion of their churches as isolated islands of holiness in a sea of worldly wickedness. Successful church leadership in challenging times requires not only a strong pastor, but able church officers, and a supportive congregation. It takes a special kind of faith and courage to stand decisively in opposition to an all but overwhelming malevolent power. Thus it has always been only a select few churches, at critical moments in history, that have been able to combine visionary and unfearing leadership with a supportive membership and adequate resources to confront injustices and difficulties head on. All the churches have important roles to play in providing various platforms for social expression, but it has been left to just a small number of them to carry out the indispensable role of vanguards for the redemption of a disinherited people; it is they who must open a way through which all others may follow.

53. King, 86. People who had been separated by the artificial barriers of social status and class found a unifying purpose as they prayed and sang together for freedom and human dignity. These domestic workers, teachers, lawyers, unskilled laborers, businessmen, and farmers found common ground in a struggle for justice. The mass meetings cut across class lines, but there was not proportional representation. The churches were filled with working people, and only a smattering few from the professional classes, but this was not due to any fault of the churches. The

Black church is not anti-intellectual; men and women of intellectual acumen and achievement have always been welcome. It is the elitist, arrogant, and materialistic nature of Western-oriented scholarship and academic training that is decidedly hostile toward African spirituality.

54. In July 1960, the ACMHR leaders M.E. Shortridge (a community leader and mortician) and Georgia Price organized the Movement Choir, under the directorship of the then 18-year-old composer, Carlton Reese. The choir's repertoire combined traditional hymns with gospel music. Crowd-pleasing favorites included: "Ain't Gonna Let Nobody Turn Me Around," "Ninety-nine and a Half Won't Do," "We've Got a Job," and "Freedom Is Just Ahead." The soulful sounds energized the mass meetings. (White, 16.) The unheralded heroines in the Birmingham Movement were the women who kept the movement moving. The women ran the day-to-day operations of the Alabama Christian Movement for Human Rights. They included: Lola Hendricks, Corresponding Secretary; Julia Range, Corresponding Secretary; Georgia Price, Executive Committee Member and Officer; Lucinda Robey, Officer and Youth Division Director; and Ruby Shuttlesworth, Youth Division Director. Mrs. Price and Mrs. Robey were influential voices on the Executive Committee. Mrs. Hendricks served as liaison to the SCLC coordinator with Wyatt T. Walker during the joint SCLC-ACMHR campaign of the spring of 1963. Mrs. Ruby Shuttlesworth, a nurse by profession, organized the activities and helped provide resources for the youth in the movement. She and her husband, the Reverend Fred Shuttlesworth, witnessed the bombing of their home in 1956. Mrs. Shuttlesworth was stabbed in the hip as she was attempting to enroll her child in Phillips High School in 1957.

55. Martin Luther King, Jr., *Where Do We Go from Here: Chaos or Community* (New York: Harper and Row Publisher, 1967), 23–24; Paul Good, "The Meredith March" (summer 1966), 9; "Black Power," *New York Times*, June 21, 1966.

56. Oates, 400. Stephen Oates points out that the term Black Power may have been used previously. And it would not seem improbable that a term composed of two commonly used words might have been employed prior to the James Meredith March Against Fear. However, the usage of the term Black Power in 1966 was important not because it was a new combination of letters or words, but because it was courageously invoked to perfectly capture the spirit of the moment, a spirit that would inspire many young African Americans to go on and make advances in business, politics, and academia throughout the 1970s and 1980s.

Many White moderates and liberals had a hysterical reaction to the emergence of Black Power ideology. In the wake of the riots and a shift toward more race consciousness and cultural appreciation, Black leaders from the churches and academia responded to White outrage over the boisterous and unsettling appearance of Black Power. A national conference of Black churchmen was convened and they drafted a statement explaining the meaning of Black Power on July 31, 1966, as well as a statement on Black Theology on June 13, 1969. The churchmen found that the power to implement justice was necessary: "The conscience of black men is corrupted, because having no power to implement the demands of conscience, the concern for justice is transmuted into a distorted form of love, which in the absence of justice, becomes chaotic self-surrender." (Milton C. Sernett, *Afro-American Religious History* [Durham, N.C.: Duke University Press, 1985], 465–488.;Floyd B. Barbour, *The Black Power Revolt* [Boston: Porter Sargent Publisher, 1968], 42.)

57. Albert B. Cleage, Jr., *The Black Messiah* (Kansas City: Sheed Andrews and McNeil, Inc., 1968), 39; Sydney E. Ahlstrom, *A Religious History of the American People* (New Haven: Yale University Press, 1972), 1077. Grant S. Shockly, *Heritage and Hope: African American Presence in United Methodism* (Nashville, TN: Abingdon Press, 1991), 250–251. The Civil Rights movement also helped to inspire the Religious Heritage of the African World at ITC by Ndugu T'Ofari-Atta in 1965. The threefold mission of the institute has been to 1) assist pastors and other civic leaders in promoting knowledge of African history and heritage, 2) avocation for reconciliation and reunion of Africans in the Diaspora and those on the continent, and 3) promotion of economic empowerment for Africans across the world.

Bishop Joseph A. Johnson also gave an important voice to the development of Black theology as he focused on making Christian teachings relevant to the experience of African Americans and their struggle to maintain a meaningful collective identity: "Black Americans are aware of the pressures and coercion which have been placed on their very being—their uniqueness as men, children of God. Integration has meant, in too many instances, that black Americans must become white Americans. Attempts were made to mold black Americans into the image of the white man, thereby destroying their uniqueness, characteristics, and distinctiveness as a people. For black Americans to become white would really mean the annihilation of their very persons, something that God would never intended for them to do…Black Americans, too, have a history – unique, glorious; a history which has shaped them and which they have shaped…They possess a uniqueness and a significance which can only be appreciated and understood in the light of the history which is theirs to possess. Knowledge of this history is one of the means by which black Americans possess themselves." (Joseph A. Johnson, The Soul of the Black Preacher [Pilgrim Press: Philadelphia, 1971], 78, 79.)

58. C. Eric Lincoln, *The Black Church Since Frazier* (New York: Schochen Books, 1974), 110. Lincoln indicates that the principal raison d'être for the Black Church is the rejection of Blacks by Whites. And is it true that African spirituality

was systematically suppressed in White churches, and even the physical presence of Blacks was repulsive to many Whites. However, the ultimate driving force behind the formation and perpetuation of Black churches is found in the need to express African spirituality, and to thereby realize some sense of communal self-determination. Otherwise, the people could have engaged a more determined effort to suppress their natural inclinations so that they might remain with the Whites. Instead, the spirituality of the people demanded a more appropriate venue for expression.

The renowned scholar C. Eric Lincoln coined the term "neo-Pentecostalism" to describe the new spiritual phenomenon that engulfed many Black churches in the last quarter of the twentieth century. There was also a Pentecostal or charismatic movement taking place in many White churches as well during this period, but there were some differences in outlook, especially concerning social issues. Dr. Lincoln wrote, "In contrast to the white churches in which Pentecostal spirit and political conservatism seem to appear in tandem, the majority of black pastors and their churches in the neo-pentecostal movement tend to be politically progressive." (C. Eric Lincoln and Lawrence Mamiya, *The Black Church in the African American Experience*, 386). It is our view that the long-term growth and vitality of Black churches will basically follow along two lines: 1) those churches that adopt some kind of Pentecostal focus in worship and 2) those which strongly embrace a social gospel mission with a community-centered or African-centered focus. This is because, although not always appreciated, Pentecostal expressions are strongly related to the African ancestral heritage of African Americans. Congregations that are not challenged to serve a higher calling by serving the greater community tend to become stagnant, insular, and susceptible to corruptions with numerous outbreaks of petty personality disputes. Also, America is facing declining economic fortunes, the weakening of traditional family and community ties and the resultant increases in social tensions and general turmoil. Under such difficulties, strengthening and developing the sense of rootedness and grounding in authentic spiritual, cultural, and ethnic foundations will provide the necessary supports for collective survival and success in the coming decades. Authenticity in this sense being more so determined by strivings, struggles, and sacrifices on behalf of community, and less so determined by charismatic expressions, displays of material wealth, prestigious titles, association with religious relics and rituals or claims of some mystical connection with the divine. Churches that decline to adopt programs centered on one or both of the above foci will likely face incoherence of mission, increasing irrelevance, and possible dissolution.

59. James Cone, *Black Theology and Black Power* (New York: The Seabury Press, 1969), 91–115.

60. W.E.B. DuBois, *The Souls of Black Folk* (New York: Barnes and Noble Classics, 2003), 135.

61. Morris, 183–187. Besides providing a format for political and economic developments in Black communities, Black churches have also frequently served as platforms and training grounds for performing artists. And it should be noted that the rhetorical styles and the rhythmic cadence of call-and-response oration primarily advanced by the Black preachers have often been appropriated by others who speak before audiences of African Americans—politicians, social activists and various intellectuals—although many of them are loath to openly acknowledge the contributions of the Black church.

62. Ibid., 224.

63. Aldon D. Morris, 88.

64. Martin Luther King, Jr., wrote the "Letter from a Birmingham Jail" in response to the published statement of eight White fellow clergymen, including Bishop C.C.F. Carpenter, Bishop Joseph A. Durick, Rabbi Hilton I. Grafman, Bishop Paul Harden, Bishop Halon B. Harmon, the Reverend George M. Murray, the Reverend Edward V. Ramage, and the Reverend Earl Stallings. (*Birmingham News*, April 16, 1963.)

65. Burns, 443–444.

66. Ibid.

Chapter 8: Conclusions

1. To study pathological conditions among the oppressed without investigating the origins, disposition, and pathology of those who have subjugated them indicates an absence of either lucidity or sincerity. For further descriptions, documentation and discussion of White privilege, see Robert Jensen, *Heart of Whiteness: Confronting Race, Racism and Race Privilege* (San Francisco: City Lights, 2005) and Paula S. Rothenberg, *White Privilege: Essential Readings on the other side of Racism* (New York: Worth Publishers, 2008). For descriptions of global Euro-American political and economic hegemony, see John Perkins, *The Secret History of the American Empire* (New York: Dutton, 2007), Noam Chomsky, *Hegemony or Survival: America's Quest for Global Dominance* (New York: Henry Holt, 2003), and Michael Hudson, *Superimperialism: The Origin and Fundamentals of U.S. World Dominance* (London: Pluto Press, 1972).

Bibliography

Allen, Richard. *Life Experience and Gospel Labors of Rt. Rev. Richard Allen.* Nashville: Abingdon Press, 1983.

Ahlstrom, Sydney E. *A Religious History of the American People.* New Haven: Yale University Press, 1972.

Archives of Maryland, I: *Proceedings and Acts of the General Assembly of Maryland, January 1637, September 1664.* Baltimore: Maryland Historical Society, 1883.

Armes, Ethel. *The Story of Coal and Iron in Alabama.* Birmingham Chamber of Commerce, 1910.

Bang, Nathan. *The Life of Rev. Freeborn Garreltson.* New York: T. Mason and G. Lane, 1839.

Barbour, Floyd B. *The Black Power Revolt.* Boston: Porter Sargent Publisher, 1968.

Bennett, Lerone, Jr. *Before the Mayflower: A History of Black America.* Chicago: Johnson Publishing Company, 1987.

Ben-Jochannan, Yosef. *African Origins of Major Western Religions.* New York: Alkebulan Books, 1970.

_____. *Black Man of the Nile and His Family.* Baltimore: Black Classics Press, 1978.

_____. *We the Black Jews, Vol. I & II.* Baltimore: Black Classic Press, 1993.

Berlin, Ira et al. *Free at Last: A Documentary History of Slavery, Freedom and the Civil War.* New York: The New Press 1992.

Berlin, Ira. *Slaves Without Masters: The Free Negro in the Antebellum South.* New York: Pantheon Books, 1974.

Bernal, Martin. *Black Athena: The Afroasiatic Roots of Classical Civilization, Vol. I: The Fabrication of Ancient Greece 1785–1985.* New Brunswick, N.J.: Rutgers University Press, 1987.

Berry, Mary Frances and John A. Blassingame. *Long Memory: The Black Experience in America.* New York: Oxford University Press, 1982.

Bettenson, Henry and Chris Maunder. *Documents of the Christian Church.* New York: Oxford University Press, 1999.

Bewkes, Eugene G. *A Survey of Philosophy and Religion.* New York: Harper and Brothers Publishers, 1940.

Billingsley, Andrew. *Mighty Like a River: The Black Church and Social Reform.* New York: Oxford University Press, 1999.

Blassingame, John W. *The Slave Community: Plantation Life in the Ante-Bellum South.* Oxford University Press: New York, 1972.

Blight, David W. *Race and Reunion: The Civil War in American Memory.* Cambridge: Howard University, 2001.

Bradley, Michael. *Ice Man Inheritance.* Toronto: Dorset Publishing Inc., 1978.

Brakke, David. *Athanasius and Asceticism.* Baltimore: The Johns Hopkins University Press, 1995.

Brooks, Walter H. *A History of Negro Baptist Churches in America.* Washington DC: Press of Pendleton, 1910.

Budge, E.A. Wallis. *Egyptian Religion.* New York: University Books, 1959.

Burke, Emory Stevens, ed. *The History of American Methodism.* 3 vols. New York: Abingdon Press, 1964.

Burns, Stewart. *To the Mountain Top.* New York: Harper Collins, 2004.

Butler, Alfred. *The Arab Conquest of Egypt and the Last Thirty Years of Roman Domination.* Oxford: Clarendon Press, 1902.

Butler, John. *Awash in a Sea of Faith.* Cambridge, MA: Harvard University Press, 1990.

Byrd, Alexander X. *Captives and Voyagers.* Baton Rouge: Louisiana State University Press, 2008.

Cade, John Brother. *The Incomparable.* New York: Pageant Press, 1964.

Carney, Judith A. *The African Origin of Rice Cultivation in the Americas.* Cambridge MA: Harvard University Press, 2001.

Carson, Clayborne, Ralph E. Luker, Penny A. Russell, and Peter Holloran, eds. *The Papers of Martin Luther King, Jr.* (vol.1). Berkeley: University of California Press, 1992.

Carruthers, Jacob. *Mdw Dtr: Divine Speech: A Historiographical Reflection of African Deep Thought from the Time of the Pharaohs to the Present.* London: Karnak House, 1995.

Chadwick, Henry. The *Early Church.* New York: Penguin, 1967.

Chidester, David. *Christianity: A Global History.* New York: Harper Collins, 2000.

Clarke, Jacquelyn. *These Rights They Seek: A Comparison of the Goals and Techniques of Local Civil Rights Organizations.* Washington, DC: Public Affairs Press, 1962.

Clarke, John Henrik. *Christopher Columbus and the Afrikan Holocaust: Slavery and the Rise of European Capitalism.* Brooklyn, NY: A&B Publishers, 1998.

Cleage, Albert B., Jr. *The Black Messiah.* New York: Sheed and Ward, 1968.

Coleman, Gregory D. *We're Heaven Bound.* Athens: C. of Georgia Press, 1992.

Cone, Cecil. *Identity Crisis in Black Theology.* Nashville: African Methodist Episcopal Church, 2003.

Corum, Fred T. and Rachel A. Harper Sizelove. "Like As of Fire," Newspaper from Asuza Street Worldwide Revival, Washington, DC: Middle Atlanta Regional Press, 1989.

Cornelius, Janet Durstman. *When I Can Read My Title Clear.* Columbia, SC: University of South Carolina Press, 1991.

Cruden, Robert. *The Negro Reconstruction.* Englewood Cliffs: Prentice Hall, Inc., 1969.

Cruse, Harold. *The Crisis of the Negro Intellectual.* New York: William Morrow and Company, Inc., 1967.

Curten, Mary Ellen. *Black Prisoners and Their World, Alabama, 1865–1900.* Charlottesville: University Press of Virginia, 2000.

Davidson, Basil. *The African Slave Trade.* Boston: Little, Brown and Company, 1980.

Davies, Samuel. *The State Religion Among the Protestant Dissenters in Virginia.* Boston: S. Kneeland, 1751.

DeLaine, Marguerite, F.S. Corbett and Cecil J. Williams. *Images of America Clarendon County.* Charleston: Arcadia Publishing, 2002.

DeLaine, J.A. Jr. *Briggs V. Elliot: Clarendon County*. Pine Brook, NJ: O. Gona Press, 2002.

Diop, Cheikh Anta. *Civilization or Barbarism? An Authentic Anthropology*. New York: Lawrence Hill Books, 1991.

_____. *The African Origin of Civilization: Myth or Reality?* Westport: Lawrence Hill and Co., 1974.

_____. *The Cultural Unity of Black Africa: The Domains of Patriarchy and Matriarchy in Classical Antiquity*. Trenton, NJ: Red Sea Press, 2000.

Douglass, Frederick. *Life and Times of Frederick Douglass*. Hartford, CT: 1881.

Dow, George Francis. *Slave Ships and Slaving*. Port Washington, NY: Kennikat Press, 1969.

Drake, H.A. *Constantine and the Bishops*. Baltimore: The John Hopkins University Press, 2002.

Drake, Richard Bryant. *The American Missionary Association and the Southern Negro, 1861–1888*. A Thesis: Emory University, 1957.

Drake, St. Clair and Horace R. Cayton. *Black Metropolis: A Study of Negro Life in a Northern City*, Vol. 2. New York: Harcourt, Brace and World, Inc. 1945.

DuBois, W.E.B. *The Negro Church*. Atlanta: The Atlanta University Press, 1903.

_____. *Africa, Its Geography, People and Products* and *Africa, Its Place in Modern History*. New York: KTO Press.

_____. *Black Reconstruction in America 1860–1880*. New York: Atheneum, 1972.

Egypt, Ophelia Settle and Rawick, George P. *Unwritten History of Slavery: Autobiographical Accounts of Negro Ex-Slaves. Volume 18 of American Slave*. Westport, CT: Greenwood Publishing Company, 1974.

Eliade, Mircea, ed. *Encyclopedia of Religion Vol. 1*. New York: MacMillan Publishing Company, 1993.

Elkins, Stanley. *Slavery: A Problem in American Institutional and Intellectual Life, 2nd ed.* Chicago: University of Chicago Press, 1969.

Eskew, Glen T. "Black Elitism and the Failure of Paternalism in Postbellum Georgia: The Case of Bishop Lucius Henry Holsey," *Journal of Southern History* 58. November 1992, 637-66.

_____. *But for Birmingham*. Chapel Hill, North Carolina: The University of North Carolina Press, 1997.

Esposito, John. *The Oxford History of Islam*. New York: Oxford University Press, 1999.

Essien-Udom, E.U. *Black Nationalism: The Search for an Identity*. Chicago: University of Chicago Press, 1962.

Fage, J. D. *The Cambridge History of Africa, Vol 1*. New York: University Press, 1982.

Farish, Hunter Dickinson. *The Circuit Riders Dismount*. Richmond: The Dietz Press, 1938.

Fauset, Arthur Huff. *Black Gods of the Metropolis*. Philadelphia: University of Pennsylvania Press, 1944.

Felder, Cain Hope, ed. *The Original African Heritage Study Bible*. Nashville: The James C. Winston Publishing Company, 1993.

Fleming, Walter L. *Documentary History of Reconstruction*. Cleveland, Ohio: The Arthur H. Clark Company, 1907.

Foner, Eric. *Reconstruction: America's Unfinished Revolution, 1863–1877*. New York: Harper and Row Publishers, 1988.

Frazier, E. Franklin. *The Negro Family in the United States*. Chicago: University of Chicago Press, 1939.

Gallagher, Buell G. *Color and Conscience: The Irresistible Conflict*. New York: Harper and Brothers Publishers, 1946.

Garrow, David J. *Bearing the Cross*. New York: Vintage Books, 1988.

Garvey, Marcus. *Message to the People: The Course of African Philosophy*. Dover: MA: The Majority Press, 1986.

Gates, Henry L. *African American Lives*. New York: Oxford University Press, 2004.

_____. *Wonders of the African World,*. New York: Alfred A. Knopf.

Gatewood, Willard B. *Aristocrats of Color: The Black Elite, 1880–1920*. Bloomington: Indiana University Press, 1993.

Genovese, Eugene D. *Roll Jordan, Roll: The World the Slaves Made*. New York: Vintage Books, 1976.

Gonzalez, Justo L. *The Story of Christianity, Vol 1*. New York: Harper Collins Publisher, 1984.

Gordon, Grant. *From Slavery to Freedom: The Life of David George, Pioneer Black Baptist Minister*. Hantsport, Nova Scotia: Lancelot Press, 1992.

Grady, Samuel L. *Human Possibilities*. Washington, DC: Hoffman Press, 1977.

Grant, Joanne, ed. Alabama Christian Movement for Human Rights, "People in Motion: The Story of the Birmingham Movement," in *Black Protest History Documents and Analyses*. Greenwich, CT: Fawcett Books, 1968.

Gray, Sara Louis. *Baptist Heritage: Bethlehem Baptist Church of Christ, 1823–First Baptist Church, 1973*. Covington, Newton County, Georgia.

Grenier, Richard. *The Gandhi Nobody Knows*. Nashville: Thomas Nelson, 1983.

Gutman, Herbert G. *The Black Family in Slavery and Freedom*. New York: Vintage Books, 1976.

Harding, Vincent. *There Is a River*. New York: Vintage Books, 1983.

Harris, Joseph E. *Africans and Their History*. New York: Penguin Books, 1987.

Harris, Sara. *Father Divine*. New York: Collus, 1971.

Haynes, Henry W. "Cotton Mather and His Slaves," Proceeding of the American Antiquarian Society, New Series, Vol. 11. Worcester, MA: American Antiquarian Society, 1889.

Heard, William H. *From Slavery to the Bishophric in the A.M.E. Church*. 1924; reprint, New York, 1969.

Herring, George. *Introduction to the History of Christianity*. NY: New York University Press, 2006.

Herskovits, Melville J. *The Myth of the Negro Past*. Boston: Beacon Press, 1991.

Hoffmann, R. Joseph. *Celsus on the True Doctrine*. New York: Oxford University Press, 1989.

Hofstader, Richard. *America at 1750: A Social Portrait*. New York: Alfred A. Knopf, 1971.

Holt, Thomas C. *The Problem of Race in the 21st Century*. Cambridge, MA: Harvard University Press, 2002.

Hudson, Winthrop S. and Carrigan, John. *Religion in America*. Upper Saddle River: NJ: 1992.

Humez, Jean McMahon, ed. *Gifts of Power: The Writings of Rebecca Jackson, Black Visionary, Shaker Eldress.* Amherst, MA: University of Massachusetts Press, 1981.

Jackson, John G. *Introduction to African Civilizations.* New York: Kensington Publishing Corp., 1994.

James, George G.M. *Stolen Legacy.* Chicago: African American Images, 2001.

Jones, Eldred. *Othello's Countrymen: The African in English Renaissance Drama.* London: Oxford University Press, 1965.

Jordan, Lewis. *Negro Baptist History.* Negro Baptist Convention. Nashville: Sunday School Publishing Board, 1930.

King, Martin Luther, Jr. *Stride Toward Freedom.* New York: Harper and Row, 1958.

_____. *Where Do We Go From Here: Chaos or Community?.* New York: Harper and Row Publisher, 1967.

Klingberg, Frank J. *An Appraisal of the Negro in Colonial South Carolina.* Philadelphia: Porcupine Press, 1975.

Kluger, Richard. *Simple Justice.* New York: Vintage Books, 1972.

Lakey, Othal H. *The History of the C.M.E. Church.* Memphis: C.M.E. Publishing House, 1985.

Leakey, Richard E. et al. *Origins: The Emergence and Evolution of Our Species.* New York: E.P. Dutton, 1977.

Lewis, David. *King: A Biography.* Chicago: University of Illinois Press, 1979.

Lincoln, C. Eric and Mamiya, Lawrence. *The Black Church in the African American Experience.* Durham: Duke University Press, 1990.

Lincoln, C. Eric, ed. *Martin Luther King, Jr..* New York: Hill and Wang, 1970.

_____. *The Black Church Since Frazier.* New York: Schocken Books, 1974.

_____. *The Black Muslim in America.* Trenton, NJ: African World Press, 1994.

Lindley, Susan Hill. "You Have Stepped Out of Your Place," *A History of Women in Religion in America.* Louisville: Westminster John Knox Press, 1996.

Littlefield, Daniel C. *Rice and Slaves.* Baton Rouge: Louisiana State University Press, 1981.

Lochbaum, Julie Magruder. *The Word Made Flesh: The Desegregation Leadership of Rev. J.A. Delaine*. Pine Brook, NJ: The O. Gona Press, 1999.

Logan, Rayford W. and Winston, Michael R. *Dictionary of American Negro Biography*. New York: W.W. Norton and Company, 1982.

Lynch, Hollis R. *The Black Urban Condition: A Documentary History, 1866–1871*. New York: Thomas Y. Crowell Co., 1973.

Madal, Edward. *A Right to the Land*. Essay on the Freedmen's Community. Westport, CT: Greenwood Press, 1977.

Manhard, Marilyn. *"Free People of Color in Mobile County, Alabama,"* M.A. thesis, University of South Alabama, 1986.

Mannix, Daniel P. *Black Cargoes: History of the Atlantic Slave Trade 1518–1865*. New York: Penguin Books, 1962.

Mather, Cotton. "The Negro Christianized." Boston: B. Green, 1706.

Mbiti, John S. *African Religions and Philosophy*. Garden City, New York: Anchor Books, 1970.

McMichael,H. A. *A History of Arabs in the Sudan: And Some Account of the People Who Preceded Them and of the Tribes Inhabiting Darfur*. Cambridge University Press, 1922.

McPherson, James M. *The Negro's Civil War*. New York: Vintage Books, 1965.

McEvedy, Colin. *The Penguin Atlas of African History*. New York: Penguin Books,1980.

McManners,John. *The Oxford History of Christianity*. New York: Oxford University Press, 2002.

Meier, August and Rudwick, Elliot. *Along the Color Line*. Urbana: University of Illinois Press, 1976.

_____, ed. *Black Protest Thought in the Twentieth Century*, 2nd ed. Indianapolis: Bobbs-Merrill Co., 1971.

Milavec, Aaron. *The Didache*. New York: The Newman Press, 2003.

Miles, Margaret R. *The Word Made Flesh: A History of Christian Thought*. Malden, MA: Blackwell Publishing, 2005.

Miller, William Robert. *Martin Luther King: His Life, Martyrdom and Meaning for*

This World. New York: Weybright and Farley, 1968.

Mitchell, Faith. *Hoodoo Medicine: Gullah Herbal Remedies*. Columbia, SC: Summerhouse Press, 1999.

Moore, Carlos, ed. *African Presence in the Americas*. Trenton, NJ: African World Press, 1995.

Morris, Aldon D. *The Origins of the Movement*. New York: Free Press, 1984.

Nelson, Douglas J. "For Such a Time as This." Ph.D. dissertation, University of Birmingham, England, 1981.

Norwood, John N. *The Schism in the Methodist Episcopal Church, 1844*. New York: Alfred, 1923.

Oates, Stephen. *Let the Trumpet Sound*. New York: Harper and Row, 1982.

Painter, Nell Irvin. *Exodusters: Black Migration to Kansas after Reconstruction*. New York: Alfred A. Knopf, 1977.

Paris, Peter J. *The Social Teaching of the Black Church*. Philadelphia: Fortress Press, 1985.

Parrinder, Geoffrey. *African Traditional Religions*. New York: Harper and Row, 1976.

Payce, Eward. *The Origins of Southern Sharecropping*. Philadelphia: Temple University Press, 1993.

Payne, Daniel. *History of the A.M.E. Church*. Nashville: Publishing House of the A.M.E. Sunday School Union, 1891.

Pinn, Anthony B. *The Black Church in the Post-Civil Rights Era*. Maryknoll, NY: Orbis Books, 2002.

Preson, Elizabeth Ware, Editor. *Letters from Port Royal, 1862–1868*. New York: Arno Press.

Raboteau, Albert J. *Slave Religion: The "Invisible Institution," in the Antebellum South*. New York: Oxford University Press, 2004.

Ray, Benjamin C. *African Religions: Symbol, Ritual and Community*. Upper Saddle River, NJ: Prentice Hall, 2000.

Reddick, Lawrence D. *Crusade Without Violence: A Biography of Martin Luther King, Jr.* New York: Praegar, 1970.

Robinson, John W., ed. "A Song, a Shout, and a Prayer." In *The Black Experience in Religion*. New York: Doubleday Press.

Rodney, Walter. *How Europe Underdeveloped Africa*. Washington, DC: Howard University Press, 1982.

Rose, Willie Lee. *Rehearsal for Reconstruction*. New York: Vintage Books, 1964.

Saakana, Amon Saba. ed. *African Origin of the Major World Religions*. London: Karnak House, 1988.

Sanders, Cheryl J. *Saints in Exile*. New York: Oxford University Press, 1996.

Sanneh, Lamin. *West African Christianity*. Maryknoll, New York: Orbis Books, 1983.

Sernett, Milton C. *Afro-American Religious History*. Durham, NC: Duke University Press, 1985.

Sherman, William T. *Memoirs of General William T. Sherman*. Bloomington: Indiana University Press, 1957.

Shillington, Kevin. *History of Africa*. New York: St. Martin Press, 1995.

Shotwell, Willis A. *The Biblical Exegesis of Justin Martyr*. London: S.P.C.K. , 1965.

Simms, James M. *The First Colored Baptist Church in North America*. Philadelphia: J.B. Lippincott, 1888.

Singleton, George A. *The Romance of the A.M.E. Church*. New York: Exposition Press, 1952.

Smith, Amanda Berry. *The Story of the Lord's Dealings with Mrs. Amanda Smith, the Colored Evangelist Containing an Account of Her Life's Work of Faith and Her Travels in America, England, Ireland, Scotland, India and Africa, as an Independent Missionary*. Chicago: Meyer and Brother, 1893.

Smith, H. Shelton. *In His Image But: Racism in the Southern Religion, 1780–1910*. Durham: Duke University Press, 1972.

Smith, Warren Thomas. *Harry Hosier*. Nashville: The Upper Room, 1981.

Snowden, Frank M. Jr. *Blacks in Antiquity: Ethiopians in the Greco-Roman Experience*. Cambridge: Harvard University Press, 1970.

Sobel, Mechal. *Trabelin' On: the Slave Journey to an Afro-Baptist Faith*. Princeton, New Jersey: Princeton University Press, 1988.

Sonn, Tamara. *A Brief History of Islam*. Malden, MA: Blackwell Publishing, 2004.

Spears, John R. *The American Slave Trade: Its Origin, Growth and Suppression*. Williamstown, MA: Corner House Publisher, 1970.

Stout, Harry S. and D. G. Hart. *New Directions in American Religious History*. New York: Oxford University Press, 1997.

Stuckey, Sterling. *Slave Culture: Nationalist Theory and the Foundations of Black America*. New York: Oxford University Press, 1987.

Tatian. *Address to the Greeks. Tatiani Oratio ad Graecos*. New York: W. De Grufter, 1995.

Taylor, Alrutheus Ambush. *The Negro in South Carolina During Reconstruction*. New York: A.E.E. Press, 1924.

Thomas, Richard W. *Life for Us Is What We Make It*. Bloomington, IN: Indiana University Press, 1992.

Tindall, George Brown. *South Carolina Negroes 1877–1900*. Columbia: University of South Carolina Press, 1952.

Tinney, James B. and Sephen Short, eds. *In the Tradition of William J. Seymour*. Washington, DC, Spirit Press, 1978.

Tertullian. *Prescription Against Heretics*. Whitefish, MT: Kessinger Publishing, 2004.

Thomas, Hugh. *The Slave Trade*. New York: Simon and Schuster, 1997.

Thornberry, Jerry John. "The Development of Black Atlanta, 1865–1885," Dissertation; 1977, University of Maryland.

Thornton, John. *Africa and Africans in the Making of the Atlantic World, 1400–1800*. New York: Cambridge University Press, 1998.

Van Sertima, Ivan. *They Came Before Columbus: The African Presence in Ancient America*. New York: Random House, 1976.

_____, ed. *The African Presence in Early Asia*. New Brunswick, NJ: Transaction Publishers, 1987.

_____. *Great African Thinkers: Cheikh Anta Diop*. New Brunswick, NJ: The State University.

_____. *Egypt: Child of Africa*. New Brunswick, NJ: Transaction Publishers, 1995.

_____. *The Lost Sciences of Africa: An Overview*. New Brunswick, NJ: Transaction Books,1984.

_____. "African Presence in Early Europe." New Brunswick, NJ: *Journal of African Civilizations*, 1985.

_____. "Black Women in Antiquity." New Brunswick, NJ: *Journal of African Civilization*, 1987.

Von Campenhausen, Hans. *The Father of the Latin Church*. London: A&C Black, 1964.

Welsing, Frances Cress. *Isis Papers*. Chicago: Third World Press, 1991.

Wesley, Charles H. *Richard Allen: Apostle of Freedom*. Washington, DC: The Associated Publishers, Inc., 1935.

West, Cornel. *Prophecy Deliverance: An Afro-American Revolutionary Christianity*. Philadelphia: Westminster Press, 1982.

Whelchel, Love Henry, Jr. *Hell Without Fire: Conversion in Slave Religion*. Nashville: Abingdon Press, 2002.

White, Marjorie L. and Manis, Andrew M. *Birmingham Revolutionaries*. Macon, Georgia: Mercer University Press, 2000.

White, Marjorie L. *A Walk to Freedom*. Birmingham: Published by the Historical Society, 1998.

Williams, Chancellor. *The Destruction of Black Civilization: Great Issues of a Race from 4500 B.C. to 2000 A.D.* Chicago: Third World Press, 1987.

Williamson, Joel. *After Slavery: The Negro in South Carolina During Reconstruction 1866–1887*. Chapel Hill: The University of North Carolina Press, 1965.

Woodson, Carter G. *The Education of the Negro Prior to 1861*. New York: G.P. Putnam's Son, 1915.

_____. *The History of the Negro Church*. Washington, DC: Associated Publishers, 1921.

Zartman, I. William, ed. *Traditional Cures for Modern Conflicts: African Conflict "Medicine."* Boulder, CO: Lynne Rienner Publishers, 2000.

Glossary of Selected Terms

Abrahamic Religions—Judaism, Christianity, and Islam all trace their roots back to the patriarch Abraham. This traditional relationship is derived from the story of Abraham and his two sons, Jacob and Ishmael. Jacob, the son of Isaac, became the progenitor of the Jews and his brother Ishmael the progenitor of the Arabs. It was God's covenant with Abraham that is the basis for the claim that the Hebrews are a "chosen people" and it was promised to Abraham that he would become the father of many nations. Other monotheistic faiths are also sometimes referred to as Abrahamic religions.

Alabama Christian Movement for Human Rights (ACMHR)—an organization formed in Birmingham, Alabama, in the aftermath of the outlawing of the NAACP in 1956 in order to support the movement for civil rights and social justice for African Americans. The organization organized protests, boycotts, and legal challenges to segregation. ACMHR was critical to civil rights struggles as it helped to establish a beachhead for civil rights struggles in what was at that time "the most segregated city in America."

Apostles' Creed—a public acclamation of faith devised by Christians in the early church in order to defend the faith against heretical beliefs, especially Gnosticism.

Arianism—the belief that Jesus Christ was created and is therefore in some way subordinate to the Creator. Arianism is derived from the teachings of Arius, a priest who resided in Alexandria, Egypt in the 4th century, and he insisted that Christ was divine, not by nature but rather by adoption. Unlike the Creator, the Word who became incarnate in Jesus did not exist prior to Creation. Therefore, "There was when He [the Son of Man] was not." The Arians were considered heretics after the Nicean Council and orthodox teachings held that Jesus Christ was co-equal and co-eternal with God the Father.

Beta Israel—Beta Israel, which means "House of Israel" in Ge'ez, is the formal name of the Ethiopian Jews who have resided in regions of northern Ethiopia since as far back as 1,000 B.C.E. They are also called Falashas (foreigners), which they consider to be a derogatory term.

Biblical Idolatry—worship of the Bible or any other sacred script or literature as an idol. Holding sacred literature to be equivalent to the divinity or just as much worthy of praise and reverence as the spirit which inspired the literature; equating the one who sends the message with the means by which it is delivered. During slavery many African Americans revered the Bible as the means for opening the doors to a new status and new opportunities. Learning to read the Bible was the chief source of inspiration to literacy for many African Americans at that time. For some the Bible itself became an object of worship. People of various cultures and faiths have often elevated their sacred literature to the status of inviolate truths. But, this approach taken to an extreme becomes an expression of materialism and idolatry which exalts the sacred text above the deity it represents; the fixation on literature about the religion supplanting the process and actual practice of religion.

Black Nationalism—the ideology and philosophy that African Americans are a "nation within a nation," and that they therefore must collectively build and maintain the institutions and social structures needed to provide for their own economic and social welfare. Martin Delany was the first person to use the term "nation within a nation" in connection to conceptualizations of Black Nationalism in the 1850s. Early proponents of Black Nationalism included Henry Highland Garnett and Bishop Henry McNeil Turner.

Black Power Movement—a movement of activists that emerged in the 1960s with the aim of radically transforming the condition of Black people in the United States by encouraging them to take control of the political and economic resources needed to facilitate the welfare of their own communities. In the broad sense, Black Power is simply an expression of the presence of Black people. It can be observed as they organize themselves to plan and set priorities for the development of their families and communities, and to facilitate their cultural expressions, perfectly natural and sane behavior which has been greatly impeded and at times viciously suppressed by American chattel slavery, peonage and various programs of racial subjugation. Black churches, business enterprises, educational institutions and civic organizations may be seen as expressions of Black Power although currently most of them do not publicly acknowledge any specific Black Power ideology. The Black Power Movement has ideological roots in earlier Black Nationalist movements and its incarnation in the 1960s was connected with the activities of the Civil Rights Movement.

Call-and-Response—patterns of interaction and communication in which expressions, both verbal and nonverbal, encouraging, affirming, or redirecting the discourse are spontaneously engaged, most often with a rhythmic interplay. Call-and-response discourse stems from traditional Africa, and among African Americans it is associated most closely with musical presentations and preaching. Call-and-response is an element of worship brought to America from the Motherland. In the African American Christian worship experience there is frequently a dynamic discourse between the pulpit and the congregation which is more reflective of African spirituality than Eurocentric Christianity.

Call to Preach—term used to indicate the emergence of an urge, vision or intention to enter the ministry; for some the receiving call to preach can be a dramatic, life-changing experience, for others it is the conclusion arrived at after much contemplation; from the antebellum period to the present the "call to preach" for Black preachers has often been a means of obtaining recognition and leadership status in the community.

Chattel Slavery—a form of slavery contrived to impose upon human beings the status of simple property; especially that form of slavery practiced in the United States which attempted to reduce enslaved Africans to the level of farm animals (chattel), backed by legislation denying them political and civil rights, the right to form their own families, or develop independent social institutions, and which furthermore attempted to systematically separate them from their African heritage, legally permitting a regime of wanton and brutal mistreatment. Chattel slavery is sometimes referred to as America's original sin and birth defect.

Circumcellions—radical disciples of Donatism who identified with the poor and disinherited. They considered it an honor to lose their lives in their struggle. They were resistant to the growing materialism of the Roman Catholic Church.

Council of Chalcedon (451 C.E.)—the church council which decreed a definition of faith and which determined that the Father, Son and Holy Spirit were of one substance.

Council of Ephesus (431 C.E.)—the church council which addressed the manner in which the humanity of Jesus was united with His divinity. There were two factions; The Alexandrians were willing to sacrifice the humanity of Jesus in order to protect His divinity, while the Antiochenes argued that Jesus had to be fully human and that His physical being must not be sacrificed for the sake of His divinity.

Council of Nicea (325 C.E.)—the church council called by Constantine to reformulate and standardize church doctrine and practices marking the first major intrusion by political authorities into the affairs of the church. It was at this council that Jesus was declared to be co-equal and co-eternal with the Father.

Creoles—population originating in Louisiana claiming descent from the region's earliest French and Spanish settlers.

Cult—a religious group lying outside of the established and widely accepted social institutions, which maintains beliefs and practices at variance with those of the dominant culture. Cults were formed in the early twentieth century by some Blacks partly in response to White racism and Black elitism.

Donatism—the belief that the moral character of a priest may determine the value of the sacraments which he performs. Donatism arose during the political struggles of the early church after Constantine began his efforts to reshape Christianity. In Carthage, Caecilian was selected and consecrated as bishop to replace Danatus, who was supported by the African Christians, but who did not have the support of the Roman authorities due to his refusal to compromise. Danatus and his supporters then claimed that one of the consecrating bishops was unworthy of the episcopacy, and that the act of consecration was therefore invalid; they found that all authority of the consecrating bishop had been forfeited by his apparent faithlessness. Their argument constituted a direct challenge to Constantine's program since if ecclesiastical powers were more a function of moral character or spiritual presence than ritual protocol, then there would be no way to assume complete control over the activities of the church. Rituals, insignia, appointed titles, documents, and ceremonies are material forms and therefore tractable, but movements of the Spirit are subject to neither prediction, or control; spiritual awareness of the most essential nature is intuitively engaged by faith and with the doing unto others as one would have them do unto self or persevering in what is right, such perseverance being capacitated by faith and such faith being demonstrated by perseverance.

Elitism—Elitism arises from the view that there exist some persons endowed with relatively rare and superior qualities, making them the most suitable to assume authority and leadership over the rest of society. All human beings have creative potential. However, the acquisition of highly specialized skills and knowledge only accrues to a few at any given time. There will always be differences in the quality and intensity of personal motivations, experiences, and expressed talents among any group of human beings. Thus, some people may be considered elites because of the value of their accumulated experience to the rest of society. However, for at least the past half millennium, all elitist hierarchies have increasingly tended to operate not for the benefit of society as a whole, but primarily to pursue programs of exploitation and the general oppression of the masses of people. The term elitism as used in this work refers not only to a select group of influential people, but also to the tendency of such groups to pursue wealth and privileges restricted to their exclusive circle, often turning to unethical means for doing so, and a growing inclination by those in established leadership positions to manifest extremely selfish or psychopathic behaviors. Among African Americans, Black elitism is the direct descendent and absolute dependent of its White counterpart. Black elitism originated when the slaveholders divided their slaves into house servants and field servants;

the house slaves were often the enslaved offspring of slaveholders and they frequently received preferential treatment relative to their equally enslaved field-hand siblings. Highly motivated by social status, the elite Blacks are mostly avid imitators of the symbolisms, protocols, and styles of their social betters. Indeed, absent the supporting mechanisms of the White elites, it is not clear how the Black elites would sustain themselves or whether they even could at all. Almost every cultural creation of lasting value has emerged from the masses, but not elites. Spirituals, gospel, jazz, blues, and hip-hop all originated among the masses. The most accomplished and celebrated heroes of the people—people like Sojourner Truth, Harriet Tubman, Nat Turner, Mary McLeod Bethune, Malcolm X—almost all sprang from the lower socioeconomic strata. And of course the Black church itself originated among the enslaved in the unpretentious "bush harbors" of the invisible institution. Ironically perhaps, under White supremacy, the most autonomous and self-determined of the Blacks tend to come from among the poorest and those untrained by formal educational institutions, their independence being bought at the high cost of material impoverishment.

Field Order #15—As a result of the 20 Black religious leaders convening a meeting with General William Sherman and Edward Stanton, Secretary of War, Sherman issued Field Order #15 on January 16, 1865, which had the following provisions: (1) Land including Charleston, Beaufort, Hilton Head, Savannah, St. Augustine, Fernandina, and Jacksonville was set aside to be occupied and settled by African Americans and (2) the land was required to be allocated only to families with two parents as head of household, thereby encouraging the building of strong Black families.

Great Migration—the migrations of millions of African Americans from the rural South to cities in the North, Midwest and Western United States from the turn of the century through the 1950s. This movement significantly altered the demographics of some northern cities and opened a new era of social and economic opportunities for many African Americans.

Individualism—the notion that human beings as individuals possess qualities and capacities completely independent of social interaction with other human beings, and that therefore they ought to pursue their own choices, prerogatives, and opinions irrespective of society at large, the needs of the community or the common good. Individualism is based on an outlook that tends to alienate the individual from the rest of society, stimulating personality types which are intrusive, truculent, selfish, and obnoxious. The extreme case of "malignant individualism" leads to antisocial behaviors, predatory and exploitative activities, and general discord. Notions of individualism have long been used to rationalize regimes of oppression, blaming individual shortcomings for the effects of systematic oppression, and individuating outcomes of economic structures contrived to consistently advantage the elite few. Yet, even among rugged individualism glorifying materialists, it is readily observed that the most significant and consequential activities are carried out by tightly organized and carefully coordinated formations in contrast to disconnected individuals. Among Westerners, when pursuing their most coveted objectives, they organize and establish government-sanctioned business corporations and military organizations. In business enterprises or the military, individuals who do not strictly conform to the objectives and standards set by the establishment or collective leadership are terminated or expelled from the group.

Invisible Institution—gatherings of enslaved Africans secretly in remote thickets and swamps to worship freely away from slave owners and overseers. These gatherings or conclaves were also known as "bush harbors," where enslaved Blacks could engage in worship practices more closely resembling those practices they had known in Africa.

Mass Meetings—gatherings most often held in Black churches, usually in the form of worship services in which issues related to the general condition of the community would be addressed. These meetings served as key means of informing and inspiriting the community and getting people involved, and they were an important component of civil rights protest movements.

Middle Passage—term used to refer to the horrendous ordeal endured by captured Africans as they were brought to the Americas to be enslaved. The Africans were brutalized, packed onto ships, and bought and sold like animals. Voyages of the Middle Passage took place from the early sixteenth century through the middle of the nineteenth century.

Monasticism—a movement that originated in the African wing of the early church in the third century C.E. embracing a lifestyle of ritual discipline and spiritual purity. The movement represented a negative reaction to the growing materialism in the church by those who believed the gospel was incompatible with materialistic living; the early monks and nuns found that it was not possible to serve both God and Mammon.

Monophysitism—doctrine first espoused by early Christians who believed that Jesus Christ was of only one nature—divine. Monophysitism advances two main principles: (1) *Eutychianism,* which holds that the human nature of Jesus was completely dissolved into the divinity of Christ and (2) *Apollinarianism,* which holds that the mind or perceptivity and reasoning capacity of Christ was informed by Divine Logos. Donatism and Monophysitism had strong appeal among those in the African wing of early Christianity. The fourth Ecumenical Council, held at Chalcedon in 451 C.E. condemned this belief. The Orthodox Tawahedo Church of Ethiopia, along with other Eastern Orthodox churches, is considered to be a monophysite church.

Montgomery Improvement Association—an organization formed in December of 1955 in order to facilitate the activities of the Montgomery Bus Boycott and address issues of concern to the African American community in Montgomery.

Mother Africa—term used to denote the role of the land and people of Africa as the progenitors of humanity and human civilization.

Mother of the Church—status sometimes achieved by women in African-American churches in which they effectively become spiritual advisors and moral standard bearers for their congregations. Church mother or mother of the church is not a formal title, but this role is widely recognized in Black churches. Women who play this role are usually elderly and esteemed for their character, they are often affectionately addressed by the title mother, and they are sometimes considered to possess "spiritual gifts." The scholar C. Eric Lincoln has pointed out that the deeply respected institution of church mother frequently found in Black churches has no parallel in White churches.

Mourners' Bench—pew situated toward the front of the church sanctuary designated for the unsaved who seek salvation. During revivals and camp meetings the unconverted would be seated on the seeker's pew as it was also called until they "came through," or became "born again."

Nicean Creed—a statement of belief acknowledging and agreeing to the decisions of the Council of Nicea. Such a statement was needed to defend against heresies and because of the many controversial issues taken up by the council. The calling of the council by Constantine, a temporal authority, was itself controversial. Athanasius was an apologist for the creed.

Pangaea—the original supercontinent or land mass which existed about 175 million years ago. It is hypothesized that the continents broke off from the central African land mass in a continental drift to eventually achieve their current formation.

Quadroon—persons thought to possess three quarters white blood or one quarter black blood by having only one Black ancestor among their grandparents, or being the offspring of mulatto and white parentage. The quadroon designation was part of a classification system used in the Spanish colonies and in Louisiana during the slave trade, and it placed value on a person's humanity according to relative amounts of white or black blood. Such classification schemes were related to the generalized hierarchy of races or scientific racism, which maintained that Europeans are the superior race, with Africans at the bottom, and Asians and Native Americans perhaps a little above the Africans but certainly well below Europeans. Though based on myths of racial superiority, such classifications as mulatto, quadroon, octoroon, and mestizo are still sometimes used. Notions of "mixed blood" abound even as the most reliable evidence indicates that all human lineages eventually converge back to the basic Black foundation of humanity. Historically, only colonized or subjugated indigenous people are subdivided and classified into "mixed race" or "mixed ancestry" types based upon supposed differential concentrations of ancestral blood while the dominant group claims for itself genetic purity or racial unity.

Rites of Passage—term used to describe traditional African ritual practices usually associated with moving from one phase of life into another such as an adolescent becoming an adult. Various African culture groups have traditionally employed sets of interrelated rituals as a means of introducing community members to new responsibilities, expectations, and privileges engaged at each new phase of life. These ritual systems helped to facilitate an interlinking and harmony between body and soul, the spiritual and physical realms, males and females, youths and elders, and individuals and the community. Rites of passage could be utilized for every stage of life from birth to adulthood to elderhood to ancestorhood.

Sect—a relatively small religious group which leaves some parent body, usually not so much to form a new faith or creed but to reaffirm and emphasize virtues from which the sect members believe the parent body has strayed; both early Christianity and early Islam may be seen as cults or sects.

Society for the Propagation of the Gospel (SPG)—a missionary organization formed in the eighteenth century by the Anglican Church with the initial purpose of providing organized and systematic training to American colonists, but then expanding its efforts to also include conversion and training for Native Americans and later Africans.

Southern Christian Leadership Conference (SCLC)—a civil rights organization formed by Black ministers in 1957 in order to facilitate the coordination of protest movements which were springing up across the country. The organization continues to support an agenda of human rights around the nation and internationally.

Three Christian Kingdoms of Nubia—Makuria, Alwa (Alodia), and Nobadia were ancient Christian nations located in the regions of southern Egypt and the Sudan. They maintained an organized Christian presence in this part of Africa until the sixteenth century.

Unmuntu ngumuntu ngabantu—Zulu proverb which literally means that a person is a person through other persons; a person's humanity can only be meaningfully expressed through relationships with other human beings. An individual's humanity cannot be fully capacitated, highly developed or flourishing in the absence of community or an organic network of inter-dependencies involving mutually respectful, harmonious and supportive interrelationships with other human beings. This proverb is representative of the profound wisdom and underlying communal values of traditional African cultures. This perspective stresses the importance of developing balanced, wholesome relationships among families and communities.

Watch Night Service—a service held each New Year's Eve which originated with the Moravians in Europe and was later brought to the Americas by the Methodists. The services gained historical significance for African Americans in 1863 as congregations across the nation gathered to pray in hopes of swaying the wavering mind of Abraham Lincoln to sign the Emancipation Proclamation. Lincoln had already signed a preliminary proclamation on September 22, 1862, declaring that if the Confederate states in rebellion had not returned to the Union by January 1, 1863, he would sign a declaration freeing all slaves in rebellious states.

White Supremacy—the practices, beliefs, ideologies, attitudes and sentiments that support and maintain the political and economic dominance of people of European descent throughout the globe and the preeminence of European cultural values primarily accomplished through the degradation and exploitation of non-European cultures. Scientific racism and similar principles provide the underlying conceptual rationale for White supremacy, and the European Slave Trade and European Imperialism established the economic and political structures of the system. White supremacy has been the historical project of White power elites in major business enterprises, academic institutions, ecclesiastical establishments, and governmental bodies. Currently, Anglo-Saxon Protestant elites mostly in Britain and the United States are the chief architects of the perpetuation of White supremacy. All people of European descent may benefit from White supremacy in varying degrees, but most White people have not played a direct role in setting policies and shaping the practices of the system. Also, White supremacy is often implicitly upheld by non-White elites as they jockey for positions of social status granted by the dominant group.

Index